Theodore D. Woolsey

**Manual of political Ethics**

Designed chiefly for the use of Colleges and Students at Law - Vol. II

Theodore D. Woolsey

**Manual of political Ethics**

*Designed chiefly for the use of Colleges and Students at Law - Vol. II*

ISBN/EAN: 9783337132958

Printed in Europe, USA, Canada, Australia, Japan

Cover: Foto ©ninafisch / pixelio.de

More available books at **www.hansebooks.com**

OF

# POLITICAL ETHICS,

DESIGNED CHIEFLY

FOR THE USE OF COLLEGES AND STUDENTS AT LAW.

Lex, communis reipublicæ sponsio.—SENECA.

BY

FRANCIS LIEBER, LL.D.,

CORRESPONDING MEMBER OF THE INSTITUTE OF FRANCE, ETC.;

AUTHOR OF "ON CIVIL LIBERTY AND SELF-GOVERNMENT," "PRINCIPLES OF LEGAL AND POLITICAL INTERPRETATION," ETC., ETC.

VOL. II.

SECOND EDITION, REVISED.

EDITED BY THEODORE D. WOOLSEY.

PHILADELPHIA:
J. B. LIPPINCOTT COMPANY.
LONDON: 10 HENRIETTA STREET, COVENT GARDEN.

Entered, according to Act of Congress, in the year 1874, by
MATILDA LIEBER,
In the Office of the Librarian of Congress at Washington.

# CONTENTS.

## BOOK III.

### CHAPTER IV.

Ambition.—Its various Manifestations.—Is it radically bad?—Political Apathy a great Evil.—Political Ingratitude.—Jealousy.—Political Modesty.—Self-Esteem.—Vanity.—Titles without Office, and External Distinctions, such as Ribbons.—The Chinese.—De Ruiter.—Personal Affection.—Friendship: in ancient Times; in modern.—Its high Value.—Epaminondas.—Abuse of Friendship and of the Word.—Favoritism: in Monarchies; in Ministers and all other Citizens.—Its ruinous Effects.—Washington and Pym.—Family Affection.—Providing for Members of the Family.—Papal Nepotism.—Its Character when highest . . 9

### CHAPTER V.

Gratitude fully discussed.—Ingratitude.—Excess of Gratitude aids Usurpers.—Cæsar, Napoleon.—Distinction between Gratitude and Popularity.—Popularity.—Sudden and Passing Popularity; Lasting Popularity.—We have no Right to seek Popularity, but must suffer it to seek us.—Power of spontaneous Popularity; peculiar Power of spontaneously returned Popularity.—Slavery of Popularity.—Danger of Popularity, in Free Countries, to the Individual.—Crowds to receive distinguished Men.—Great Danger of Personal Popularity for Liberty.—Pericles.—Demagogues.—Athenian Demagogism.—Monuments.—The Duty of Attention.—Observation of Primary Agents and Elements.—Truth and Justice connected with it.—Obligation to study the History of our Country, its Institutions and their Classical Periods.—It is necessary in modern Times to read Newspapers . . . . . . . . 35

### CHAPTER VI.

Continency.—Political Evils of Incontinency; of Prostitution.—The primary Foundation of Society, the Family, is undermined by it.—Evils of general Incontinency in the highest Classes, and the lowest.—Religion.—Its Universality.—Its importance for Morality; for Society; for the State.—Fanaticism.—Fanaticism of any kind.—Religious Fanaticism.—The Bible.—Revelation.—Both exclusively religious.—Persecution.—

Direct and indirect Persecution.—Political and social Persecution.—Hypocrisy and Desecration of Religion.—Regulation of political or social actions by Tenets . . . . . . . . . 63

## CHAPTER VII.

Patriotism.—The Patriotism of the Ancients; of the Moderns.—Some have rejected Patriotism.—National Conceit, Pride.—Narrowness of Feeling a Counterfeit of Patriotism.—What is true Patriotism?—It is noble and necessary for Liberty.—Loyalty.—Public Spirit.—What it consists in.—Calamitous Consequences of a Want of Public Spirit.—Veneration for the Old; Forefathers.—How far just, necessary.—When injurious.—The Age of Action under Forty; of Conservatism over Forty.—Do Times grow worse?—When are we more experienced than our Forefathers?—Stagnation and Heedlessness . . . . 80

# BOOK IV.

## CHAPTER I.

Education.—What it is.—Strong and universal Tendency to form Habits and continue them.—Great Importance of Education in Politics, not only of elementary and general School Systems, but also of superior Education and literary Institutions.—Expeditions, Libraries, Museums.—Industrial Education.—The Rich as well as the Poor ought to be actively engaged in some Pursuit, whether purely mental, or industrial.—Law of Solon.—Connection of Crime with want of regular industrial Education in modern Times.—Statistics.—Habits of Industry, of Obedience, of Independence, of Reverence, and of Honesty.—Ancient History for Children.—Concentric Instruction.—Gymnastics.—Sexes.—The Woman.—Difference of physical Organization, Temperament, and Powers in Woman and Man.—The Family (and through it the Society of Comity and the Country) is the sacred Sphere of Woman's chief Activity.—The Connection of Woman's Activity with the State.—Woman is excluded from Politics.—She is connected with the State by Patriotism.—Lady Croke.—The Petitioning of Women.—Lady Russell a Model.—History of Woman.—Is the Woman represented though she cannot vote at the Poll? . . . . . . . . . 108

## CHAPTER II.

Obedience to the Laws.—How highly the Greeks esteemed it.—Obedience to Laws one of Man's Prerogatives.—Absolute Obedience impossible.—Ad Impossibilia Nemo obligatur.—Ad Turpia Nemo obligatur.—Viscount Orthes.—Unlawful Demands made by lawful Authority.—High Importance of the Judiciary with reference to Obedience to the

Law.—Not all that is not prohibited may be done by the Citizen, any more than all that is positively permitted.—Penalties are not equivalents of Crime.—Malum in se, Malum prohibitum: Is the distinction essential, and can we found any Rule of Action upon it?—The Question of Obedience to Laws a Question of Conflict.—Obedience in the Army and Navy.—Articles of War.—Obedience in the Civil Service.—How far is the Citizen bound to obey the Laws?—Justifiable Disobedience.—Necessary and morally demanded Disobedience.—Noncompliance with the Laws, or passive Resistance.—Active Resistance.—Armed Resistance.—Insurrection.—Revolution.—Resistance formerly considered lawful and received in the Charters.—Mobs and Mob-law, so called.—Duty of Informing: in the Officer; in the Citizen at large.—Professional Informers for Rewards.—Secret Police.—Delatores and Mouchards.—The Obligation of Informing against intended or committed Offences . . . . . . . . . . 139

## CHAPTER III.

Associations.—Associated Means, Endeavors.—Associations for the Promotion of Morals.—Pledges.—Trades-Unions.—Ancient Guilds.—Unlawful Combinations for Purposes lawful if pursued by the Individual.—Evil Effects of Trades-Unions.—Disclosures respecting them in Scotland and England . . . . . . . . . 194

## CHAPTER IV.

Liberty of the Press.—Primordial Right of Communion.—Journalism.—High moral Obligations of Editors.—Temptations in the Way of Editors.—Power of Leaders, good or bad, rests upon their seizing upon that Principle which is the moving Agent of the Mass.—In what the Power of leading Papers consists.—Conditions which give great Power to single Papers.—Populous Capitals in Connection with the Influence of Papers.—Obligation of Veracity peculiarly strong for Editors.—Political Importance of gentlemanlike Tone.—Publishing private Letters.—Dangers of Newspaper Flippancy.—The Political Position of the Clergyman.—Opinion of ancient Theologians.—How far the Clergyman ought to share in the Politics of his Country . . . . . . 205

# BOOK V.

## CHAPTER I.

Voting.—Principle of Unanimity; of Majority and Minority.—Deliberative Procedures.—All who have a Right to vote ought to vote.—According to what Rules.—(Election Statistics.)—Voting for Officers.—When we ought to abstain from Voting.—Influencing Elections.—Canvassing.

—Intimidation, individual and official.—Bribery.—Severe Laws against it at Athens.—Mutual Insurance Companies for Bribing at Athens.—Bribes of common Voters.—Bribing Judges; Legislators.—Bribes by a Government of its own Citizens.—Bribes by foreign Powers.—Betting on Elections.—Election Riots and Disturbance around the Poll.—Various other Election Malpractices . . . . . . . 226

## CHAPTER II.

Parties.—Has any free Country existed without Parties?—Can a free Country possibly exist without Parties?—Is it desirable that a free Country should exist without Parties?—Historical Parties and passing ones.—Conservative and Movement Parties.—Characteristics of a sound Party.—Dangers of Party Zeal and factious Passion.—Party Signs.—Misunderstanding of Language in high Party Spirit.—Ought a conscientious Citizen to attach himself to a Party?—The Law of Solon.—Independents.—Trimmers . . . . . . . . . 252

## CHAPTER III.

Opposition.—Government.—Administration.—What is a lawful Opposition.—A well-understood Opposition the essential Safeguard of Liberty.—The Opposition a great Institution of Modern Times.—As such it dates more especially from the Times of Walpole and Pulteney.—It is lawful to oppose the Majority, which is not always right.—(Order of Sitting in Legislative Assemblies.)—Public Opinion and General Opinion.—Ethical Rules relating to Opposition and to Parties in general.—How far ought a Citizen to go in his Opposition, especially in times of War?—Coalitions.—Parties formed on the Ground of foreign National Extraction . . . . . . . . . . . 268

## CHAPTER IV.

Public Men.—Leaders.—Self-examination before a Citizen embarks in Public Life.—Physical, Moral, and Mental Qualities desirable in a Public Man.—Necessary Knowledge for a Public Man.—Caution in entering upon Public Life . . . . . . . . . 284

# BOOK VI.

## CHAPTER I.

Extra-constitutional Meetings.—Their Necessity.—The Representative.—Summary of his Duties.—He is the Guardian of the public Treasures.—When ought he to vote liberally?—The Framing of Laws.—Legislation upon the Principle of mutual Accommodation.—Importance of a

CONTENTS. 7

gentlemanly Character for the Representative.—Instruction.— History and the various Constitutions show that the Right of Instruction has been claimed and disclaimed as promoting and as injurious to Liberty, according to the Circumstances of the Times.—The Representative Government is not a mere Substitution for direct Democracy.—Essential character of the Representative Government.—The different characteristic Principles of Ancient States, the Middle Ages, and Modern States.—Nationalization of States; Socialization of Population.—National Representation the great Feature of Modern Times.—Difference between Deputative and Representative Systems.—Oath in New Jersey and the Netherlands to promote Public Welfare.—How does the Representative faithfully represent?—Advantages of Representative Government.—Objections to the doctrine of Instruction.—Instruction belongs to the Deputative System . . . . . . . . . 295

## CHAPTER II.

The Subject of Instruction with particular Reference to the United States.—The ancient Articles of Confederation founded upon the Deputative System.—The Articles of Confederation compared to the Constitution of the former United Provinces of the Netherlands, the Swiss Act of Mediation, the present Constitution of the Swiss Confederation, and the Germanic Confederacy.—The Constitution of the United States boldly changed the former deputative character of the Confederacy into a representative one.—Senators are not Ambassadors.—In Leagues the strongest Member of those on terms of parity according to the letter must sway.—Hegemony in Greece, Phœnicia, the Low Countries, etc.—Relation of the State Legislatures to the respective Senators elected by them.—The History of Instruction in modern times, as connected with the Representative System . . . . . . . . . 339

## CHAPTER III.

Responsibility of the Representative.—Pledges.—Implied and positive, general and specific Pledges.—Are Pledges moral, and consistent with general Liberty and Justice?—When are they so?—Pledges originated with the Court Party and Aristocracy.—Strong Power of Implied Pledges.—Breaking Implied Pledges, and throwing one's self upon the Constituents by Resignation.—Duties of Presiding Officers of deliberative Assemblies; Speakers . . . . . . . . . 363

# BOOK VII.

## CHAPTER I.

Executive Officers.—Difficulty of controlling them.—Their Interference with Elections; in Athens, Rome, France, England, the United States.—Plato's Opinion of the Duties of Officers.—Post-Office.—The Chief Executive Officer.—Confidential Officers.—Official Interpretation of Constitutions and Laws.—The Veto.—Ancient and Modern Veto.—Absolute, suspensive, and conditional Vetoes.—Privilege of Pardoning in Monarchies; in Republics.—Danger and Difficulty in Republics.—For what Purpose is it granted?—Rules which ought to be observed in making use of the Power of Pardoning . . . . . . . . 373

## CHAPTER II.

Judge, Juror, Advocate, and Witness.—Official, external and moral Independence of the Judge.—Sanctissimus Judex of the Romans.—The Judge, where there is doubt, must interpret in Mercy, in Penal Cases; in Favor of civil Liberty, in all.—The Institution of the Jury.—The sacred Office of the Juryman.—What is he to do when the Law is contrary to the universal Conscience?—The Institution of the Advocate.—Moral Obligation of the Advocate.—Political Relations of Lawyers in Free Countries.—Duties of the Witness . . . . . . . 401

## CHAPTER III.

War.—Definitions.—Present Exaggerations against War.—Christian Religion does not prohibit just War; neither the Bible, nor the early Writers of the Church.—Objections against War on the Score of Morality; of Reason; of Political Economy.—Just and Patriotic Wars have morally raised Nations.—Eternal Peace.—Arbitration by a Congress of Nations.—Just Wars.—National Debasing Effect of suffering national Insult and Injustice without Resistance.—The Age of Louis XIV.—Wars do not absolve from Obligations to the Enemy.—Who is the Enemy?—Are Citizens of the hostile State Enemies?—What Means of injuring the Enemy are admissible?—Treaties containing Provisions for the Case of War between the Contracting Powers.—Shall Confidence be abused in War?—Does War allow Deception?—Capitulations are sacred.—Destruction in War.—Carrying off Works of Art, Archives, etc. Duties of the individual Soldier . . . . . . . 426

# POLITICAL ETHICS.

## BOOK III.

(*Continued.*)

## CHAPTER IV.

Ambition.—Its various Manifestations.—Is it radically bad?—Political Apathy a great Evil.—Political Ingratitude.—Jealousy.—Political Modesty.—Self-Esteem.—Vanity.—Titles without Office, and External Distinctions, such as Ribbons.—The Chinese.—De Ruiter.—Personal Affection.—Friendship: in ancient Times; in modern.—Its high Value.—Epaminondas.—Abuse of Friendship and of the Word.—Favoritism: in Monarchies; in Ministers and all other Citizens.—Its ruinous Effects.—Washington and Pym.—Family Affection.—Providing for Members of the Family.—Papal Nepotism.—Its Character when highest.

XXXVI. The English word ambition is used for very different degrees of the same affection of the human soul, from its laudable original principle to its immoral or criminal excess, for which some other languages have different words. This want of terms has not unfrequently exercised an unfavorable influence upon the views which have been taken of the subject. By ambition we designate a desire of distinction or superiority, whether it only prompts to legitimate emulation, increases to a longing for distinction, or degenerates into a craving and ultimately into an ungovernable passion for it. If we comprehend all these gradations under one term, namely that of desire of distinction, I believe that we do no violence to language. Of course we must waive the Latin etymology of the word ambition, since the meaning originally attached to it in that language has entirely faded away in our own idiom. The question is, Is ambition a legitimate desire, laudable, beneficial, or must a conscientious citizen extinguish it, and can he do it, or is it an original, elementary, and therefore necessary principle in our soul, so that we ought to cultivate and moderate rather than eradicate it?

We have seen that men are ordained to exist as individuals, not only physically so, like the animals, not only each with his own moral value, but also with an infinite variety in the combination of mental faculties and ethical inclinations, a variety far greater and more surprising than that which we observe in the combination of matter around us. Diversity, taken in its deepest meaning, and not sameness, is the law of everything that lives; the propelling agent, most especially, of society. Closely connected with, and indeed directly resulting from it, are emulation and competition. Without them little energy would be roused, and it is not only justifiable in, but it is demanded of us, that in whatever line we are conscious of possessing peculiar powers we should strive to emulate those who are before or above us, to rise, if possible, superior to them, since we have enjoyed already the advantage of their example and acquisitions. Desiring, then, to distinguish ourselves is far from necessarily implying vanity, but it may, and indeed ought to, be a desire to develop our individual nature, stamped upon us as our peculiar intellectual compound character, to the utmost extent, so that we may be all that which our Maker destined us to be, and distinguish ourselves by perfection, if he has given us peculiar faculties. In this view ambition, or a desire of distinction, is not only legitimate, but it is one of our great duties. Skill, knowledge, wisdom, and virtue may thus become in a variety of spheres, humble or high, the object of laudable ambition, the vis motrix of society and civilization. Without it there would be stagnation, inanity—listless barbarity. But it has been asked, How is this ambition compatible with that modesty which all systems of morals must hold up as a virtue, that humility of mind which the Christian religion especially demands? I believe the question would never have been asked, had not an erroneous view respecting men and society been taken, according to which a state of perfection, towards which we were bound to strive, was believed necessarily to consist in a state of sameness; but we have already seen that where there is individuality there is diversity, and this diversity of combination seems to be one of our Maker's greatest laws of life, by which his greatness, inconceivable by man, appears nevertheless the more holy the longer and deeper man contemplates it and follows it out as far as his limited faculties will sustain him. If we take the opposite view, that perfection of life does not consist in infinite combinations of character and infinite mutual relations, necessary in order to keep society joined together, but also necessarily founded upon variety and contrast, because without it society would dissolve into equal and equally inert atoms, we must ultimately arrive, if we consistently reason, at that state held up by the wisest Hindoos as the state of perfection, in which we are "indifferent to all pairs of opposite things, as honor or dishonor, and the like, remaining absorbed in the Divine Essence."[1]

XXXVII. Desire of distinction is just and all depends upon these points, that we desire to excel or distinguish ourselves in something laudable, that after calm examination this appears to be within the reach of our faculties, endowments, and position, so that we mistake not the aim pointed out to us by our individual combination, that the desire do not become excessive, or a diseased function of the soul, and that consequently we do not desire distinction because it is such but because it is in a good cause and our duty calls us to excel in it as we have the endowments for it, and therefore do not envy or hate those who excel in the same paths, but, on the contrary cherish, them as striving for the same good and noble end.[2] Many persons have entirely missed their

---

[1] Ordinances of Manu, translated by Sir William Jones, London, 1799, vol. iii. p. 237.

[2] * The very ruinous effect of small vanity, which is highly dangerous in all truly free governments, is strikingly illustrated in the following extract from Sir Samuel

aim by striving to excel in poetry while they were made perhaps to be sound practical men; many have ruined the usefulness of their life and their happiness by not proportioning their ambition to their faculties or other means; many, by placing it upon worthless subjects; many, again, by criminally placing it upon subjects legitimate in themselves. And in this latter point of view, in which it becomes especially important in politics, we must not forget that it is closely coupled in gifted minds with that urgency to action which we find always to exist in proportion to a man's faculties, and from which rises the love of power, not wrong in its principle, but often carried to such insatiate excess that it bewilders the mind, deranges all other functions of the soul, and ends in a monomania. Yet, though ambition has frequently intoxicated superior minds and led less gifted ones to many follies, we can in politics as little dispense with ambition as in the arts, sciences, or literature, in the school, the house, or the various avocations of practical life. For if ambition in those gifted citizens who by their peculiar mental organization are fitted for officers or as leaders is extinguished, either by disgust at a de-

---

Romilly's Narrative of his own life, in Memoirs of the Life of Sir Samuel Romilly, 2d edit., London, 1840, vol. i. p. 107. He had paid a visit to Paris at the beginning of the revolution, and says, "What struck me as most remarkable in the dispositions of the people that I saw, was the great desire that everybody had to act a great part, and the jealousy, which in consequence of this was entertained of those who were really eminent. It seemed as if all persons, from the highest to the lowest, whether deputies themselves, declaimers in the Palais Royal, orators in the coffee-houses, spectators in the gallery, or the populace about the door, looked upon themselves individually as of great consequence in the revolution. The man who kept the hotel at which I lodged at Paris, a certain M. Villars, was a private in the National Guard. Upon my returning home on the day of the benediction of their colors at Notre Dame, and telling him that I had been present at the ceremony, he said, 'You saw me, sir?' I was obliged to say that I really had not. He said, 'Is that possible, sir? You did not see me! Why, I was in one of the first ranks—all Paris saw me!' I have often since thought of my host's childish vanity. What he spoke was felt by thousands. The most important transactions were as nothing but as they had relation to the figure which each little self-conceited hero acted in them. To attract the attention of all Paris, or of all France, was often the motive of conduct in matters which were attended with most momentous consequences."

generate state of things or their own haughtiness, and if it be not properly kindled in the rising generations by directing their attention to the noblest examples of civic worth in the history of their country or that of other great nations, one of the greatest and most ruinous evils of a state must unavoidably befall it, that of political apathy or indifferentism, which always foments political demoralization, as it partly arises from it; until it finally extinguishes all public spirit and patriotism.

If the best, the well-informed, the honest, do not strive for the honors of the commonwealth, the wicked, ignorant, or dishonest will; if all matters of political distinction, be it in the way of parliamentary honor, distinction of high office, on the bench, or in whatever other manner, be disregarded or derided, matters of justice and politics themselves soon will be treated so too. If the substantial citizens become indifferentists and do not vote, perhaps because they are too proud to mingle in the crowd, or unwilling to exercise so high a privilege of liberty at the expense of some personal inconvenience, they ought to know that others will not do the same, and that the "fæx infima populi," where such have a right of voting, will infallibly be at the poll. Indifferentism in politics leads to what was called in a previous passage political atony, a dissolution of the political ties, and of course to the death of justice and liberty, an awful state of things, out of which convulsive revolutions alone, accompanied with suffering and violence, can develop a new order of things.

XXXVIII. We ought not to forget that distinction in sciences or other branches may be acquired not indeed without sacrifices, for there is no good to be acquired without proportionate exertion and sacrifice, but without those sacrifices from which nobler minds would shrink. The movements of liberty, however, are in their nature not unfrequently of a rough character, because they are the affairs of masses, in which we cannot always expect delicacy of relations. Without ambition, without love of distinction, there would then not exist sufficient incentive for those who have the mind and mould of soul to become great citizens.

For this reason, however, it is also necessary not to withhold from the excellent or great the just reward of their ambition, not to instil into them by unworthy ingratitude the poison of jealousy, or contempt of popular acknowledgment, not to permit that honorable ambition, which respects and obeys the public voice, to degenerate into the love of power for its own sake, the most reckless and unscrupulous of passions Habitual ingratitude produces one of two things: either it leads those who long for power to use the people while they despise it, or it drives the best minds from the stage of politics. Niebuhr, in his History of Rome, says, " M. Manlius, the preserver of the capitol, of whom the chronicles relate that in birth and valor he was second to none, and in personal beauty, exploits, eloquence, vigor, and daring superior to all, found himself bitterly disappointed in his claims to gratitude and honor. Camillus, his enemy, to whom he felt himself at least equal, who had not shared in the distress of the siege, who had imprecated curses on his country, was repeatedly raised by the houses to the dictatorship, and by the comitia, which were under the influence of the aristocracy, to the military tribunate: while he, though a consular, found himself excluded from all dignities. This insulting neglect in return for an action standing foremost but not alone in a heroic life, the energy of which was still unexhausted, poisoned his heart with virulent rancor. He was one of those powerful-minded men who have received a calling to be the first among their countrymen, and feel an unconquerable longing to fulfil it, while low minds, envying and disliking them, are resolved to keep them back from the place which is their due; one of those, the superhuman vehemence of whose character, when drawn forth by such a conflict, makes even honest but timid natures shrink. For indeed it is their doom to be haunted by a spirit against the snares of which nothing can protect them but the confidence and esteem of honorable minds. God will require their souls from those who have driven them into fatal courses: their faults he will judge more mercifully than the faults of those who ruined his noblest work. These mighty characters have always an intense inborn feeling in behalf of justice, truth, and whatever is glorious; they are animated by love and pity, by hatred and indignation of the right sort: these become subservient to their fierce passions, but do not die away: it is glaringly unjust, even when they have gone irretrievably astray, to regard actions, which in a man of blameless life would be extolled as noble and praiseworthy, in any other light in them, although vulgar souls may do the same things from selfish motives."[1] So far the historian of Rome. We shall return to the subject of gratitude and popularity in politics.

XXXIX. If excessive or unfounded jealousy towards great and honorable citizens is blamable, it marks no less an evil disposition if the ambitious show it towards one another, and allow themselves to be carried away so far as to sacrifice their country, or even its partial welfare, to these animosities which are below a truly great mind.

The danger when a man's ambition is greater than the resources within him, has been already alluded to. If his position is such that he cannot effect much except by the power which he could only acquire by a superior mind, the injury is not only on his side; he will earn disgrace; but it is also greatly owing to this disproportion in the endowments of many men that we meet with so many restless, turbulent, and noisy politicians in their limited spheres, men who have too much ambition to remain quiet, and too limited a mind to comprehend what is truly noble, great, or good, and whose petty pride makes them jealous of all true distinction and influence in others. They are very troublesome members of the community, and become sometimes highly injurious. It is the duty of every true citizen to keep within his proper sphere. This disproportion between the impulse and the

---

[1] Eng. trans., Amer. ed., ii. 451.

faculties is of immense danger in disturbed times, when rapid changes are unavoidable, and in persons who by their position, acquired by adventitious circumstances, have for a time at least power or influence. How easily may not a country be ruined by the ambition of a weak-minded man, whether monarch or demagogue, in such times of danger! The duke of Norfolk, who conspired against Elizabeth, in order to marry Mary of Scots, queen of England, is represented by Hallam[1] to have been such, and therefore to have fallen by "a sentence amply merited, the execution of which was indispensable." The French revolution shows many examples of this species of character in a most glaring and appalling light.

XL. Ambition, as first limited, is not incompatible in any way with modesty, a virtue which is indeed no less amiable in private life than in public. Nor is modesty incompatible with self-esteem.[2] Anaxagoras, when exiled in Lampsacus, was pitied because he now was deprived of Athens: "Rather Athens of me," he replied.[3] Whether this proud answer was well founded in the case of Anaxagoras, is not the place here to investigate; but certain it is that there are great men who are as valuable to their country as that is to them, who, because they are of a great and comprehensive intellect, cannot but see clearly their position, and surely would not act morally if they should attempt to hide the consciousness of their own

---

[1] Constitutional History of England, vol. i. pp. 181, 182.

[2] * Pitt (afterwards Lord Chatham) is said to have expressed, in 1757, these words to the duke of Devonshire: "My lord, I am sure I can save this country, and nobody else can." Walpole's Memoirs, vol. ii. p. 271.

So did his son William Pitt, at a very early period, "prefer the profession of the law to any official connection with an administration of which he did not form a part." Soon after he declared publicly that he had determined "never to accept any subordinate office,—meaning an office which did not entitle him to a seat in the cabinet." (Tomline's Memoir of William Pitt, 2d ed., vol. i. p. 66.) The consciousness of his talents entitled him to do this. Cases of great emergency would of course make an exception. The delicate hand of a Phidias would be justly placed to the rope in cases of impending shipwreck.

[3] Diog. Laert., ii. 10.

importance by hypocrisy, one of the great evils in politics. Yet, as in all morals so in politics, we must beware of extremes, and political arrogance is as dangerous a rock in politics as hypocrisy is undermining. Theodatus Gozon, as we learn from the chronicle of the Rhodian Knights, in addressing the conclave which had convened for the purpose of electing a grand master of that heroic order, after making a review of all the qualities and virtues necessary for a commander of the illustrious order in its dangerous duty of warding off the Mohammedans and of preventing them from overflooding western Europe, and mentioning the solemn oath he had taken to propose the proper person, uttered these closing words: "Thus, I find no one fitter to rule the order than myself." He was almost unanimously elected, and the order found no reason to rue the election.[1] These are extraor-

---

[1] Having mentioned the Order of the Knights of St. John on account of this instance of political self-esteem, I cannot forbear mentioning it on account of the glorious and almost superhuman perseverance of the Knights in resisting the gigantic power of Mahomet II., who intended to conquer the West of Europe, and, though death prevented him from carrying his cherished plan into execution, had it engraven on his tomb-stone, "I meant to conquer Rhodes and fair Italy." If we thus see in the resistance of the Order under Villiers a noble instance of fortitude and calm perseverance, coupled with the greatest heroism, we find in that same siege an instance of the infamous guilt to which jealousy may lead, in the case of Amaral, who, forgetting duty, religion, humanity, was bent on delivering Rhodes into the hands of the Turks and thus laying open to them a farther progress towards the West. The siege of Rhodes is an instance of some political virtues so nobly displayed, and its history is every way of so thrilling an interest, that it cannot fail to sink deeply in the mind of the reader, especially of the young, whence it may rise again as a supporting and encouraging example in a time of need. Vertot, History of the Knights Hospitallers, 5 vols., Edinburgh, 1770.

In appending this note I am reminded of two striking instances of self-esteem or consciousness of worth, though not of a political kind. Most of my readers will remember the clause in Lord Bacon's Testament, " My name and memory I leave to foreign nations; and to mine own countrymen, after some time be passed over." In Eckermann's Conversations with Goethe during the Last Years of his Life, 2 vols., Leipsic, 1836 (in German), we are informed (vol. i. p. 143) of the following and, in my judgment, just opinion which Goethe had of himself: " Tieck [a distinguished German poet] is a star of superior order, and no one can appreciate his merits more than myself, but when they attempt to elevate him

dinary cases, and in general it may be given as a sign of political modesty if a citizen betrays no eagerness for place or honor, but dutifully accepts whatever place he is called to and for which he feels himself capable, always keeping strictly the public benefit in view. There is perhaps no more striking trait in the whole life of Washington than that on no occasion during his whole political career did he seek or solicit a single place or appointment, still less, of course, did he intrigue for one. Yet in paying this just and great tribute to that illustrious citizen let us not be unjust towards others, and not forget that this abstinence from striving higher is not always possible and would not be right for every citizen. The American revolution was no internal revolution; it was the severing of colonies from their mother country. When intestine wars devastate a country, when the horrors of civil war demand a remedy at the moment, a citizen who is conscious of resources within and power without would certainly neglect his duty were he not boldly to strive for that position in which alone he could be of service. Would Spain, in her bleeding state, not bless such a citizen, if there were one sufficiently great for the task?

XLI. True ambition is incapable of vanity, a vice by which rulers but too often have found it possible to attach to a bad cause numerous men who without it might have well deserved of their country. Ambition seeks distinction in reality; vanity is satisfied with outward distinction, or its form, without substantial basis, and if common and habitual in a nation it deprives it of the proper manliness indispensable for civil liberty. Marks of distinction seem not only to be wise but just, because by it the opinion which is invisible and may be evanescent is embodied and condensed in a permanent sign;

---

above himself, and to raise him on a level with me, they err. I may say this as a plain matter of fact, for what is it to me? I have not made myself. It would be the same if I were to compare myself to Shakspeare, who neither made himself, and yet is a being of a superior kind, to whom I look up, and whom I must venerate." Eckermann was the daily and domestic companion of Goethe.

it is gratitude made visible and symbolically expressed; the person who receives it is by the feeling of acknowledgment and gratitude in turn more closely connected to those who thus palpably show their feeling towards him, his friends feel cheered in the acknowledgment of merit in him, and the community at large have in their act a representation of the virtue or merit which dwells among them, and the encouragement it meets with at their hands. It is the same principle which prompts the passengers of a wrecked vessel to present a silver tankard to the pilot who may have saved their lives. Among these public marks I count the thanks of Congress or Parliament, swords voted to deserving officers, the bestowing bounties upon meritorious citizens—for instance the land granted to Lafayette—the civic crown of the Romans, the sword of honor bestowed by Napoleon upon the brave, or, where there exist different privileges in the civil fabric of a nation, the bestowing of these upon the most meritorious. If France believes that peers for life are necessary or salutary in the organization of her government, I consider it as a very noble trait, and am bold enough to claim it as a general good sign of the times, that she raises to this political dignity and influence, among others, men who have evinced the influence which they exercise by no other power than that which the gifted always must exercise over the less gifted minds—in short, to literary and scientific men. There are now above sixteen peers in France who had no other claim to the peerage than that of thought. He who denies that such examples are not inciting to others has in my opinion no correct view of mankind. Britain, though formerly far in advance of France by admitting commoners to the high peerages, has now remained behind her; and all the distinction that science can aspire to in England by way of political honor is knighthood, once so degraded under James I. that people would pay fines rather than accept it. Strange that no minister has sought additional strength by boldly bestowing the peerage on scientific men; while mere riches in many cases have obtained the peerage. Yet, if the French have thus nobly broken the path—it was Napoleon who first saw how wise it was—they stand in another respect much behind the English, namely, by promoting petty vanity in the citizens through the profuse bestowment of those outward signs—ribbons—which appear to the national taste of the Anglican race beneath a manly spirit. A friend of liberty could not read, without a degree of mortification, the many debates on the "cross of July" which began almost as soon as the smoke of the guns at the barricades had vanished. Ribbons, and titles unless they serve for an expression of something substantial, for instance as that of peer of France, which in fact is no title, but merely the name of a station, are mere play of vanity, and cannot possibly be conducive to a lastingly healthy state of the public. The world has done without mere titles, and it will do so again. Already is no title of nobility conferred upon a French commoner when made peer. Canova, the great sculptor, was made marquis of Ischia. Who knows it? He himself never used the title. But when Frederic the Great ordered the number 66 to be placed in the coat of arms of Major Chazat, whose regiment had taken sixty-six standards in the battle of Hohenfriedberg, there was more substance in the token. The whole continent of Europe has greatly suffered in consequence of the trifling and unworthy spirit manifesting itself in empty titles, that is, titles of offices without office, or of rank without privilege. These and crosses and orders came into vogue when popular liberty and substantial civism gave way more and more to court politics and court government; and in the same degree as civil liberty shall return to those countries where the abuse exists now, empty titles and unmeaning ribbons will give way, because in popular and national politics the question is respecting the real character which a citizen has been able to found for himself. The Chinese government is also in this respect of much interest to us, because similar causes have produced similar effects. We find there, as in some European continental states, a court government with a thoroughly organized and vast hierarchy of officers, and we find there likewise a variety of merely honorary titles, promotions of rank independent of promotion of offices, and signs of court favor and official distinction, such as the peacock feather, together with presents which seem to correspond to the snuff-boxes with brilliants frequently given by continental monarchs to favored persons.[1] These marks of distinction, essentially belonging to the epoch of court politics, have already, it would seem, begun to diminish, both in frequency and the estimation in which they are held.

Filippo Strozzi, the distinguished Florentine and opponent of the Medicis, though connected with them by marriage, said, when his fellow-citizens would give him the title of Messire (Mr.), " My name is Filippo Strozzi ; I am a Florentine merchant, and whoever gives me a title offends me." Orders bestowed by the executive alone should always be considered as injurious to true liberty ; for they give a considerable power founded upon a paltry motive, and may be entirely independent of all that which ought to confer real distinction. The grants of the order of the Legion of Honor by Louis XVIII. furnish a striking instance.

In matters of morality examples are cheering and reassuring. I may be permitted, therefore, to conclude these observations with mentioning the great admiral de Ruiter, as an example of great modesty united to undaunted courage and valor, in which Lord Collingwood was not unlike him. That great naval hero of the United Provinces often said, " I willingly dispense with all praises if I only satisfy my conscience and follow the commands sent me." He would never grant

---

[1] * Yet it is very curious that distinction not only by title, but actually by ribbons, crosses, and stars, seems to have had a very decided effect upon the whole career of Nelson, and he owed his death to the wearing of his orders in the battle at Trafalgar. See A Narrative of the Battle of St. Vincent, with Anecdotes of Nelson before and after that Battle, by Col. Drinkwater Bethune, F.S.A., author of the History of the Siege of Gibraltar, 2d edit., 8vo, pp. 97, London, 1840. Colonel Bethune was present and reports a curious conversation with Nelson after the battle of St. Vincent, showing how eagerly Nelson coveted the order of the Bath. Extracts from the above book are to be found in the London Literary Gazette of August 8, 1840. See likewise the extract from the London Literary Gazette of May 2, 1840.

permission to publish from his log-books the most important acts of his eventful life. His repeated answer was, " Not I, God has done it." Frequently, when relating some of his remarkable exploits, he would suddenly stop when his son-in-law asked for the date of an event, because he was afraid it would be used for a biography. The king of Spain made him a duke, but the patent arrived after his death; his son requested the king to grant him a more modest title.[1]

XLII. Personal affection between particular individuals, whether it grows out of relations of consanguinity, out of the difference of sexes, out of a proportional coincidence and disagreement of dispositions, gifts, and acquisitions, or out of mutual service, belongs to the primary agents of all human society. Let us consider the last-mentioned affection, friendship, first. The ancient philosophers held friendship to be a subject worthy of their fullest attention. Aristotle treats of it in two books, the eighth and ninth, of his Ethics; Plato, Pythagoras, and after them Cicero, speak of it as one of the most sacred means of cultivating virtue. The poets celebrate this union of souls no less, from Homer, who ends his eighth song with the words, " Not less indeed than even a brother of the same blood is an honest friend, kind and judicious in mind," down to the latest. The ancients indeed considered friendship a wedding of the souls, and not unfrequently the act of concluding friendship was accompanied by religious consecration. The same intensity and specific character of friendship, perhaps, no longer exist; the causes of this fact may be various. Our practical life is more movable, our social intercourse and hence our personal acquaintance vaster and more changeable, our mind is occupied with a much larger variety of subjects in science as well as literature, our states are wider, and our religion points at a morally perfect being towards whom all minds are directed as their

---

[1] Brandt, De Ruiter. Van Kampen, History of the Netherlands, Hamburg, 1833.

great example, so that necessarily, it would seem, the attention to a specific personal relation must be lessened, unless very extraordinary causes are added. The same perhaps would be applicable to our matrimonial relations, which nevertheless are certainly stronger and intenser, generally speaking, than in ancient times; but the reason of this apparent inconsistency seems to lie in the circumstance that the position of woman has risen in the course of civilization; and the greater importance of the family with us is of itself one of the causes to account for the phenomenon of which we speak.

Yet, although friendship may not any longer be so often as in antiquity of that fervor and religious intensity with which the ancients considered it, it remains an important element of society, and, like every moral good, ought to be carefully cultivated; the nobler the souls the greater the blessing of friendship. Friendship is a mutual affection, or intensity of feeling towards another, arising from an inmost pleasure in the soul of a good man, which it feels in honoring, admiring, and cherishing what is good, pure, or great, and in being honored and cherished by the good and pure, together with the feeling of delight which the soul enjoys at being fully and wholly understood in this world of general misunderstanding or necessary difficulty of mutual comprehension,—the thrilling delight of confidence, of mutual repose. There is an essential approach of souls in friendship as in love of the highest sort, or a finding out of one another's essence, stripped of all adhesion, accident or what may arise from different position, nay, even sometimes stripped of the difference of opinion; and as we fervently believe that the Creator will develop in another world that which was good and pure in each man here beneath, though single and separate, and which led the different individuals in this nether world to different or even opposite opinions, and separated the republican from the monarchist, the rationalist from the enthusiast, the cautious from the bold, and will thus expand and mature what He laid in each individual, and unite them all in greater perfection, so does He allow men in this world faintly to foretaste in friendship the bliss of a future world, where no accident of difference can any longer exist.

As the love of Romeo and Juliet elevated their souls above the strife of their houses, so can friendship elevate two hearts above the struggles of their time, though the individuals be even engaged in it; while those friends who happily walk the same path cheer and strengthen each other by their mutual example; and, since essential confidence can exist between good men only, they propel each other in the path of virtue: for it is a primary law of all intercourse, that if two or more of the same inclination, pursuit, or character—good, frivolous, or wicked—are brought into close contact with one another, in that same direction they will propel one another still more rapidly. Friendship must rest on mutuality; it is one of its essential qualities; for one of its requisites and blessings is the enjoyment of confidence—a luxury to good men; and Æschylus is right when he says that kings suffer one evil, they do not know how to confide in friends; while the reason that was given of Trajan's having friends, is that he was a friend himself.[1]

Friendship thus cultivates disinterestedness, forbearance, liberality, kindness, and generosity; it improves our judgment by admitting the counsel of the friend in whom we confide, and who views our case, though interesting, yet less personal to him, as a physician prescribes for a brother of his profession in his illness; it makes the cultivation and practice of that primary virtue, justice, easier to us, because it accustoms the mind to view occurrences not solely with reference to ourselves; and since friendship is partly founded upon the peculiar personalities of men, and these personalities may on

---

[1] "Habes amicos quia amicus ipse es." (Plin., Panegyr.) Christ, to prove to the apostles that they are what he calls them, his friends, mentions confidence, the fact that he trusted the highest truth to them: "Henceforth I call you not servants; for the servant knoweth not what his lord doeth; but I have called you friends; for all things that I have heard of my Father I have made known unto you." John xv. 15.

account of some prominent feature lead to the friendship with one person, and on account of some other prominent feature to the same or a similar relation with another, it unites mediately more than two individuals. Friendship thus becomes a ramified bond of society, a tie of good will between individuals who otherwise might remain insulated.

XLIII. It is evident from the foregoing remarks how very important an element friendship is in the social order, and how carefully we ought to cultivate it wherever it is offered by the circumstances of our life; for being an affection it cannot be forced. Yet although a man may be more or less successful in meeting with that individual whose nature is so happily conformed to his own that the relation of friendship follows as a matter of course, it may be safely assumed that in a community in which free and various action is not suppressed, and in which, especially, public life exists, a man who has never succeeded in forming some strong friendship or other must, if not unusually unfortunate, look for the causes of this great privation within himself—to his egotism.

That friendship, as designated above, in its highest degree, cannot be obtained by every one is clear, and, as is the case with all other relations, it necessarily exists in a variety of gradations; but it is an abuse of terms, too common at present, to apply this sacred word to the relation subsisting upon mere acquaintance, to persons perhaps known to us only by a chain of intermediate recommendations, or among those who but temporarily are united for some selfish or evil ends. Those are companions or followers, but not friends, of whom the Bible gives so severe a test. (John xv. 13.)

As a rule for a life in general as well as in politics in particular, it is far more important, in order to secure all the advantages of friendship, moral or practical, to make one or a few close friends who will "stick closer than a brother" (Prov. xviii. 24), than many whose friendship consists rather in the negative character of an absence of ill will, or merely in a general and undefined but not very active good will, not in a positive affection of the inmost soul, which rejoices at the success of the friend and grieves at his grief. "It is of far greater importance to a statesman" (it is so to every man) "to make one friend who will hold out with him for twenty years, than to find twenty followers in each year, losing as many."[1]

And here a question of importance offers itself: "How far, in politics, should we carry our friendship, taking the term in its intense meaning? Of course we are not allowed to assist in doing the wrong which the friend may contemplate or actually commit, or to do injustice to others, to sacrifice truth or public welfare to this special relation; but there are cases which are not so easily decided. Our friend may have committed an error which we would disapprove of and would loudly censure were we his opponents; or our friend may commit a positive fault: how then? I would answer, The more you find that public clamor sets violently in against your friend, the more loudly his fault is discussed, and the more vehement the cry against him, the more consider yourself in this public trial his natural advocate, endeavoring, as in a trial of justice, to show whatever may be favorable for him, which no one will do if you do not, so that whatever is redeeming in your friend may not be swept away in the general excitement. Stand by him so long and so far as your conscience will permit, and as your perfect consciousness of your own disinterestedness supports you, and believe that by exhibiting an example of generous faithfulness, and of trying all in your power even for a fallen friend, you do a great service to public morality. But of course this allows of no weakness, of which such innumerable instances are preserved in history, of men who disapproved thoroughly of a measure, who declared it criminal, and yet, when they found their friend irresistibly bent on it, finally yielded and assisted. It is a great thing to know we have a friend who will stand by us; it is a great misfortune to have none who will boldly sacrifice us, if unfortunately bent on wrong, to justice, right,

---

[1] Taylor, The Statesman, London, 1836.

and truth. We may firmly cling to Plato, but must cling more firmly to Truth.

The friendship of great souls, founded upon pure patriotism, may produce the greatest effects. It may shine on a Thebes like a suddenly rising sun. Whether the friendship as it existed between Pelopidas, the rich and ardent, and Epaminondas, the poor and far-seeing, be the noblest and most inspiring example of the excellence of friendship between two patriotic souls and have its equal in history or not, I feel convinced that my younger readers will do themselves a great service by reading the biography of Pelopidas in Plutarch. No heart in which there is a generous spark can ponder it without delight at their nobleness, patriotism, mutual love, absence of jealousy, and disinterestedness, despite their great diversity of character and fortune.

XLIV. Quite different from friendship, and yet frequently cloaked with its name, because the term "friend" is abusively extended to followers, adherents, and adherents' adherents, is what we will call favoritism in politics, the bestowing of favors without regard to justice, merit, and public welfare, or in direct contradiction to it. Favoritism is one of the most dangerous vices of governments, because it may steal in under the garb of that which in itself is good and right, of gratitude to those who served us, of liberality, or, as we have seen, of friendship. We need not discuss that favoritism which sets out from vice or from an egregious affront to all justice, as we see it exemplified in the "minions" of some of the most corrupt periods of the French court or that of Spain, or in the Dorsets and Buckinghams, Gavestons and others in England, or in the corruptest periods of some republics, since it is too glaringly vicious to deserve especial notice. We might with equal justice treat of murder as a highly reprehensible crime in rulers. But favoritism is highly dangerous also in other places, and arising out of sources which may be originally pure, as more difficult to resist. Elizabeth, the great statesman, as Richelieu called her, earned no substantial advantages from her partiality to Leicester or Essex. Is it not, then, a bitter condition of monarchy that rulers must studiously avoid allowing personal inclinations, the friendships of private life, to acquire such control that they can no longer be resisted, but have acquired a preponderance over the interests of the public welfare? Undoubtedly it is so; but we must not forget that although monarchy is necessary for many states, it is in itself an expedient to avoid certain evils; it is a government which, not viewed with regard to practical utility but in the abstract, contains always this contradiction, that we adopt for the highest, most important place a principle which civilization steadily eliminates in wider and wider circles, as injurious to society, respecting all other offices of any importance,—that of inheriting them without reference to capacity. Even those who do not see in the monarch the highest officer, but something more and higher, must at least admit that among other things he is an officer or magistrate likewise, unless they claim a confused essence in the monarch, according to which he is the mystic shrine of sovereignty, a view which I endeavored to refute in the first volume. But nowhere can we depart from strict principle and resort to compromising expediency, however necessary or right, without proportional sacrifice. The monarch who does not obtain his place by his talent must allow himself to be surrounded with fetters which for the private citizen would not be endurable.

The favoritism of a monarch becomes still more serious in countries in which the expediency of hereditary government is carried still farther against abstract principle, and the crown is suffered to descend upon that sex which otherwise is justly excluded from all public employment. While favoritism has with female sovereigns the additional incentive of difference of sex, which by no means needs on that account to be founded upon unlawful affection, it is, generally speaking, for them more difficult to overcome the feeling of partiality by reason alone; since the soul of the woman is by nature more active in the spheres of affection and feeling than in that of the reasoning judgment. It is necessary therefore that ruling princesses and their advisers most especially guard against this dangerous political fault. These remarks do not hold good against real friendship in a monarch. On the contrary, if he is himself capable of friendship, and if he has a friend on terms which are very different from capricious favoritism in the one or interested submission in the other, friendship is one of the greatest blessings to monarchs. I do not know that anything in Henry IV. of France is a truer sign of greatness of soul than that he could be so true a friend as he was to Sully, nor could any event in his reign be called happier than that he found Sully and concluded a friendship with him. They were united in the great desire to live for France, in a generous, candid, manly friendship. But the narrower the mind of the monarch, or of any man of power, the more danger exists that favoritism will steal in under the garb of friendship.

Favoritism is, however, not only dangerous in monarchies, or there in the monarch only; it is equally dangerous in republics, and in every citizen according to his sphere. If it becomes general, it tramples justice, the foundation of the state, under foot; it stifles virtue and exertion of talent, because they do not avail; it leads to party rancor, because it bestows places of profit or honor upon "friends" alone, not for past merit and future benefit to the commonwealth, but for past and future party services; or it substitutes altogether caprice for reason, and leads infallibly to a state of general public dishonesty, in which public places are considered as berths of enrichment, of pilfering, or of family aggrandizement; it leads to the appointment of incompetent men and to general public disgrace and apathy, to servile adherence and ruinous flattery. There are letters of Washington's which might show how utterly unjust and subversive of the best interests of the state he considered favoritism. Pym is another striking example of perfect freedom from this vice. "He knew neither brother, kinsman, nor friend, superior nor inferior, when they stood in the way to hinder his pursuit of the public good." It was a saying of his, "Such a one is my entire friend, to whom I am much obliged, but I must not pay my private debts out of the public stock."[1] "To such a degree and with such sincerity did he act upon this principle, that when his friends frequently put him in mind of his children and pressed upon his consideration that although he regarded not himself yet he ought to provide that it might be well with them, his usual answer was, 'if it were well with the public his family was well enough.'"

XLV. The family is not only important for the stricter political reasons which have been dwelt upon in previous passages, but likewise as affording those relations out of which mutual affections grow, feelings strongly connected with public spirit and patriotism. The love of our family, of our kinsmen, is not only innocent, but necessary and a powerful agent in society, an incentive to exertion and a source of public spirit. Yet, like all other original agents, it must be judiciously watched lest it grow stronger than it ought to be, lest it transcend its legitimate and natural power. Not to have greater forbearance towards members of our own family than to others, so long as strict duty allows of this forbearance, would certainly be wanting in duty; but to allow family considerations to outweigh higher and the highest considerations is either pusillanimous or dastardly. If William III. saw, as I for one believe that he did, that England was in danger of being ruined and of being forced into retrograde steps or into a political system similar to that of France and Spain, appalling indeed to every honest man; if he felt convinced that James had become a rebel against the country and constitution, and saw that he himself could rescue England, when called upon by circumstances and by many of the endangered nation, he would have shown extreme weakness of

---

[1] These two extracts are from Stephen Marshall's Sermon preached before Parliament at the Funeral of Mr. Pym, 4to, 1644, as quoted in the Westminster Review for July, 1833, in an article on the life of Pym, from which likewise the next following quotation in the text is taken.

mind in allowing family relations to weigh against this sacred calling of the welfare of Britain and of Europe.

Yet as the undue attachment to friends or favorites assumes the dangerous form of favoritism, so does the excessive attachment to the members of one's family become nepotism. The name of this political vice comes from the government of the papal hierarchy, and has been chiefly restricted to it; but the evil principle is visible elsewhere too, and there is no reason why we should not use the term in a general sense. Nepotism, or the showering of riches, power, and honors upon the nephews (*nepoti*) of the pope (hence the name), became actually a state institution, not unlike to the keeping of royal mistresses in France, until, finally, endowed and powerful relations of the pope were considered necessary for the honor of the pope and despatch of business, even by some of the highest clergy in Rome, who do not always seem to have had flattery in view.[1] Indeed, the government was so badly contrived, the cardinals so divided and subservient to foreign courts, and the state of Italy so utterly demoralized, that the pope was not expected to trust all his secrets to any stranger out of his family; yet the business required some minister or other who had the confidence of the pope. Who then could be this person except a relation of his?

There is indeed no danger at present that nepotism, as it existed towards the end of the fifteenth and the beginning of the sixteenth century, can reappear there or in any other state; yet it is one of our duties to weigh attentively any institution or fact in which we find a general principle, good or bad, developed distinctly and in all its consistency, in all its beauty or hideousness. We shall then better understand the

---

[1] I believe that papal nepotism, in its various historical phases, has nowhere been so thoroughly and amply represented as by Ranke, History of the Popes, Eng. trans. (in the Amer. ed. of 1841. See especially vol. i. pp. 46, 51, 99, 274, 275, 301). See also the remarks of Macchiavelli on this subject in the first book of his History of Florence. That not only nephews were promoted by th s nepotism, but, under the name of *nepoti*, the natural sons also of popes, as for instance under Alexander VI., is a well known fact.

less distinct manifestations of the same principle at other periods or in other spheres. The crime and plunder which were connected with nepotism were appalling: state property was alienated and changed into hereditary principalities for the *nepoti*, until at last these treasonable procedures were prohibited by the pope and cardinals themselves; the *nepoti* obtained money for selling justice, or, what is perhaps most curious and strikes a professional politician as a choice rarity, —as the naturalist is interested by some peculiar monstrosity, —the "cardinal *nepote*" gave (and of course sold) "*non graveturs*," which were immunities against all future procedures by way of justice, amounting to more than an anticipation of pardon of a general kind, as the English kings formerly gave them in cases of impeachment.[1] Lorenzo de Medici writes to Pope Innocent VIII. that other popes had not waited so long in bestowing property upon their family, and that should he hesitate longer, other reasons would be suspected. "Zeal and duty," he continues, "oblige me to remind your holiness that no man is immortal; that a pope signifies as much as he chooses to signify; his office cannot be made hereditary; only the honor and benefices which he bestows upon his family he can call his own."[2] The very theory followed by some prime ministers! Washington, in a letter, dated February 20, 1797, to John Adams, when president, expresses his hope that promotion will not be withheld from Mr. John Quincy Adams "because he is your son."[3] Equally striking are letters written by that pure and single-hearted man,

---

[1] Under Urban VIII., for instance. See Ranke, as above, vol. i. (also vol. ii., *i.e.*, vol. iv. of Princes and Nations of Southern Europe), p. 442, extract from MS. by Cardinal Cecchini.

[2] In Fabroni Vita Laurentii, ii. 390.

[3] This letter happens to be preserved in a pamphlet entitled Correspondence between the Hon. John Adams and William Cunningham, Boston, 1823, published by the son of the latter. Washington adds that if he were now to be brought into the diplomatic line he would not disapprove of the caution hinted at in Mr. Adams's letter, "upon the principle which has regulated my own conduct," but he says that the case differs. The question is only promotion of a valuable public servant.

when president, to relatives who solicited offices.[1] It is universally considered odious to see the relatives of a minister, distant or near, like so many birds feasting upon the carcass of the public revenue, and mere decency ought to prevent an undue favor towards relations;[2] though it is true, on the other hand, it would look much like political prudery if relationship should actually impede. It is advisable on the score of mere prudence that a high officer should never appoint a near relative to another high office near him, for the public feel insecure and naturally uneasy at it. Very many constitutions prohibit such appointments. Brothers and sons of the doge of Venice were excluded from high appointments. The constitution of Geneva prohibits more than two persons of the same name and family from sitting in the council of state,

---

[1] Washington's Writings; such letters as those to Bushrod Washington, New York, July 27, 1789, and to Benjamin Lincoln, Mount Vernon, March 11, 1789. Mr. Sparks gives part of a letter in a note to page 478, vol. ix., which contains the following passage: "Among all these anxieties, I will not conceal from you, I anticipated none greater than those that were likely to be produced by applications for appointments to the different offices which would be created under the new government. Nor will I conceal that my apprehensions have already been but too well justified. Scarcely a day passes in which applications of one kind or another do not arrive; insomuch that had I not early adopted some general principles I should before this time have been wholly occupied in this business. As it is, I have found the number of answers which I have been necessitated to give in my own hand an almost insupportable burden to me.

"The points in which all these answers have agreed in substance are, that, should it be my lot to go again into public office, I would go without being under any possible engagements of any nature whatsoever; that, so far as I knew my own heart, I would not be in the remotest degree influenced, in making nominations, by motives arising from the ties of family or blood; and that, on the other hand, three things, in my opinion, ought principally to be regarded, namely, the fitness of characters to fill offices, the comparative claims from the former merits and sufferings in service of the different candidates, and the distribution of appointments in as equal a proportion as might be to persons belonging to the different States in the Union."

[2] Earl Grey, universally esteemed, even by the opposition, probably suffered no severer attacks than those founded upon the reproach that he provided too anxiously for his extensive family relations. It will be remembered that it was favoritism and nepotism which furnished Junius with the materials for some of his most caustic sarcasms.

composed of twenty-four members, and more than five individuals of the same name and family in the representative council, composed of two hundred and seventy-four members.[1] In so small a state, where frequent intermarriages produce powerful family affiliations, this may be a serviceable law; but since the powerful agency of the public press has become a vital political agent, such matters are in most cases better left to public opinion, until it shall be found insufficient. Besides, laws of this sort rarely prevent the evil, if there is a disposition to engender it, except that it is well enough thus decidedly to express by a law the opinion which society entertains of the subject.

---

[1] Constitution du Canton de Génève, tit. iv. 89, and tit. iii. 42.

## CHAPTER V.

Gratitude fully discussed.—Ingratitude.—Excess of Gratitude aids Usurpers.—Cæsar, Napoleon. — Distinction between Gratitude and Popularity. — Popularity.—Sudden and Passing Popularity; Lasting Popularity.—We have no Right to seek Popularity, but must suffer it to seek us.—Power of spontaneous Popularity; peculiar Power of spontaneously returned Popularity.—Slavery of Popularity. — Danger of Popularity, in Free Countries, to the Individual. — Crowds to receive distinguished Men.—Great Danger of Personal Popularity for Liberty. — Pericles. — Demagogues. — Athenian Demagogism. — Monuments. — The Duty of Attention. — Observation of Primary Agents and Elements.—Truth and Justice connected with it.—Obligation to study the History of our Country, its Institutions and their Classical Periods.—It is necessary in modern Times to read Newspapers.

XLVI. INGRATITUDE has at all times been held one of the worst of vices; it proceeds from meanness of soul, and annihilates one of the indispensable and most genial ties among men. To requite good with evil, or to remain untouched by the good conferred upon us, shows a callous heart; and of whatever changes the human heart is capable, the change from meanness or callousness to nobleness or warmth is the rarest of all, because a whole deep-rooted disposition and turn of feeling and thought is to be changed, which can be effected by a long training only; but this requires in the commencement a degree of nobleness of purpose. Gratitude, in all its manifestations, towards the living and the dead, who directly or indirectly have conferred good upon us, even though it be in no other way than by leaving us an encouraging, cheering, or inspiring example, ought to be cultivated from the earliest period in education. Public ingratitude, wanton disregard of the best men and the best exertions and purest sacrifices, is no less vicious and injurious to public welfare than private ingratitude is in its own sphere. It proceeds from sordidness and promotes it. Noble souls find a pleasure and deep enjoyment in warmly acknowledging real benefits and genuine kindness, and in reverencing what is good and great; it is the little-minded and narrow-hearted, or the evil-disposed, who are troubled and haunted by fretting jealousy, who see in all greatness of action or elevation of thought, and in the acknowledgment by the public of the virtues of others, a reflection on themselves, as well as a danger to the public. They, judging from their own selfishness, believe that no greatness can exist without injury to the common liberty, and have at times even publicly proclaimed the "danger of talent," thus becoming rebels against God's own order of things and the fairest works of his hands; but "there is a congeniality between vast powers of thought and dignity of purpose. None are so capable of sacrificing themselves as those who have most to sacrifice, who in offering themselves make the greatest offerings to humanity."[1] The wicked and the little-minded are ever leagued against grateful reverence of high-minded patriotism; and he that cannot be grateful or feel esteem deserves neither love nor esteem. His soul is void of some of the best impulses.

Why do we love liberty? Why does mankind eternally struggle for it? If liberty necessarily required the sacrifice of the noblest traits and imprints of humanity, if the sameness of mediocrity were its condition, it ought to be shunned as the most unfortunate state in which society can be placed. We love liberty, we sacrifice everything to her, as the last and highest good, because it is that state of things which most corresponds to God's order of things, which promotes the freest development of thought and action; because man, made for thought and action, is most really man if protected by her. Were it otherwise, liberty would be the most unnatural state, opposed to the highest calling of humanity. Let a nation for any length of time systematically cast aside its best and loftiest characters, those of which it ought to be proud as finding its spirit and endeavors nobly represented and concentrated in them; let a community for a series of

---

[1] Rev. Dr. Channing.

years reward its purest and most gifted citizens with ungrateful neglect, and with unworthy partiality for servile flatterers; let a monarchy adopt the policy of overlooking those upon whom public opinion bestows grateful honor, or a republic requite faithful and generous patriotism, civic wisdom, and stanch justice with petty jealousy or chill disrespect, and they will soon lose public dignity, morality, and elevation, and sink into sordid and corroding egotism — the most unfailing of national dissolvents.

XLVII. Yet is it not true that nations have as often sinned by way of gratitude as of ingratitude? Have not free nations, in far the greater number of cases, lost their liberty because they were intoxicated with gratitude or admiration of real or imagined benefits received at the hands of the usurper? Is not the willingness with which the mass give up their liberties, with which they sometimes press upon the usurper the surrender of freedom on their part, frequently due to this cause? By what indeed are in most cases usurpers supported and emboldened, if not by the acclamation of the people? To destroy the rights or liberties of one part they must necessarily have the support of the other, if the question is of intestine revolutions and not of conquests by foreigners.

In order to answer these questions correctly and see the subject in all its bearings, it is necessary to make careful distinctions.

In some cases the act of the usurper is but the final accomplishment and ratification of a radical change prepared and effected throughout a social system from a period long antecedent to that of the usurpation; and the existing system, bestowing franchises upon some, once salutary, has, by the change of circumstances and of the people's spirit, become galling or ruinous to the mass, or the people have become unable any longer to uphold the institutions of former liberty. Such was the case when Cæsar grasped the reins. Rome was no longer Rome. It is indeed no subject fit for the present occasion to inquire whether Cæsar belonged in mind to the class of mean usurpers, who prefer the purple and an elevated throne in the hall of audience to a lofty place in history, and are willing to exchange for a regal title, which has graced the worst as well as the best, the proud name of a great citizen; but certain it is that even if Cæsar had been one of the best, full of calmness of soul and love of justice like Washington, placed as he and the Roman commonwealth were, rotten as the whole framework of government and demoralized as the public spirit were, he would have been bound, with his power and insight, to consummate the fall of the old order of things and establish a new one. The constitution of Rome, grown out of a totally different state of things and calculated for it, had become a nuisance. Civil war and fermentation were the order of the day; the aristocracy factious, the democracy lawless and indolent, while both were rapacious. In a crisis of this serious import it is very natural that the people should willingly throw more power than he before had into the hands of a powerful man, and should even rejoice, by a natural instinct, if he assumed more and more, because they first of all desired protection against bloodshed and extortion. Whether we admire Napoleon or not, whether we consider his saying to Las Cases, "If I had aped Washington I should have been guilty of a mere silliness; all that I could strive for was to be a crowned Washington," as empty words or not, whether we believe that he criminally abused his power and neglected every opportunity of developing a civic spirit or of sowing its seeds, as the only means of strengthening, restoring, and permanently healing France, there can be no manner of doubt that, had he been as pure as Doria,[1] he still would have been

---

[1] Andrew Doria, whose name, the historian Rotteck says, calls up the name of Timoleon, was born at Genoa, in 1466, a period when his republic was rent by factions and northern Italy was the unceasing battle-field of the European continental powers. Genoa had lost her fairest dominions. Galeazzo Sforza, duke of Milan, ruled likewise over Genoa, once free and powerful. He had ordered to draw ropes where walls should be erected from the castle to the sea, as an additional means of security against the Genoese. The assembled multitude was gaping at this token of subjugation, when a bold man, Lazzaro Doria, stepped forward and severed the ropes in presence of Galeazzo's servants. The

called upon to break up the ill-jointed and injuriously-working machine of government that then existed, and popular applause would have been justly bestowed upon him.

XLVIII. Secondly, we must not mistake popularity, of whatever sort, for the expression of public gratitude, which was designated above as a virtue of high importance in politics. Popularity is a subject of magnitude, and it behoves us to examine it well.

What is popularity? To speak plainly, it is the being liked and cherished by many; being acceptable to the people. A man, a measure, a tune, a color, may thus be popular. The power of popularity, therefore, rests essentially on sympathy,

---

people were roused; but their excitement vanished; the best citizens emigrated, to avoid servitude. Columbus left Genoa at this time, and Andrew Doria, having served against the Turks, went to Urbino. Genoa revolted against Mantua, and acknowledged France. Doria took service under the king, Louis XII., but he never forgot his country. When Francis I. had succeeded Louis, had broken his oath taken to Charles V., and suddenly fallen upon Italy, and the troops of Charles fled to Naples, and everything seemed to indicate the ascendency of Francis, feared by all Europe, and Italy especially, Doria hoisted the imperial flag and turned the scale. He acted very differently from the Constable Bourbon; Doria was not subject to France, and Francis tyrannized over Genoa. She hoped for deliverance at the hands of this hero. He entered the city victoriously, and expelled the foreigners; the people, carried away by gratitude, greeted him as their prince. Doria might undoubtedly have established a dynasty, nor did he need to found it with blood. His fellow-citizens urged a crown upon him; but he was greater: he declined, although his family had been for centuries allied with emperors and kings. He exhorted his fellow-citizens to be united and virtuous, that they might be free, in a speech which ended, "With pride and emotion I call myself a free citizen of Genoa. This and your friend I desire to be, not your ruler; and may it never be said of Doria that when he served his country he had selfish ends in view." He used the favorable spirit of the people to establish with their co-operation a new constitution, by which the tyranny of the aristocracy and the lawlessness of the people, which had so often distracted Genoa, were avoided—a constitution which lasted three hundred years, until the great revolutions of Europe hurried away this with so many others, in their sweeping course. Doria died ninety-four years old, honored and loved as a very father by his republic. His tomb bears this inscription: "Andreæ Auriæ, civi optimo, felicissimoque Vindici atque Authori publicæ Libertatis, Senatus Populusque Genuensis posuit."

the adaptation, assimilation, or prominent development of the feelings and likings of the community, or the set of people with whom we are popular. This leads us at once to two distinctions. The feelings from which this sympathy arises may be good or bad; a leader of robbers may be popular with his band by humoring or satisfying their bad feelings and propensities, as Doria was popular with the good by good measures; and popularity may be passing or lasting, suddenly excited by suddenly humoring a feeling strongly excited at the moment, or well founded upon the esteem of some prominent quality which is valued as an important one by the people, and which they have reason to believe exists in an eminent degree in the popular person.

The good citizen can of course cherish the popularity of the good only, as a welcome cheering on the path of duty and a power to do good. But how must he obtain it? Popularity is not an ultimate object; the ultimate object is to do right. We are not allowed, therefore, to obtain popularity by sacrificing right or duty. We must not seek popularity as an end, which may ultimately determine our actions, because thereby we should establish an arbitrary and extra-ethical standard for our actions. We must allow popularity to come to us; if it comes in consequence of our acting right, and gaining the sympathy of fellow-citizens because we feel in common with them and for them, well and good; if it does not, we have not to answer for it. No moral code makes the demand, Thou shalt be popular. The moral code says, Try to obtain the esteem of the good, but before all act right, although all should abandon you. It is a happy fact, however, that, with very few exceptions, no surer means exists to obtain lasting popularity, a popularity which, though it may be lost for a time, will return, and, if so, with redoubled strength, than that which is founded upon the esteem of our fellow-men. Esteem does not necessarily constitute popularity, which, we have seen, rests on sympathy, and there are many reasons which thus may withhold it from an honorable man. He may not share the feelings of the public;

all his chief endeavors may be directed to a point uninteresting to the community; his manners may not be pleasing. Nor is popularity the infallible reward of the good for good and pure endeavors. The best may be misunderstood, the more easily so the farther they are in advance of their age, while less elevated endeavors, perhaps mediocrity, for the very reason that it can be understood by the many, may meet with general popularity, if it happens successfully to strike common sympathy. How many instances are recorded in history of overwhelming popularity of contemporaries, which vanished like clouds with posterity, and of neglect by contemporaries of men whose names posterity has placed highest on the list of great and wise men! Popularity, therefore, is as little an ultimate criterion as it is an ultimate moral object. But this remains certain, that esteem forms necessarily an essential ingredient of lasting political popularity with the good; and such alone we ought to value.

XLIX. Popularity is pleasing, it delights the heart, not only in politics, but in all spheres. How could it be otherwise for man, a being created for society? This is only a stronger reason why we ought not to make it the standard of our actions. So soon as a man does this, he submits to the worst species of slavery—that of mind and heart. He throws away his own standard within, and seeks for one without, a changeable one withal; he loses self-esteem and strict rectitude, and in short is a mental slave. There is no institution in this nether world which has not together with its advantages its dangers, and the danger of civil liberty and publicity of politics—the one cannot exist without the other—is the danger of popularity. The power of public opinion, the just principle that we ought in many cases—not indeed in all—ultimately to submit to it, and in part to regulate our conduct by it, are so many inducements which will lead the fainthearted to yield to this servitude. The dread of unpopularity has ruined many statesmen, led authors to abjure truth, seduced citizens to crooked paths, and shows its unfortunate effect with the young in the schools and colleges of free countries. There is no teacher, I suppose, who has not seen or felt the evil influence which a positive desire of popularity or fear of unpopularity exercises upon many young men in institutions for education, seducing not a few even to vice and final ruin. It is, therefore, one of the first duties of the young, early to learn manfully and unequivocally to do right for its own sake; and for their teachers to imbue their souls early and deeply with this element of rectitude. It will be one of the best preparations for future and public life, for the support of the commonwealth and genuine patriotism. Once more, the danger of free countries is morbid desire of popularity.

L. The ingredients of sound popularity are esteem at home and the sympathy of the people. This popularity in truly free countries begins generally at home, a circumstance of still greater importance in vast countries, in which the people at a distance cannot judge of the private character of a citizen except by the name and standing he enjoys at home. Popularity begins in the house and family, extends to village, county, state, and moves in concentric circles over the country. Keep, therefore, your house and affairs in good order, treat your wife well, and educate your children carefully; be a benevolent neighbor and public-spirited member of the community; and you will generally lay a firm foundation for popularity. Or if degenerate times despise these elements, if the people banish even an Aristides, all you have to remember is that popularity is no duty, but only a welcome effect of duty if it comes of itself.[1] On the other hand, as popularity is a power, and, if just, a lawful power, as in many cases the leading citizen cannot act without it, and as it depends at the same time upon sympathy, it is clear that he

---

[1] Mirabeau frequently exclaimed, "J'expie bien cruellement les erreurs de ma jeunesse," and Dumont says he knew that Mirabeau would have gone through fire to clear himself, not, certainly, on account of morality itself, but on account of the injury his popularity continued to suffer from his former reputation.—Dumont, Souvenir sur Mirabeau, etc., chap. xiv.

must not slight it. There are national feelings, and even prejudices, unimportant in themselves yet strong on account of extensive and historical or other associations, which it would be wanton unnecessarily to offend; and by "unnecessarily" I mean if they do not stand in the way in the obtaining of a laudable object, or actually produce evil. In the latter case it may not be your duty to attack them, either because you are not quite certain regarding them, or because you have no adequate power to overcome them and by an attack upon them would fritter away the influence and means you might use for other purposes. One man cannot do everything. A citizen engaged in reforming the penal laws of his country may observe great and even injurious errors in the literary taste of his countrymen. He is not bound on that account to engage in a contest against perverse taste. Very many citizens have deprived themselves of all power to do good by attacks which did not come from an intention to overcome and extirpate an error, but rather from a weakness which deprived of the power of silence—a power as great as that of speech. But in no case ought one to favor directly or indirectly what he believes to be absolutely wrong, or sacrifice to it; in no case ought he to give way to national follies; he should make due allowance for prejudices, and not ruin the best cause by throwing away the whole because he can only obtain part, or by presumptuously setting up a standard of perfection; but in no case should he administer to passion, wickedness, or crime, either by remaining silent when silence must be construed into approval or by giving in a cowardly manner a qualified approval.[1]

---

[1] Within sixty years there were executed in Geneva one hundred and fifty witches; yet Calvin does not once express his dissatisfaction with this error in his many writings and innumerable letters. We are justified, therefore, in concluding that he shared the general error of the times, although he does not speak in favor of the trials, because we must expect that he would otherwise have felt himself bound to pronounce his opinion; his silence necessarily appears as qualified assent. That Calvin does not pronounce dissent, I mention on the authority of Mr. Henry, Life of John Calvin, in German, page 489.

The citizen who is to act must be understood by the community; but we are not understood by word of mouth only; we must have the sympathy of the hearer,—this constant interpreter of human words, which are but broken accents without it. "How difficult is it," exclaimed Cato when the last time before judges, "to defend one's self before men with whom one has not lived!"

LI. There is a subject not unconnected with that of popularity, which deserves a moment's attention—the crowds which at times receive distinguished citizens. As a faithful and distinguished citizen must be scrupulously on his guard against the full tide of popularity in general, since it is but too apt to throw him off his guard, under most pleasing, stirring, or even inspiring forms; so he must not mistake the meaning of crowds. It may be well imagined that it must be animating to a citizen or general to see thus visibly and strikingly the feeling of his country towards him represented by thousands of eyes turned upon him, as perhaps the sole cherished object of the attention of all. Who would envy him the enjoyment of so elating and electrifying a moment if he deserves it? But he must remember that of itself it shows little,—proves nothing; for, though thousands may be present, many more thousands may not be. When Charles II. made his entry into London after the death of Cromwell, and saw the many people rejoicing at his return, he exclaimed, "Where are my enemies?" There were enough, but they were not present, or, if so, could of course not be discerned. Who, that ever has seen it, can forget how multitudes and crowds were never wanting to stare at enemy after enemy that made his entry into a populous city, during the many changes in the times of the wars of Napoleon? When Riego entered Madrid, he was greeted by crowds; when Ferdinand followed, he was greeted likewise. It is not necessary to suppose that these crowds were entirely composed of the same persons; but it shows that crowds in large cities prove little, unless the mere excitement itself may, as in fact sometimes it does, prove something; as when a citizen not high in official station is received by thousands. There are always very many who go to see a sight—no matter of what kind—because others go, and very many people to whom huzzaing of itself seems to be an enjoyment. There are persons who, when the bells begin to toll in indication of fire, will suddenly break forth in a lusty shout, as if an opportunity only had been wanting for their shouts to go off. The same persons will throw their hats and hurrah loudly for any one, whoever he be. Yet princes are very frequently deceived by assembled crowds and their huzzas. I do not speak of those crowds which the police at times have paid for hurrahing; but bona fide crowds with bona fide shouts amount to little, and are rarely faithful indexes of anything which might be of importance, except they are overwhelmingly strong, or are silent, for "the silence of the people is the censure of kings." Princes, instead of allowing flatterers to pay them compliments upon the assembled multitudes, would feel rather humbled, if they considered that it is the show which brings the greater number together. They can serve as no foundation for any political satisfaction. The coronation of few monarchs was attended more numerously than that of Charles X., yet his crown was not for all that the faster on his head.

LII. Popularity, if sought as an object worth obtaining for itself, is not more dangerous to individuals seeking it than it is to the people, who do not grant it for virtue and talent but on personal or capricious grounds and in spite of the law. Nothing indeed is more dangerous to liberty than the permitting a citizen to lead or rule on account of great popularity, and the greater the popularity and the longer the sway, the more ruinous will be the effect; because the political energy of the state concentrates in him, and receives from him its impulse, the institutions lose their energy, the law as law loses its vigor, and the community becomes unfit for civil liberty. If the leader, thus placed beyond the line which no citizen ever should be allowed to overstep, is restless and nuprincipled, he may become a usurper; but even if he be naturally of a most generous mind, and have the general welfare alone before his eyes, the effect is always disastrous. If the people are willing to confide the government into the hands of even so glorious a leader as Pericles, on account of his personal popularity, and allow him momentous influence besides and beyond the law, because he is great and glorious, if they confide in him, the individual, because they are charmed by him and not because he acts out their institutions, they must be content to follow, when the mortal lot befalls this glorious leader, so low and puffed-up a demagogue as Cleon. So no monarch properly provides for his state who does not powerfully promote institutions, but makes the government essentially dependent upon his personality, however brilliant this may be. The most gifted monarchs are frequently those who are most easily betrayed into this political error.

LIII. Free nations who value their liberty ought jealously to frown down all leading and ruling popularity which does not strictly keep within the limits of the law, and to allow no essential influence except within its institutions, none whatsoever on account of a mere personal, still less a capricious, popularity. This does not exclude a sound and healthy opposition, of which we shall treat presently. I speak of that popularity which does not merely oppose the administration but infringes the laws and their spirit, and stands instead of administration. Out of this spirit arise demagogues—men who gain popularity and sway by unlawful or wicked means and by flattering or pampering the evil dispositions of men. After Pericles, or through him, demagogism was raised in Athens, we might almost say, to a state institution, as we have seen that nepotism was under the popes of the fifteenth century—a most melancholy condition for democracies. For it has this peculiarity, that while it clips and stints more and more the lawful operation of established institutions, which demagogues never fail to do in order to flatter the crowd, it gives on the

other hand more and more essential power to the undefined
and unrestricted influence of the demagogue, under the delusive garb of giving power to the people—another and substantial reason against democratic autarchies, in addition to
those which we found in the first volume. Neither Pericles,
the guardian of Alcibiades, nor Socrates, his teacher, was able
to regulate his ambitious temper, because the indulgent love
of the people spoiled and ruined him. He became a traitor
to his country. The history of Athens after Pericles almost
concentrates in a series of demagogues, Cleon, Hyperbolus,
Callias, Alcibiades, and whatever their names were. Opposite
to the demagogue rose the oligarchist, dealing in treachery,
and a vile tribe of sycophants prospered in the struggle, while
the people were carried madly to their ruin.[1]

LIV. Before we dismiss the subject of national gratitude I
desire to add a few words on statues and other monuments
erected in honor of events or persons by authority or the
community at large. Ought we to erect such? It has been
often said, "Much better that the memory of a person or event
live in the hearts of the people than that it be perpetuated in
stone." No doubt it is; so it is better that knowledge be in
the head than in books, but still books are not only useful
but necessary. I for my part am decidedly in favor of judicious

---

[1] Frederic the Great has a whole chapter on flatterers in his Anti-Macchiavelli.
There is a remarkable passage in the Mémorial de Sainte-Hélène, which I
give because worthy of reflection, and, though we shall not entirely agree with
Napoleon, that which he advances respecting what people say applies at least more
or less to all excited times. The emperor, having spoken of popularity and *debonnaireté*, adds, "Thus we ought to serve the people worthily, and not occupy ourselves with pleasing them. The best way of gaining them is by doing them good;
nothing more dangerous than to flatter them: if after that they do not obtain all
they desire, they become irritated and believe that faith has not been kept with
them; and if we resist, they hate so much the more, as they believe themselves
duped. The first duty of a prince is doubtless to do that which the people wants;
but that which a people wants is hardly ever that which it says: its will, its
wants ought rather to be in the heart of the prince than in his mouth." Page
110, vol ii., Paris ed., 1824.

monuments, and my reasons are these. I consider them moral, honorable, elevating, and useful.

Whatever has a tendency to impress man with the fact that he is a member of society, influenced and influencing—of a society which is closely connected with the past; whatever leads man to feel attached to mankind has a tendency to elevate him, to suppress or soften that which is selfish or brutish; whatever tends to insulate man, to stifle the consciousness in him that he is an integrant part of society, produces egotism and crime, because it weakens humanity in him, which is in a great manner founded upon sociality. Hence the great use of studying history: it makes us conscious that we belong to a great union of beings, existing for important purposes. Sismondi, in his History of the Fall of the Roman Empire, justly says, "The morality of a nation is preserved by associating its sentiments with all that is stable and permanent: it is destroyed by whatever tends to concentrate them on the present moment. So long as our recollections are dear to us, we shall take care that our hopes be worthy of them; but a people who sacrifice the memory of their ancestors or the welfare of their children to the pleasures of a day are but sojourners in a country—they are not citizens." The study of history and every means of commingling its reminiscences with our soul make us modest, yet firm and persevering; history gives substance, earnestness, and a necessity of action, not of talk, to the mind. All periods which have been most fruitful to a nation or mankind at large, most active in building and sowing, not in destroying and uprooting, have ever distinguished themselves by an earnest zeal to understand the past ages, which generated the present; all periods which destroyed and ruined without developing, which are distinguished for superficial clamor and theories without character, substance, or sense, are distinguished for arrogant disregard of any knowledge beyond the present day, which is considered as overflowing with wisdom. Man never studies the past without earnestly thinking of the future; but so soon as man's thoughts dwell upon the past and meditate the future destinies of that which surrounds him, so soon as his affections are roused by that which is absent, he feels elevated, and returns to the consideration of that which now exists and is close before him, to the present moment and himself, with an expanded heart and a greater soul; and he is only thus able to consider the present and himself individually without selfishness. So soon as man, on the other hand, dwells upon the present without any connection with the past and the future, he exposes himself to sordid views and arrogant conceit. The truth of this position may be tested in a proportionate degree by every one in his daily life and smallest transactions, as in the actions and performances of whole nations. Since monuments, however—be they columns, inscriptions, entire fabrics, or whatever else—are means to connect our thoughts with the past, and thus lead us to dwell upon the possible future, they are desirable for any nation which feels that its destiny is higher and nobler than the mere care for the present moment could indicate. Monuments are impressive tokens and illustrations of history, and not merely for those who do not read, nor even most so for them, but the impressions received through the eye in shape and form are strong and lasting. A thoughtful man will dwell upon a monument with fruitful thoughts, while the volatile are arrested for a moment, reminded of one that was great, good, heroic, and one more name, one more date, will be stored up in vivid remembrance. The image of a statue or monument, frequently passed by the school-boy, will sink with many associations deeply into his heart, so that the busiest life of later periods will not make it vanish again. A public monument honors those who erected it. In viewing it we feel that a debt of gratitude in some manner is paid; we feel that we live in a community sensible to worth, merit, nobleness of action, and willing to acknowledge them. To the active, monuments are incentives: no Boston school-boy feels the worse for having viewed Chantrey's statue of Washington, and if he could view in his early dreams another of Hancock it would not harm him. A column has been erected to Walter Scott in Glasgow, with the inscription, "that it may record their [the citizens of Glasgow] admiration of his genius, their deep sense of the honor which his name reflects on his country, and their gratitude for the delight which they have received from his writings." A statue of Fulton, with some similarly appropriate inscription, in some conspicuous landing-place at New York, would be a just tribute, harm no one, and do good to many. The lion erected at Thermopylæ in honor of Leonidas must have told a pregnant story to many a Greek. Monuments show and testify palpably and strikingly that society is not always occupied with material interests alone, but allows the nobler sentiments their proper sphere. Whoever can view Westminster, or the Pantheon in Paris, without stirring feeling, must be without sympathy for anything great; whoever can believe that those places do not exercise their moral and inciting influence, not only on those who visit them but on the nation at large, cannot be acquainted with the human heart. By monuments we take the fine arts, one of the choice flowers of civilization, into public service, and in turn promote them; and society is deeply interested in their promotion. They humanize, soften, and refine, and at the same time elevate the standard of taste, one of the most efficient agents of national industry.[1] Bacon says, "Imo citra omnem controversiam, artes emolliunt mores, teneros reddunt, sequaces, cereos, et ad mandata imperii ductiles: ignorantia contra, contumaces, refractorios, seditiosos: quod ex historia clarissime potet, quandoquidem tempora maxime indocta, inculta, barbara, tumultibus, seditionibus, mutationibusque maxime obnoxia fuerint."[2]

The expense of money for monuments or other works of art is one of the most common objections against them. If money is spent in erecting them, and objects of more press-

---

[1] On this subject I have given my views more fully in the Report on Girard College.

Repeatedly has the vast usefulness of diffused taste and pleasure in the fine arts, with reference to industry, and the duty of governments to promote them as far as in them lies, been amply acknowledged in the British parliament.

[2] De Dignitate et Augmentis Scientiarum, lib. i.

ing necessity are neglected, it is of course folly, in this as in any other case, to attend to the less important in preference to the more important. On the other hand, if there are sufficient means for both,—and judiciously managed means may effect much,—it must not be forgotten that money laid out in anything which promotes essential civilization promotes thereby, directly or indirectly, harmony of thought and feeling, and peace among individuals, security, intercommunion, and the standard of social life and comfort; and thus not only is the value of exchangeable articles enhanced, but civilization imprints, with every progress, the character of exchangeableness upon things, performances, and various species of skill and labor, which without it remain without any exchangeable value. We have but to look around us, and every day will furnish us with numerous examples. We must never forget that taste forms an essential ingredient of national industry no less than necessity; that the *wants* of civilization, upon which all industry is founded, consist as really in the wants of taste as of necessity. If the leading motives to industry are wants and security, both are more or less directly promoted in part by the cultivation of the fine arts.

Monuments promote — who would seriously deny it? — glowing patriotism. Whatever is good or great it is well to impress symbolically and compactly on the mind. It is not because we are of a gross nature that we require this; it is because concentrated signs and forms make concentrated impressions. The badge of office makes a sudden, palpable impression. No German passing through Wittenberg requires to be reminded that this is the place where Luther lived, fought, and died; his mind will be filled with recollections and reflections. Still, the iron statue of the Reformer at that place will contribute to present still more vividly the man and the period which affected his country so deeply and lastingly. Few men who travel to the battle-field of Lützen will stand in need of being reminded that there Gustavus Adolphus fell. Yet is there a great difference between this general reminiscence of history, and the ideas which crowd upon the mind when we sit down near the stone which marks the spot where the great man fell, or when we see the spot in the town-house of Lützen which to this day exhibits the floor marked by the blood of the expiring king. It was a praiseworthy custom of the Romans to deposit the ashes of their distinguished men in suitable tombs near the high-roads. In travelling along between rows of sepulchres a man was reading the annals of the great state written in deeply impressive symbols.

It shows no grossness if we love to admire the wisdom of God in the wonderful construction of a small insect's wing and make it thus a symbol of his vast power. So it is not gross when we present great deeds, illustrious men, or periods to which we owe what we are, symbolically in form and shape, by monuments or statues, and when the ingenuity of men is employed to find fit forms delicately to express complicated actions or characters, the spirit of exalted periods, or the sentiments of the founders of states.

But have not monuments been greatly abused? Has not repulsive flattery often erected them? So has religion, so has everything of any general interest to men, been abused. Nor is the love of the fine arts an infallible indication of elevation of the soul. It is not an unfrequent phenomenon that peculiarly corrupt natures, even cruel to excess, have a strong tendency to sentimental emotions, and please themselves in them;[1] but would these enormities be seriously urged against the general influence of the fine arts, if, as is always made a condition, other important objects are not neglected, and the object is the erection of patriotic monuments? Let it be adopted as a rule that no statue shall ever be erected to a living person, but only after the survivors or posterity have pronounced upon the merit, as the censors used to give their judgment upon the doges of Venice after their decease. If,

---

[1] Several Roman emperors are striking instances. In 1830, a woman, Margaret Gottfried, was executed for having successively poisoned more than thirty people, and to her last day she liked sentimental emotions and would at times cry at the recital of poems. See her Biography, published by her counsel, Bremen, 1831.

however, monuments do exist, it is a sacred duty of the citizen to preserve them inviolate, and to bring up the young with a fear of falling into the vandalism of injuring public property in them or in any other shape.

LV. There is a general duty and consequent virtue of the last importance, which for want of a better term we may call the virtue of attention, comprehending therein observation and reflection upon what has been observed. We have seen that the intellect forms an ingredient of man's ethical character, and that the human race constitutes a continuous society, collecting and transmitting knowledge and improving by experience. The animals, "quæ natura prona atque ventri obedientia finxit,"[1] have but a limited degree of observation; man's erect posture, "his eyes turned towards heaven," no more indicate his destiny, as the ancients said, than his duty of free observation around him. We cannot learn and reflect without observing the phenomena around us, and our mind, like our eyes, remains dull and unable to distinguish, if not trained by practice. Observation and attention do not mean a hasty and fretful curiosity, undirected by a concentrated and composed mind which glances at the surface without receiving a lasting impression—mere craving for news and change; but they mean that attention which is the effect of a desire to know the elements of things or principles of phenomena, and their mutual connection with and bearing upon one another—the truth of things, their essential character. Every experience or observation, without it, is shallow and unsound, and propriety, judiciousness, wisdom, and even that primary virtue, justice, depend essentially upon this attention. If we pay the slightest attention to the subject, we shall find that every man is successful in his sphere, from the humblest to the most elevated, useful to his neighbors, and efficient in his calling, in the same degree as he unites with a peculiar skill or talent for his specific calling a knowledge of his subject which is the fruit

---

[1] Sallust, Bell. Catilin., i.

of patient attention to its primary elements and agents alone. We receive no proper knowledge of a tree by satisfying ourselves with a general view of its outward size and bulk. To know it thoroughly we must examine, among other things, a fibre under the microscope. We are cheered in our attention when by closely observing one fibre we gain the knowledge of millions of fibres of the same class.

Those men who may be considered the leaders of mankind, the philosophical minds,—by which I mean all who with a philosophical, that is accurate, analyzing, and comprehensive, mind, examine and grasp their subject, historians, rulers or statesmen, poets, artists, and moral teachers,—will be found to have influenced society so far as and no farther than they combined with a native activity of mind a penetration of reality around them, a comprehension of the nature and operation of the elements or integrant parts of society and all its relations and conditions, and discarded wayward or arbitrary fancy.[1] In this as in so many other respects the ancients ought to serve us as models. Their laws as well as their literature show in an eminent degree, which cannot be sufficiently weighed by us, their clear and lively perception and keen penetration of the real state of things.[2] In this alone lies the advantage of experience, in this the power of the school of misfortune. They

---

[1] [Polybius has a fine passage (ix. 22) in speaking of Hannibal. Dr. Lieber cites the passage in his manuscript notes. "So truly great and wonderful is a man and a soul properly fitted according to the original constitution of its nature to any human work to which it may bend its efforts."]

[2] I have elsewhere spoken of our obligation not to lose by negligence what has been gained at earlier periods and under more fortunate circumstances for a particular subject, but perhaps at great expense to society or under totally different circumstances, which it is not in our power to bring back, or not right for us if we could. Christianity and modern civilization have very materially changed the relation in which the individual stands with the world. We have a world within, with which we strive to bring the outer world in connection and harmony. The real world was the problem of the ancients. We ought surely not to return to their view, but are in duty bound to learn whatever good may have been produced by it without paying the same price. We theorize too easily; we start from ideas and carry them over into the material world: the ancients started from the *fact*, the *object* without.

force knowledge and penetration of reality upon us; if they do not succeed in doing this, they have no improving effect, as we may frequently observe with persons of a dull mind. The necessity of observation, which Bacon so urgently and solemnly presses upon the student of nature,[1] is no greater for him, not even as great as for the student of men and society. Many sufferings and misfortunes have afflicted mankind because their rulers or legislators perceived the important phenomena of society outwardly only, and did not penetrate to the component parts and to their principle of action and mutual relation to one another. Frederic the Great acknowledged that as an administrator of a realm he had gained invaluable knowledge when his father obliged him to act the part of a subaltern officer in one of the administrative courts at Cüstrin. He there studied the fibres, the first and last operation of the agents of society, those minute elements which make up the bulk of what we call society or state; he became acquainted with the action of laws, not only with their words. The essence of a law does not lie in what its words decree, but in the effect which they have upon the given state of things. Nor is it difficult to perceive by perusing the letters and biography of Niebuhr, alluded to before, how that historian was enabled shrewdly to unravel some of the most perplexing questions in Roman history, and to penetrate Roman and past reality, by his constant attention to present reality around him, by never sneering at any knowledge, however humble in appearance, provided it led him to perceive the connection of things. His knowledge of the various relations of the soil to its owners in his native country alone gave him an important key to the corresponding relations with the Romans. So Gibbon, in his Miscellaneous Works (vol. i. p. 136, ed. 1814), says of himself, "My principal obligation to the militia was the making me an Englishman and a soldier. In this peaceful service I imbibed the rudiments of the language and science of tactics, which opened a new field of study and observation.

---

[1] Novum Organum.

The discipline and evolutions of a modern battalion gave me a clearer notion of the phalanx and the legion; and the captain of the Hampshire grenadiers (the reader may smile) has not been useless to the historian of the Empire."

It is painful indeed to observe how many persons walk through life with an obtuse mind and dull eye and yet do not feel prevented from boldly pronouncing their opinion upon all occasions. Many persons are not struck either by the characteristic form or even the color of things, and when they have to give an account it is undefined, unsatisfactory, erroneous, or exaggerated, one way or the other. The most delicate phenomenon in nature, the surprising and admirable connection of a chain of causes and effects, agents of awful simplicity and magnitude, can be laid before them without eliciting their inquiry. Nothing which constitutes the framework of society and gives it its peculiar character attracts them: they do not ask in what relation the tiller of the ground stands to the owner of the soil; how the taxes are decreed, assessed, and levied; what are the pastimes of the people; how often they eat meat in a week; what their standard of comfort, their habits of cleanliness are; in what relation their religion stands to their morality or practical life; whether the people read or not, and what. Still less do they inquire into the most important institutions, and how they became such. They never look, as Bacon calls it, "abroad into universality."

Without this attention we insulate our mind, or the things which may happen to interest us, and cannot see them in their connection, that is in their truth.

LVI. This duty of attention, enjoined upon man because he has received reflective faculties and has the general obligation of truth in all its bearings, is of singular importance in politics, for every one who has to act; hence in free countries for all citizens. The virtue of attention is one of those which require most practice; it cannot begin too early. Whatever we see or hear we ought to try to understand, attempt at least to learn its connection; of a word, term, thing, institution, person, or event, its peculiar character, meaning, history, elements, and causes. A single set of casters on our dining-table, if viewed in all their connections, may teach a vast lesson of political economy, geography, and civilization. We ought not to read the name of a place without combining the idea of its situation with it, or of a law without that of its operation. We thus not only acquire the knowledge of the thing itself, but our horizon expands, one species of knowledge supports others in our mind, our intellect acquires the proper classification of things—a fixed frame-work for further acquisition; it gains clearness and retentiveness, and above all we learn to see things more and more in their true light and bearing, and as our knowledge becomes firmer, truer, and more substantial, we enable ourselves to become juster, and are less exposed to be swayed by casualties or impulses which originally may not have been bad. The judgment of some men upon the whole English revolution has been swayed by the exclamation of James II. when he returned to London and found that Princess Anne had fled: "Good God, my child too has left me!" He who can read this without emotion must have a hard heart; but so natural an exclamation of the afflicted father will weigh very little with him who views the infatuated king in his whole connection with the country over which he so injudiciously ruled. Hardly had the world ceased to applaud the French for manfully resisting a criminal executive outrage, when many not only lavished their sympathy upon the duchess of Berry for attempting to raise a civil war, and in their admiration of her spirited conduct forgot her licentious course of life but actually turned their feeling against Louis Philippe. It may be hard for the duke of Bordeaux to be deprived of a throne, but if we view him in his whole connection we may not find reason to wish him back in the Tuileries.

LVII. We must gather experience: without it no man would be wiser at forty than he was at fifteen, nor England be safer after her Protestant settlement, with its various organic laws, than she was under Charles II. But what is experience? It is not the mere witnessing or going through the perils or drudgery of a thing, nor the bare knowledge that a fact has happened. It is the knowledge we derive by reflection upon that which happens. Men may pass through a variety of scenes without gathering any experience, as an obstinate physician may kill hundreds by the same physic in the same cases, because he refuses to reflect upon what he witnesses. Attention, therefore, to what we witness, see, or learn, constitutes an ingredient of experience, and this experience may be personal or not, that is, we may see with our own eyes or not, perceive with our own senses or not. This distinction, however, is far less definite than is generally supposed. For if personal experience relates to effects upon my own senses or person alone, it is necessarily extremely limited. If we extend its meaning, and would comprehend within it what has happened at our own times, the distinction becomes arbitrary; for we may or may not know an event of our own times more thoroughly than one of past periods. It is the certainty of knowledge which is important, and this may at times be much greater when we were not present at an event than when we were. Experience, true knowledge, a just view of the things and relations among which we live, or whatever we may call it, demand of every citizen two things, that he know the society he lives in as thoroughly as with his means he is able to do, and, in order to do it, that he know the history of its growth and of the development of its character (its generic history).

There is an absolute duty of the citizen to make himself acquainted with the history of his country, for, whatever it is, it did not spring forth yesterday, but it became such gradually, and the institutions which surround the citizen, which form the essence of his government, are not known from their casual appearance as it may strike him at first glance, but from their operation, which is but their history; nor can we possibly know whither they tend, and whether they work good or evil, without knowing the causes from which they sprang, and the mode in which they have operated. Besides, no genuine and firm patriotism is possible without its receiving aliment from the knowledge of our institutions, the history of our country. Without it we shall feel and act as selfish insulated ephemerals—"sojourners in our country, not citizens," as Sismondi expressed it. Cicero very truly compares those who do not know history to children, because they are deprived of experience. To rule or legislate for one's country, one must know it; to know it, one must study it; but our country is not these few millions who happen to be alive at this precise moment, nor this land on which they stand, which they cultivate—but our country, patria, is this land, with all the relations subsisting between it and the dwellers upon it, their institutions, their growth and history. "In it alone can the citizen study his obligations and rights,"[1] which he really enjoys and ought carefully to preserve, and transmit inviolate to his children; through it alone he can learn how to appreciate what is good in it, and discover what requires amending, and how it ought to be amended.

A nation does not live an equally active and productive life at once in all spheres. A variety of circumstances must combine in order to produce a period in which, by the united activity of many, a certain branch, a certain institution, a certain part of the public law, will be cultivated with peculiar felicity and effect. General attention is directed with peculiar intensity to one or the other subject; many of the most gifted minds being engaged in the same pursuit or animated by the same idea propel one another in their common or similar career; one discovery leads to another; while the public, being influenced by the same spirit and common circumstances, incite and reward by their interest the peculiar votaries of that branch which is the flourishing one of the times, and at the same time public opinion, keen as to this branch, acquires tact and taste, and modifies what may be extravagant or retards what may be over-zealous in those who give their whole

---

[1] Jovellanos, Complete Works, Madrid, 1830, vol. ii. p. 438.

mind to that particular subject. Thus are produced what I have called on another occasion the classical periods of these peculiar branches.[1] It is thus in literature and the arts, in law and politics. If, then, we do not study history, and try faithfully to learn in what persons have excelled, what are the results of a specific branch in its own classical age or in the period in which it was cultivated with success, when by fortunate circumstances the public mind was rendered peculiarly sensitive respecting it, we neglect the true fruits of civilization and disregard one of the most solemn duties of man as a social being; that is, as a being who is not only called upon to live in social relations with the living, but who owes his social, his human relation to the continuity of society and is socially connected with past generations—that he is a social being not only within the limits of his generation, but also by a lineal connection with the past generations, through influences derived from them, and with the future generations, by influencing them. In order, therefore, that man may know his true position, he must understand the past likewise. This is the solemn and sacred character of history.

If we do not train our minds in duly finding and appreciating the elements of phenomena around us, we shall be unguarded against that fault in reasoning to which all men, without exception, are but too liable, namely, the mistaking of the co-existence of two things for a sufficient proof that they stand in the relation of cause and effect—a fault which has produced very grave evils in politics. Nothing is more common than that public men or an administration are charged with the evils under which the country happens to suffer, merely because those men happen to be at the helm, although there may be no more connection between the two than between a general epidemic and the administration at the time. If we do not learn to discover the elements of the phenomena around us, we shall continually fall into that grave error which has convulsed large nations, namely, the

---

[1] I have dwelt upon this subject at some length in the Hermeneutics.

mistaking of great social evils for merely political evils; for a remedy of which we seek, therefore, in a change of laws or institutions, while the seat of the disease is in a totally different region, and the cure must, consequently, come from different remedies.

As to the general duty of attention to the present society and times, in and through which we are what we are, I wish to add only that, since we do no longer assemble in the market, and our states have become extensive political societies, and since, at the same time, printing has become so powerful and active an agent of transmitting knowledge and thoughts, it is our duty not to slight those vehicles which bring us information of the daily occurrences of life, near and far, important and trivial, cheering and saddening—in short, of life such as it is. It is the duty of a free citizen to read attentively some newspapers. Without it he lives in the dark as an Athenian would have done who had not visited the agora. We seize with avidity upon the letters written in past periods, even the gossiping ones, because they bear the imprint and breathe the spirit of the period in which they were penned. Newspapers are letters. It indicates, in my opinion, very little knowledge of our whole human character and calling, if persons, as I have actually found some, assert with superciliousness that they never look at a paper. Let the newspapers of some countries differ ever so far from what they ought to be, or the feeling of hauteur at the society around those persons be ever so great, still the papers are the channel through which alone a mass of the most important knowledge respecting our society can be obtained, and the country remains the society in which we live and to which our sympathies ought to belong. The noblest and the worst things may happen, and to penetrate reality we ought to know both. A Ross may return from his three years' expedition and be received by the people of Hull in a manner which reminded the public of the reception of Columbus after his first voyage public defalcations may be discovered, improvements of all sorts may take place; crimes or noble deeds may be performed, or portentous signs foreboding evil may show themselves, without ever being noticed by so negligent a citizen. Only let us read the papers attentively, and not merely to fill vacant time. The gradual enlargement of knowledge by a serious and regular newspaper reading, with the proper aid of books of reference, is very great, and—it ought to be observed, especially for the young—there is much knowledge of details irretrievably lost, knowledge perhaps of great importance at some future period, when unexpectedly we may greatly need to possess it, in the sweeping course of the news of the European race, if we do not store it up gradually as it is offered, and endeavor to keep on a level with facts and events in the political as well as scientific life of the civilized nations. This species of acquiring knowledge can be abused, like everything else. As to the importance and duties of editors, they will be touched upon farther below.

# CHAPTER VI.

Continency.—Political Evils of Incontinency; of Prostitution.—The primary Foundation of Society, the Family, is undermined by it.—Evils of general Incontinency in the highest Classes, and the lowest.—Religion.—Its Universality.—Its importance for Morality; for Society; for the State.—Fanaticism. —Fanaticism of any kind.—Religious Fanaticism.—The Bible.—Revelation. —Both exclusively religious.—Persecution.—Direct and indirect Persecution. —Political and social Persecution.—Hypocrisy and Desecration of Religion. —Regulation of political or social actions by Tenets.

LVIII. CONTINENCY, a virtue demanded by all moral systems and purer religions, is a moral element of great importance in a civil point of view. The legislators of all times have acknowledged it, both by the direct support and countenance given to lawful marriage and well-constituted families, and the serious discountenance given to prostitution, from ancient times to modern. Hardly had the attempt been made during the first French revolution to pronounce by law that dissolution of some of the most elementary ties of human society, which had been eating itself into its vitals for upwards of two centuries, when, on the simple ground of public necessity, many of the violent political fanatics petitioned for legislative repression of universal profligacy, or, placed in authority, urgently recommended measures of the kind.[1] It is not only

---

[1] Some of these reports are contained in a work of the saddest, indeed, but also the deepest interest for every reflecting man who studies human society with that earnestness and truthfulness which is anxious to know the real state of things and society in all its elements, not shuddering or averting the face from truth and fact, even though it be loathsomely hideous, as no physician allows himself to be repelled by the most sickening suffering, or, if he does, is a worthless votary of the healing art. I allude to the work De la Prostitution dans la Ville de Paris, considérée sous le Rapport de l'Hygiène publique, de la Morale et de l'Administration, etc., par A. I. B. Parent-Duchatelet, Paris, 2d ed., 1837, 2 vols. 8vo. It is a work of the first importance to the moralist, philosopher,

because prostitution at large is invariably coupled with crime that it becomes so dangerous to the state, as the experience of all periods and all nations, ancient and modern, without exception, proves that general incontinency becomes a dangerous political vice. There is another reason, and, in my opinion, of much greater import still. We have seen how indispensable the family is for civilization as well as virtue; we called it the hearth of the best traits of man, of virtue, of generosity, of patriotism. We have seen that monogamy is justly considered as one of the most important elements, perhaps the most important of all to which Europe owes her early and great superiority over the Eastern world, where yet civilization was of much earlier date. If we carefully examine Roman history, I believe no one can fail to observe that a very great part of all that we feel ourselves bound to admire in it, the great power which the word law acquired in that city, and that peculiar trait in her politics which we may call Roman steadiness, was owing to the early acknowledgment of the family in its sacredness, and the consequent esteem of womankind, especially of wives and mothers—the high character which the Roman attributed to the matron, who therefore stands prominent in their history from an early period, some of the traditions of which are mixed with fiction, but which nevertheless prove, even in this shape, the state of national feeling. We shall return to this subject when we treat of Woman. In the middle ages, and especially in that period which more particularly is designated as the age of chivalry, few things served to restrain the lawlessness of the times, in some degree at least, more effectually than the rising esteem of woman, extravagant and distorted as even this feeling generally was, or however extravagant the views of many persons to this day respecting the universal purity of this feeling at those times may be. It is a fact that it formed one of

---

politician, criminalist, and statistician, to every one who studies man considered individually or socially, and gives a deep insight into one of the darkest, lowest sinks of vice, avarice, and crime.

the essential points from which modern civilization started anew.[1]

LIX. If the family, however, is so important, it is evident that continency, its very support and life-blood, is so likewise. The former cannot exist in its purity and in that solidity which is necessary to make it a substantial element of political welfare, without the latter, without the purity of woman. Yet this does not exhibit the whole importance of continency. So soon as continency is generally disregarded or slighted, selfishness will likewise become general, because families are not formed—that circle where disinterestedness is fostered most,—and the more lasting connection between the two sexes, if formed, is founded upon selfish gratification only; the claims of children upon their parents for education, the pride of parents in their children, that they may do honor to the name, is weakened or entirely destroyed; and woman sinks from the position of a companion to the father and an honored mother to the offspring, to a mere means of gratification. In short, the first principle from which civilization starts, and that from which at all periods it draws the most substantial support, is undermined. There are four different impulses which, more than any others, prompt man to generous actions, elevate him above the calculation of interest, and imbue his soul with those motives without which utility and expediency would remain as the only causes and prompters of action: these four are religion, love, patriotism, and the feeling of justice. Love, that peculiar sympathy between men, and which we have considered in friendship, one of its prominent manifestations, is intensest and most general in the sympathy which exists between the two sexes, so much so that the poets of all ages have been naturally led to it, as the surest means to excite interest on the largest scale. That disinterested spirit of love, which is often called the romantic spirit, has

---

[1] Hallam's History of the Middle Ages, mentioned here, out of so many others, only on account of its greater accessibility to most readers.

not unfrequently led to extravagances, errors, sometimes to vices and crimes; yet this is only because it is so general, and if it were blotted out from the human heart it would scarcely be possible to keep human society together, aside from the extinction of many of the noblest exertions. But general profligacy does extinguish it, and we find therefore that at all times those classes which are not touched by public opinion, and give themselves up to libertinism, which become callous and selfish, disavow the obligations of continency and of family life, and in doing so become dead to many of the most sacred calls of morality, are of extreme danger to the whole commonwealth; whether such a class be in the social scale at the head, as the libertine nobility in France, England, and several other countries in the seventeenth and eighteenth centuries, or at the bottom of that scale, as the poorest classes are at present, in England, for instance, and several other highly-peopled countries.[1] Whether squalid wretchedness or arrogant profligacy deaden the power of public opinion, the effect and the danger, though not the same, are equally great, with this difference, perhaps, that the wretched may still be coerced by a strong government into submission to the laws in some degree, while the others soon may become daring rebels against the most sacred interests of society, having necessarily a considerable part of authority and power in their own hands. In this respect, too, the history of Roman dissoluteness furnishes us with admonishing facts and experience. There were many reasons why France could not remain without a deeply penetrating revolution but one of them will always be found

---

[1] I refer here to the various Reports of the Poor Laws Commissions to Parliament since the whigs have formed the administration. The work I have used in particular is the Report from the Commissioners for inquiring into the Administration and practical Operation of the Poor Laws, published by Authority, London, 1834. Several works of value have been published by private individuals on subjects connected with the above, for instance, " The Manufacturing Population of England, its Moral, Social, and Physical Conditions," etc., by P. Gaskill, London, 1833. Some of the first British political economists have likewise written on the subject; nor can Malthus on Population be forgotten here where we speak of the effect of general unchastity in a political point of view.

to have consisted in the profligacy and shamelessness of a
very large part of the higher classes, which made even Burke
give so sad and contemptible a picture of the French nobility
before the revolution, so much more dangerous, though probably not in itself greater, than that of the court of Charles II.
and James II., because it had lasted longer and settled down
far more into a certain code and system.[1]

LX. Society is deeply interested in religion. If we comprehend within this term all belief, true or erroneous, in an
agent or agents overruling the actions and destinies of men,
possessed of a power surpassing human power, which extends
to the changes in the physical world, we shall find that men
have never existed without some religion, whether it be in the
form of the grossest fetish religion, adoring bodies which do
not even represent real or imagined animate beings, or polytheism, or monotheism. The consciousness of our dependence and of the great limitation of our power, fear or hope,
desire of superior aid, or a longing for support and comfort
in adversity, which every man feels that he himself or his
fellow-man are incapable of affording, has invariably led man
to acknowledge a superior agency of some sort or other.
Man has always adored. If, therefore, there were no other
reason why we should promote pure religion—and there are
many indeed—this would be a strong one, that man will not
and cannot live without some religion, of whatever character;
and if he has not a true one he will embrace a false one; if
he has not belief or a pure faith he will resort to superstition,

---

[1] The historical memoirs, a branch of literature so peculiar to France, furnish most melancholy proofs of the enormous height to which unchastity as a social and political evil had risen in that country. Quite lately a new contribution to this history of vice has been made in the Memoirs of the Duchess of Nevers from 1713 to 1793. We can hardly trust our eyes when we read the attending circumstances of the well-known fact that Cardinal Fleury, prime minister of France, was the person who deliberately seduced the then young monarch, Louis XV., still attached to his wife, to adopt the countess du Mailly as his mistress, and thus began a career of vice which during a long reign extended its fatal influence over a country doomed to the greatest sufferings.

or rather his heart will naturally engender it. But if a religion acknowledges a God " who is of purer eyes than to behold iniquity," who is love and all-pure, it needs no farther discussion to show how deeply the whole society is interested in maintaining the diffusion of such a faith, which affords the two most powerful agents of morality, namely, on the one hand, the mental communion with a being who is purity himself, and, being omniscient, does not judge by signs or outward actions but searches the motives in the deepest recesses of our heart, and who, being almighty, affords support to all who seek it in purity from him; and on the other hand, the belief in the immortality of the soul. It extends at once the whole sphere of action; its effects and tests go beyond the mere calculation of expediency, and thus the belief must needs become the most powerful primitive impulse to good action, uprightness, disinterestedness, kindness, love of truth, and admiration of what is truly good, beautiful, noble, and great.

The promotion of religion in a community takes place chiefly by instruction in the family, and by that society which is founded upon the principle of religion, called the church. It belongs to the province of natural law to inquire whether the state as such, that is the jural society of men, has the right, and, under certain circumstances, the duty, to support that particular ecclesiastical society or church which is founded upon the religion professed by all members of the state or the majority, and to exercise a supervising or regulating authority over all the religions professed by the various members of the state. But to the science of politics proper it belongs to discuss those means which may be best warranted by experience as well as by principles of strict right to carry out that supervision or direct promotion, should it be found either that it is necessary or right; in short, to discuss the important subject of how far any connection between church and state can or ought to subsist, for instance as in England, where the established church has, in some respects, a political form and substance, or as in France, where the churches of the various denominations are supported by the state, but otherwise distinctly separate from it, since the revolution of 1830. We have already seen, in the first volume, that in no case whatever has the state the right to interfere with the religious belief of the individual, that is with his relation and communion with his Maker. A few remarks on religion will be added when we shall come to treat of education. In political ethics one of the subjects connected with religion, which claims especially our attention, appears to me to be fanaticism.

LXI. By a fanatic we understand an individual who is actuated by a false zeal for some general principle or truth, real or supposed, so far that he commits wrong. A bigot is, in the attachment to what he holds to be true, illiberal and narrowminded to those who think differently. Fanaticism includes bigotry, but the bigot need not be a fanatic. The falseness of the zeal in the fanatic may consist in the excess of its degree, or a zeal for something wrong of itself, or in the fact that the zeal and fervor of the individual mislead him to carry principles and standards of action into spheres which ought to remain entirely foreign to them. It was fanatical when a revived spirit of religion, after papacy had sunk lowest, carried some popes to the destruction of ancient works of art; it was fanatical when the admiration of the fine arts in antiquity induced people to write against Christianity. I believe that according to common adaptation the word fanatic always implies action injurious to others, especially persecution, or to ourselves (as persons have crucified themselves), while the word enthusiast, perhaps, denotes only the excess of zeal. So long as the two musical schools in Paris at the time of Rousseau carried their zeal only to an excess of love of music, forgetting in their ardor many important duties, we would call them musical enthusiasts; but when they began to injure one another, I believe we must call them musical fanatics. It is very clear that the enthusiast will in most cases be ready, if opportunity offers, to become a fanatic.

As the zeal with which we are animated for the prosecution of anything may degenerate into excess, so there may be fanaticism in the pursuit of any truth or principle, real or pretended. The Nominalists and Realists in the middle ages became actual fanatics in their philosophical zeal. So there have been frequently political fanatics, who have persecuted one another for the sake of political principles or truths, and all party excitements are liable to the danger of political fanaticism. Indeed, whenever we forget the aim, and in excessive zeal mistake the means to obtain the aim for the aim itself—the very general error of which I have spoken already—we are close upon the limit where fanaticism begins. Anything engaging the zeal of men may degenerate, I repeat, into enthusiasm, as the innocent love of flowers did at one time degenerate into the actually disastrous tulipomania; and so soon as enthusiasm acts injuriously to others, by blinding men to their due interest or inciting to injustice and persecution, it is fanaticism. I remember an instance when a juryman could not be persuaded by his eleven fellows to agree to a verdict of guilty, although the evidence of theft left no doubt whatever of the crime, and finally declared he would not consent to the verdict, because the prisoner belonged to his own political party. If this was not on the ground of some sordid interest, it was, I believe every one will agree, political fanaticism. But no species of fanaticism has been more common or more disastrous than religious. The reasons are clear. Religion, true or false, is, as we have seen, one of the most universal principles, and hence its fanaticism is likewise so. All feel interest in some religion or other; not all in the fine arts or in philosophical systems. As religion occupies itself with the relation of man to his supreme ruler, men who take a confined view of religion and of their maker, as all fanatics do, imagine that religion, with reverence be it spoken, is the peculiar province of God, and forget that every truth and true principle, for instance justice and its pure administration, is his likewise. The religious fanatic believes that everything which does not belong to religion as he imagines it is worthless or the evil production of man. God willed the state and the relations of justice among men as much according to his divine intentions as he willed the church. The fact alone that he willed it is proof of the truth; for in him everything is infinite and eternal, and in his will every principle is of equal importance. The struggle of the Catholic church and some other denominations to supersede the state and make it a mere vassal of the church was founded upon this erroneous view. The religious fanatic believes that God is peculiarly honored by peculiar measures, and therefore proportionably offended by their omission or opposition. Everything, therefore, in his opinion, ought to give way to these particular measures, even justice, which he conceives to be of human origin. Crimes have been at times committed or palliated because it was blasphemously believed that they were for the promotion of the cause of God, as if the purest being, and the only all-pure and all-powerful being, could be served by untruth, or injustice, or impurity; as if his honor could in any way depend upon the actions of finite and impure beings, and as if there was any other way of serving him than that of truth and right. The enthusiast, moreover, has arrived at his views by processes which are not deducible from reasoning; there is therefore in him that instinctive and restless fear of unsoundness or of taking offence at others not agreeing with him, as if their disagreement cast reflection upon his belief—sentiments which, in default of the power of truth, lead to persecution either by way of revenge or propagation of its tenets. Radical conviction is calm; superficial conviction restless, heated, angry.[1]

LXII. These remarks apply to fanaticism in all religions; but there are some features peculiar to Christian fanaticism, arising out of the peculiar character of the Bible, that code on which the faith of the Christian is founded. The Bible is a

---

[1] [Enthusiasm in a good sense is a generous ardor for that which is good, true, humane. In a somewhat degenerate sense it is ardor disproportionate to the magnitude of the object. Fanaticism is that one-sided zeal united with hatred.]

book composed of various parts, which have a different character; it contains inspired truths and revelations, it contains records of facts, or, in other words, historical accounts, and the political laws calculated for a peculiar government, a theocracy of a particular nation, the Hebrews. To what melancholy errors and unspeakable sufferings the mistaken impression has led, that those historical parts which record facts contain, in addition to the truths legitimately drawn from their aim and purpose, others applicable in totally different spheres, for instance in science and politics,—how consciences have been coerced and the purest religion has been degraded into a handmaid of sordid passions, every one who has but glanced at history knows well. The whole code of laws destined for the Jews and adapted to the specific state of their civilization and to the object to be obtained by that specific theocracy, has led to fearful fanaticism, applied, as it has been, to objects for which it was never intended. The Mosaic law of property, of government, of administration of justice, especially the penal laws, would be subversive of the most sacred interests of society if put in practice in our times, for many of them are repulsive to the feelings of humanity which have become developed by the intervening diffusion of Christianity, in consequence of that very civilization which those laws contributed to bring about.

The Bible has not nullified man's moral or intellectual character; it contains absolute prescriptions of principles, not absolute prescriptions of specific actions, such as the officer for instance receives from his commander.

LXIII. Respecting the inspired parts of the Bible, which reveal religious truths, I must remind the reader of what was said in the first part, of the character of those truths which Christ taught, namely, that he limited himself strictly to religious truths. A similar remark applies to the whole Bible. Two different views may be taken of revelation through the mouth of man. Either the inspired writer utters words by way of dictation, or he pronounces in human language what revelation, a direct communication from the divine to the human mind, leads the latter to pronounce. The translations of the Bible into modern languages will somewhat explain the latter view. They contain the full revelation, yet the words conveying them were not inspired dictation. Whichever view may be taken, it appears that the inspiring Spirit did not purpose to stop by this act the course of the development of mankind, but only to reveal so much as was necessary for religion; and therefore religious truths only. The inspired men were not made divinely omniscient; their minds were led to promulgate truths, and these alone were inspired. As they had to deliver their inspiration in human language, so they remained men of their own times, in all that had no direct relation to religion, in many of their views respecting public or domestic government, for instance, the arts, the sciences, or other branches; and God has allowed other nations far to exceed the Hebrews in very many branches, which yet are of the highest importance to mankind. The Greeks, for instance, far excelled the Jews in the fine arts, in composition and criticism, and in all the sciences; and it would be no greater error to seek for the principles of architecture, mathematics, dramatic poetry, or botany, in the Bible, than to derive an equitable and safe system of justice or the organization of government for a civilized and free people of our times from the laws of the Jews. The Bible was not intended to make men inert copyists. We are destined to exert ourselves, and to pursue with those powers with which the Creator has benignly endowed us the aims he has prescribed in his wisdom. Still less are we justified in accusing those of irreligion who conceive the Bible to be a book of religion, and I believe they act impiously if they take it as a book of science, politics, or the arts. There are very strong passages in the works of some of the Reformers against the abuse of the Bible in using it for foreign purposes. A modern writer, archbishop Whately, speaking of the unhallowed attacks which have been made upon political economy under the cloak of religion, makes some remarks which agree so well with what I hold to be true that I shall be excused for subjoining an extract from them.[1] Who would doubt but that by the revelation of a few

[1] "Till the advocates of Christianity shall have become universally much better acquainted with the true character of their religion than universally they have ever yet been, we must always expect that every branch of study, every scientific theory that is brought into notice, will be assailed on religious grounds, by those who either have not studied the subject, or who are incompetent judges of it; or, again, who are addressing themselves to such persons as are so circumstanced, and wish to excite and to take advantage of the passions of the ignorant. 'Flectere si nequeo Superos, Acheronta movebo.'

"Some there are who sincerely believe that the Scriptures contain revelations of truths the most distinct from religion. Such persons procured accordingly a formal condemnation (very lately rescinded) of the theory of the earth's motion, as at variance with Scripture. In Protestant countries, and now, it seems, even in Popish, this point has been conceded; but that the erroneous principle—that of appealing to revelation on questions of physical science—has not yet been entirely cleared away is evident from the objections, which most of you probably may have heard, to the researches of geology. The objections against astronomy have been abandoned rather perhaps from its having been made to appear that the Scripture accounts of the phenomena of the heavens may be reconciled with the conclusions of science, than from its being understood that Scripture is not the test by which the conclusions of science are to be tried. And accordingly, when attention was first called to the researches of geology, many who were startled at the novelty of some of the conclusions drawn, and yet were averse to enter on a new field of study, or found themselves incapable of maintaining many notions they had been accustomed to acquiesce in, betook themselves at once to Scripture, and reviled the students of geology as hostile to revelation; in the same manner as, in pagan and Popish countries, any one who is conscious of crime or of debt flies at once to the altar and shelters himself in the sanctuary."

. . . "Historical or physical truths may be established by their own proper evidence; and this, therefore, is the course we are bound to pursue. The Christian will indeed feel antecedently a strong persuasion that such conclusions as I have been speaking of, or any others which are really inconsistent with the Bible, never will be established; that any theory seemingly at variance with it will either be found deficient in evidence, or else reconcilable with the Scriptures. But it is not a sign of faith—on the contrary, it indicates rather a want of faith, or else a culpable indolence—to decline meeting any theorist on his own ground, and to cut short the controversy by an appeal to the authority of Scripture. For if we really are convinced of the truth of Scripture, and consequently of the falsity of any theory (of the earth for instance) which is really at variance with it, we must needs believe that that theory is also at variance with observable phenomena, and we ought not therefore to shrink from trying that question by an appeal to these. The success of such an appeal will then add to the evidence for the truth of the Scriptures, instead of burdening them with the weight of defending every point which they incidentally imply. It is for us to 'behave ourselves valiantly for our

principles in natural philosophy for instance, or political economy, many of the gravest errors and much consequent bloodshed might have been prevented; yet he who did not choose to reveal these principles and allowed mankind in due time to find them out must have had his wise ends. Since he has denied revelations except on religious truths, we act irreligiously if we misapply his revelations for ends for which they were not intended.

The government of the Hebrews was a theocracy, and everything in it was subservient to this one great object, the protection of the worship of a single God against contamination, until at length monotheism should cease to be a national religion and become that of the world. So soon as this moment had arrived, the Hebrew government, solely calculated for that object, and for the Jews in their then state, lost its meaning, and it is utterly unfit to be imitated by other nations, who have to solve totally different problems. It is just, therefore, to say that no book is less fit to be imitated in politics than the Old Testament, because no system of politics has been calculated for so entirely peculiar a state of things; and yet, since Christ does not touch politics, we find that at all times fanatics, if they turn for politics to the Bible at all, will naturally be chiefly attracted by the Old Testament. I have mentioned elsewhere already for what opposite and often awful political systems and pretensions the Bible has been abused to serve as a foundation. Catholics and Protestants have equally erred on this subject, and while some denounced all force and constraint exercised by government, and preached the most revolting licentiousness, all the time pretending to rely for every proposition of theirs on the Bible, Bossuet could write his Politics drawn from the proper words

---

country and for the cities of our God,' instead of bringing the ark of God into the field of battle to fight for us. He will, at all events, we may be sure, defend his own cause, and finally lay prostrate the Dagon of infidelity, but we, his professed defenders, more zealous in reality for our own honor than for his, shall deserve to be smitten before the Philistines." Lect. ii., Introductory Lectures on Political Economy, London, 1831.

of holy writ, almost entirely in biblical phrases, and yet produce a work in the spirit of his absolute master, Louis XIV., and in his own spirit of a careful courtier-prelate to such a master.

LXIV. If we call religious fanaticism all perversion of our actions by undue application or influence of religious doctrines in spheres which are not strictly religious, we shall be led to the following truths and rules respecting political and other social relations:

Persecution is not only irreligious, but there is likewise no earthly right of using political power and authority for religious persecution, because political power is power arising out of the state, which is the society of right, and right has nothing to do with matters of faith.

Persecution, however, though it be not of a political character, may be highly oppressive and yet remain essentially social. A man may be deprived of his good name, necessary intercourse or subsistence, by social action, and yet be unable to use political protection against it. It is one of the worst species of persecution, because there is no protection against it. But lately a very disgraceful instance took place in England. The bishops of Durham and Norwich, having subscribed for a copy of a work written by a Unitarian, were so loudly and vehemently clamored against by clergymen and laymen that they believed themselves obliged to write what cannot be termed other than submissive letters.[1] Thus a

---

[1] The letter of the bishop of Norwich bears date November 1, 1838. The bishop of Durham had previously written one. Both found it necessary to excuse their subscribing on the ground that they did it on account of politeness to Mr. Turner, the Unitarian author, according to them a man of unblemished character and great talent. Requisitions to the archbishop of Canterbury, to institute an episcopal commission to inquire into the conduct of the two bishops " in having subscribed to a work intended to promulgate the infidel heresy of Socinianism," were signed by the clergy of the several dioceses. The epithets given to the two prelates remind one of the worst and bitterest times of controversy when the church preached and supported the doctrine of divine right and absolute obedience. They were called " consecrated culprits," " obscene and

theologian would not even be allowed to study all books on theology. The articles written and the speeches made against them showed sufficiently the profane hypocrisy and political rancor against these two prelates, they having been appointed by the whig administration in power. And this is one of the necessary consequences of all fanaticism, that it lends aid to and promotes hypocrisy, and on the other hand seeks for the proof of essential religion in specific acts, without consideration of their whole bearing, thus making of the most spiritual and divine things a gross matter of outward signs.

The same must be said of that indirect persecution which favors, in the mutual dependence of society, persons according to tenets. The danger is invariably that on our own part we expose ourselves to all the dangers of fanaticism, because we are carrying by this very means principles of religion into spheres to which they are alien; for instance, if we decline to buy from an honest and poor merchant, because he is not of our sect. And on the other hand we promote hypocrisy and desecrate religion, because we make tenets the test of actions and of intercourse which ought to have nothing to do with them. I know of instances where commercial credit was given on a recommendation of a minister on strictly so-called religious grounds. Is not this desecration? The only safe rule, I believe, is this, that we regulate our intercourse of mutual dependence solely by the honesty, purity, skill, and claims of

---

flippant pamphleteers," "time-serving remonstrants," "rotten liberals," "hardened criminals," "men at the thought of whom the soul sickens," "liberal and Protean bishops," "loose and lowly priests," "Judases," "perfidious prelates," "surpliced traitors," "white-robed ministers of Satan," "pet sons of the devil,"—and many more names as disgusting. All these invectives were in articles of tory papers, which sanctimoniously pretended to write for the true cause of Christ, and the crown of England, frequently in strains of blasphemous hypocrisy. Indeed, seeing at the distance, as we did, those articles of virulence and acrimony garnished with passages from the book of peace and love, we could hardly believe that they belonged to our times. It is the duty of every well-wisher of his species firmly to look truth in the face, and fix upon evils, if dangerous, without fear. It is in this spirit that this note has been written. Let us all take an example, and call scandal what is scandalous, disgraceful what disgraces, and gloss nothing over in fear or sectarian party spirit.

dependence in the individual himself. For, the moment that we direct our daily actions of common intercourse by the profession of religious tenets, we desecrate religion, and promote hypocrisy on the one hand or chilling and ruinous irreligion on the other.

In doing this we likewise fetter the mind, and prevent free and conscientious inquiry, and expose ourselves to one of the most grievous errors, that of hiding the faults or crimes of those who profess the same tenets with ourselves. The Catholic orders as well as many Protestant sects have frequently committed this grave fault of mistaking the means, the uniting into a sect or church, for the object, truth, religion, active piety. I have mentioned already the just view of Augustine on this subject, that it is better that scandal arise than that truth and justice suffer. This false spirit is not peculiar to religious societies; all bodies of men have that esprit du corps and weakness of shrinking from exposing their fellow-members; but, as fanaticism always believes that everything it does or suffers is for the honor of God, so is religious fanaticism peculiarly apt to mislead in this particular.

Of vast danger is religious fanaticism in politics if it seizes upon free nations and introduces into politics the test of religion—which, if this word is applied to large masses and by way of distinction, means of course the profession of certain tenets. The state is the jural society, and as conscientious citizens we have no right to judge by anything but relations of right. We act unconscientiously if, for instance, in voting for or against a citizen, we are influenced by other tests than his uprightness, honesty, capacity, and general fitness for the particular object. It is indirect persecution if we are influenced by dogmas, for he has a right to have his own, as we have ours; we turn the state from its true end, we promote the mere profession of tenets, that is hypocrisy, and may, for aught we can calculate, pave the way to open and cruel persecution. The history of the Western and Eastern Empires after the conversion of Constantine, when dogmas became the most active elements of politics, and led to indescribable misery and wretchedness, physical and mental, as well as the many instances of the unfortunate and unhallowed application of dogmas to politics by both Protestants and Catholics, arising out of the religious struggle of the times of the Reformation, ought to be taken as a lesson too grave ever to be disregarded. I repeat that persecution may be violent, undermining, and ruinous, without showing itself in bloodshed. It may be strictly social, and thus may degrade that which is the best of all things that man can possess—a pure and true religion. The more a man values his religion and the sacred communion which the infinite Deity permits a finite individual to hold with himself, the less he will be apt to desire its desecration by making his belief a test of external intercourse with society at large. The more men pretend to intermix politics or the intercourse arising out of mutual exchange with religion, the surer we may always be that they are either blinded by fanaticism or prompted by selfish ends, or, as is most common, jointly by both.

# CHAPTER VII.

Patriotism.—The Patriotism of the Ancients; of the Moderns.—Some have rejected Patriotism.—National Conceit, Pride.—Narrowness of Feeling a Counterfeit of Patriotism.—What is true Patriotism?—It is noble and necessary for Liberty.—Loyalty.—Public Spirit.—What it consists in.—Calamitous Consequences of a Want of Public Spirit.—Veneration for the Old; Forefathers.—How far just, necessary.—When injurious.—The Age of Action under Forty; of Conservatism over Forty.—Do Times grow worse?—When are we more experienced than our Forefathers?—Stagnation and Heedlessness.

LXV. WE have seen, in the first volume, that with the ancients the individual, as far as rights were concerned, was almost absorbed by the state; all they were felt to be they were in and through the state; and not only was their state a political institution, but a separate religion, with peculiar national deities and distinct national dogmas, was closely interwoven with it. The national religion thus aided in separating the specific state or nation from others—a circumstance powerfully promoted by another fact. The Greeks, and after them the Romans, were so far advanced in civilization beyond the other tribes known to them that they looked down upon them as benighted beings of an inferior kind; the stranger was a barbarian. In the attachment, therefore, which an ancient felt for his state, in his love of country, his patriotism, were united and amalgamated nearly all the intensest affections which animate the human breast—religion, with all the powerful associations of poetry, legends, and mythologic history; the affection for his kindred tribe and native land, its institutions and history, its language and literature; and consciousness of superiority, disdain of foreigners, and hatred when they became invaders and threatened to smother this superior civilization. When the Persian attacked the Greek, not only were his life and property endangered, but his higher life, his whole being as an individual, which we believe will last beyond this earthly existence, was in jeopardy. Patriotism, therefore, comprehended the acme of all virtuous feelings, of piety, of love of civilization; it was the meridian of man's most noble existence. Christianity severed religion from the soil, from earthly citizenship. He was told that religion is above, beyond the difference of language, color, kindred, descent, or country. Chivalry arose, and became a tie beyond national affection; the church with its monasteries became a super-national society, which with its common language, the Latin, with the monastic orders extending over many political limits and under one common discipline, the seminaries, mingling the youths of various nations, the pilgrimages to distant lands,[1] and the frequent emigrations of priests, produced a common feeling, despite the many feuds between parts and particles in this European society. Vast enthusiastic movements, such as the crusades, aided still more, if not in cementing nations (for the feudal systems prevented this), in extinguishing that form of patriotism which it had naturally assumed among the ancients. In the course of time, however, three great historical processes took place in the European race: first, that which we may call the nationalization of tribes and governments; France became gradually one France, Spain one Spain; then the growth of national languages, poetry, and literature, in opposition to the Latin, by the rise of nations and great minds among them. Dante, who dared to sing in "vulgar Italian," and pressed at once the seal of his genius upon the idiom of the unlettered, felt still obliged to ask pardon that he did not continue to compose in Latin, as he had begun, on so sacred a subject as

---

[1] Among others, Frederic Rühs, in his Manual of the History of the Middle Ages, Berlin, 1816, mentions the pilgrims as one of the means by which mutual knowledge of one another among the nations of Europe was kept up, a slender means, yet in the absence of other and powerful ones in the darkest periods not undeserving of attention. I quote from memory, but believe I am correct as to the above author. Whether this be so or not, I consider it a fact that the innumerable pilgrimages, attended with many evil consequences, had also the mentioned good effect of aiding to keep alive sympathy among the Western Christian nations.

his was. Finally, the Reformation. This event or process of civilization broke in many countries the uniting tie of the church. But a new common bond had arisen, and was rapidly increasing in strength, a general pursuit of knowledge, the tie of common European science, promoting in its turn intercommunication, both mental and, owing to the gradual fusion of the sciences and arts, physical also, which was still more increased by the greater security caused by the gradual nationalization of states and governments. Sciences naturally lead to general views; they have, in the main, a strongly cosmopolitan character; and, above all, we have seen that natural law, that science which treats of the rights of men, flowing from their nature, of justice, and not merely of positive or historical law, arose, and was and is cultivated by the moderns, while the Christian religion must ever continue to exercise a more and more cosmopolitan character, the more purely it dwells among men. There was thus no possibility of a return of patriotism in its ancient manifestation.

LXVI. It was felt and seen that ancient patriotism, heightened to national or state egotism, could no longer exist or be endured. "The barriers are broken which severed states and nations in hostile egotism. One cosmopolitan bond unites at present all thinking minds, and all the light of this century may now freely fall upon a new Galileo or Erasmus."[1] On the other hand, it was observed how churlish, narrow, unjust, or even wicked that frequently is which is claimed as patriotism, how directly opposed to truth, how blind in its selfishness.

I do not speak here of clannishness, which is at its height and extreme perhaps in the Scotchman, and which by the great painter of his country's customs has been represented, no doubt in strong yet in true colors, as rising at times beyond everything, even the fear of final eternal doom;[2] nor of the

---

[1] Schiller, Inaugural address on: "What is, and for what purpose do we study, universal history?" first delivered in 1789. It is contained in his works.

[2] Walter Scott depicts this fearful feeling of attachment to the chief of the clan, family, etc., in Elspeth in "The Antiquary," etc., especially in chap. xii. vol.

petty and selfish feeling, the utmost extent of which is the town limit; but I speak of that national egotism which is blind to truth and callous to justice beyond the nation's frontier, and which has been used for various and opposite evil ends, so much so that men have not been wanting who not only looked upon patriotism as beneath a true elevation of mind, but have actually declaimed against it. A late writer exclaims, "What misery has not already been caused by the love of country! How much has not this counterfeit virtue excelled all acknowledged vices in wild fury! Is the selfishness of a country less a vice than that of an individual? Does justice cease to be a virtue so soon as we exercise it towards a foreign nation? It is a fine species of honor, indeed, which prohibits us from declaring ourselves against our country when justice no longer stands by its side!"[1] If patriotism is founded upon selfishness, and therefore cannot but lead to injustice, if it tends to blind us against truth, then indeed it is one of our first and most sacred duties to pluck this rank

---

ii., in colors which every foreigner would certainly consider beyond all possibility, did he not know that Scott never, probably, gave a wrong account of manners, national feelings, etc., except from want of knowledge, which in the above character cannot well have been the case.

[1] Louis Börne, a late German writer of much keenness and boldness, who was obliged to leave Germany and take up his abode at Paris, where he wrote many a bitter, many a witty, many a true, and many a false thing. He belonged to a party, if such it can be called, in Germany, who wish to unite their endeavors with that which gives itself the singular name of *la jeune France*, thus raising, probably for the first time, age into a political party distinction. These parties seem to think that liberty has yet to be born, and that this new god will be brought forth by the union of the two great nations to whom all this procreation of new liberty seems to have been assigned, the French and the Germans. The Anglican tree of liberty, which is an oak of centuries, is thus treated as if its mighty branches did not reach already over many countries, and over France and Germany too. But I must stop, lest I should make of a note an historical discussion. As to the above passage, to which this note is appended, I have for the present to say only that the author is mistaken as to the degree of fanaticism which has arisen out of patriotism. I know of no fanaticism which has so repeatedly affected mankind in so great a degree as religious fanaticism. His whole argument would thus turn more strongly still against religion were it correct in its conclusion.

weed out of our heart. Justice is above all; truth is the only legitimate sphere of the human mind and soul.

LXVII. If patriotism consisted in national vanity, pride, or self-sufficiency, which are its counterfeits, and one or the other of which we meet with in all nations from the Chinese to the Americans, it should be avoided by every wise man. But is it so? does there not exist a real virtue, compatible with purity of heart and general good will, and which has produced the best effects, which is deeply planted in the human breast and ought to be most carefully awakened and cultivated?[1]

Reflecting men have frequently fallen into two serious errors, of which the one is, indeed, a consequence of the other. In seeking for truth, and hence for distinctness and clearness, they have often conceived that only to be real, sound, or true which can be established by the calculating or analyzing understanding, of which the plain end and object,

---

[1] To give instances of national vanity would be a task difficult on account of the difficulty of choice only. I will merely mention that quite recently I have met with a passage in a distinguished French work, which speaks of the French as being at the head of civilization with an assurance which resembles the manner in which Napoleon spoke of "the Great Nation." In another work, soon after, I saw it stated that Prussia stands at the head of European civilization. In an address of a large sect to Queen Victoria, the British nation was called the greatest on the face of the earth; and that the Americans in their turn are the first in the world, we may easily find by turning to any of their endless and innumerable addresses. Of all the feelings connected with this subject pride is nevertheless the least evil, while small conceitedness, as we find its prototype in the last stages of Athenian democracy, is a serious disease without any redeeming quality. It affords a handle to narrow-minded demagogues and unfits the people for any just or enlarged views and elevated feelings. There are rules of good breeding of social intercourse gradually settled by good sense and mutual regard. Among these rules it is now universally adopted that gross flattery shows excessive ill breeding, and is taken rather as an insult than a compliment. When shall we have our rules of good breeding in politics? When will flat and gross, dull and cumbrous flattery in a public speaker be taken as an insult by his hearers,—as a young lady would feel grossly offended were we to address speeches to her which were given as pattern speeches to ladies in works on politeness two hundred years ago?

the use as well as the origin, can be stated in so many words; forgetting at once that as finite beings we must begin to reason from a finite beginning, and that the ultimate object must be beyond utility, because utility expresses only a serviceableness for an object, so that the ultimate object itself must be good in its own nature. We may show how one thing serves for another; but we must needs end somewhere, that is, we must arrive at a final object which is its own end.[1]

The second error is that men have been misled to consider their subject as totally separate and insulated, forgetting that everywhere there are gradual and connecting transitions between those points where things show themselves in their fullest and most developed character—transitions which exist no more between the animal and the plant, for instance, than between the arts, or institutions, or ideas, as the Useful and the Ornamental, the Just and the Fair, or anything that is mental, social, or human. It is not only right but necessary, in order to obtain the clearest possible insight into any subject, first to consider it absolutely, that is in its essentials, by which it wholly differs from all other things, for which purpose we must examine it when at the highest degree of perfection peculiar to itself. If we omit this, we shall obtain but indistinct ideas, leading to a thousand erroneous conclusions. But having done this it is equally important to view the same subject in all its transitions, through which it is affiliated and joined, in the various directions, to other things. By doing this we can alone discover its position and bearing. As an instance I will take the courts of justice. They have to administer justice, they have to do with right. This is the characteristic of this institution. The opposite extreme to strict justice is self-denying love. Between the two stands

---

[1] I have met with an old German sermon in pamphlet form, entitled "The Utility of Eternal Bliss" (*Ueber den Nutzen ewiger Glückseligkeit*). It was in the hands of a seller of old books, and I have often regretted that I did not purchase it; but I did not then know how often in my life I should be reminded of this unique instance of extravagant consistency in the utilitarian theory.

fairness; and we shall not obtain a perfect and partial view of courts of justice if we do not consider, among other things, the very subtle transition from the strictly just to that which is fair, and if we do not consider that, although the law is the rule by which the judge is bound to decide, this very law, being made by man and drawn up in human language, is not absolute like a mathematical formula, but in many cases must be interpreted in its application. These rules, the omission of either of which has misled many philosophers, are of great importance in all meditations on subjects connected with the state, and, as we shall see presently, on patriotism.

LXVIII. One of the strong impulses to action is interest, but alone it would altogether fail to effect many necessary things; and a stronger impulse than is afforded by interest is that of sympathy. It gives in many cases the first impulse to action, and often supersedes interest or that which is clearly to be proved by the understanding. Men were destined, as we have seen, to establish families; from them civilization proceeds: yet neither did men originally nor do they generally now unite in marriage after having calculated their interest, nor, in most cases, after having clearly represented to themselves the pleasure they may derive from domestic happiness. Sympathy attracts them, and weds closer than either of the other two motives could do. Nor does a man who feels deeply attached to one woman among so many thousand thereby declare that he holds her to be better, wiser, purer than all the rest. He merely shows that sympathy draws him to her in particular. We are commanded to love our parents, which means of course to love and cherish them in particular, but by obeying this commandment we do not mean to express that we consider them better than all the rest of mankind, nor that we hate the others because we love these in particular. The commandment directs particular attention to the lawful effect of a peculiar sympathy, and to the callousness of a heart in which this primary sympathy has no effect. Yet it cannot be proved by the mere understanding. The parents in many cases may indeed not deserve the warm thanks of their offspring; they may have done no more than what in the common relations of society they could not well help doing. The children may have many reasons for dissatisfaction, and yet sympathy is not on that account extinguished. It is the same with patriotism: it is not to be calculated according to interest, nor is it a duty first established by a train of reasoning; but we reason upon the feeling already existing, and then find how great an agent it is in God's household. The immense power of association, in all its varieties, from the nursery song to the highest national epic, forms, sounds, colors, things and persons, joys and pains, all have seized upon us, and we feel attached to our country, we love it; but we do not hate others on that account. We may value other countries higher, in the abstract. We might say, We believe if we were to be born again, and were to have the choice, with present knowledge and without present feelings, we would choose a certain other, and yet would love our country, such as we now are, because our soul feels there at home. We may see our country engaged in a wrong war, and yet we shudder at the bare idea of fighting against her. We may reprove her follies or vices, may strive to correct them and justly acknowledge that other countries have no such vices, and yet we feel closely attached to her. We may not be able to arrive by mere reasoning at the result that we should labor for our country or sacrifice ourselves for her. We might say, Is not the state that institution which exists for the great purpose, among others, of protecting my life? how then is it reasonable to expect that I should expose it for the state, or rush to offer it when not called upon? and yet would feel *that* within us which prompted Sir John Eliot calmly to assign over every portion of his extensive estates to relatives in trust for the benefit of his family, make all directions respecting the education of his children, dearly beloved by him, and then go to the "great, warm, and ruffling" parliament of 1626, where he expected, and, unfortunately, met with, all the danger for which he had prepared himself.[1] We may honor Eversteen of Holland, whose father and four brothers had fallen by the enemy, who yet asked for re-appointment in service, so that he might likewise fall "on the bed of honor."[2] We honor Aristides, whom injustice banished, and who still loved Athens. And why? Because we love our country.

LXIX. But it is not sufficient that we see that it is so. The question is whether it ought so to be. Most assuredly it ought to be so. For all nobler pursuits there must be one primary impulse, beyond interest, and which binds us religiously to that pursuit. We ought to do good even without any selfish ends; why? Because the love of the good impels us to acknowledge it. It is the religion of morals. The scholar pursues his science; for interest's sake? It may be directly against it. For the promotion of ease, or quiet of mind? He may be led to much anxiety, and yet not give up his career. It is the religious love of truth which impels him, the yearning for action, for the use of those faculties with which he is peculiarly endowed. The artist produces his works of art. He might enjoy greater tranquillity, perhaps, in other spheres. His religious love of the beautiful impels him. The patriotic citizen acts for the benefit of others; not for his interest, but because that sympathy and impulse, patriotism, impels him to share dangers, to work out liberty for those who are not yet born, to preserve liberty. Patriotism is the religion of liberty and the state, and at all times have tyrants and sordid politicians been at pains to deride it, unless they expected to turn it to their own account.

Without patriotism, we might easily show that a free state could not possibly endure, for, extinguish patriotism or public spirit, a species of the former, and all must dissolve into dreary, heartless egotism. But even to regret such an

---

[1] Forster's Life of Sir John Eliot, vol. ii. p. 38, of British Statesmen.
[2] Van Campen, History of the Netherlands, vol. ii. p. 196.

occurrence and strive to prevent it requires patriotism in all cases when we can gain nothing for ourselves, or when in all probability we shall sacrifice more than we can obtain. We can see its necessity from those higher points of view from which we perceive that society is a continuous union, with the great ends of justice and civilization; but no man indeed can prove by enlightened self-interest what earthly interest I ought to take in future generations, or what it matters to me personally whether the literature of my country flourishes or is eradicated by a barbarian foe.

LXX. Patriotism forms likewise the transition and link between the state as the jural institution, and the society as the aggregate of living men, with their associations arising out of their history and the soil—in short, the country; it stands between the abstract demand of justice and love of kindred. It is that sympathy which brings affection into the state, and without which the state would often be deprived of its primum mobile; for right is based, as we have seen, on individuality, interest may unite, but it may also sever. Without patriotic spirit, men would separate into different sects, hostile parties, companies, schools of science; and interest alone or abstract right would not be able to supply the bond. Those Asiatic tribes which for centuries have passed from one conqueror to another, and Rome ever since the downfall of the republic, afford us melancholy instances of the absence of patriotism. If then we mean by patriotism the "whole body of those affections which unite men's hearts to the commonwealth,"[1] it is for any nation a most indispensable element of civil success, which cannot be supplanted by any utility; it infuses life and vigor into all parts of the nation, and produces mutual support, magnanimity, and elevation of public action; it is a virtue as much as the love of parents. Still, we do not say that it is an affection to which all others must absolutely give

---

[1] This is the definition which Mackintosh gave of public spirit in Peltier's trial. (State Trials, vol. xxviii. p. 573.) But I believe it designates patriotism.

way. "Patria cara, carior libertas." If those elements which make up what we call our country (patria) — the land, the people, their history, their institutions, their liberty—separate, we must adhere to the higher and highest, in preference to the lower. If we cannot have liberty in our native country, and cannot aid in establishing it there, if we are oppressed, we are surely not bound to stay, although we may feel pain at the separation even then, and often look back with a homesick heart.

Patriotism is an affection for our country, made up, as are all deep-rooted affections, of a thousand associations and influences. Patriotism in modern times, when the stages of action, knowledge, and our very feeling to all men are so much enlarged, in comparison with what they were in ancient times, requires a *country*, to be deep and fruitful. Our reminiscences and attachments must be national; the glory in which we delight must be that of the country, the glory acquired by our nation in the fields of science and the arts, of literature, and of arms in defending her institutions and liberty; the sympathy and powerful associations must be sufficiently distinct from those of the men of other countries, to make patriotism an intense feeling; but a small community, for instance a city, does not supply a sufficient amount of affections to seize upon the whole inner man, and consequently does not afford a marked line by which to distinguish these strong affections from those of others; as for instance the patriotic affections of a German for Germany are distinguished from those of a Frenchman for France. In ancient times this was different. Languages, literature, historic reminiscences, extend over *countries*. And even in ancient times, when was the Greek more nobly and more admirably and truly Greek than when he was Grecian in a national sense? Whether at Olympia or at Marathon, he was greatest when he felt himself wholly Greek. Sismondi's work on the Italian Republics in the Middle Ages contains a passage in one of the concluding chapters (end of chapter cxxvi., vol. xvi., ed. of 1818) which illustrates the preceding remarks in a pointed manner: "Italy," says the celebrated historian, "towards the end of the eighteenth century had always soldiers, riches, a large population, flourishing agriculture, commerce and manufactures which presented still great resources, men versed in the sciences, others whom nature had made fit to acquire them soon; but the feeling and life were missing; and when the French revolution broke out, there was no one in Europe who could not see that Italy had neither the will nor the power to defend her independence, and that a nation which had no longer a country (*patrie*) could not resist, either to defend itself or its neighbors." Mr. Von Raumer, speaking, in the sixth volume of his History of Europe, of the endless sufferings to which Germany was exposed by Louis XIV., says that so it always will be when the Germans forget that they have one common country, and that they ought to have one common national feeling, into however many parts they may be politically divided.

Patriotism is much connected with loyalty, a warm attachment to the institutions of our country, and an upright desire to act according to the true spirit of its laws. In monarchies loyalty has often been used to designate a warm attachment to the royal person, which has not unfrequently existed indeed, but has also often been supposed to exist when the real feeling was for the country, and the monarch was only its visible sign, its standard—a distinction which is seen as soon as the monarch ceased to represent the country. The history of all times, especially since Napoleon, who produced so many changes, furnishes many examples. The attachment is warmest for the country, that is for the land, the people, and their history; that for a king, personally, must always be comparatively weak in a vast country. When Nelson meant to inspire his sailors before the battle of Trafalgar, he told them that England expected every man to do his duty. It told well. Had he said, parliament expects, it would have been much weaker, yet not without effect, for it is a vast institution. Had he said, the king expects, it might have had very little effect; and surely it would have sounded very odd, and stirred no soul, had he said, George III., or the regent, expects, etc. The name of an institution is well calculated to inspire men with a feeling of duty by way of obedience. Congress have sent orders to such or such an effect, would be a weighty expression with an officer in war; but if men were expected to act with noble inspiration, it would be necessary to remind them of "their beloved country."

LXXI. It was significant that with the Romans the word *impius* comprehended at once failing against the gods, the country, and the family. They felt that a temerity or baseness of heart subverting society in its elements was requisite for impiety in all three cases. Patriotism is founded upon what was called in the first volume national allegiance, that indestructible sympathy and attachment which every uncorrupted heart feels towards its own country, not necessarily the native land, but the land of one's parents and history; that "allegiance" which in reality and not in theory "is of a greater extent and dimension than laws or kingdoms, and cannot consist by the laws merely, because it began before laws, it continueth after laws, and it is in vigor when laws are suspended and have had their force,"[1] as Lord Bacon said of personal allegiance. This allegiance can consist, as we have seen, with a desire or duty of emigration, but it will ever prevent a man of any true feeling from fighting against his country, except perhaps in cases of invasion of his adopted country by an army of his native one. A man who can do it has ever been despised as a dastard. It is not easy in some cases to say where or what the country is. On the one hand

---

[1] State Trials, vol. ii. p. 596. Bacon as well as Coke was desirous, as is well known, to prove in Calvin's case that the post-nati, or Scots born after the accession of James I. to the throne of England, were natural subjects of the king of England, and they did it by claiming personal against national allegiance. I have spoken more fully of the subject in the first volume. Every one must now admit how untenable a ground is the principle advanced by Bacon; for it places the king, and the primitive relation of the subject to him, entirely beyond the law. The whole famous case contains many positions that are more than doubtful.

it is sufficiently plain that Thrasybulus did not fight against his country when he returned to Athens with his army to deliver her from the Spartan yoke; on the other, no one fails to be struck with the arrogance of the French emigrants during the first revolution, who actually called their assemblage at Coblentz, France. It is likewise plain enough that calling in armed foreigners and fighting with them against the army or part of the army of our own country is one of the greatest evils. The French have often declared it to be, under any circumstances, treason of the worst kind, and have never forgiven Moreau for having joined the allied princes, nor Bernadotte for having commanded his Swedes against France. Of the latter case we do not speak. A king is an institution, and Bernadotte would certainly have acted treacherously towards his new country had he consulted for one moment his own feelings. Although he was not then king but only crown-prince, the crown was already fixed upon his brow. Had he, in that situation, not felt wholly assimilated to Sweden, but, as Napoleon demanded, remained a Frenchman, because he was so before he entered into a solemn covenant with Sweden, and had he allowed his actions to be influenced by this feeling to the injury of his adopted country, treason would have lurked in his heart. In the case of Moreau, our decision must partly depend upon the point whether he considered Napoleon and his government national, or not. If he faithfully believed that France was irrecoverably tyrannized over so long as Napoleon ruled, and, besides, that a change would be produced long ere the allied powers should enter France, he certainly cannot be placed on a par with Hippias, who infamously led the way for the Persians to his native Attica and Greece. Yet, though we do not feel the execration at Moreau which the baseness of Hippias excites, does not every one feel the strongest repugnance, and pause with pleasure, in the account of the same wars, at the example of Carnot, who had never joined Napoleon, but the moment when foreigners set foot on French soil forgot the government, thinking but of France, and offered his services?

His gallant defence of Antwerp showed how earnest he was.

How careful we ought to be in pronouncing upon this subject an absolute rule, declaring, for instance, that without exception the bringing of foreigners into our country is the greatest of all calamities, is shown by the case of William III. Were not those Englishmen right who came over with him and were ready to fight against the established government of the country? Would they have deserved well had they scrupled to go over from Holland with a foreign army? The circumstances were peculiar, I own. The fact that the republic of the United Provinces was comparatively but a small power, so that a conquest could not take place, and the chief work must remain to be done by the English themselves, either by fighting for William or by readily receiving him, was of the greatest importance. This shows that there are exceptions. On the other hand, all that Demosthenes said of foreigners being called in against Philip remains generally true, and the consequences proved that the Athenian was right. We do not here speak of cases such as that of the duke of Bourbon's leaving the French army and fighting against his native country. He merited the reproach of the dying Bayard.

LXXII. That genuine patriotism enlarges instead of narrowing our views, should have appeared from the previous passages. It is therefore a poor counterfeit of patriotism or public spirit if foreigners, though their services should be considered necessary, are excluded from this service. It is against the spirit of our times, which acknowledges a general union of civilization too much to admit of so narrow a view. In sciences and arts in particular, foreign scholars and artists have for centuries received calls from one country into another. If it is perhaps less so at present in some countries than in the middle ages, it is only because the chairs can now be more easily filled with natives. Spain, which rapidly rose under Ferdinand and Isabella, owed her glorious rise in a great measure to her rising universities, which no natives probably contributed so much to elevate as the foreigners placed in their chairs, as for instance Peter Martyr. Erasmus in England is another striking instance.

Among the foremost citizens in loyalty when times are gloomy, foreigners who are citizens by choice and not by chance will always be found. The American revolution is full of such examples; nor should we forget the names of Columbus, Vasco da Gama, Cabot, William I. of Orange, William III., all of whom served in faith and peril or brought glory to their adopted countries.

LXXIII. The term public spirit has often been used for patriotism, the word patriot having become somewhat objectionable at some periods. Words are unimportant. By patriotism we designate perhaps more specifically that sacred enthusiasm which prompts to great exertions and has the welfare, honor, reputation of the country at large in view; by public spirit, a practical disinterestedness and cheerful readiness to serve the community and promote its essential success in every way. A perfect stranger to a country might still show much public spirit.

Hume says, "A man who loves only himself, without regard to friendship and desert, merits the severest blame; and a man who is only susceptible of friendship, without public spirit or a regard to the community, is deficient in the most material part of virtue."[1] The freer a country, the more it

---

[1] Essay III., on Politics a Science. — Self-forgetting, not self-denial, delights us wherever we meet with it, so universal is the admiration of disinterestedness, the dislike of selfishness, although our interests betray us continually into it. If we are attentive, we shall find in how great a degree in all branches the principle exists. An author delights most when we see he has entirely forgotten himself and is but the spokesman of his subject; we admire a work of art when we see how entirely free from vanity and selfish conceit the artist was, and that he forgot himself entirely in his work. It goes so far that a sentence or a conceit never intended to be heard or seen frequently gives pleasure, although it is neither witty nor interesting enough to do so, so soon as we know it was not intended to be heard. Nothing touches the heart so deeply as to become ac-

stands in need of public spirit and the more baneful becomes isolating selfishness. But it may well be asked, How far shall public spirit prompt a man to act? There are some who ruin their own affairs or who become burdensome in consequence of mistaken public spirit. A citizen who attends every meeting but neglects his own affairs, or lectures on education and brings up his own sons as idlers, cannot be said to have public spirit, for one of those things in which a community is primarily interested is that every one keep his own affairs in a sound state. Public spirit shows itself chiefly in substantial and noiseless ways, and prompts the citizen to perform those elementary functions on which he knows the existence of society depends, even at the price of some inconvenience or loss of time, without any hope of reward in public acknowledgment. A public-spirited man will vote, though he need take no active part in party measures; he will willingly serve on a jury, and he will aid in his proportion with money and time in any fair and reasonable project, without seeking to promote thereby his own interest.[1] It has been mentioned too often already to dwell here any longer on this subject, how useless all laws become, and that no community can expect success, when public spirit has fled; but the reader will find below to

---

quainted with great or good deeds long after they were performed in a manner which shows that they were done without any expectation of their ever becoming known.

[1] We were once marching on a road broken up by the rain and the passing of many troops. At each step we sank deep in the clay. It was a toilsome march; and any impediment in the road was much disrelished by the weary men. In the midst of this road happened to lie a stone covered by the mire, but of sufficient size to hurt any one who knocked against it. Each soldier, as he knocked himself, grumbled and passed on. The colonel observed this, and stopped, whilst the troops passed. At last a soldier arrived who likewise knocked and hurt himself severely. He showed it by the expression of his face, but immediately went to work to remove the stone, and then passed on. "Stop," called the colonel: "what's your name? More than ten men have passed here and hurt themselves, and you are the first who had public spirit enough to remove the stone. You shall be one of the first corporals." This was real public spirit, in however humble a sphere.

what political misery and extravagance the absence of this elementary principle may lead.[1]

---

[1] Where sound patriotism and healthy public spirit are wanting, factious spirit and selfishness united with boldness must be rife. This selfishness may have ends of avarice, ambition, or revenge. We all know into how deplorable a state the South American States have been thrown in consequence of their want of public spirit, of disinterestedness applied to politics, since they have broken their allegiance to Spain. Even that public spirit which may partly arise from interest, yet interest well enlightened respecting its real advantage, is entirely wanting in the great mass of the people. We not unfrequently meet with accounts from those regions that the polls of a certain place were entirely deserted, no citizen appearing to think it worth his while to vote. Apathy leads to, or is the effect of, anarchy and lawlessness; armed faction succeeds faction; and so frequent has this been in some states that a judicious traveller, Mr. Chevalier, was enabled to write a certain theory of these factious movements in Mexico. As the causes and men are always similar, it is very natural that the different stages of an insurrection should succeed in a similar and certain order. "In Mexico," says Mr. Michel Chevalier, in a series of letters written from that country, and published, in 1837, in the Paris journals, "insurrections have become an act of mere common life. There have gradually been established perfectly well-defined forms for it; which, like the rules of the noble game of tric-trac or the receipts of the *cuisinière bourgeoise*, it is understood, admit no deviation. The procedure is sufficiently simple, and in Mexico sufficiently humane likewise: it resembles, if not a battle at the opera, at all events a harmless enough guerilla warfare. The first act of a revolution is called *pronunciamiento*. An officer of any grade, from that of general to that of lieutenant downwards, *pronounces* himself against the established order of things, or any institution which he does not approve of, or anything else of any description. He collects a party, a company, or a regiment, which generally hastens to place itself at his disposal. The second act of the revolution is called *grito*—the *cry*, in which the motives and objects of the insurrection are reduced to three or four heads or articles. When the subject is of some importance, the *cry* assumes the name of a *plan*. In the third act, the insurgents and partisans of the government come into each other's presence. There are skirmishes, there are reconnoissances of their respective forces. In the fourth they come to action definitively. But, according to the improvements which have been introduced recently into the art of revolution-making, this is done in the most guarded manner and at the most respectful distance. There must, however, be a victor and a vanquished. If you are beaten, you *unpronounce* yourself; if victorious, you march upon Mexico. In the fifth and last act, the conqueror, whoever he is, makes his triumphal entry into the capital, whilst the vanquished embarks at Vera Cruz, or Tampico, with all the honors of war." With the exception, perhaps, of the bloodlessness of these movements, which reminds us of the captains in Italy towards the end of the sixteenth century counting the num

LXXIV. The word old, denoting in its strict and primary sense a length of time that an object has existed,[1] came, by a natural transition from designating the old people, also to designate the times in which they lived, and these once being called old, the previous ones would be still older; old came to be used for expressing what we now more strictly call ancient; in short, old is used not only to denote length of years but also distance of time in the retrospect, an ambiguity which has at times exercised a certain effect in politics; which obliges us to dwell for a moment upon this subject. In treating of it I shall not restrict myself to the consequences of the ambiguity alone, but treat of old applied to the living, to ancestors, and to institutions, in so far as this is of moment in politics.

It belongs to the province of ethics in general to point out the respect, forbearance, and peculiar kindness we owe to old age, and the reasons why this is a duty, the absence of which is always considered by the virtuous as an indication of a heart in which anything which might be called generous must have given way to obdurate selfishness or a callousness which easily may pass over into brutality. We not only feel a degree of respect for gray hairs, but it affects us deeply to see an old man arraigned or convicted of a crime, because it contends so directly with the feeling which we desire to entertain for advanced age. A feeling so general, the absence of which indicates so much more than a mere dereliction of a single duty, is of course of itself important to the community in politics. Its extinction would indicate general selfishness and callousness, incompatible with the essential success of any community. Montesquieu goes so far as to say that "nothing maintains morals more firmly than an extreme subordination of the young towards the old." This, it would seem, is extravagant; for the veneration of the old

---

bers opposed to each other, without fighting, the same theory applies pretty much to the changes in Portugal.

[1] The word *old* is derived from the root *al*, to "grow," Latin *al-* and *ol-* in *adolesco;* Gr. perhaps in ἄλσος, and found also in Gothic, High German, and Irish. Comp. Curtius, Gr. Etymol., 4th ed., No. 523, b.

may be coupled with or arise from other causes not propitious to morals. In no country is the subjection of the young to the old more complete and systematically as well as religiously carried out than in China, a country which we would certainly not place at the head as to morality, however willingly we may acknowledge its superiority in this respect over most other Asiatic countries. But this is certain, nowhere can sound morality subsist, or liberty endure and be prevented from degenerating into licentiousness, folly, fickleness, where the young are without modesty, respect and deference for superior age and experience, and a sincere veneration of those who by their works and continued labors have proved the sincerity of their zeal or have added honor to their community or country.

LXXV. Authority, which begins in the family and passes over to the similarly situated elders of the tribe, is naturally connected in all early times with old age, so that the names of offices and judicial or legislative institutions are in most early nations derived from the words indicating old age.[1] They by the mere fact of being older enjoy a degree of respect, they have experience and know the laws better than the young, because the latter have not yet been able to learn them from tradition. When nearly all that can and must be learned respecting public affairs is to be learned by oral transmission, and when the various classes of society are as yet little separated from one another, but the education and knowledge of all are nearly on a par, old age of itself must necessarily be of considerable importance and weight. It is different when laws, finances, and other branches require study, and study leisure, which by the difference of fortune is allotted in very different degrees to the various classes. In this state of society it is frequently the case that a young man

---

[1] It will be hardly necessary to remind the reader of the word *senatus* derived from *senex*, of the Greek γερουσία, counsel or senate, (from γέρων, an old man, and many corresponding terms in ancient times and the middle ages, as Signior, Patrician, Alderman, Presbytery, Council of the Ancients.

may have read, heard, seen—in fact, lived more—than an old one; and in a state of a populous society far advanced in civilization we cannot any longer assign the same official importance to old age which naturally is attached to it in earlier periods. Men but too frequently run into extremes, and, while we allow the above position, we must also acknowledge the absurdity of attaching wisdom to youth, and making youth, as it were, a party-sign and qualification, as seems now to be actually the case in some countries. That there have been great and rare minds who at the age when others are yet learning wielded the helm of vast affairs or brilliantly shone in the sciences, we all know. Pitt, Napoleon, De Witt, Grotius, Laplace, and many other distinguished names among the moderns and ancients, prove it abundantly; but they were extraordinary men, geniuses, the very character of which consists in leaping beyond what for others is the natural course. From exceptions we cannot draw our rules. Macchiavelli rightly observes, "If we choose a youth, he must have shown himself already worthy of this election by something distinguished." It is right, then, not to withhold from them a station due to their genius and nobleness of soul; but we must first have this pledge, and not trust to favorites, to Buckinghams, *despite* their youth.

In the common course of things we know that the young are the readier and bolder for action, prompted by a more lively temperament, and not yet tamed and chilled by repeated failures and bitter disappointments. The distinctive age as to readiness of action is about the fortieth year. The average age of the signers of the American Declaration of Independence was nearly forty-four; yet if we deduct of the fifty-five signers the age of seven citizens who were sixty years old or above, the average age comes down to forty.[1] Most of those who first embraced the Reformation were about forty years

---

[1] Of fifty-five signers there were under thirty years 2, both twenty-seven years old; thirty, and less than forty, 17; forty, and less than fifty, 22; fifty, and less than sixty, 8; sixty, and less than seventy, 6; seventy, 1.

old, or younger.[1] Far the greater number of the most distinguished generals have been young, and, when all other circumstances were nearly equal, the young general opposed to an old one has almost always been victorious.[2]

Those governments therefore which contain the principle of movement, which give a field or call for prompt action,

---

[1] The Venetian ambassador at the court of France, Micheli, reported in 1561 to the doge that except among the common peasantry, "who continue to visit the churches zealously," "the young men under the age of forty, almost without exception," belong to the new doctrine—that is, Protestantism. According to a despatch in 1562 from the Venetian ambassador in Spain, there were many Huguenots throughout Spain. (Ranke, History of the Popes, etc., vol. ii. pp. 16 and 21.) Passion and action together belong chiefly to the male sex from twenty to thirty, during which age therefore by far the greatest number of crimes are committed.

[2] We must remember here, however, that these young generals had always tried and experienced soldiers around them. They counselled and planned; the young gave energy, promptness, boldness, on which victory, after a good plan has been made, so much depends. Alexander, Cæsar, Frederic, Napoleon, were young when first victorious; Themistocles, at Salamis, twenty-six; Leonidas, when he fell, twenty-one; Scipio Africanus, when he conquered Hannibal, little above twenty; Eugene, at the battle of Mohacz, twenty-four; Charles XII., at Narva, eighteen; and many more might be cited. Camillus is said to have been but fifteen years old when he performed the heroic deed which soon elevated him to the censorship, and in his eightieth year he was dictator the fifth time—a full life indeed!

[Dr. Lieber's examples are to be taken *cum grano salis*. Themistocles, if born, as seems probable, in 514 B.C., was thirty-four years old at the sea-fight of Salamis. Leonidas had been king, before he fell, nine years. His niece and wife was, according to Clinton, twenty-nine at that time. His brother Dorieus, soon after the accession of their half-brother Cleomenes, who reigned nineteen if not twenty-nine years (Clinton), left Sparta to found a colony, and Leonidas was born, as Herodotus says, "right after Dorieus." (V. 41.) All this shows the story that he was only twenty-one at Thermopylæ to be a fable. Scipio Africanus, again, probably born B.C. 234, and seventeen years old at the battle of the Ticinus, when he first encountered and defeated Hannibal at Zama in 202 was thirty-two. Prince Eugene did not command at Mohacz, but the duke of Lorraine. His great victory at Zenta, of which Dr. Lieber was probably thinking, was gained in 1697, when he was thirty-four. The story of Camillus being chosen a censor not long after he was fifteen is ridiculous. He was censor probably in 403 B.C., and died in 365, so that, if eighty years old at his death, he was forty-two when elected censor. Charles XII. remains,—hare-brained in his youth, hare-brained until his death.]

bring men upon the stage of action at a comparatively early age. Many of the most prominent Athenians were very young when they first acted; while in Sparta, founded upon conservatism, the citizens acquired consideration and privileges with the different advances of age. Liberty in general is favorable to bringing forward men in the prime of life. On the other hand, the conservatism which is an indispensable element of all true liberty, and not a cant or desire to retain what ought not to be retained, the spirit which arises out of a conviction that no healthy government can spring into existence as by a magic wand, but that development of the laws wisely founded upon the existing facts is necessary,—this is more generally a characteristic trait of those beyond forty years of age. They have experience, not only the mere knowledge which amounts to no more than the remembrance of that which we have seen, but the convictions and impressions and vivid consciousness with which the operations and effects of laws and institutions, and the forcible illustrations and interpretations of history afforded by what we witness ourselves in practical life, deeply imbue our mind; they, the old, have in many cases acquired tact or instinct of great importance in those numerous cases in which mere reasoning and counterbalancing the advantages and disadvantages, as Cecil used to do, cannot lead us to a decisive result. This tact, indispensable wherever we have to act in very complicated cases, may be native in genius, but its possessor must be a genius if it be native. If the old are on some occasions too reluctant to do what ought to be done because it is new, the young are on the other hand apt to adopt measures because they are new. In times therefore like ours, in which new and powerful moving agents have been brought into play in politics, such as the power of the daily papers and the swift mails, it behoves us to allow their full share to the principles and elements more strongly represented by the old in public matters.

LXXVI. Veneration for our forefathers arises, if real,—and we do not occupy ourselves here with hypocritic cant,—from two causes; the one just, the other erroneous. It is one of the most indelible feelings in the human breast that we honor the memory of our parents. The basest criminal, dead to almost all other feelings, will resent a reproach cast upon his parents; few things sting the heart of a man so deeply, even of the vulgarest, as reproach cast upon father or mother. A good name is, with all honorable men, an expression of vast import. Nothing is so sad for the receding Indian as when he "takes leave of the land in which the bones of his fathers lie;" nothing so solemn in the Old Testament as when the Hebrew is admonished by the God of his forefathers.

It would seem that Providence has made this feeling one of the primary agents to unite society, one generation with the other, to make of communities continuous societies, and to prevent them from crumbling and disintegrating into mere masses of selfish particles. This feeling, as we have seen, extends farther back than to our own bodily parents. We feel grateful for the blessings, which may be the effects of the endeavors of our forefathers, perhaps of their struggle and suffering. If we enjoy well-founded liberty, it is they who must have established it or provided for its growth; if it cost them sacrifices, they must have been prompted to bear them by the consciousness that they would thereby obtain it for us; they lived, toiled, and died for their country, and that country includes the thought of future generations. If, however, we ascribe superior wisdom to our forefathers, we must have a specific reason for it; they may have established an institution when peculiar circumstances favored them to obtain superior wisdom as to this subject, or to see with greater disinterestedness, because the times may have been fitter for it. Enthusiasm for what is great and good may have been more general, as, for instance, when our forefathers struggled for independence. But this may also not be the case. An Englishman who should carry his veneration for his forefathers so far as to look upon the courtiers of Charles II. or his judges as upon men of superior probity or wisdom would deviate from all truth. If, however, we have reason to be grateful to them, it must be an active gratitude, not an oral one, which frequently is but a cloak to our own indolence, or our vanity, or pride of descent,—to lower others by comparison. Our gratitude must consist in acting out farther and farther what they have begun, not in a desire to remain stationary and to consider that which they were able to obtain under their circumstances as the last degree of perfection that may be obtained. The ideal of a nation, that for which it strives, must lie onward, not be believed to consist in something absolute established in former ages and the keeping of which in that precise state forms the highest duty. The Hindoos, the Chinese, thus look back, not forward. The excellence of all laws depends upon their fitness—that is, upon the sound principle judiciously applied to the existing state of things; these things, however, change in the course of time; real standing still is therefore impossible, and if we do not move onward, if we force the same laws upon changed circumstances, we must ruin the state.

The erroneous cause of the veneration of our forefathers is the popular and very old belief that times grow worse and worse; not a little promoted by the feeling of discomfort which must befall all old people when men and things around them change. This belief is very old. Even Homer makes Pallas say, "Few children indeed are equal in virtue to their father, many are worse, and but very few better."[1] History does not justify this dictum, and Homer himself, since he has been quoted once, says in another passage, "We claim to be much better than our fathers." Hallam, treating of the period of Elizabeth, and speaking of the Tower, says, "It seems like a captive tyrant reserved to grace the triumph of a victorious republic, and should teach us to reflect in thankfulness how highly we have been elevated in virtue and happiness above our forefathers." And in a note appended to this passage he adds, "There is no line in Homer which I repeat more frequently or with greater pleasure than the boast of Sthenelus: Ἡμεῖς τοι πατέρων μέγ᾽ ἀμείνονες εὐχόμεθ᾽ εἶναι. This is a truth of

---

[1] Odyssey, ii. 277.

which the impartial study of history persuades us; and yet, like other truths, it has its limitations."[1] Let us not forget that even the Spartans, certainly the most conservative of the prominent Grecian tribes, appeared at one of their national festivals in different choruses. The chorus of the ancients chanted, "We were brave in days gone by." The chorus of men responded, "We are brave, come who may to try it;" when the chorus of the boys concluded, "Brave we shall be; our deeds shall outshine yours." In the only branch in which the Spartans were proud to excel, they acknowledged that an onward endeavor was the only spirit to maintain what they valued most highly—national valor.

Not only has it been believed that a regular course of moral degeneracy is going on, but at a very early period it was believed that men became feebler and more diminutive with every generation.[2]

The reason of so general a belief is that we see and feel the evils of the present time, but not those which belong to the past, while dissatisfaction with the present time or real suffering causes us to magnify the virtues of our ancestors, to which a general respect for our own parents and grandparents already naturally inclines us.

LXXVII. The advantage which old persons possess over young ones is experience. Respecting the world in general, then, we are the old ones compared to our forefathers, provided always we have endeavored to possess ourselves of their experience and that of our own times, and do not presumptuously think that the mere fact of our being born after them makes us wiser. We must truly study and respect their endeavors before we can say that we are wiser. Bacon's remark to this purpose appears to be a mere truism as soon as distinctly stated; yet not unfrequently the old times are appealed

---

[1] Constitutional History of England, i. 202.
[2] There existed formerly a nursery-story, founded upon this belief, which predicted that men would become so small that the ovens used by us would become their palaces.

to as authority as we would appeal to old persons.[1] But it is very necessary to keep some points distinctly in our mind respecting old institutions. I will state them briefly:

The more ignorant a person, and the less acquainted therefore with what has been done, said, tried, suffered, what has miscarried or succeeded, what difficulties are in the way, or what evils, no longer visible, have been suppressed by a certain institution not inconvenient itself; the less a person is conscious of the great multiplicity of actions and operations in society; the more forward he will be found to intrude his new thought or system upon men, as if happiness or sense should date only from the day when his system was introduced; the more he believes in an absolute goodness of laws; and the less substantial the qualities of his mind; the more prone he will be to destroy rather than maintain, develop, enlarge.

The inexperienced and ignorant alone believe that a projected institution can, in all its bearings, be comprehended at once without practical application, and that laws and institutions are finished if drawn up on paper, regardless of the state of things in and with which they have to operate.

Those institutions are the best which, if good at all, have their roots deep in the soil of the nation, whose body of laws consists mainly in the alluvial soil deposited by the course of time, since thus alone institutions which have grown and have developed themselves in the course of time meet with the spontaneous action of the people; they have been checked, expanded, fashioned as the course of history required, and have become endeared to the nation as blessings, as realities.[2]

Old institutions have the advantage of being tried, and

---

[1] Bentham calls the reason which is derived from the oldness of an institution a one in its favor the Chinese argument. Archbishop Whately, in the Appendix to his Elements of Logic, has a few words on the term "old."

[2] Cicero de Respubl., ii. 1. "Nostra republica non unius [est] ingenio sed multorum; nec una hominis vita sed aliquot constituta sæculis et ætatibus; . . . neque cuncta ingenia conlata in unum tantum posse uno tempore providere, ut omnia complecterentur sine rerum usu et vetustate."

hence are known, while of new ones we have yet to see how they operate, and what ultimate effects they produce.

Old institutions ought not to be pulled down except evil is perceived to be produced by them.

We must be especially careful in touching those laws which were made by those whom we know to have lived in better or more favorable periods.

It is a wicked idolatry to sacrifice the living to the memory of the dead, and obstinately to insist upon old laws simply because they are old, although bad, and perhaps cruel.

Stability is of itself a most desirable thing; it promotes probity, and gives moral tone to society; but to preserve that which is bad is either foolish or immoral. The star-chamber was an old institution: should it have been preserved? The institution of the vizier in Asiatic despotism is older than any British one: is it on that account good? The cause of civilization and of a liberty worthy of man is neither promoted by Asiatic stagnation,—whose Koran says, Every new law is an innovation, every innovation is an error, and every error leads to eternal fire,—nor by the arrogance of a jacobin declaring war against everything that exists and has existed.[1]

---

[1] Dumont, speaking of Paine, in the Souvenirs sur Mirabeau, ch. xvi., says, "He was a caricature of the vainest Frenchman. Paine said to Dumont that if it were in his power to annihilate all libraries he would do it without hesitation, in order to destroy all the error deposited in them, and to commence a new chain of ideas and principles with the Rights of Man." How many Paines in their respective spheres, and more or less bold, have we not seen since, and are we not seeing daily!

# BOOK IV.

## CHAPTER I.

Education.—What it is.—Strong and universal tendency to form Habits and continue them.—Great importance of Education in Politics, not only of elementary and general School Systems, but also of superior Education and literary Institutions.—Expeditions, Libraries, Museums.—Industrial Education.—The Rich as well as the Poor ought to be actively engaged in some Pursuit, whether purely mental, or industrial.—Law of Solon.—Connection of Crime with want of regular industrial Education in modern Times.—Statistics.—Habits of Industry, of Obedience, of Independence, of Reverence, and of Honesty.—Ancient History for Children.—Concentric Instruction.—Gymnastics.—Sexes.—The Woman.—Difference of physical Organization, Temperament, and Powers in Woman and Man.—The Family (and through it the Society of Comity and the Country) is the sacred Sphere of Woman's chief Activity.—The Connection of Woman's Activity with the State.—Woman is excluded from Politics.—She is connected with the State by Patriotism.—Lady Croke.—The Petitioning of Women.—Lady Russell a Model.—History of Woman.—Is the Woman represented though she cannot vote at the Poll?

I. EDUCATION, the transmission of knowledge, skill, and morality, that principal tie by which one generation is connected with another and thus mankind becomes a continuous society, is a subject of the first magnitude in everything that relates to society. I waive the great importance of education in developing and perfecting, humanizing and elevating the individual as such, on which a few words were given in the first volume, when the views taken by the ancients respecting education were compared with the light in which this subject appears to the civilized modern nations.

Society is deeply interested in general education: in no subject more so; in very few equally so. In educating we ought to strive by aiding and cultivating to develop the whole man, as much as all the given circumstances admit. We have seen throughout this work that man, destined for civilization as well as moral independence, has a social and individual destiny, and man to be fully man must be a citizen, that is a member of the state. It is one of the unalterable destinies prescribed by Providence for our existence. The future citizen, or active member of the state, is then to be included in the objects of education. All education consists in storing and training the mind, if we comprehend within the latter term the purifying guidance in morals and religion as well as the training of the intellect, imparting method and vigor by exercise and habit; and, finally, the imparting of sound habits, which again may be moral, intellectual, and social habits, a subject of the utmost importance, because it is, as Bacon already quoted said, custom that governs man in far the greatest number of practical cases hourly occurring. Indeed, the constant tendency of man to custom and habit, to uniformity in manner, opinions, and desires, "the centripetal power of custom," as Hallam calls it, is one of those agents without which society could not possibly exist, which operates long before reflection makes us conscious of it, and after reflection has made us conscious operates far more effectually, generally, and constantly than mere reflection would be capable of doing. This primitive tendency, strongly founded upon the impulse of imitation, from which the development of the mind in earliest childhood starts, but which remains a powerful agent throughout life, naturally carries along with it its evil effects;—as we have observed, in previous passages, of other elementary agents or impulses in the human soul. It leads men to perpetuate evil customs, to accommodate themselves to erroneous opinions, to continue upon bad precedents; but it would be as impossible, and, were it possible, as disastrous to society, to extinguish this elementary tendency of uniformity and custom, of imitation and perpetuation, on account of its evil effects, as it would be to quench the desire of union between the different sexes on account of its evil effects; as, we all know, has been attempted by many enthusiasts of all periods for many thousand years, if not in all mankind at least in certain classes and societies and as an additional means of attaining greater perfection. Customs, habits, therefore, will be formed; and, for the same reason which was adduced respecting religion, we are bound to cultivate good habits, even had we not other and urgent considerations for so doing. If we do not cultivate the habit of industry, we may be sure that by this very neglect we cultivate the habit of indolence; if we do not promote the habit of propriety and modesty, we directly aid in forming the habit of indecency and boldness.

II. The reader will, of course, not expect in the present work a sketch of a whole system of education. I must confine my remarks to a few general observations, and some hints, which experience has taught me to consider as not unimportant with regard to education as related to politics. Education, we have seen, aims at developing the whole man: we may consider man, however, either as a moral and religious being, as an intellectual being, as a social being, as a physical being, or as an æsthetic being, that is a being endowed with taste, in other words, who has a sense for the beautiful; and as no man can be a good and sound citizen who is not a good and sound man, so the best education for future citizens will be that which is the completest and fullest education of the individual as an entire man. Let us keep in mind that all education, adapting itself to man in his various capacities just mentioned, may be training, that is invigorating and producing habits, or storing, that is imparting knowledge. Finally, all education is either domestic education, school education, industrial education,—by which, for want of a better word, I mean all education for a trade, profession, or station in life; or social education, by which we may designate that indirect yet highly important training which every man receives by his living in and with a society—the formation of his mind by the influence of his society and age.

III. How important nay, how indispensable, domestic education is, both in training and storing, morally, intellectually, and physically, is clear to every one who has paid the slightest attention to the subject. For it is in the family where those earliest impressions are received and habits formed which adhere longest to a man, or go with him as far as to the last goal of his life. Example, powerful everywhere, is most so at home; because it there presents itself earliest, most frequently, and most authoritatively—in that authority which is stronger than that of king or law, the authority of the parent. Yet division of labor, necessary everywhere, is likewise so in education: hence the necessity of school education; and as it is out of the power of many whole communities, and of large classes in most communities, to provide for a sound school education, either for want of individual means or knowledge sufficient to select or obtain the best teachers, general systems of school education have become highly important for all civilized nations. It is one of the peculiar traits of the latest times that all the most civilized and elevated nations have with much care and earnestness established general school systems or are actively striving to establish them. And it is a fact no less pleasing that of late the whole science and practice of education have become so diffused and honored that in some countries, for instance in Germany and partially in France, the word School is used in as comprehensive a meaning as the word Church was used in former times, or as we are wont to use the word Law or Bar, meaning thereby the whole system, organization, members, and the distinct acknowledgment of its importance by society. Jovellanos said perhaps too much when he pronounced that "the fountains of social prosperity are many, but all originate from one and the same well, and this is public instruction;"[1] but, although using too strong terms when he recommended a measure so much neglected by his countrymen, this excellent man was certainly not far from truth and only erred in the expression of a principle itself true and essential. Modern

---

Complete Works, Madrid, 1831, vol. iii. p. 292.

nations cannot fulfil their duty, nay, they cannot even protect themselves sufficiently against evils otherwise unavoidable, the consequences of civilization and density of population, without general and public instruction.[1]

\* Although single persons may have the means to provide for the education of their children at home, the sons nevertheless should go to school. Every one is destined for civilization, for society, and an education is very incomplete if the mind of the boy has not been fashioned among others, under the influences of society. This begins earliest and most effectually in the school. In the school the boy steps out of the close family circle, where it is possible to pay attention to a thousand minute details, into a larger society, yet not so public as public life — but still it is a sort of public life. There the boy forms the earliest attachments beyond those of kindred, has his angular points rubbed off, learns to judge for himself more freely, and stands much more upon his own legs. The King of the French has shown in a remarkable manner how strong *national* society is at present by sending his sons to the schools of Paris, open to all citizens' boys— common schools inasmuch as they are open to every one.

IV. It is, however, a grave error into which some have fallen, who believe that the state as such, or civil society, is interested only in the promotion of education among the poor, in other words in systems of public instruction restricted to the diffusion of elementary knowledge among large masses. This is the opposite error to that which in former ages so frequently induced governments richly to endow a few institutions of learning and totally to neglect common education. A complete system of public instruction comprehends all institutions which are necessary for the society, and which nevertheless cannot or will not be established by private means. Society at large, down to the lowliest cottager, is

---

[1] I must again refer, respecting this point, to my Letter on the Relation between Education and Crime.

deeply interested in the highest possible degree of cultivation of the sciences; for they shed light and diffuse civilization by a thousand rays and in a thousand channels over the whole of society. If science, untrammelled and unconcerned about any immediate application, does not boldly press forward, since its application to practical life always necessarily follows at a considerable distance, the actual state of science will stand still or retrograde. The Chinese, spurning every species of knowledge, every experiment, which cannot be proved at once to be of direct use, furnish us with a very impressive illustration of this fact. Had Laplace always thought how his soaring calculations might be applied at once to navigation, he would never have produced his Celestial Mechanics, which nevertheless will effect great practical benefits, not only by having led our race a step farther on its great road of civilization, but by way of actual use. Science is not a mere luxury. Well it is that science is a luxury to some minds to reward them for many privations or disheartening disappointments. For society the sciences are of imperative necessity, and fall entirely within the province of that civilization which we found to be the destiny of man. The sciences are like the sun of heaven. When his rays descend upon the blade, the blossom of the tree, you do not see them unfold themselves at once. Yet when he has passed onward in his heavenly course, the ray of noon is still effecting its enlivening and transforming processes even in the humblest and minutest herb or the moss which derives its modest existence from the bounty of the lofty tree. The state is directly interested in sustaining the highest institutions of learning, which require means hardly ever at the disposal of private individuals; nor has it any right to wait for private contributions towards the foundation of public seats of learning, however cheerfully it may receive them if offered. Every citizen, as such, low or high, simply as a member of the state, has an undoubted right to demand this, just as much as he has an absolute, natural, primitive right to demand an establishment of some sort or other to administer justice. Even if political society were nothing but an agglomeration of atoms, if it were not as we have found it to be a continuous society, it would still be the state's duty to promote these institutions, for on the one hand they are of general utility, on the other hand the pursuit of the sciences requires means which the individual, who must turn his industry towards objects which by direct exchange will furnish him the means of subsistence, does not possess. These means are chiefly leisure and money. Instruments, libraries, those conductors, concentrators, and bridges of civilization, collections, expeditions, measurements, scientific surveys, are all wholly or in part of a character not to be obtained or executed by private means, especially by the means of those who generally are the peculiar votaries of knowledge and feel the greatest direct interest in these subjects. Had not governments effected the measurements of a degree, what private person would or could have done it? Yet the more accurate knowledge of the earth's formation has already proved of great importance to society at large in a thousand ways. The more knowledge multiplies and branches out, the vaster our experiments and inquiries become, the more time the various patient investigations require, the more necessary also becomes public support of knowledge. Had the Greeks felt the same want, had sciences obtained with them the same importance, and their pursuit been attended with the same difficulties, as with us, they would have simply taxed their Girards or Rothschilds with a "liturgy," to send an expedition to the north pole. We cannot and must not do this. Who, then, can do it? Society, of course; and let me add, how small are these expenses compared to so many others of less and even of doubtful importance! how incalculable their benefits!

The fine arts are, as we have seen, of great national importance, in an industrial, moral, and patriotic point of view. Museums, therefore, if more important subjects are not sacrificed to them, and if they remain national institutions and national schools, are subjects justly claiming their due and proportionate support of the state.

V. Let us return to the subject of general education. If general school education, imparting that elementary knowledge without which an individual nowadays is a sort of outcast from the common pale of civilized society, is of great importance in politics, that species which was called industrial education (by which, I beg to remind the reader, I intend by no means a training in schools for certain trades) is not less so, and is perhaps even more so. Every citizen without exception, in some sphere of activity or other, strictly industrial or mental, should apply himself, and manifest himself as a real and active member of his society. Without it he loses his hold upon society and becomes dangerous, whether he be prompted to do so by riches or poverty. Man is not made for indolence; he loses his inward equipoise, and becomes morbid or criminal, fanciful or self-willed, if he is not acting. He neglects his duty towards society if he thus severs himself from the common course of action and plunges into undefined and indolent selfishness. As to those who cannot be seduced into such a course because they do not possess wealth, it is necessary to observe that among the most fruitful sources of all crimes a neglected habit of industry is the foremost. Solon, according to Plutarch, decreed that the son was not bound to support his aged father—one of the most sacred obligations in his code—if the latter had not brought up his son to some trade. This is very striking. Very positive experience must have induced that sage to express in so forcible a form the observation of a political result. Observation in modern times will furnish the same facts. I do not speak of riots, or political disturbances, which, when they are not founded on a substantial evil, are in most cases chiefly promoted by those who are not engaged in industrious pursuits, but limit myself to the commission of crime.[1] In my

---

[1] Idleness as a political evil reached its "classical age" in the worst periods of Grecian democracy, and in Rome. In the former, presence in the popular assembly came to be paid for, as in the worst time of the French revolution. During the decline of Rome, the idling wretches sank so low that, too cowardly to march against the conquering tribes, they nevertheless were delighted at seeing

inquiries respecting education, industry, and crime, I have found among other remarkable results this: that of three hundred and fifty-eight criminals two hundred and twenty-seven had never been bound out to any trade or regular occupation, seventy-nine were bound out but ran away before they had stayed out their time, and only fifty-two were bound out and remained with their respective masters until the completion of their proper time; and that the average time of the sentence of imprisonment in the case of those who had served out was a little less than four years, but of those who ran away, a little above five years, thus indicating a much greater degree of criminality. Here it might be objected that the running away from the master is the effect of vicious habits, and not the cause of the future crime; but whether the one be the cause of the other, or both the effect of the same cause, it is for our purpose the same: it shows how closely the want of industry is connected with viciousness and criminality, and how right it is, like Solon, to insist upon universal industrial education.

It would be well could the right of voting be connected not only with a degree of education, but also with some steady employment. This, however, belongs to Politics proper.

I ought to observe here for the general reader, that binding out is not restricted to mechanical trades, but extends, with us, to agricultural pursuits likewise.[1] The facts ascertained

---

the agony of the dying gladiator. When Treves was devastated by German predatory tribes, the first thing which the inhabitants, deprived of house and property, asked for, was Circensian games. Salvian de Gub. Dei, vi. 146.

[1] Mr. Wood, warden of the Eastern Penitentiary in Pennsylvania, and Mr. Yard, keeper of the New Jersey Penitentiary, have with much kindness made at my request inquiries and furnished me with statements respecting the industrial education of criminals, and the age at which criminals lost their parents, of high interest, the results of which I shall not omit to make public on some proper occasion. The Rev. Mr. Barrett, chaplain to the Connecticut State Prison, has furnished me likewise with valuable statistics as to the age when the criminals lost their parents. I made this point one of my inquiries, because it shows the probability of moral and industrial neglect in the convict when young, if he has lost his parents early; the great value, therefore, of sound education, and—it may be added—of judicious-orphan asylums. For some im

in other countries corroborate the observation made above. The training for vice, as testified to before parliamentary committees, and the harvest of crime growing on the luxuriant soil of indolence, is appalling.[1]

VI. Besides the habit of industry, the four following are of much importance in education applied to politics; the habit of obedience, of independence, of reverence, or whatever it be called,—by which term I wish to express that earnestness in contemplating things which strives to know their real character and connection, and the absence of arrogant forwardness and self-sufficiency, which considers everything silly, useless, or unmeaning because not agreeing with its own views or not showing its character at once to the superficial observer,—and, lastly, the habit of honesty. We have seen that it is the high prerogative of man to acknowledge superiors and inferiors, to have laws and to obey them; but since individual interest as well as the pleasure or allurement of resistance and opposition is in itself frequently very strong, as selfishness is but too apt to grow up like a rank weed, we ought to imbue the young early with true loyalty, that is with a sincere desire to act as members of a society, according to rules not arbitrarily prescribed by themselves, and with a submission of individual will and desire to that of society. They ought to learn that it is a privilege of men to obey laws, and a delight to obey good ones. That these habits, early and deeply inculcated, may lead to submissiveness and want

---

portant remarks on the connection between habits, morality, and labor, and its quality, see H. C. Carey, Principles of Political Economy, Philadelphia, 1838, vol. ii. p. 207, et seq.

[1] An article in the London Times, of December, 1838, contains extracts from statements made before parliamentary committees in 1837, respecting the careful and effectual education in crime practised in London, of great importance to the criminalist and philosopher. Mr. Wakefield has attentively inquired into this hideous subject, and written upon it. It were desirable that the French penal statistics, issued yearly with such laudable zeal by government, would in future include some statement by which the industrial education might be ascertained, as likewise statements of the age when the convict lost one or both his parents.

of independence, is only to be feared where education is imperfect or liberty at a low ebb. The greater the liberty enjoyed by a society, the more essential are these habits, especially in modern times, when various new and powerful agents of intercommunication and diffusion of knowledge have produced a movability and thirst for inquiry which cannot leave in us any sincere fear on the ground of dull tameness in the adult, wherever liberty is at all established. The ancients knew the value of these habits, and all their wise men insisted upon them. Nations which lose the precious habit of obeying, that is of self-determined obedience to the laws because they are laws, lose invariably likewise the precious art of ruling. Greece, Rome, and Spain, for the last centuries, as well as the worst times of the feudal ages, are examples.

I believe, moreover, that an individual destitute of that reverence by which he feels linked to his fellow-men, present and past, is as unfortunate as he is dangerous. It is a sad thing to be imprisoned in selfish arrogance. The habit of independence includes the love of justice, of right, of acting manfully by principle, of disdaining popularity when need be, of holding up the head in spite of the heavy blows which fate may inflict—of being honestly, bravely, yet calmly, a true man. Lastly, the habit of honesty in the smallest details, and apparent trifles, both as to truth and property, cannot be too early and too anxiously cultivated. It is not sufficient that the young learn early to shun pilfering, but it is necessary that a sacred regard for property, in all its manifestations, be early instilled into their souls; a regard which must increase in the same degree as the protection of property is wanting, and towards public property, even though consisting only in the school or college utensils, as much as towards private property. That greatest aim of all moral education, to make men just and true, kind and self-controlled, is also the most important moral education for the state. Let men be just and true, and what is not gained!

As regards the instruction of the child with reference to its future citizenship, I would mention that the soul of the child is best awakened by noble examples. We ought to make it early acquainted with some of the best in history, and, as ancient history is far more striking and symbolical, simpler and more direct, as well as more significant in forms and signs, than modern history, which is more complicated and covered, if I may use this expression, the former will always be found to be far more appropriate to warm, incite, and occupy the child. Plutarch, or some parts of Herodotus, cannot be supplanted by books on the history of late centuries. At the same time, that *concentric* instruction which starts from what is near us and extends in wider and wider circles, indispensable, in my opinion, for leading the child to vivid perceptions, is highly advisable likewise in leading the young to a just appreciation of distant actions and institutions and to a habit of observation and attention. It is in political instruction as in geography, in which the course of the largest rivers, and the laws which they obey, can be best shown by following the course of a rill or rivulet near at hand. At a successive period the history of our own country in connection ought to follow, and finally a more particular acquaintance with our political duties and responsibilities, for which the instruction in history gives opportunity in a desultory yet very important manner from its first commencement. The attempt to teach political economy to children is one of the ludicrous effects in our times of a disregard of the various conditions resulting from different ages, sexes, and other circumstances—a folly resulting from superficiality, not unfrequently from sordid desire of gain in those who offer instruction, and of ignorance in the parents, who do not know that learning formulas by heart, and printed answers for printed questions, drawn up moreover not unfrequently in an injudicious manner, does not constitute teaching and cultivating the mind of the young. Conscientious education cannot be carried on in so hasty or wholesale a manner.

It is hardly necessary to mention gymnastics. They are of such decided moment that I do not know what to say of them except that they are even morally of the first importance, without entering into a discussion the length of which would be unsuited for the present work. They are far too little regarded as an indispensable branch of education, and ought invariably to be connected with public instruction. Our climate, with its great changes of heat and cold, our exceeding ease of travelling without physical exertion, our free institutions, and our entire dependence upon the people at large for the defence of the country, demand it imperatively.

VII. I have spoken here chiefly of elementary education only. As to superior education, the classical department will always be of the highest importance. It is a principle in all education that its efficiency, thoroughness, and completeness depend in a high degree upon the question whether it is founded upon the main elements of that civilization in which the individual to be educated lives and has to act, and which he is expected to promote in turn. Now, the factors of that product which we call our civilization—the civilization of the West Caucasian race—besides those factors without which no civilization whatever can exist, namely, accumulated experience (knowledge) and accumulated labor (skill and capital), are Christianity, antiquity, and the Teutonic element. From these three elements arose, and still arises, our peculiar and high civilization, through them alone we can find a key to it, and upon them we must found our education, if we endeavor thereby to develop the mind in such a manner that it may harmonize with the civilization we breathe. Every time that an attempt has been made to discard one or the other, experience has shown that injurious deficiency must be the consequence. The history of education amply proves it.

It appears to me that the gigantic effect of Chinese education is owing to the fact that it is strictly founded upon the factors of Chinese civilization. Whatever we may think of the latter, and however fettering instead of developing and invigorating we may consider Chinese education, it cannot be denied that the effect is gigantic; perhaps more so than that of any other extensive national education. Nearly four hundred millions of bustling and industrious people, in an overpeopled country, without a religious element which induces them to consider this life as a minimum existence to be regulated in part with reference to an endless existence hereafter, —or if part of these people, the Buddhists, believe in a future existence, they believe it to depend upon certain performances rather than the morality of their acts in this life — and all these many people under a weak government, which does not even share in this latter religion — and yet they live in peace, and form an unbroken whole. It is by education alone that the Chinese government rules this colossus, and this education does produce this surprising effect, as it appears to me, only because it is strictly founded upon the chief factors of their peculiar civilization, being entirely a civilization of their own. It is not a patriotic education, but a most essentially Chinese one. I need not repeat that I have mentioned this instance only with reference to the magnitude of its effect.

VIII. In the whole scale of our terrestrial creation we find that the higher life rises in its functions, and therefore the nobler the organism is of which it is the result, the more distinct and prominent becomes the difference of sexes. Vegetable as well as animal life exhibits this important phenomenon. In the very lowest animals no difference of sexes exists; with the higher station of the animal in the long chain of organic bodies the marked distinction of the sexes increases, until we find it in man, the concluding link, more prominent and thorough than in all other animals. It is a divine order of things, and has been early acknowledged as such by the various nations, as the ancient religions and systems of philosophy show. So striking is this difference in the great household of organic life that men have frequently applied the same principle to inorganic matter, and even to abstract principles,[1] while they likewise naturally expressed

---

[1] Most of the religio-philosophical systems of the East have adopted in their accounts of creation a principle by which they typify a mysterious union of

their feeling and conceptions by applying the different grammatical genders to inanimate objects around them, as the early and original languages do, I mean those idioms which did not originate by the process of mixture at a period when the people were comparatively advanced and reflection prevailed over impulse.

The female of the human species is smaller, the chest narrower, the muscular system little developed, the voice an octave higher, and the nervous system predominant; hence her sensibility is greater. The peculiar state of her lymphatic and cellular systems, and the circumstance that her sanguineous system is less active than in man, are the causes of her greater whiteness and transparency of skin and roundness of form, in short of her greater charm, of her less activity, and of a greater want of fiercer passions, which characterize the bilious temperament. She is framed and constituted more delicately, and in consequence of this marked difference of organization has advantages and disadvantages compared to the male sex, differences which are fundamental and of the last importance for the obtaining of those ends for which man and mankind are placed on this globe, and from which likewise different positions, callings, duties, and spheres of activity result.

The woman is more timid, more affectionate, keener in feeling, hence sprightlier in those thoughts which originate from acute sensitiveness; she is less ardent in far-reaching plans, more uninterruptedly busy in a sphere of quiet activity, more graceful in soul and body, more attractive, more patient and

---

the masculine and feminine principles, from which the first existence of things takes its origin. The dogma, in certain mythologies, of the supposed intervention of a masculo-feminine principle in the development of the mundane egg, bears a singular parallel to the Chinese Tai-Ky, a mystic figure which represents the union of Yang and Yn, the male and female principle. [The Tai-Ky really denotes the absolute, that beyond which there is nothing more. Wuttke, Gesch. Heidenth., ii. 14.] Davis, The Chinese, vol. ii. p. 65, gives an account of it. Respecting the Hindoo philosophy on this point I must refer to the History of Ancient Philosophy, by Ritter (iii. 349-418, Hamb., 1834). So did the Pythagoreans enumerate among the primeval elements of nature the Masculine and Feminine. Arist., Met., i. 5, 6.

cunning in obtaining her objects, more confiding and believing. Man is stronger, bolder, more energetic and active, and of consequence more exhausted by his efforts, thus standing in greater need of deep repose; he is more judging and inquiring, hence more just if his passion is not roused; less patient and enduring; less willing calmly to submit; more ardent and much stronger in the powers of combination and comprehension; his mind has greater grasp; he is more independent, freer in action and thought, bolder in braving the opinion of others. These mental differences are no less important for the constitution of the family (as it rises in character with the progress of civilization) than the physical difference which the Creator has ordained as the necessary condition of procreation for nearly all organic life, and upon which those differences of disposition and faculties are founded.

IX. From this different organization arise different relations, as has been observed already. The woman is fitter for all those actions which must be impelled chiefly by affection; hence she is more fit to foster and educate the young, and to nurture in turn their hearts with affection; she is more disposed to cling to a protector, and far readier to consent to sacrifices; she graces society, and—sentiment being one of the spheres in which she is most active, and chastity her first virtue and honor—she is the chief agent in infusing delicacy, gentleness, taste, decorum, and correctness of morals, so far as they depend upon continency, into society at large. These in turn attract the male sex, and inspire the sterner bosom of man with those feelings of romance and delicate reverence which form, however extravagant they may at times appear, not only a salutary but a necessary element of high civilization. It belongs to the province of general ethics to discuss the question, why continency is the chiefest virtue of the woman and inseparably connected with her honor, and why, according to the universal sentiment of mankind, incontinency in the male sex, however immoral, does not create the same feeling of disgust with which it is viewed in the other sex. Thus much only may be stated here, that Providence, ordaining that the family in its purity and inviolateness should form the nucleus of civilization, and that it should be formed by the union of sexes, seems to have imposed as one of the primitive elements of human society, on man, not only the desire for this union, but the choice of his desire, on the one hand, and the acute feeling of bashfulness of woman on the other hand, so that man's desire should partake of reverence and be more than mere appetite, from which circumstance attachment and perpetuity of union arise. If the desire in man were not strong, selfishness might prevent the existence of families; if the woman were not bashful, an equal disorder would arise. When the family has been formed, the actual knowledge of the child's parentage—that knowledge which is derived from the evidence of the senses, and not from moral conviction—is confined to the woman alone; and as the family, with the affections between the parents and their offspring, forms an absolutely necessary element of man's ethical and political relations, the continency of the woman, on which the purity and intenseness of family feeling depend, becomes naturally the more important, so that moral conviction of the child's parentage as far as concerns the father may fully supplant the want of conviction by the senses.

X. The true sphere of woman's best and noblest activity, and a sacred one it is, assigned to her in the distribution of the degrees of affection and intellect, ardor and reliance, is the family, where she acts as wife, mother, daughter, and sister, and through it that society which we have called the society of comity, where she graces, humanizes, and reconciles, and, through both, the country. In what way her activity is connected with the country, and mediately with the state, is the subject which will now occupy us.

The nature and consequent duties of woman exclude her from public life; her timidity, bashfulness, delicacy, and inferior grasp of mind, as well as the necessity of acting out those sacred duties more especially assigned to her, require her being more retired than the other sex. A woman loses in the same degree her natural character, as woman, as she enters into publicity. There are, of course, women whose extraordinary mental organization is such that they form exceptions; but wherever this fundamental principle is abandoned as a general rule, evil ensues, as in every other case of deviation from the laws of nature. The woman cannot defend the state: if she were physically able to do it, she would necessarily lose her peculiar character as woman, and thus a necessary element of civilization would be extinguished. Here, too, emergencies may make exceptions—exceptions of the noblest and proudest kind; but should they cease to form exceptions, a subversion of the whole moral order of things would be the consequence. She does not preach, she does not judge in court, nor debate in the legislative halls, nor take a direct part in politics; if she does so, it is always to the injury of society, be it by way of court intrigue, as was the case in so eminent a degree in France before the first revolution, or by way of popular excitements, as was frequently the case in Scotland during its most agitated periods in the seventeenth century,[1] or in a hideous degree during the French revolution.

We have seen that the family in its unity and purity is necessary, and that to produce and maintain these the retiredness of woman is equally necessary. A natural consequence of this circumstance, in addition to the fact that her affections and feelings are stronger than those of man if not blunted by corruption or absurdity, is that she is naturally less apt to judge of public business, and to allow the principle of right, of justice alone, full weight. Her situation in the family gives her less opportunity to cultivate this feeling of mere justice than she otherwise might do. Women, therefore, are carried away by that which naturally operates most actively in them,

---

[1] Raumer, History of the Sixteenth and Seventeenth Centuries, illustrated by Original Documents, London, 1835, vol. ii. p. 337, and previous passages.

by sentiment, even in spheres where it is of the utmost importance to repress it as much as human frailty will permit.[1] Hence the fact that if women once enter into politics, and especially take part in party strifes, they show themselves less scrupulous than men, are apt to be entirely carried away by personalities, and to trespass much farther than men upon the limits of fairness, justice, and truth.

There are other reasons, however, why women should be strictly excluded from active politics. The woman, weaker by nature, hence gentler and more dependent, is naturally given more to intrigue if she once transgresses the line of her proper sphere. Boldness, strength, and public action being denied her, originally or as a natural consequence of her position, she will the sooner resort to intrigue, and as she naturally acts more by attraction and charm she becomes necessarily the more dangerous. No true civilization is possible where there does not largely exist that chivalric feeling in man which gladly yields, wherever possible, to the weaker and more delicate, gentler and more graceful sex. This feeling, however, operates in politics, where Right should rule alone, very dangerously. If woman were to be admitted to an active participation in politics, she must do it at the price of her whole peculiar nature, her grace and her attraction, and would henceforth be distinguished from man by her greater weakness alone, and in consequence become greatly oppressed. If woman claims to be admitted as a member of a jury, she must allow herself to be sworn in as a constable. The woman who should go to the poll must have disrobed herself of her essential nature as woman, and either be treated as men are, which would lower her character and position in society, or she must be treated with deference, which would be disastrous to the fundamentals of the state.

The family is necessary not only for procreation, but for the promotion of morals and civilization; unity, love, forbearance

---

[1] In this respect women are like people living in countries in which there is no public political life. They do not learn to modify their opinion by seeing it opposed, or to respect the perfect right of others to oppose it.

in it are necessary; the woman stands in need of protection and support; the man, of being led to the sphere of affections, to the unselfish love of his wife and children. But if the woman were to take an active part in the politics of free countries, the unity would be disturbed, husband and wife would no longer be one; the most gloomy consequences must follow, it would be impossible for womankind long to retain modesty and continency, and thus society would hasten to speedy dissolution. She would likewise lose her great privilege of softening and pacifying society, of being the bond which unites many discordant elements. If we look around us, we see how daily and hourly woman, because she enjoys her peculiar position, brings elements in contact, if she does not reconcile them, which otherwise would bitterly war with one another. "She shall have peace in market or fair, whether the feud among men be never so great," says the ancient law of the Visigoths. The most sacred interests, then, of man, of woman, and of society demand, as much as strict justice, that she should not meddle with politics.

XI. There is, nevertheless, a cord by which the woman is strongly connected through her liveliest sentiments with the state—it is patriotism. Let it not be said that this virtue cannot be strong in her if we deny her an active part in the daily political affairs. On the contrary, that feeling is frequently strongest by its native vigor in those individuals whose feelings have not been exposed to the blunting effects of political strife and rancor, for patriotism is the love of country, not the love of the state only. Through her husband and children and brothers she is connected with the actions of the state; let her cultivate the noblest feelings, let her be both a support and an incentive to her husband, let her in herself represent to him the country which is worth living, toiling, dying for, let her early imbue her children with this sacred love, and, when finally need shall be, let her act boldly and heroically if she have the constitution, bestowing an honor upon her country. Let the woman look upon the numberless Roman wives and mothers who, though so strictly domestic, willingly could die for their country, and then say whether their lot is low. I believe it can be said without contradiction that in all periods of free nations, in which the noblest deeds have been performed and the greatest sacrifices made to liberty, and in which the nation has evinced a spirit that stands as an enkindling example to the latest periods, woman has stood in this her true position, as wife and mother, linked most closely to her country through husband and son.

It seems to me one of the great destinies of woman that, not being ordinarily called upon in the great order of things to mingle in the turmoil of life, in the strife and struggle of the times and the bustle of business, or in those pursuits of knowledge or practical life which make men acquainted with the selfish, criminal, and foul aberrations of human nature, she is more able to keep the simple and elementary sentiments and impulses untainted in their native freshness and purity. Men in this respect appear to me like the lawyers or judges, who, by long practice, seeing so much, weighing so much for and against, must frequently become blunted in their native quick feelings of right; but women, like the lookers-on, unprofessional yet deeply interested in the issue. And should it be necessary to add that men, frequently seeing so much corruption abroad, are apt to be influenced by the lower standard around and above them? It becomes, therefore, the more necessary that in the wife, not exposed as she is to these unhallowed effects, and cultivating as she does in the stillness of the house the virtue of her children, the broad and pure principles of patriotism should continue to be represented. When the sentence respecting Hampden's ever-memorable ship-money case was to be pronounced, and the British court used its whole influence to obtain an opinion of the bench favorable to the unlawful usurpations of the crown, but subversive of one of the most elementary principles of the British constitution, and nearly all the judges, dependent creatures of the crown, had made up their minds to support them at all hazards, Justices Croke, Hutton, and Denham alone dared to side with justice, honor, truth, and their country. Croke, however, before he gave his final opinion, had wavered, not because undecided as to the great question of right, but because he saw that his seat on the bench was at stake. It was then that his patriotic and high-minded wife "implored him not to sacrifice his conscience for fear of any danger or prejudice to his family, being content to suffer any misery with him rather than to be an occasion for him to violate his integrity." Her name ought to be held dear and in living remembrance forever.

XII. It is high-minded patriotism which, among other deep seated motives, may induce women in times of emergencies to perform the most heroic deeds, boldly braving danger or supporting all the suffering that human nature can endure. We need not seek for instances in Telesilla, who valiantly defended Argos when the youths of her country were slain, or in Leæna, who, tortured by Hippias to compel her to betray the secrets of her lover Aristogiton, bit off her tongue for fear she might be unable to resist the pain;[1] we find many of the proudest instances of heroism and devotion in all periods of struggle for a noble object. The history of the Dutch war of independence is full of the brightest examples, and we have seen in our own times the women of Saragossa abide by their fighting husbands unto death,[2] and the Prussian women of all ranks attend the hospitals, in organized societies, and do every work, the most arduous or loathsome not excepted, which the state of the wounded required, in the years 1813 and 1814, when every able-bodied man was in the field: at which time they did not shun the malignant typhus fever, then raging in the hospitals and carrying off many of these ministers of humanity, who did not exclude from their care their wounded enemies! It is sufficient to read the papers of the day in order to be satisfied, by the accounts of ship-

---

[1] [Comp. Plut. de Mulier. Virt., iv.; Pausan., i. 23.]
[2] Napier, Peninsular War, book v. ch. 3.

wrecks for instance, of what heroism woman is capable.[1] Yet let us remember that in those periods of extremity in which woman has performed so noble a part, she had not prepared herself for these arduous deeds by previously misplacing herself in society, or by intruding into spheres which would have deprived her of her character. It was the loving mother, the faithful wife, not the female politician or the spinster who had delivered public speeches, that could suddenly step upon the wall and look into the enemy's face.

I believe, then, that the most important calling of the woman respecting politics is, that, as wife, she identify herself with her husband in his best endeavors, and aid him in keeping alive and active the purest principles, and as mother, that, besides the whole cultivation of her children, which in so eminent a degree depends upon her, she sow with religious zeal the seeds of lofty patriotism in their hearts from early infancy. For this purpose she ought to make herself acquainted with the best examples in the history of her own and other countries. A story received in early youth from a mother's lips' sinks deep into the soul, and becomes a very part of it.

On the other hand, I believe that woman transgresses the proper line, to her own injury and the detriment of society at large, if she takes public part in the ordinary politics of the day. I think it highly objectionable, unfair, and injurious if women canvass for elections,[2] and highly dangerous for their position and character if they hold public meetings and publicly debate, as several times they have done of late in Eng-

---

[1] * It is a great omission that the French women of the revolution were not mentioned here; for, while the fishwomen of Paris were loathsomely vile and bloodthirsty, all France literally abounded with the greatest heroines, who sacrificed themselves, as wives, mothers, sisters, daughters, and friends. See by all means Raumer, Histor. Taschenb., Neue Folge, vol. i., 1840, essay 3 : " die Frauen der Französ. Revolution."

[2] There is perhaps no more striking instance of ladies canvassing for election, however common in England, on record, than when, previous to the famous Westminster election in 1784, the duchess of Devonshire and Mrs. Crewe canvassed for Fox, and the countess of Salisbury for Sir Cecil Wray. Wraxall gives an account of it in his Posthumous Memoirs.

land;[1] and I believe it manifestly out of place if they petition legislative bodies respecting public measures, unless it be against a direct injustice done to them as women, of which indeed they do not stand in much danger in our times. Women ought to abstain in particular from petitions for pardoning criminals. Their sentiment as well as their want of acquaintance with practical life inclines them naturally towards charity as soon as sentence is pronounced upon a convict; they forget his crime, and the cause of morality and society, little thinking what injury may be inflicted by frustrating the course of law, and in particular by the new crimes which the pardoned criminal will not be unlikely to commit. I shall say more on pardoning in general in another place; suffice it here to say that petitions for pardon from women are unjust and unfair in the highest degree. Either they study the particular case or not: if they do not, it is preposterous to solicit a pardon; if they do, they throw away one of their first privileges in life, that of being exempt from the necessity of making themselves acquainted with the foulest diseases of society. I speak here of those written petitions with a number of names, of which we all know with what degree of ignorance of the case in question they are signed. Who would consider it wrong in a single woman to implore mercy in cases which do not touch common and base crimes and which interest her individually?

Were I asked which of the women known in history signally embodies those qualities which appear to me essential to the modern woman, not by way of exception or rare distinction for talents, but as eminently showing those qualities which ought to be in all, in short showing the modern wife and mother in the noblest light, I should point out Lady Russell, wife of Lord William Russell. Kind and considerate to children and husband, she always invited him to unbosom

---

[1] I would certainly not go so far as to pronounce against all meetings of women, placed in so peculiar a situation, for instance, as those working in some of the American factories. But even there they ought always to take care not to endanger their essential female character by entering into publicity.

himself to her in his patriotic anxieties; she understood him; she felt with him; when he was imprisoned, she did all possible service to him; when he was tried for his life, she was not overwhelmed, but stepped forward in court and took notes for him; when he was sentenced, she lost no time in bewailing his doom, but attempted every lawful means to avert the blow, and to comfort her lord in prison by her own high-minded composure; and when, on the evening before his execution, she took her last farewell from a husband she loved better than aught on earth, and whom she knew to be unrighteously sacrificed, even then she had the greatness of soul to stand the trial. "He kissed her four or five times; and she kept her sorrow so within herself that she gave him no disturbance by their parting."[1] This fortitude, and the patience with which she bore her affliction through the rest of her life, was greater heroism than any ancient or Asiatic self-immolation could have proved.[2]

---

[1] "After she was gone," continues Burnet in his journal, from which this account was taken, "he (Lord Russell) said, 'Now the bitterness of death is past,' and ran out into a long discourse concerning her—how great a blessing she had been to him; and said, 'what a misery it would have been to him if she had not had that magnanimity of spirit, joined to her tenderness, as never to have desired him to do a base thing for the saving of his life, whereas, otherwise, what a week should I have passed, if she had been crying to me to turn informer and be a Lord Howard!'" Lady Russell's whole character may be seen from Lord John Russell's Life of William Lord Russell. I hope I do not trespass the limits of a note, if I add a few words on the widow of Barneveldt. Maurice, stadtholder of Holland, caused the wise patriot to be executed; at any rate, he did not, as he had the power to do, prevent it, when the most unfortunate religious excitement against the poor Remonstrants ran high. When, some time after, the son of Barneveldt had shared in a conspiracy against Maurice, and been sentenced to die, the mother threw herself at the stadtholder's feet to implore mercy for her son. He asked why she could beg now for her son, and had not done so for her husband,—whom, it ought to be mentioned, the stadtholder declared himself at the time ready to save, if he would implore mercy; but the old man would not belie his innocence, as Russell declined the same. The heroic answer of the afflicted mother but proud widow was, "My husband was innocent, my son is guilty." Her prayer was not granted. Van Campen, History of the Netherlands, vol. ii. p. 43.

[2] See also Letters of Lady Rachel Russell, from the Manuscript in the Library at Woburn Abbey, etc., 6th ed., London, 1801.

XIII. The history of woman in her domestic and social as well as in her civil relations, and more particularly in her jural position and social influence, is one of the most interesting and important branches of the history of civilization, which, so far as my knowledge of literature extends, has not yet been treated with the profoundness of thought and extent of knowledge that the subject deserves, although valuable materials have been collected for this inviting task.[1]

In the earliest times, when physical subsistence and bodily protection form the absorbing objects of human activity, it is natural that woman should occupy a very subordinate position. She was not only considered mentally, but also morally, inferior to man, as she was physically inferior to him. She was so little considered a human individual of herself, that not only most essential rights were denied her, but, as a natural consequence, also moral responsibility, even to a late period, not only metaphysically but legally, so that it became necessary to restore legal responsibility to her.[2] Man, being conscious of the necessity that the woman should associate with him and form an ingredient of the family, could not at once acknowledge this necessary association and yet at the same time her entire moral individuality. Though from early ages affection has prevailed over power, the daughter, like her brother, was considered the property of her father, and when married she was sold to the wooer. The ancient

---

[1] There have been several collections of the biographies of distinguished women. Alexander, History of Women, 2 vols. 4to, 1779; Ségur, Les Femmes, 3 vols., 1802; Communications from the Lives of Distinguished Women (in German), Stuttgard, 1828; with many other works. Meiners wrote a History of the Female Sex (in German), Hanover, 1788-1800, 4 vols. For any one who desires to inquire thoroughly into what has been written on this subject, as well as on the influence of Christianity upon the position of woman, and other points connected with the general subject, it would be well to examine the list of works appended to the article Woman (Frau) in Krug's Dictionary of Philosophical Sciences; though it is far from being complete.

[2] King Magnus Erichsen of Sweden "was able to decree, in 1335, that 'the woman shall suffer for her crimes like the man, especially for crimes touching life.'" Geijer, History of Sweden, Hamburg, 1832, vol. i. p. 273. The words "was able" are very significant.

history of Asiatic nations, for instance the Bible, and of other tribes, shows this, as well as the customs observed to this day by the tribes of the East.[1] Polygamy, legitimate even with the Hebrews,[2] though not favored or general,[3] did not rapidly promote the jural or social emancipation of the woman. In Europe, among the Greeks and Romans as well as other tribes, monogamy existed from early times, and we consequently find the woman there in a very different position. She has now become the companion of the husband. Greek history records many of the brightest examples of women as wives or mothers, but the annals of no nation probably exhibit so many as those of Rome; instances of heroic devotion, which continue far into the corrupt periods of the Western empire. The Teutonic tribes, which hastened the downfall of crumbling Rome, showed, from the earliest periods in which we find them mentioned, no less than in their whole mythology, a peculiar regard for the female, which, together with the humanizing influence of the church in general, and its direct efforts in many instances to improve the position of woman, had a salutary effect on the European population. When chivalry sprang up, in which religious ardor, desire of adventure, and devotion to woman were romantically blended, the exaltation of woman became, in one class at least, an absorbing concern of life. Though this adoration of woman led to many fantastic and even immoral aberrations,[4] and had far less effect upon the essential

---

[1] Niebuhr the elder, Burckhardt, and all the other travellers in the East. So do we find instances of the buying of wives in Odyss., xi. 281; Iliad, xi. 244; Herod., i. 196; Strabo, p. 745, etc.

[2] Michaelis, Mosaic Law, ii. 85; Saalschutz, Mos. Recht, chap. 103.

[3] Michaelis, ii. 95; Jahn, Arch., i. 2.

[4] The morals of the twelfth, thirteenth, and fourteenth centuries were of the most licentious character. Chateaubriand, in the third volume of his Etudes Historiques, gives instances, such as establishments in imitation of nunneries with vows of immorality. Whoever is in the least acquainted with the morals of those ages, with the peculiar government and corporate privileges of the prostitutes in the various cities during former periods and with the courts and monasteries of those times, will consider the advance of morality in our race during the last two centuries, despite all existing irregularities, as one of the most signal traits

position of woman in general, and the morals of the age, than many persons, satisfied with insulated and poetic accounts, rashly believe, still every one acquainted with the history of civilization will admit the romantic devotion of the middle ages to have been one of the factors in producing a better state of things and in somewhat tempering even the miseries of part of the worst periods. The cities, with their industry and wealth, rose in power and number, governments became more general institutions, the feudal lords more subdued; peace was more and more established, and the rights of the commons, of the people in general, and also those of the women in particular, became gradually more clearly defined, extended, and valued. Woman was more and more acknowledged in her own moral capacity. Laws became juster towards her. When the period of re-discussion of all human rights began during the last century, inquiry naturally was extended to the position and rights of woman, which, the more these attracted attention, became in many instances very limited indeed as to extent, though acute as to the single object which happened to be under discussion; and finally a series of writings appeared, beginning perhaps with Mary Wollstonecraft's Vindication of the Rights of Women, published towards the end of the last century, which, in determining the proper sphere of action in society and the state for man and woman, altogether lost sight of the different organization of the two sexes, and the pervading divine order of things founded upon it. One step led to another, and finally writers appeared, both male and female, who endeavored to break up that institution which was already considered by the ancient philosophers, poets, and priests as forming together with the institution of property the only firm foundation of all civilization—the institution of matrimony. Two late writers in particular, a man and a woman, have written upon this subject and the intercourse between the two sexes, with so disgusting

---

in modern history. The change which has taken place is far beyond what any one who has not perused the histories and chronicles of the times can imagine.

a temerity that I seriously doubt whether any previous period has been disgraced by compositions of equally loathsome immorality, pitiful and superficial reasoning, and gross ignorance.

XIV. Neither the literary progress of women and their distinction in the province of letters, on the one hand, nor, on the other, the question why females should be allowed to sit upon a throne, when excluded from all other public business, is a subject to be discussed here. The one belongs to the history of literature or female civilization, the other to politics proper. It is nothing more than a mere question of high political expediency. Yet although the subject of voting by females does not belong, strictly speaking, to our province, but to natural law and politics proper, as defined in the first part, I may be allowed to give here a very few additional remarks on the subject.

Either we acknowledge the difference of sexes, and consequent different spheres of action, as necessary and founded in the great order of things, or not. If the former, then there is no more denial of right in excluding women from public business than there is in not calling on them to take up arms or to work, by way of taxation, in repairing high-roads. If the latter be the case, we ought not only to allow them to vote, for that is a very specific and limited political act indeed, but they ought to be in every respect admitted and consequently called upon to do all that men do. It is erroneously supposed by some that voting is a natural and absolute right, inherent in each individual. This is a very great mistake; for though every one's interest ought to have its due weight in the devising of public measures, whose degree of justice depends upon the average benefit they bestow upon the whole, it is not necessary that this be effected by his voting. Universal suffrage is a term too vast for what is meant to be expressed. There are always persons excluded from voting. Soldiers do not vote, and ought not to vote for instance in their barracks; the French constitution of Hérault de Séchelles excluded domestics from voting, because too dependent in their situation;

many constitutions exclude the clergy from voting, because their influence, always great, is feared if they interfere with politics. Nor is the question of universal suffrage to be otherwise decided upon abstract ground. Universal suffrage in Illyria or in any semi-barbarous tribe in near contact with civilization would be a very melancholy thing. So no civilized nation in which, from whatever cause it may result, there are vast classes, ignorant, rude, and poor, excluded from the common stream of civilization, can endure universal suffrage. Those who insist on the natural birthright of man to vote cannot in my opinion demonstrate the legality of a representative government, nor of any other government except that of a tribe which daily decides by a simple numerical majority of all its members upon every subject. Yet we are told that, allowing all these positions, the woman is not even represented. This too rests upon an error. Is not the whole life of the husband daily, hourly, and most thoroughly influenced by her and by his position towards her? And if he takes, as he necessarily must do, this whole frame of mind with him into legislative proceedings, is his wife unrepresented? The agriculturist is far less sure that a merchant of his district will represent his interest than the wife is that her husband represents her.[1] How are the sick or the old represented who cannot go to the poll? If indeed by true representation be meant that each one should have a direct spokesman, and not the political organism through which we arrive at the public opinion and public will of the whole, after those of the parts of society have modified one another, I do not see how indeed the minority is represented in any representative government, or how a law of the majority in an absolute democracy can

---

[1] It is always a painful, sometimes a dangerous, task to be obliged to touch upon important and highly debated points without being able to give and develop the whole: for it is not agreeable to be misunderstood on such topics. I can of course not explain my whole view of governments, etc., but I may be allowed to add at least that I consider it a principle in politics that the right of voting, if it exist at all, ought to be extensive, and not restricted, or it will work far more mischief than good.

have any binding power upon the minority. For it is certain that in the former case the representative does not directly represent the minority, since he says and does things totally at variance with their opinion; nor is the law in the latter case the direct law, that is the public will of the minority.

I conclude with a passage of Mr. Guizot's, and only add that he is the husband of a lady highly distinguished even in literature. He says, "Society, however simple may be its structure, has other affairs than such as are merely domestic to engage its attention; affairs that demand an extent of capacity not possessed by females and minors. Let us suppose a discussion to arise in some savage tribe, or in some state already civilized, relative to a warlike expedition or the adoption of a civil law: neither women nor minors are capable of deciding upon interests of this description; Providence has destined the former for a state of existence purely domestic, while the latter have not yet attained to the plenitude of their individual existence and the full power of their faculties. Naturally, then, and by the operation of one of those truly providential laws in which fact and right are so very harmoniously blended, the right of suffrage does not belong to them. Capacity, then, is the principle, the necessary condition, of right. And the capacity here spoken of is not merely due to intellectual development or to the possession of this or that particular faculty; it is a complex and profound whole, comprising spontaneous authority, habitual situation, and natural acquaintance with the different interests to be regulated; in fact, a certain aggregate of faculties, knowledge, and methods of action which animate the whole man, and which decide, with more certainty than his spirit alone, upon his course of conduct and the use which he will make of power."

# CHAPTER II.

Obedience to the Laws.—How highly the Greeks esteemed it.—Obedience to Laws one of Man's Prerogatives.—Absolute Obedience impossible.—Ad Impossibilia Nemo obligatur.—Ad Turpia Nemo obligatur.—Viscount Orthes.—Unlawful Demands made by lawful Authority.—High Importance of the Judiciary with reference to Obedience to the Law.—Not all that is not positively permitted may be done by the Citizen, any more than all that is positively permitted.—Penalties are not equivalents of Crime.—Malum in se, Malum prohibitum: Is the distinction essential, and can we found any Rule of Action upon it?—The Question of Obedience to Laws a Question of Conflict.—Obedience in the Army and Navy.—Articles of War.—Obedience in the Civil Service.—How far is the Citizen bound to obey the Laws?—Justifiable Disobedience.—Necessary and morally demanded Disobedience.—Non-compliance with the Laws, or passive Resistance. — Active Resistance. — Armed Resistance.—Insurrection.—Revolution.—Resistance formerly considered lawful and received in the Charters.—Mobs and Mob-law, so called.—Duty of Informing: in the Officer; in the Citizen at large.—Professional Informers for Rewards.—Secret Police.—Delatores and Mouchards.—The obligation of informing against intended or committed Offences.

XV. "STRANGER, tell the Lacedæmonians that we lie here in obedience to their laws." [1] This was the simple inscription, composed by Simonides of Ceos, to commemorate the heroic and conscious devotion of the faithful band of Leonidas at Thermopylæ; and in which a nation of peculiar sagacity, and promptitude of mind as well as ardor of soul for liberty, a nation with whom "freedom was what the sun is; the most brilliant and most useful object of creation—a passion, an instinct," thought to express the highest acknowledgment of a deed which every Greek remembered with national pride. It was not merely the happy conceit of an individual; it was the true expression of the public spirit. Of all that was noble and great in this patriotic act, the noblest and greatest seemed to them that the gallant citizens had been obedient to the

---

[1] Herodotus, vii. 228.

laws and their country even unto death. Youthful reader, whose noble and happy lot it is to be born in a free country, an heir to the laws of liberty, weigh well this inscription, in which one of the noblest nations of the earth has concentrated its lively spirit and dear experience, a lesson for every one who cherishes freedom, and intends to make it prosper, as far as in him lies, as the best cause of mankind.

XVI. To make, acknowledge, and obey laws is one of the high prerogatives as well as duties of man among all the animate beings of the visible creation. Obeying a law, in this case, means conforming our actions willingly to laws, that is, to rules in which principles, as applied to a class of cases, are pronounced. The individual himself, as well as society at large, stands in need of laws; without them there would be physical and moral disorder. The individual who does not adopt general laws of conduct or principles of action is exposed to all the dangers of being carried away by impulses which may arise from causes wholly unconnected with what is good, right, or wise, by selfishness and vices; and society does not only stand in need of laws that it may avoid violence and consequent suffering, but also because without laws society would lose its moral character, man would forfeit his destiny as a social being, and civilization, that produce of united exertion, would be impossible. Man is wholly man only in society; society is what it ought to be only through laws; laws are virtually laws only when obeyed: therefore man's destiny requires obedience to laws. Obedience to laws, then, is necessary, for without their being followed they are no longer laws in essence, because no longer rules of action. Habitual disregard of laws in a society not only produces confusion and clashing of action, but it leads to a want of energy, of mutual reliance, and of public spirit, as well as to a want of manly independence in the individual. It invigorates the soul, lends energy and gives precision of action, and promotes a general feeling of right, if the individuals obey the laws they have chosen to obey. Few things promote more the formation of a manly character and a deeply-seated sense of justice in the young, than decisive and good laws or precepts, strictly acted out. Even the severest laws, if but clearly pronounced and strictly enforced, may leave some feeling of independence; but dependence upon humor gives an insuperable feeling of slavishness. He who obeys laws only as so many insulated regulations, depriving him of more or less individual liberty which he has given up for the public good, has not penetrated to that high degree of civic sense which makes obedience to the laws an inspiring cause of nobility of character.

Yet we have seen that man cannot divest himself of his moral individuality and responsibility; the will of another cannot virtually become his own will; and, therefore, absolute obedience is impossible, and, were it possible, immoral. Every approach to it becomes in the same degree immoral. Absolute obedience can be claimed for the commandments of the Deity alone; but even here it must be observed that the evidence that such commands do proceed from the Deity is to be judged of by the individual; reason and conscience must decide upon the character of the authority which demands compliance with the command presented as coming from the Deity. A law presented by Mohammedans as a divine law would not be obeyed by Christians in Turkey, at least not as a divine law. In all matters between man and man absolute obedience would destroy the moral as well as the jural ground on which their relations are founded. Nevertheless, passion, as well as temerity of partial reasoning, has repeatedly induced man to claim absolute obedience for some authority or other, in ecclesiastic spheres as well as political. I have stated already that it seems to me to be one of our obligations to pay serious and particular attention to any act or institution in the whole range of history or of our own observation in which a principle, virtue, error, or vice has been most consistently carried out. In the one case we become acquainted with a degree of perfection perhaps unattainable at the times we live in, yet worthy of being approached as much as possible; in the other case we see the evil acted out in all its hideousness, and therefore the danger increasing with every degree of approach: they distinctly say to us, "To this it will come." In either case we observe truth in its fulness. Respecting absolute obedience I know of no more striking instance of its being carried out in daring consistency than that which the Jesuits demanded from the inferior to the superior, and we may well say to those who demand it in any other sphere, "To this it will come."[1]

XVII. Indeed, all promise of absolute obedience would virtually amount to taking archbishop Laud's famous and absurd "Et-Cætera Oath," by which people should bind themselves to "maintain the government of the church by archbishops,

---

[1] "But one thing shall exist instead of every other relation, every impulse of activity, namely, obedience, obedience without any reference to what it extends." (Epistle of Ignatius "Fratribus Societatis Jesu qui sunt in Lusitania," 7 Kal. Apr. 1553, 3.) The superior shall appear as the representative of Divine Providence, the "Locum Dei tenens" (pars 5, cap. 3, Constit. Ignat.); even a sin, if demanded in the name of Christ, or in virtute obedientiæ, shall be committed. Well may Mr. Ranke, in quoting the two following passages from the "Constitutiones" of the society, add, "we hardly trust our eyes when we read this:"

"Et sibi quisque persuadeat, quod qui sub obedientia vivunt, se ferri ac regi a divina providentia per superiores suos sincere debent, perinde ac cadaver essent." Constit., vi. 1.

"Visum est nobis in domino . . . nullas constitutiones declarationes vel ordinem ullum vivendi posse obligationem ad peccatum mortale vel veniale inducere, si superior ea in nomine domini Jesu Christi vel in virtute obedientiæ juberet " Const., vi. 5.

Is it to be supposed that this iniquitous passage was understood to mean that nothing, in reality a sin, would be demanded in the name of Jesus Christ, although, according to all appearance and common notion, it might appear so to the inferior? If this be the case, waiving the still remaining audacity and danger, it would only prove that absolute obedience cannot be carried through, and must stop somewhere. The passage contained in part vi. ch. 1 of Const. Ignat. is not much better: "Nec solum in rebus obligatoriis, sed etiam in aliis, licet nihil aliud quam signum voluntatis superioris sine ullo expresso præcepto videretur."

Bacon, although he has but just bestowed fulsome flattery upon a monarch at once one of the meanest and most arrogant, says, even to a James I., "Nam qui cæcam obedientiam fortius obligare contenderit quam officium oculatum, una opera asserat, cæcum manu ductum certius incedere, quam qui luce et oculis utitur." De Dignitate Scient., i.

bishops, deans, chapters, et cetæra."[1] Yet, although absolute obedience has been so frequently demanded in theory, practice has always shown its impossibility, and those who demanded it most have generally proved the least ready to submit to it, so soon as it did not suit their position. The Jesuits have had at times violent struggles within the bosom of their society; though they took the additional vow to go whithersoever the pope might send them, they would not obey him had he commanded anything against the doctrine of the church. They would say that he does not do this as pope; and this is all that ever a sober mind has insisted upon for the vindication of the right and duty of disobeying laws—that is, that they are no longer, or never were, lawful; or that the authority demanding it is not, in doing so, any longer lawful.

There is no government ever so absolute in theory which has not sanctioned acts of disobedience even to the command of the prince, because done on account of the still more important interest of the same prince. How often have monarchs wished that they had been disobeyed! Napoleon was, according to Bourrienne, on some occasions highly pleased when he learned that he had not been obeyed. In short, obedience is always acknowledged in practice as something relative, and of this the individual, of course, must judge. Nowhere in political spheres, probably, was the theory of absolute obedience more roundly acknowledged than in the Prussian army, to its head, the king, under Frederic William I.; yet when his son was tried for attempted escape from his insufferable treatment, and the king appeared at least to insist upon the blood of his son, a colonel[2] rose, tore open his vest, and said, "If your majesty want blood, take mine: that there you shall not have as long as I can utter a word." The king, vehement as he was, did not carry out the theory of absolute obedience, but was silent; and the colonel was not prevented from promotion.

---

[1] Laud caused this oath, attached to certain new canons, to be passed by the convocation of 1640.

[2] The name of this independent man was Buddenbrock.

From ancient times the maxim has been acknowledged, Ad impossibilia nemo obligatur; that which is impossible, therefore, need not be attempted, though ordered; nor is the omission of attempting it punishable; and, farther, that Ad turpia nemo obligatur; no one is bound to do what is iniquitous. Mankind have uniformly agreed in applauding resistance to that which is iniquitous, because they have always either acknowledged or at least felt that man cannot lose his own moral value, his independent moral individuality, and that authority, even if supposed to rest upon some divine origin, may be and ought to be either disobeyed or opposed if it perverts its character and demands things against God's laws, as expressed by revelation, nature, the feeling of humanity, morals, reason, or physical necessity. When Charles IX. of France, or his mother, issued orders to slaughter the Protestants in the provinces as they had been murdered in Paris on the eve of St. Bartholomew, several governors and other officers—Sully mentions seven—declined obedience. Viscount Orthes, or Ortez, commandant at Bayonne, wrote back, "Sire, I have found in Bayonne honest citizens and brave soldiers only, but not one executioner. Therefore they and myself supplicate your majesty to use our arms and lives in possible (*feasible* is the original) things."[1] He was right to call this demanded murder an impossible, an unfeasible thing for an honest man. Iniquitous things (turpia) are as to obedience as impossible (impossibilia) as physically impossible things.

The difficulty, however, which arises out of the two necessities, that I cannot give up my individuality, my responsibility and judgment, on the one hand, and that I am obliged to obey the laws, on the other, is not thus easily solved. There are laws which though not atrocious ought to be dis-

---

[1] The original is, "Sire, je n'ai trouvé parmi les habitans et les gens de guerre que de bons citoyens, de braves soldats, et pas un bourreau. Ainsi eux et moi supplions V. M. d'employer nos bras et nos vies à choses faisables." All the original historians of the times have it. Count de Tende was another officer who dared to disobey. Both died soon after, it was supposed by poison.

obeyed, others which may be disobeyed, and still others which may be or ought to be resisted; and again there is a difference between a just law and its unjust execution or the mere order of an officer, even in countries where this distinct difference has not, as in England or the United States it has, been acknowledged. These points I propose to consider in the following sections. Long and vehement as the discussions of the right of resistance have been, they seem to me not to be more important nor so difficult as a clear view of the various questions touching obedience and noncompliance which are of daily occurrence. We have seen that obedience is necessary, in general; disobeying or noncompliance is the exception; hence it is difficult to find general principles of solid and practical value; yet the subject is so important that it deserves our fullest attention, and, remembering Bacon's "Ut nihil veniat in practicam cujus non fit etiam doctrina aliqua et theoria," we must endeavor to discover this general theory or those principles which may guide us.

XVIII. The freer a state, the greater is the authority of the law, as such and not as the personal direction of an individual, and less circumscribed at the same time is individual action. These are not so much, as we have seen, necessary consequences of civil liberty, as essential attributes. The freer, therefore, a state, the greater is the necessity of reverence for the law. Despotic governments may far more easily dispense with moral compliance to the law; they may coerce, and thus maintain their character; free states stand in need of willing compliance with the law, because it is law; otherwise disorganization, instead of advance of society, must follow. Civil liberty shows in this, as in so many other respects, its superior character. Force may greatly support absolutism; liberty is of a moral nature. Yet we must needs know what is the law. Is every demand in the name of the law, every order of an individual clothed with authority by the law, that law which the conscientious citizen is desirous of obeying? Can no law though made by the proper authority transgress its rightful limits? Do not laws themselves, if applied to practical cases, contradict each other at times, so that it becomes impossible to obey both at once? And, finally, cannot laws, the organs of the state, injure or destroy the very objects of the state, and are there no cases in which refusal of compliance or even positive resistance becomes the necessary and the only duty of the citizen? All these questions have been, at various times, more or less comprehensively discussed, generally under the excitement of disturbed times, when passionate partiality, or a judgment warped by considerations foreign to the jural character of the state, has induced men to assert extravagant opinions beyond the proper limits of truth one way or the other. Or men, anxious to carry out with consistency one theory or the other, have arrived at opposite results, the one as far removed from truth as the other. It was natural, besides, that the views entertained of this subject should partake of all the errors or necessary peculiarities incident to the gradual progress of political civilization. Power is the most striking attribute of the state, and we have seen already that that part of government which wields it most signally is, in the course of political progress, for a long time mistaken for the government itself, a mistake which misleads farther, so that he or they who have supreme public power come to be considered the state itself. Had these political errors not existed, disobedience to officers would not have been considered equivalent to disobedience to law, non-compliance with law ar refusal to yield obedience to orders of one branch of government only equal to resistance, and resistance equivalent to insurrection. So deeply seated has become, in the course of time, the idea that the executive, or the executive in conjunction with the law-making power, is the whole government, that many writers to this day, although belonging to the liberal portion of mankind, consider the acknowledgment of the principle that somewhere in the state an authority may exist which can decide upon the legality of government measures, to be an " engrafting of revolution upon the state," classing the ancient Justicia (chief justice) of Aragon[1] in the same category with the ephori of the Spartans or the council of the hundred in Carthage. We cannot discuss here the best means of watching over the legality either of executive measures or of laws themselves, in how far they agree with or differ from general laws or principles declared to be fundamental. It is a subject which belongs to politics proper; but the principle, so far from being revolutionary, is the only conservative principle of free and civilized nations, as we have seen when speaking of the all-important subject of an independent judiciary. It is a fact that an authority, for the purpose of watching over the lawful course of the high authorities of the state, either has or has not power superior to them. If it have not, it is inefficient, and becomes only the more dangerous by apparently legalizing the respective measures; if it have, it is the supreme authority, and requires in turn to be restrained and watched. It seems, therefore, that no expedient will be discovered so efficient, safe, and lawful in its operation as the independence of a judiciary, which in each practical case may declare unlawful and without authority an order, measure, or decree purporting to be a law; an operation far more extensive than at first glance it might appear, because every decision of a single case settles or distinctly pronounces the essential principle involved in the whole class of cases. The independence of the judiciary may, indeed, frequently be

---

[1] If the reader will refer to the Introduction of Prescott's Ferdinand and Isabella, he will find the high authority of the Justicia, and admit, I suppose, that although those early times had not yet discovered many expedients which we possess to insure the easy operation of the law against executive encroachment, nor that of making responsible ministers answerable for every act of the monarch, yet the essential idea in the Justicia was the insurance of the law against power, and that this institution, considering the general state of the times, so far from engrafting revolution on the state, was, on the contrary, fitted to insure much more quiet. That it did not develop and modify itself, and become more and more a blessing to the state, seems to be owing far less, if at all, to any inherent incongruity with sound government than to powerful extraneous circumstances, —the vast and rapid increase of power in Spain in general, connected as much with domestic as with general European causes.

unable to calm the high seas of power, but it may, like firm rocks on shore, break the single wave and disperse it into harmless spray.[1]

The danger that in turn the judiciary may become the supreme authority and may err as well as the others, is greatly obviated by the following circumstances, which have in part been mentioned already. The judiciary has neither honor nor places to bestow; it is accompanied by no pageant; its power rests more essentially upon moral power than that of any other branch; it gives the reasons of its decisions after discussion; it is comparatively no compact body, and its decisions may in time be overruled. I cannot conclude this

---

[1] In England, proclamations, etc., of the executive are, as a matter of course, subject, as to their legality, to the decisions of the courts, and every officer executing an unlawful order, even were it from the king in council, does it at his own peril. But Lord Coke (8 Coke, 118), Chief-Justice Hobart (in Day *vs.* Savage, Hob. 87), and Chief-Justice Holt (City of London *vs.* Wood, 12 Mod. R. 687) held and decided that even in England, where parliament is technically termed omnipotent, acts of parliament may be controlled either by common law or by natural equity. This natural equity is what Cicero beautifully calls the reason of God: "Lex vera atque princeps, apta ad jubendum et ad vetandum, ratio est recta summi Jovis." (De Legg., ii. 4.) In the United States, as was observed in the first part, the proper courts must decide whether a law, made by a legislature acting under a constitution, is in conflict with the supreme law, or not. In the state courts or circuit courts of the United States the principle had long been acted upon, when in the case of Marbury *vs.* Madison, Secretary of the United States (1 Cranch, 137), in 1803, the supreme court of the United States, through the chief justice Marshall, declared it to be " the power and duty of the judiciary to disregard an unconstitutional act of congress or of any state legislature,"—" an argument approaching to the precision and certainty of a mathematical demonstration," as Chancellor Kent (Comment., vol. i. 453, or part iii. lect. xx.) expresses it. (See the same Commentaries, vol. i. p. 448.) The report of the case is likewise contained in the collection of Chief-Justice Marshall's most important "Writings upon the Federal Constitution" (Boston, 1839), consisting of the opinions of that eminent man, delivered in the supreme and circuit courts on constitutional questions of vital importance. It is a valuable compilation, of great interest to every student of constitutional history and politics. As to obeying officers demanding unlawful things, of which I have twice already spoken, there is no civil liberty possible where the principle of the armies is followed, that the citizen must first obey, and then complain, and where the judiciary has not to decide on each particular case in due form of justice, whether the demand is lawful or not, and whether the citizen therefore is not right in disobeying.

section without remarking that since the first part of this work has been published I have been asked, from a distant country, what I precisely understand by an independent judiciary. I own that my previous observations on the independence of the judiciary were calculated for Americans or Englishmen. I will add here that the chief demands of an independent judiciary are that the decision upon law be wholly left to it, and that in no case the judge demand explanation of the law in a pending case from any person or branch soever except the law itself; that the judiciary decide in cases between the citizen and the executive; that the judge be in a situation which shall insure moral independence as much as possible; that therefore he be not removable except with comparative difficulty, for instance by impeachment, and that he hold his office during good behavior. For further remarks I must refer the reader to the chapter on judges, farther below.

XIX. Before I proceed to the consideration of the subject proper, I may be permitted to make the following brief remarks, connected with obedience to the laws. We have seen already that a conscientious citizen is not at liberty to do all that is directly permitted by law: unjust, immoral, and cruel things have at times been permitted. When the English law made it felony to teach a Catholic child in Ireland, and the informer was remunerated out of the forfeited property of the condemned, an honest citizen was not on that account in conscience allowed to make use of the law. As the British courts of law hold him answerable who does anything against law, though directed to do so by lawfully constituted authority, as having acted in that single case unlawfully, so we may suppose, if there be any responsibility at all, will God hold him responsible who does anything upon the authority of injustice passed in the form of law against his eternal laws of justice, reason, and humanity. The law does not make us unthinking and unjudging beings; it does not substitute itself for individual responsibility. We cannot, consequently, allow ourselves either to do all that is permitted or that is not prohibited. There are many evil, and even wicked things, which cannot be prohibited, or whose prohibition has not yet been called for, as the ancient Roman laws, we are told, were silent upon parricide.

A sheriff in the state of Kentucky, in a contested election case,[1] withheld the ballot-box, because the returns were against his party. There was indeed no specific positive law prohibiting this daring offence against all reason and justice. Was he on that account justifiable in doing so? The state soon after made it felony for the future. When Tiberius Gracchus ordered the clerk to promulgate the motion of his first agrarian law, his colleague Octavius steadily forbade the clerk to read it, no tribune being allowed to read it himself. Octavius had the general tribunal power of vetoing, but he nevertheless acted unjustly.

Nor are punishments equivalents to offences, or compositions, as the fines for most crimes were called in the early penal tariffs so peculiar to the Teutonic tribes. We are therefore by no means allowed to commit offences or disobey laws merely on the ground that we have previously made up our minds to submit willingly to the appointed penalty. Not to speak of the fact that, even taking the penalty as an equivalent of the offence, we should remain debtors to society so long as we have not submitted to the penalty, there remains always the moral consideration of the individual case, the injury we do to the sufferer, and to society at large; for, though all offences should be punished, increase of crime would remain equally deplorable, and punishment is by no means intended as a moral or social atonement for the offence. Yet nothing is more frequent than this belief of offenders, even though they have committed the blackest crimes. All who are acquainted with the moral treatment of convicts know well that this supposition, that the moral account is balanced by the

---

[1] In the contested case between Mr. Moore and Mr. Letcher, in Lincoln, Kentucky.

suffering of penalty, as debt and credit are in money matters, is one of the most common obstacles to finding entrance into an obdurate heart.¹ It is well known that fines are frequently the avowed equivalents for acts demanded by authority, without any reference to morality or offence; in many cases they are preferred. That these fines, not being penalties, have no connection with the above question is evident, but it is necessary not to mistake fines intended as penalties for offences for fines intended as equivalents for services. Whenever a fine is imposed for a service which may be fully obtained for that service, we have a right to consider the fine as an equivalent for the service. But it is necessary that this service must be *fully* obtainable for the money paid as fine. If the service is such that besides the work to be done it is important on account of public opinion that every citizen should cheerfully join, we must not consider the fine as a full equivalent. If the demanded service, for instance, is a share of labor in the building of a public road, the corresponding fine may in ordinary times be considered an equivalent. But if the citizens of a beleaguered town are requested to throw up redoubts, and it is important that every one should contribute to keep alive patriotic cheerfulness and readiness to do all in his power to save the town, the fine would not be an equivalent. That fines for omissions by which the community is endangered, for instance for omitting the sweeping of chimneys, or for actions by which the rights of others are endangered, as for trespassing on their grounds, cannot be considered as equivalents of the acts or omissions, is clear.

XX. The peculiar view taken of an original state of nature, according to which the state appeared something *made*, artificial, and not unfrequently arbitrary—a view which I have

---

[1] Even that remarkable criminal, the woman Gottfried, already cited, expressed repeatedly, during her last days, that a person could do no more than die for his sins, and several other opinions, which clearly indicated that she considered her moral account perfectly balanced. It will be remembered that she poisoned above thirty persons, including her parents, children, friends, etc.

endeavored to show in its whole untenableness in the first part of the work—has affected no part of the theory of law more strangely than that which treats of the degree of obedience due to the laws according to their presumed original source, namely, nature, revelation, and positive human legislation. As the original view was founded upon an error, so was the view of the obedience due to the laws equally erroneous. Jurists distinguished between mala in se, that is actions pronounced immoral by conscience according to nature or revelation, and mala prohibita, that is actions "simply and purely penal, where the thing forbidden or enjoyed is wholly a matter of indifference, and where the penalty inflicted is an adequate compensation for the civil inconvenience supposed to arise from the offence." (1 Blackstone, 58.) The commentator, who has previously called the legislating authority of the state an "inferior authority," that is inferior to the natural law, thus arrives actually at what was termed in a previous passage a tariff of penalties, and positively states that conscience is no farther concerned in the non-compliance to the law "than by directing a submission to the penalty in case of the breach of those laws" (the commission of mala prohibita, see the same place as above). Errors in original notions necessarily lead to inconsistencies, and thus we find grave ones in those passages of Blackstone in which he treats of the present subject. He instances the case of a poacher as one in which the offender may simply take the penalty as an equivalent for the malum prohibitum; but I apprehend it would be very difficult to make out that transportation, and not fine, is equivalent for unlawfully shooting deer. On the other hand, Blackstone concludes his passage on mala prohibita, and the penal theory founded on the idea of equivalents, with these remarkable words: "But where disobedience to the law involves in it also any degree of public mischief or private injury, there it falls within our former distinction, and is also an offence against conscience." Now, with what earthly subject has the state a right to meddle by way of penal law except it involve "public mischief or private injury"?

XXI. The distinction which is imagined by some writers to exist between natural law, and the law made by the "inferior authority" of the law-makers, vanishes if the view of the state which I have labored to establish be correct, namely, that the state is the sole state of nature of man. It is one of God's highest ordinances, if in a human manner we may distinguish between them, that man should live in the state. He wills the state through the laws he planted in our reason and the principles he established in our physical constitution. A legislature making laws is no less natural than the original feeling of right in man. Every wise and just law is willed by God as much as he wills that the infant receive nourishment from the mother, or that man, gifted with reason and hands and having the earth before him, shall plough it up, sow, and reap; for our intellect is his gift, our living in the state his ordinance, and hence our providing for ourselves by laws, his work. "In every law positive well made is somewhat of the law of reason and of the law of God; and to discern the law of God and the law of reason from the law positive is very hard."[1]

Secondly, the relation which the revealed law bears to the state can only be appreciated if we remember that the state is emphatically the jural society, that is, it has to do with right only, so that the revealed law can enter into state law so far only as it has to do with right; which idea of right implies, among other things, that if more mischief ensues from state interference than from leaving an evil untouched, it ought to be left untouched. Thus, natural as well as revealed law prohibits theft. Nevertheless, most codes declare that a child living in the house of its parents cannot commit theft against the latter. Yet the moral evil remains; the child commits a grievous *sin*, but the state thinks it wiser not to make it a punishable *crime*.

The reason why all mankind feel that there is a great differ-

---

[1] Words quoted in Christian's note to 1 Blackstone, 58, from the Doctor and Student, Dial. I. chap. 4.

ence as to the degree of guilt in various actions is twofold: first, the degree of danger to which the act exposes may be different, and I speak here of moral danger as well as physical;[1] secondly, the law in question may be viewed differently by different persons as to wisdom, if it is enacted for some convenience, or it may relate to a principle which every one without exception acknowledges, such as the broad and fundamental principles of morality. Blackstone calls mala in se acts which are "naturally and intrinsically wrong." But acts of themselves are never intrinsically wrong; it is the principle alone which makes them so. Thus, killing is not intrinsically wrong, for there is justifiable homicide and demanded homicide, if, for instance, I defend my wife against pirates. If a shepherd makes a fire in the field, it may be a very innocent act, but it is a highly penal act in many countries. Nor is it intrinsically wrong if the same shepherd makes a fire near the sea-shore, where vessels are constantly passing, thus exposing the lives and property of many fellow-creatures to destruction.

The difficulty, therefore, as to conscientious obedience to the laws does not lie in distinguishing between mala in se and mala prohibita, because as the general rule it *is* malum in se, it is *naturally* and *intrinsically* wrong—a positive moral wrong—to disobey the law; for it is the will of God and demand of nature that we have laws, and consequently obey them. The difficulty arises solely, as in the other cases of duty, out of conflict. No man has a right to disobey a law without reason, but he may and in many cases must disobey it when that law conflicts with superior laws; and the difficulty for the conscientious man lies in settling in many cases which is the superior law. It is in politics as in other spheres. We must obey father and mother. Yet Christ says the son will be against the father for his sake. The difficulty in many practical cases arises out of the difficulty of ascertaining to the satisfaction of

---

[1] I have given my view respecting the *moral* and *physical* danger in the Letter on Subjects of Penal Law.

the conscience whether there be a sufficient reason to disobey so true and holy a law as that requiring obedience to father and mother. It is the object of the following passages to discuss these cases of conflict in politics.

XXII. In obeying laws we must guard ourselves against interpreting them too loosely or too strictly in favor of individual interest, and against a pedantic observance of their letter beyond their spirit. In either case we do not act according to the true sense of the law. When Napoleon returned in October, 1799, from Egypt, expected by France to rescue her from anarchy and advancing enemies, it was natural for him not to stop at Fréjus, his landing-place, to perform quarantine, and for the people, believing him to be the only one who could save the country, to break through all the sanitary regulations. The rule in these cases is the common moral rule, that the important, essential, and general prevails over the trivial or particular. The practice of this rule is daily and hourly called for in life. The same applies to clashing laws. I have given my ideas more fully on this subject in the Legal and Political Hermeneutics, to which I must be permitted to refer.

We must observe here that as "it is an established rule in the exposition of statutes that the intention of the lawgiver is to be deduced from a view of the whole and of every part of a statute, taken and compared together,"[1] so it is in doubtful or conflicting cases the obligation of a citizen to examine and understand a whole law as a part of the whole political system, and to understand it in that sense in which alone any authority can be vested in the lawgiver, that is, as limited by the lawful objects of the state and the immutable principles of right and wrong. All that is to the contrary is not lawful, and, strictly speaking, not law at all, because ordained or demanded against legitimate authority. The principle is sufficiently evident and simple; the application not so, because

---

[1] Kent, Comment., i. 461.

the opinions of men differ or are strongly affected by the prevailing interest at the time.

XXIII. The efficiency of the land and naval forces depends so essentially upon unity, quickness, and energy of action, that at all times stricter and far less limited obedience has been exacted in the army and navy than in any other branch. The Roman soldier stood, in many respects, in the relation of a slave to his commanding general. Armies without discipline are not only of no use, but they are positive evils to their country; and discipline consists mainly in a universal habit of obedience throughout the whole body. History is full of the most striking instances: take, for instance, the efficiency of the navy under Cromwell, and the respect in which England was universally held as a maritime power, on the one hand, and the lax state of the navy under Charles II., when De Ruyter swept the Thames and naval disaster followed disaster, on the other hand, because there was no discipline, no obedience in the navy, most of the captains being young noblemen of families in high favor at the corrupt court, as we most abundantly learn from Pepys's Diary.[1] Not that discipline can become a substitute for patriotism or that ambition with which a great captain knows how to inspire his army. One Spartan who glories in falling for his country is worth twenty Medes who, as Herodotus tells us, were whipped into the fight by their officers against the Grecian band at Thermopylæ. Patriotism in an army, however, will become efficient only in the same degree as it is coupled with discipline. The Prussian militia in 1813 were animated by the best spirit; they loved to fight for their country; they willingly died for it; yet they became truly efficient and averted danger only in the same degree as they became disciplined. The history of the American war of independence shows the same.

---

[1] Diary of Pepys [especially notices in 1666, 1667; and comp. Knight's History of England, vol. iv. chap. xviii.].

Yet even in the army and navy absolute obedience is not and cannot be demanded. Disobedience to commands of superiors in these branches of the service may take place because the command may be unlawful. Or the command may be lawful, yet the inferior may be absolutely convinced that it was given under misapprehension, and that the superior would not have given it had he possessed the same knowledge which he, the inferior, possesses of facts as they really were at the time when the command was given, or as they have come to be since it was given; or that the execution of the command would be absolutely destructive; or, finally, that the command or order, though lawful according to the letter of the law, is unlawful according to the general and immutable objects of all law and government, that is, the security and welfare of the state, or, in free countries, the safety, prosperity, and liberty of the people.

XXIV. As to the first,—disobedience to unlawful commands, because contrary to the established law of the land,— it is now settled in England and the United States that an officer of the forces who executes the unlawful order remains personally answerable. If the highest in command, the British monarch himself, order, contrary to law, an officer to quarter his soldiers upon the citizens, to annoy and oppress them, as Charles I. did, the officer remains responsible in the fullest sense of the term to the law of the land. All that has been gained by the arduous and protracted struggle which began to show itself most signally under Charles I. may be summed up in the few words, that the law shall be superior to all and every one and to every branch of government; that there is nowhere a mysterious, supreme, and unattainable power which despite the clearest law may still dispense with it or arrest its course. This is the sum total of modern civil liberty, the great, firm, and solid commons' liberty. The British and American articles of war demand obedience to all lawful commands.[1]

---

[1] Article ix. of the American Rules and Articles of War says, "Any officer or

As obedience to commands and thorough discipline are so absolutely necessary to obtain those objects for which the forces are maintained, and as, therefore, the power given to a superior over his inferiors is much more extensive and discretionary than in any other branch, the inferior, before he disobeys, ought to be convinced that the command is most clearly illegal. He must decide it at his own peril or responsibility. But even in absolute monarchies, where the executive and legislative are one, and where the principle is adopted that all right of complaint or hope of redress is forfeited at once by not first of all obeying the superior, it is always acknowledged that under certain circumstances the inferior may disobey; for instance, if the superior were to command the inferior to commit a palpable crime or treason, or if he should show himself palpably cowardly in surrendering a fortress. The oath to be taken by every soldier, according to the Prussian articles of war, ends with these words: " I will everywhere obey the articles of war now read to me, and conduct myself, in the execution of all my duties, always in such a manner as is proper and fit for an honorable (the original is *ehrliebend*, that is, honor-loving) and undaunted soldier." He clearly can do nothing, then, against honor and conscience.

Respecting the second point, disobedience on the ground that the commander could not possibly have been sufficiently informed, we find in all wars instances which have been acknowledged as lawful. An officer would make himself highly responsible were he pusillanimously to allow a manifest advantage or victory to escape, when it was evident that the commander in giving his order could not have considered or

---

soldier who shall strike his superior officer, etc., being in the execution of his office, on any pretence whatever, or shall disobey any *lawful* command of his superior officer, shall suffer death, or such other punishment," etc. Article xiv. of the Naval Law, page 95 of the Red Book, Washington, 1826, says likewise, " No officer or private in the navy shall disobey the *lawful* orders of his superior officer," etc. So the British articles of the navy, which have served as a model to the American, say (Art. xxii.), "And any person presuming to quarrel with any his superior officer, being in the execution of his office, or disobeying any *lawful* command of any his superior officer, shall suffer death or," etc.

known of the particular combination of circumstances. There are instances of this in the wars of Napoleon. Yet here again the inferior must act upon his own responsibility, and a very high one it is: yet it is nothing more than a natural consequence of the fact that those who command are but limited and finite men, and that those who obey do not cease to be individual men with their own power and duty of reflection and responsibility. Sully, in his Memoirs, speaking of the war of Henry IV. against the duke of Savoy, says, "I did not scruple to disobey his (the king's) orders by forwarding the ammunition," etc.[1] The case is far more difficult when the inferior officer disobeys, not because he is convinced that the superior was insufficiently informed or circumstances have changed since the order was given, but because he sees the commander was in error, and a great advantage is to be gained by disobedience, perhaps impending ruin to be averted. Delicate and dangerous as these cases are, yet there have been such as would not only warrant but even demand disobedience of an honorable man. There are exceptions when we must, as in other cases of grave conflict, seriously weigh the matter, and if we feel bound to obey the higher commands of conscience, honor, and patriotism, we must do it with a full consciousness and readiness to abide by the consequences of the strict law of martial discipline should they eventually fall upon us. Of Nelson himself it was said that at times "he would look at signals, given him in battle, with his blind eye."[2] If the plain and direct order has been disobeyed, it has been generally held that the disobeying officer should be made strictly answerable, without regard to the success, even if it were bril-

---

[1] Memoirs of Sully, book xi. vol. ii. p. 26, London, 4to, ed. of 1761.

[2] * A courier arrived just before the battle of Zentha, and Prince Eugene told him to wait until after the battle. He would not open the dispatches, knowing their contents.

Major Saldern resolutely declined the plundering of Hubertsburg Castle in 1761, as "contrary to honor and duty," which Frederic the Great had ordered. Frederic ordered Icilius to do it, and was obeyed. Saldern lost nothing of the high favor in which he stood with the king. Preuss, Leben Fried. d. Gros., p. 249.

liant, of his disobedience; and this is right; for so great is the general necessity of strict obedience, and in many, nay, most cases, the impossibility of penetrating all the combinations of the commander in issuing his orders, that disobedience, were it authorized, would bring on ruin. A man who loves his country and knows likewise the nature of the service will be ready to satisfy the discipline by manfully bearing the consequences of his disobedience, which nevertheless he thinks right. Such a conflict may end tragically; yet should not a man know how to die willingly for his country, even if her call presents itself in this stern demand of her military law?

The last case is that when we know the order to be lawful according to the letter of the law, but wickedly intended against the objects for which these laws were established. This is a case of the uttermost responsibility; yet it is nevertheless true that all obedience without exception, even the military oath of obedience, is conditional; that it can be demanded only with reference to the ultimate ends of all government, the eternal objects of mankind organized in a state. The military man does not become an unfeeling, unthinking, unseeing, absolute instrument. Yet when is he to resort to this last and highest authority? Again, it is impossible to give rules, for these are cases of extremity, nor can any one else decide for the individual placed in that difficulty. If before his God he is plainly convinced that the orders of his superiors are palpably at variance with the essential objects of the state and therefore traitorous to his country, and if at the same time he is fully convinced that his disobedience, or resistance, if need be, does not bring on greater calamity than the execution of the orders, he is in conscience bound to disobey. According to the British law, the monarch is commander-in-chief of all the forces, and disposer of peace and war. Admiral Pennington had been sent by Charles I., amid the acclamations of England, seemingly to carry out a humane treaty with the oppressed and besieged Huguenots at Rochelle; but he had no sooner arrived at the place of his destination than he found himself under secret orders to give up his vessels to French command in a "murderous warfare against British honor and the Protestant religion." Here was a flagrant conspiracy of Charles and Buckingham against the state, an outrageous abuse of power executed with criminal deception, and Pennington was right not to obey, and to draw up his high-minded protest; the sailors were right who wrote "what is called a round robin against the service, and laid it under the Bible of their admiral, whose sentiments accorded with their own."[2] An officer of Charles X. of France who in 1830 was convinced that it was the government, not the people, which had daringly broken the fundamental law, was right in not firing upon the latter; the soldiers were right, they were in honor bound to join them. An English soldier who was wholly convinced that James II. had become a usurper by breaking down the law of the land was right in joining William III. So long as there is doubt in the breast, it is honorable to remain even with the unsuccessful commander; that moment at which it becomes clear to us that country and commander stand opposite to one another, the name of honor used to designate obedience to the commander has no longer any meaning; for there is no honor without doing right, and it is right to abide by the country in preference to all else.

XXV. The civil service not requiring that instant energy and decisive unity of action which is necessary to make the army and navy answer their ends, it follows that less absolute power ought to be given to the superiors, and that civil officers have a wider scope to consider the legality of an order, or may take more time for farther information from their superiors before they obey orders, than military officers. As to free countries, where, as has repeatedly been remarked,

---

[1] Brodie, History of the British Empire, Edinburgh, 1822, vol. ii. p. 70. Also, Lord Nugent, Memorials of John Hampden, London, 1832, vol. i. p. 100, and Appendix A of vol. i., where the instructions are given. See also note 2 to p. 35 of vol. ii. of Forster's British Statesmen, in Lardner's Cabinet Cyclopædia.

the law is supreme, it is clear that no officer is bound or ought to obey an illegal order. When Charles X. shortly before the last French revolution sent orders to the civil officers throughout the kingdom to vote for certain candidates for the chamber of deputies, the officers were clearly free of all obligation to obey such mandates. That the civil officer has the same right, and, as the case may be, the same duty in cases of extremity to disobey a command although within the letter of the law, with the officer of the army or navy, is evident. In ancient and modern times laws have been issued which demand disobedience to the orders of superiors under certain circumstances.[1] I shall speak more fully on some obligations of the officers belonging to the executive department in another place, and at once turn to the subject of the disobedience to law of the citizen at large.

In countries in which the people are not conceived to form the state, which is understood to be one and the same with the government, it is very clear that proportionally high notions of the duty of obedience are entertained by the rulers. If, however, the view of the state as given in the first volume is correct, many cases of just non-compliance or actual disobedience take place. We call that citizen loyal who, satisfied with the main principles of his government, although he may be very strongly opposed to the characteristic features of the administration for the time being, conscientiously endeavors to act in the main not only according to the letter, but also and rather according to the true spirit, of the laws of his land, so long as he can conscientiously do it. Laws may be, or under certain circumstances must be, disobeyed, if they are contrary to the fundamental law of the land, if they are

---

[1] Majorian, that excellent emperor of Rome, too late, however, to find a sphere for his noble soul, prohibited the infamous pulling down of ancient monuments for private purposes, and decreed the severest penalties to be inflicted upon every subordinate officer who should obey his superiors in these scandalous grants. (Gibbon, chap. xxxvi., or vol. iv. pp. 63, 64, Bohn's ed.) The Norwegian Constitution (of November 4, 1814) says, § 85, "He who obeys an order whose object is to disturb the liberty or safety of the storthing makes himself guilty of treason against his fatherland.

against the law of God, that is of morality, nature, and conscience, against primordial rights, against the spirit of the times, if I am driven by superior force to comply with other commands, and, in general, if I cannot obey otherwise than by disobeying a superior law.

XXVI. We are citizens because we are men, and in order to obtain our ends as men; and we shall continue to be moral individuals long after we have ceased to be either citizens or men. The demands of the state, therefore, are by no means the sole or ultimate laws by which in cases of extremity we must regulate our conduct. If a law prohibits, under certain circumstances, giving a degree of education to my child which I nevertheless may be convinced that its peculiar capacity deserves, I am not bound to obey; for it is one of the very first objects of man to become all that God has given him the capacity to become. In Hesse-Cassel it was found that far too many young men received a university education, thus preparing them for careers in which they could not succeed, owing to the number of applicants. A law was passed which allowed the children of certain parents only to study in the universities. Yet if a father in that country should have seen that his son was peculiarly fitted for the sciences, would he have been chargeable with any dereliction of duty if he should have evaded the law and sent his son to some foreign university? Dissenters were formerly not allowed to keep schools in England; yet in many districts there were none other but dissenters' schools. Was it disloyal for dissenters to keep a school despite the law? Was it not, on the contrary, a manifest duty to disobey, provided there was the slightest chance of success, because the state glaringly transcended its legitimate sphere?¹ A law may be disobeyed if unlawful authority

---

¹ Lord Russell, Memoirs of the Affairs of Europe from the Peace of Utrecht, says, " The Schism Bill was introduced by Sir William Wyndham,—one of the chief ornaments of their party. Its object was to prevent the education by dissenters in any way; and it went to prohibit them from keeping schools even for their own children." So I find it quoted; I have not the work at hand.

has issued it, or rather it is no law, because against the fundamental law, for instance when James I. bestowed unlawfully the soap monopoly upon favorites. We must not forget that laws may be passed in regular and lawful form, and yet be clearly against the plainest rights of the citizens, although outwardly conformable to the fundamental law. There is, however, a fundamental law superior to any fundamental charter, that is reason, right, and nature, and that superior fundamental law of all humanity requires, in cases of high conflict, first to be obeyed. An immoral law is no law, and my yielding to it or not is a mere question of expediency, just as I may or may not yield to the demands of a robber. If my government prevents me from importing what books I see fit to use for the pursuit of my studies, I have an undoubted right to evade the law if I deem it expedient, for the pursuit of truth is a law of infinitely greater authority, and therefore infinitely more demands obedience, than any law enacted by temporary authority ever can.

Laws which are manifestly against the spirit of the time, which cannot be obeyed whatever the law may demand, may and must be disobeyed. If the government neglects changing the laws according to the change of circumstances, it is not the obligation of the citizen to adhere to the law. Such are laws manifestly fallen in disuse, of which some striking ones have been mentioned in previous passages, laws which it would be morally impossible to obey. It is true, indeed, that by the strict principles of the common law an act of parliament cannot be repealed by a "non-user;"[1] yet where are

---

[1] 2 Term Rep. 275; 2 Dwarris on Statutes, 672. But the contrary has been laid down by a writer of authority, Wooddeson's Elements, 63, and it is also to be found in the Roman law, Digest, lib. i. tit. 3, § 32. I must be permitted here to give the whole of that section, because it contains true principles of right, and many of my readers out of the profession of the law may not have an easy opportunity of perusing it. The Digest says, "Respecting those matters for which we have no written law, that must be followed which has been introduced by custom and manners, and if this does not exist respecting a subject, that must be followed which lies nearest and that which results from analogy of similar cases: if nothing else can be obtained even in this way, the custom of the city of Rome

there more laws virtually fallen into disuse, which it would be impossible to act out and which it is, consequently, not immoral to disobey, than in England? Let us not forget that even Lord Mansfield, when acting as the highest organ of the law itself, told the jury to find a verdict of theft for an amount far less than the articles before the eyes of the jury evidently amounted to, in order to rescue the prisoner from the effects of a law wholly dissonant with the spirit of the time, and to give her the benefit of more humane and more efficient modes of punishment, discovered since the establishment of the ancient law. Whatever reason there was in early times for punishing almost any theft with hanging, in England, whether the state of society then required it, or whether even then the law was injudicious, sure it is that Lord Kenyon pronounced no more than a solemn truth when he said, when a girl, sentenced to be hung for her first theft, dropped down dead in court, "I then felt, as I now feel, that this was passing sentence not on the prisoner but on the law."[1]

If a law is against nature I am at liberty to disobey. It is God's order that all animal life shall be sustained by food; if then government lays so high a duty on necessary articles of food that it becomes impossible properly to support the body, as has been the case and that repeatedly, I have a right, if I am able and see fit in other respects, to import the food against the law. The duty on salt was in some parts of France before the first revolution so exorbitant that the people could not purchase it. Had the most conscientious

---

must be followed. All rooted custom is justly followed as law, and that which has been founded by custom is law. For if the laws themselves bind us for no other reason than because they have been adopted by the pronounced will of the people, that likewise binds justly every one which the people have sanctioned without writing; for what matters it whether the people declared their will by voting or by the thing and fact itself? It has therefore with perfect justice likewise been adopted as a rule that laws may be abrogated not only by the pronounced will of the lawgiver, but also in consequence of universal tacit consent by disuse."

[1] Related by Mr. Morris, in the house of commons, in 1811.—(English) Law Journal, May, 1837, 296.

citizen to reproach himself in any degree if he smuggled salt for his family? What is more natural than language? what more ungodly and tyrannical than to make the use of one's mother tongue penal? Yet governments have repeatedly passed laws to that effect. If laws are passed respecting religious beliefs, they are naught in themselves, because they aim at that which is impossible,—to believe according to command. And if I believe that a certain service is essential to my religion, I have certainly an undoubted right to disobey the law and celebrate it in secret, if I thereby do not injure any one else. If, finally, I am forced by a conqueror or usurper to obey his orders contrary to the laws of the land, I am not answerable for disobedience, for one of the first objects and duties of all governments and laws is to protect me; if they fail to do so, I am not bound, though I may choose to do so, to expose myself to the penalties of the rulers in actual possession.

To sum up the whole, then, it is evident that in obeying laws we must, wherever laws clash, obey the superior in preference to the inferior; and this superior law may, in many cases, be one that was never enacted, perhaps for the very reason that it was of itself universally binding, like the demands of physical nature; farther, in many cases of this conflict, nothing can decide which is the superior law, and whether disobeying the inferior law be justified, except the conscience of the individual. I am well aware that hasty and forward citizens, fanatics, and wicked men have asserted that their conscience commanded them to disobey, when it ought to have told them the opposite. South asserts the truth when he says, "No such instrument to carry on a refined and well-woven rebellion as a tender conscience and a sturdy heart. He who rebels conscientiously rebels heartily." Abuse, however, does not disprove the rule. Men have often pretended to change their religion for conscience' sake, when sordid interest or turpitude guided them. Should we establish on that account the rule that the conscience must not decide upon the change of one's religion?

XXVII. Merely disapproving of a law by no means gives us a right to disobey it; we must be clearly and conscientiously convinced that it may be disobeyed upon one of the main grounds enumerated, or that it does not come from lawful authority, when in fact it is not law but the semblance of law. Another question is, whether we may under any circumstances make use of or profit by a law of which we disapprove. If the law goes against our own main principles we must not expect to stay its own evil effects by partial compliance; for instance, if we were in times of violence to accept of confiscated property with a view to restore it to the owner or to rescue it out of the hands of the despoilers. That this is, however, very dangerous is very clear, for the feeling of every one marks such a procedure as a partial co-operation, and no one at present will read without disapproval or very reluctant excuse the account that some persons, otherwise standing high for their virtuous character, accepted at the hands of James II. the lands confiscated in consequence of Jeffrey's sanguinary procedures, with the declared view of making the best use of them and preventing their falling into the hands of his greedy and licentious courtiers.[1]

XXVIII. So far we have considered only the cases when a conscientious citizen may disobey or must disobey; for the latter must depend upon his conscience alone. If he believes that by obedience he positively co-operates in the furtherance of iniquity, he must disobey. This is the ground upon which the Quakers decline paying taxes towards the army. Still, it is not to be forgotten in any of these cases that obedience to the laws is of itself a duty so long as we can conscientiously obey, and that the penalty is not an equivalent; and that we must carefully guard ourselves against presumption, that is setting up our conscience against that of all who made or favor the law. The case, therefore, must always be a strong one.

---

[1] See Mackintosh's History of the Revolution of 1688.

Another question is, has the citizen the right to resist, and can he under certain circumstances go so far as to take up arms against those in power? Despite the vehement discussions on this point at periods when it was of practical importance, there has been but little difference as to the actual theory. Those monarchs who have most strenuously maintained the principle of "absolute non-resistance," for instance the Stuarts, have fostered and fomented resistance against the governments established in consequence of their own dethronement. George III., who maintained very high notions respecting the obedience due to a government, not only connived at but promoted the plan of Queen Matilda of Denmark, then residing at Zelle, to overthrow the existing Danish government, and to make herself, not what she had been before the execution of Struensee, but actually regent of the kingdom.[1] Ferdinand VII. rewarded the persons who had resisted the cortes and himself, after he had been re-established in absolute power by the assistance of Louis XVIII.' The duchess of Berry incited the people to civil war, from whom she claimed the throne on the principle of legitimacy. The pope has in repeated instances promoted resistance and fostered revolt.

So far the question has only respected resistance to the whole government on account of its entire unlawfulness. Another is, may a lawful government be resisted in unlawful demands? and, finally, may a people take up arms against a whole government, previously considered lawful? When this question has been discussed without peculiar reference to practical cases of deep interest at the time, the greater number of jurists and philosophers have allowed that there are cases in which it is lawful and necessary to resist with arms, that is to resort to insurrection. Generally writers have restricted the cases of justified resistance against monarchs to resisting atrocities on the part of the prince; in short, they

---

[1] Wraxall, Posthumous Memoirs [i. 374-418. Compare what Lord Mahon says in his History, v. chap. 50, note.]

have maintained that armed resistance is admissible only against tyrants, and among the characteristics of a tyrant, who was generally depicted in such a manner that there was no necessity of telling people that it was lawful to resist such a monster, atrocious cruelty was generally one. This was partly because writers were afraid to speak out, partly because they really feared to make resistance too easy. Times have changed, however. Physical cruelty is no longer considered as the only ground upon which resistance is admissible. Already have German and other continental writers expressed themselves very differently.[1] As to the principle there can be no doubt whatever. Every unlawful government ought to be resisted and permanently changed, if it permanently and obstinately insists upon a course injurious to the people, and if the evils accompanying the change are not greater than the blessings to be obtained by the change. In the abstract we might easily go farther; we might say, Government ought to be resisted whenever it acts unlawfully. But there arises the unavoidable difficulty of deciding when it acts unlawfully; for the people may be mistaken as well as the government. Our forefathers enacted in many cases that if the ruler distressed the people against law, it was lawful to resist him.[2] The difficulty adhering to all discussions on the

---

[1] One of the early writers who treats the subject with great freedom is Hubert Languet, in his Vindiciæ contra Tyrannos, sive de Principis in Populum Populique in Principem legitima Potestate, Stephano Junio Bruto, Celta Auctore, Edinburgi, 1579. A work I recommend to the student.

[2] Charles the Bald, grandchild to Charlemagne, was obliged to sign in 856 A.D. a charter in which it was pronounced that the nobility should have the right, unitedly, and with arms, to resist whenever the emperor should demand anything unjust. The Magna Charta says, " Ipsi Barones cum communitate totius terræ distringent et gravabunt nos modis omnibus quibus poterunt, scilicet per captionem castrorum, terrarum, possessionum, et aliis modis quibus potuerint, donec emendatum fuerit secundum arbitrium eorum." [But in the Charta this is made the end of a series of attempts to obtain justice. See art. 70.] Andrew II. of Hungary granted the right of resistance in case the then concluded compact should be broken. King John of Denmark acknowledged the right in the three kingdoms subject to his power, if he should not listen to their complaints of grievances. (Schütz, Universal History, v. 194.) Alphonso III. of Aragon

practical application of the right of resistance, which has ever been acted upon by the people when it comes to the last, and will be acted upon so long as the world stands, has been increased by the two circumstances of which we have spoken already; that the executive has been, and still frequently is, mistaken for the government, and resistance against the executive, though it should be in defence of the law, as in France in 1830, is taken for resistance against the whole government; and, secondly, that monarchs have been erroneously surrounded with an extra-political halo. A relation between the subject and the monarch on religious grounds beyond the foundation of the state and law is imagined; a sacred, indelible, and indestructible allegiance is supposed to exist. Yet that the Bible does not teach the theory of non-resistance we may easily gather from the Old Testament; and it is a fact that Christ does not speak of politics, and that none have so much disagreed on the subject as the theologians. Indeed, they have advocated resistance, under circumstances which to them seemed to warrant it, more freely and positively than any other writers.[1] No set of theologians have, I believe, so stanchly and unequivocally, though by no means in all cases consistently, maintained the principle of non-resistance as the writers of the Church of England during the seventeenth and eighteenth centuries. They did not in-

---

granted in 1287 to the barons by the two Pacts of Union the right of insurrection against the king if their liberties should be infringed after they had protested. (Prescott, Ferdinand and Isabella, Introduction, xci.) Of the Polish rocoss I have spoken previously. I might increase the instances. [See what Mr. Guizot says of the right of resistance in feudalism, History of Civilization, i. 100, ana History of Civilization in France, iii. 96, 97, Amer. ed. of transl.]

[1] Even Luther did not hesitate to sanction resistance to the emperor who will not follow "signed privileges" (beschriebene Rechte), and considered an emperor lawfully dethroned if the empire and electors unitedly dissolve the allegiance. Luther saw this case of a German emperor clearer because he was an elected prince. For us there is no difference. All princes are conditionally monarchs, that is for the good of the people. None is by intrinsic legitimacy so. The mild Melanchthon thought tyrannicide admissible. Loci Theologici, De Magistr.

deed maintain the doctrine of absolute obedience, for they demanded "passive obedience" only, and allowed therefore non-compliance.[1]

XXIX. Of the force of allegiance we have spoken already. Yet even where the theory which I have endeavored to establish in the first volume is not admitted, it is certain that no man can be lawfully bound or lawfully promise to do what is unlawful. This is self-evident. Even the canon law says, "In malis promissis non expedit servare fidem." So that neither allegiance nor oath can bind to obey that which is unlawful. This therefore would absolve every one from absolute obedience. Yet if we merely decline to co-operate or obey but do not in cases of uttermost emergency resist, we leave all power to do that which we hold to be unlawful in the hands of the government. In the opinion of those who sincerely believe that dynasties or certain specific governments are from God, we ought to suffer everything at their hands as so much punishment inflicted by the Deity. That this idea does not agree with our views of government supported throughout this work is clear. The government is an organism for the purpose of obtaining the great ends of the state, the state an institution to secure the great social and individual ends of humanity, and if the former ceases to obtain its object, either from want of energy or because it endeavors systematically and constantly to undermine and destroy those ends, society has no doubt the simple right of establishing a new one, even where there is no particular compact between the rulers and the ruled. The government is no longer a lawful one, though established according to all the formalities of the law, because no longer answering the purpose or obtaining the ends and objects of the law. Mankind have always acted upon this principle. Yet so necessary is a government, so unrighteous is it not to deliberate in all matters relating to society whether

---

[1] Hallam, Constitutional History, in various places, among others, vol. ii. p. 625, et seq.

we may not injure others more than we assist them, so doubtful, calamitous, and frequently demoralizing are the effects of insurrection and of civil war, so easily is the individual deceived respecting his own rights and the probable success of measures which may appear suitable to the temperament of our mind at the time, so much increased is the evil of tyranny in case of unsuccessful attempts at resistance, so frequently does resistance, even though successful against the government, lead to a tyranny worse than the previous one — to military government — and so often does it open an arena for the worst passions and for a shallow mediocrity, noisy, forward, and unconcerned about the harm it produces, that he who on slight grounds resorts to force against the existing government indeed commits treason against society.[1]

An insurrection may take place on the strict ground of resistance; that is, people may take up arms to resist every attempt to enforce a certain law or measure, without the intention of going farther than this resistance. This may especially take place when single provinces rise. In very many cases in history such insurrections have had salutary results; because government learns practically that it cannot go beyond a certain line. Every measure of sufficient magnitude and radical importance may be sufficient to warrant armed resistance; but as it necessarily leads to political interruption, and especially as a partial insurrection may lead to a revolution though originally intended for armed resistance only, it is necessary both that the cause be of sufficient magnitude, and that all common and regular means of redress have previously been fairly and honestly tried. By revolution I understand a violent change of the fundamentals, or one fundamental, of the government; a violent change of the administration would be a rebellion, or rebellious riot. Aristotle (Pol., v. 1, 4) mentions two species of revolutions, those by which the constitution is changed, and those which leave the

---

[1] See the judicious remarks of Mackintosh in his History of the Revolution of 1688, chapter ix.

constitution but bring another set of men into power: he does not mean, however, by another set, another administration, but other rulers, for he instances the monarchy and oligarchy. The change of persons in these states, that is, the change of the power-holders, is evidently a change of one of the fundamentals of the government, and thus falls within our definition.

As to revolutions, they can never be justified by a single executive measure—except it be a *coup d'état*—but by a perverse course of ruinous, unjust, and malevolent or infatuated measures, and after all civil means of redress have been tried in vain; and there must be either fair hope of success, or the people be driven to desperation, so that a serious risk shall seem more endurable than the existing state of things. For revolutions are most grave, bitter, and uncertain processes.

On the other hand, it must be admitted that there exists no nation with well-established freedom which has not been obliged to resort at some period to resistance and does not owe some of its choicest blessings and most deeply-founded liberties to armed resistance or revolution. There is rarely a clear understanding between the government and the people of free nations unless at some period or other they have passed through this process and crisis. It is a maxim ascribed to the duke de Sully, and adopted by Burke,[1] that there are no unprovoked revolts. If we understand by revolts insurrections of the people, and not conspiracies of the nobility or generals, the remark is certainly true. Thus Sully must have meant it, for otherwise his own times would but too abundantly furnish us with instances to the contrary, while we have but to look at South America to see unprovoked army revolts happening in almost uninterrupted succession. Revolutions are fearful, yet they are at all times not only unavoidable but salutary. The whole political institution of a country may become so corrupt or so thoroughly unfit for the existing

---

[1] Sully's Memoirs, and Burke, Thoughts on the present Discontents [Works. i. 310, Bohn's ed.].

and changed state of things that it engenders misery and
political immorality and altogether loses its jural character.
Revolutions then become unavoidable and just; nor should
any conscientious citizen then shrink from them. What the
great Boerhaave says of fevers, " Febris sæpe sanationis optima
causa," applies with equal force to political diseases. I do
not speak here of separations of colonies from their mother
countries, which we call likewise revolutions in the English
language though they differ materially from domestic revolutions.[1] Whatever power affections may have, and they are in
many instances salutary, it is certain that so soon as a distant
colony has the power of maintaining its independence, and can
promote the whole social interest by independent domestic
laws, she has the right and, it may be, the sacred duty of
entering into the lists with independent nations.

XXX. If there is danger in the right and necessity of resistance or in justifying revolution, there is much more danger
in the doctrine of non-resistance; for, while power naturally
and by inherent quality tends to increase, the people are reluctant to resort to resistance except in cases of extremity,—
a powerful and privileged class always excepted. The uncertainty of success, the difficulty of united action, the natural
disposition in the citizen to follow the law and authority much
rather than to disobey it, are no mean guarantees against the
wicked application of the right of resistance. Moreover, we

---

[1] Revolutions may be of a very different character. They may be revolutions of the people against the domestic government, as the English and French revolutions were; or against foreign, imposed governments, as the revolution of Portugal against the Spaniards, that of Masaniello in Naples, or of Hofer in Tyrol, if the latter be not called mere insurrections on account of failure of success; or the separation of colonies or distant provinces, as the North and South American revolutions; or the separation of part of the country, as in the late case of Belgium; or the re-establishment of independence, as in Portugal when the Spaniards were expelled; or the expulsion of one branch of the family by another without participation of the people, as not unfrequently in Asia; or a revolution of the prince against the state, for instance when an elective monarch makes himself hereditary.

ought to remember that the resistance or revolt of no people is so fearful and calamitous as that of those who have not been accustomed to freedom. The resistance of the freest nations has been the freest from those atrocious crimes which sully the civil wars of nations that shake off the chain of bondage, so that the very acknowledgment of the right of resistance, as an accompaniment of liberty, becomes a guarantee of its being used rarely and of its being attended with less evil than if the right were denied.

The necessity of resistance has, as we have seen, often been acknowledged. I will not speak of the emperor Trajan, who, when he handed the sword of the prætorian prefect to Saburanus, said, "Use it for me if I rule well, if not, against me."[1] As a sentiment it is fine for a Roman emperor; but acted upon as a political principle it would be a sort of janizary constitutional law, and make Saburanus a strange super-emperor. Hume says that the laws ought to be silent on the right of resistance, but he guards himself against the suspicion that he desired to prevent its discussion. If by resistance is meant the citizen's resisting any procedure against him contrary to the law, then the laws of England and the United States have in a great measure sanctioned it, and there is indeed no firm and substantial civil liberty imaginable without its acknowledgment. If resistance against laws themselves, as contrary to the fundamental law or on any other ground, be meant, it would be useless and inconsistent were the laws to acknowledge it beforehand; for who shall decide whether the law be lawful or not? If the citizen for himself, nothing is gained; if some authority, except the courts in the regular course of expounding and administering law as to the specific case, then this authority again, whoever it might be, might abuse its power. The constitution must acknowledge some highest legislative power, and cannot at the same time call upon the people to resist if this power should be abused; this

---

[1] [Dion Cass., lxviii. 16; Victor, de Cæs., 13, who mentions the prefect's name.]

would require another power to resist the abuse of the latter. The French therefore had gained nothing when they declared in the rights of men enumerated in the constitution of 1793, "If the government violates the rights of the people, insurrection is for the people and for every portion of the people the most sacred and most indispensable duty." Insurrection belongs strictly to political ethics, and must in cases of extremity be decided upon by the most solemn act of the conscience; it cannot be made a subject of politics proper and be drawn into positive law; but resistance may so far be made matter of positive law that an authority may be appointed by the constitution which shall decide—after the resistance has taken place—whether the resisted law, measure, or demand was conformable to the fundamental law or not, and, consequently, whether or not resistance was warranted. And the courts of the United States have actually such power.

XXXI. Entirely different from resistance, yet frequently confounded with it, or justified on the same ground, is what by a contradiction in the term itself has been called of late mob law. A mob—the ὄχλος of the Greeks, and *turba* of the Romans, is a lawless multitude impelled by a common desire for the obtaining of some immediate object, or drawn together by a common impulse, for instance curiosity.[1] A mob, it

---

[1] Mob is the abbreviation of mobile (the movable), which we find used at length in the diaries and familiar letters written at the time of James II. and Charles II. I do not remember that it occurs in Pepys. It is of frequent occurrence in the Ellis correspondence, edited by Lord Dover, London, 1828. The abbreviation was probably brought into use by the newspapers, like so many others, for instance scrip. Whether the word mobility, which Walter Scott puts in the mouth of a courtier of James I. (in the Fortunes of Nigel), it should be presumed without anachronism, preceded the introduction of the word mobile, or vice versa, I do not know. It is evidently a word of derision closely resembling that of nobility, and must have come in use when the masses attracted at least so much notice as to be derided by the privileged, which always precedes that period when the masses really obtain power. It was so in Rome, the Netherlands, France, England. For the barbarous word mobocracy, that is the aristocracy of the mob, though properly speaking the rabble is meant in this case.

would appear, need not be the rabble, by which we designate more especially a tumultuous congregation of the vulgar or their aggregate in the abstract. The term "dregs of the people," the fæx, *fæx infima*, of the Romans, designates the abject class of a population visited with ignorance and poverty and consequently stricken with vice and crime. They were also most significantly called by the Romans, carrying out the trope of the vessel of the state, the bilge-water of the republic, expressing at once their loathsomeness, danger, and fickleness, which, together with a gust of wind, may indeed throw the vessel on her beam-ends. "Sin tu exieris, exhaurietur ex urbe tuorum comitum magna et perniciosa *sentina* rei publicæ." Cic., Cat., 1, 5, 12.

When Suetonius (Julius, xiv.) tells us that, when Cæsar insisted upon punishing the Catiline conspirators by confiscation alone, "a body of the equestrian order, holding up their arms, threatened him with immediate death," they acted as a mob, though they were originally lawfully assembled there as a guard. Thus the British commons have been hyperbolically called at times a mob, to designate their occasional planless procedures. I have already spoken of the grievous and mischievous error in politics[1] when a mob take the law into their own hands, as it is inappropriately called, for the law ceases to be such at the instant it is taken out of the hands of the legitimate officer, be this by prince, officer, or mob. On that occasion the error was chiefly considered in the light of justice and natural law. In this place I shall add a few observations respecting the ethical character of the subject.

The most noticeable political effects of mobs are when they pretend to deal out justice, when they overawe the legislature or administration of law and destroy property for their own

---

that caricature of government when the mob claim the privileges of exemption from law, the Greek term was ὀχλοκρατία. It is one of the most uncompromising species of aristocracy.

[1] See on Lynch Law, in Part First.

supposed interest and necessary support; as was the case with the machine-breakers in England some time ago.[1]

Although the people composing mobs will generally confess that in interfering with the regular course of justice they only do so by way of exception, it must not be forgotten that no moral phenomenon is more common, of which every one upon reflection finds instances in his own life, and of which we have spoken already, than that interest, excitement, or passion presents to us that case which excites us as a particular one, deserving of exception from the principles we may have laid down for the guidance of our own action in calmer moments. One of the main objects of all justice is protection by the interposition of law between blinding interest or excited passion and the object complained of. The mob tramples down this wall of safety, and derides the majesty of the law—a term of the greatest import, however shamefully it has been abused in periods of political and legal degeneracy. The very existence of the mob is, in most cases, evidence of the excitement, hence of its unfitness to judge or execute judgment. The mob, generally, consists of the most movable part of the population, not of the steady laborer or mechanic, hence of the least reflecting and most excitable people; and of those whom it is not difficult to guide with any moderate skill in the art of the demagogue. The London apprentices, so conspicuous in British history, afford instances. In delicate times, when the best patriots labor to secure great blessings by a steady and considerate course, and when it requires all the consideration of the calmest minds not to trespass a distinct line beyond which all becomes insecure and dangerous, a mob not unfrequently rends the whole.

The mob disregards property; and everything which ren-

---

[1] How ill-guided the destroyers of the machinery were, who believed that they should lose their bread, can now be incontrovertibly proved by statistics. Machinery made cotton goods so cheap that millions could use them who formerly could not, and consumption altogether increased in an unexampled manner, so that far more hands are now employed with the machines to satisfy the increased demand than formerly without them.

ders property insecure, by whatsoever means, be it by unsettled and partial taxation,[1] or government oppression, or insecure inheritance, or mob violence, destroys one of the chief objects of the state, security of property, a chief object not only on account of mere safety, but also because insecurity of property injures the steady and moderate pursuit of property, and engenders idleness, immorality, and unfitness for substantial liberty. The fact that either there is no chance of acquiring property, or little chance of preserving that which has been acquired, has the effect, not to cause people now to strive to obtain the more in order to be the better able to sustain partial loss, but to give up altogether the accumulation of property.

The suspicion and fear of being overreached, want of confidence in themselves, and consequent fretfulness arising from the absence of organization; the consciousness of unlawful and very brief power, and consequent thirst for making rapid use of it; the fearful and natural operation of mutual excitement, of which I have spoken before; the absence of individual responsibility,[2] and the desire in many of outdoing in boldness the rest, with the unrestricted action of revenge and final cruelty, are so many reasons why mobs, when they take it upon themselves to execute what they believe to be justice, interfere most injuriously with the lawful state of mankind; and no one who loves his country, respects the dignity of man, has regard for the sacred objects of society, or reverence

---

[1] Boeckh, in his Political Economy of Athens, translated from the German, 2 vols., London, 1828, specifically mentions the *liturgy*, or special and heavy charge of rich individuals for the performance of some public act, as one of the causes of public ruin by rendering property insecure, and the author substantiates his case, not without the aid of ancient authors themselves.

[2] There is a saying of Napoleon's, in Las Cases, not unworthy to be mentioned here. At St. Helena he found an old Malay, of the name of Toby, who had been kidnapped and sold at that island. Napoleon was much affected by his recital, and said, among other things, "If this crime has been committed by the captain alone, he is no doubt one of the worst of men; but if it has been committed by the whole crew unitedly, it may have been done by persons who, after all, are not so wicked as one would think at first." Vol. ii. p. 26, ed. of 1825.

for truth and justice (which is truth enacted), will talk slightly or speak jocosely of them; which, nevertheless, is but too frequently done in our papers. The hanging at the lantern in the beginning of the French revolution, the awful and unrighteous excitement and cruelty in the times of Titus Oates, the barbarous slaughtering of the prisoners of war in Spain, when a commanding officer declared by proclamation that the people demanded the slaughter of fifty-five persons, and rather justified the act upon this ground,[1] evidently from fear, the procedures in our own country at Vicksburg in 1835[2] and at Boston against a convent, are warnings which no one ought to leave unheeded. No one who has not been present at such unfortunate procedures can have any idea of the rapidity with which suspicion rises, is received, passes on, increases, and terminates in a sanguinary act of revenge. The multiplying power of excitement in a mob by rapid circulation is perhaps the most conspicuous example of the power of reciprocal influence and sympathy lodged in our nature that human life ever presents.

To overawe the legislature or courts of justice is equally pernicious and unjust. We can trace in the history of every revolution the fact that evil consequences of the gravest kind have attended it. In France the sans-culottes at the bar, in England the people in the galleries in the times of the ascend-

---

[1] We find, in the year 1838, Juntas of Retaliation formed in Spain, and the Paris journals published a proclamation of the general commanding at Valencia, which contains the following deplorable passage: "Brave national guards and inhabitants of Valencia: The Junta of Retaliation began its labors yesterday. Conformably to its advice and the general clamor of the people, although much against my inclination and painfully for my heart, I find myself under the necessity of causing to be shot fifty-five of the Carlist captives in the prisons of this city, etc. . . . The fatal system of moderation which we have followed must cease. The enemies of the throne and of liberty tremble in learning that her majesty's government has recovered all its energy and suppressed forever all that benevolent sentiment which made us regard them only as erring Spaniards. If the despot pretends to subjugate us *by blood*, it is *in blood* that we will extinguish his projects, and it is *with blood* that we will consolidate the constitutional throne of Isabella and liberty."

[2] Niles's Register, Baltimore, August 1, 1835.

ency of the Presbyterians and Independents, and the boisterous people in the hall of the cortes in 1821, are all instances of what is here maintained; and little do those who invoke this overawing by the mob know what chains at that moment they rivet on their own limbs. Silence, therefore, in legislative halls and courts is not only a debt of respect and decency, but a political duty of grave import; not to speak of other inconveniences arising out of habitual applause or disapprobation from the galleries. It is one of the surest means to give confidence to those insipid yet ever-ready talkers of whom every assembly has some, and who constitute a political as well as social nuisance. Overawing by the mob does not only occur in times of revolution: we find an instance of it during peace, in Walpole's day, in the commons, when an outcry was made against the excise bill,[1] the people being heated into fury by the frauds of stock-jobbers at the time of the South Sea bubble; and of late, in the legislature of one of our states, another of a very serious character.

When we come to speak of the nature and essence of the representative government, we shall see how utterly incompatible with it is the influence of mobs upon the representatives — mobs which daringly assume the name of people. Mobs, if in any way allowed to influence assemblies, produce those bursts of passion or excitement, so much to be dreaded in all politics, monarchical or republican, for which the French during the first revolution had a technical term, calling them *décrets d'enthousiasme*, so that Dumont, in his Memoirs of Mirabeau, gives us an instance of a decree of enthusiasm of war. There is, we all know, such a thing as passing a proposition by acclamation; but in excited times it is exceedingly difficult to distinguish between universal enthusiasm and universal bawling respecting the passage of a measure, either to urge it forward or to denounce it. When on February 7, 1787, Sheridan brought forward his fourth charge against Hastings, and had charmed the audience by his most brilliant

---

[1] Robert Walpole's Memoirs, vol. iii., ed. of 1816.

display so much that members, peers, and strangers expressed their approbation by long-continued applause—a procedure new and irregular—an adjournment of the debate was moved and carried " to afford time for the dispassionate consideration of the question, and to avoid coming to a vote while the minds of members were under the fascinating impression of that speech." Tomline calls this reason justly an "unprecedented" one, although just. Fox opposed it, but it was carried without a division.[1]

XXXII. The obligation of informing the proper state authority against offences before or after the fact has at all times been considered a very serious one, and demands our attention. The whole subject may be considered first in regard to government officers, and secondly respecting the citizen at large. That every officer has not only the right but the duty to inform against all offences belonging to his proper sphere which come to his notice, and diligently to trace them out, is evident. For what else is he appointed, if not to support and assist in the regular course of law? An officer, therefore, is bound by the relation in which through his office he stands to society, and the object for which power and authority have been delegated to him, not only to take proper notice of offences relating to his department, if he has undeniable evidence of them, but also diligently to trace out the truth so soon as he has reasonable ground of suspicion. With respect to offences which do not touch his particular department, he has only, it seems to me, the obligation common to all citizens at large. Before we treat of this latter subject, it will be necessary to speak of some dangers and evils connected with informing.

Governments have not unfrequently held out regular rewards, proportioned to the offence or crime of which information is given. It was formerly so in England. The more a government is a government of law, and not of executive

---

[1] Tomline, Memoirs of William Pitt, vol. ii. p. 271, 2d ed.

management alone, the less effective must necessarily become, upon the whole, a preventive police; for one of the main ideas of a strict government of law and of civil liberty is that the citizen be allowed to do all he chooses, provided he do not offend against the laws, and that proper notice shall be taken of the offence only, and then only according to law, after an abuse of that right to do what one chooses has taken place, in other words, after an offence has been committed. I do not mean to say that all preventive police is contrary to civil liberty. On the contrary, it is infinitely better to prevent crimes than to punish them; and one of the means to prevent them is a preventive police. Yet it is certain, on the other hand, that a preventive police cannot and ought not to be established on so expensive and thorough a plan in a free country as is possible in a well-regulated and carefully organized absolute monarchy.[1]

The comparative inefficiency of a thoroughly organized preventive police, under institutions of civil liberty, might induce us to consider this additional means of detecting offences by holding out a regular reward for information, as peculiarly necessary in free countries; for the necessity of punishing offences remains in all societies the same. But we must consider that none but the abject portion of the community will show themselves willing to make a profession of informing for money, people who are incapable, perhaps, owing to their

---

[1] * There are two questions not distinctly stated here: Is a man bound to inform? and when is he bound not to inform? For the latter compare the following words of Lord Mansfield, when speaking of the laws against the Catholics, in the case of James Webb, at the suit of Payne, a "common informer" of that period:

"But now the case is quite altered. The pope has very little power, which seems to grow less and less daily. As for Jesuits, they are now banished out of most kingdoms in Europe; so that there is now nothing to fear from either of these quarters, and consequently no necessity of enforcing these laws; neither was it ever the design of the legislators to have these laws enforced by every common informer, but only at proper times and seasons, when they saw a necessity for it, and by proper persons appointed by themselves for that purpose; and yet more properly speaking, they never were designed to be enforced at all, but were only made in terrorem." From J. Holiday's Life of Mansfield, 1797, p. 179.

lost reputation, or unwilling, to make a living in the steady
and industrious pursuit of a regular trade. These informers,
therefore, will not limit themselves to informations of fully-
committed crimes and to lawful evidence of them, but they
have always been found prone to foment crimes, to mature
offences, which otherwise would not have been consummated,
with whatever care they could, to invent evidence and procure
perjured witnesses who share in their reward; so that the
professional informers themselves become in turn a most
criminal portion of the community, and constitute a most
alarming evil, totally inadmissible in a well-regulated society.[1]
I do not mean to discuss here how far the police should feel
authorized in thickly-settled countries, and especially in very

---

[1] Various acts to encourage the apprehending of felons were passed in England, in 1692, 1694, 1699, 1707, 1720, 1741, and 1742, granting rewards from £10 to £50 sterling. By the statute of 1699, besides the £40, an immunity from all parish offices was allowed to any person who should prosecute to conviction a felon guilty of certain crimes. The Tyburn tickets, as the certificates of exemption were called, were sold at high prices, even to £306. In 1813 the reward-money amounted to £18,000. Officers would seduce poor people, especially, to utter counterfeit money, in order afterwards to prosecute them. A certain M'Daniel confessed, in 1756, that he had caused by his testimony seventy men to be condemned to death. When he was tried with two others, the people feared so much his acquittal upon some flaw or other that they were killed on the spot. In 1792 a similar case happened, in which twenty men had become the victims of an informer. In 1817 four police-officers conspired against poor men and were sentenced to death, but released upon judicial informalities by the twelve judges. These conspirators had induced poor women to pass counterfeit money and seized them in the act; they frequently changed small offences into capital ones, for instance if a work-bag had been stolen they swore that it had been tied with a string to the arm and torn from it by violence, thus theft became robbery, and they received £50. Another revolting case happened in 1817, when two soldiers wrestled for a wager of one shilling, and with the greatest difficulty escaped death, the sentence for robbery having already been pronounced, through the perjured exaggeration of the police. Counterfeiters, well known to the police, were frequently not prosecuted, because good customers, but only the utterers. Alderman Wood asserted in 1818, in parliament, that visiting the prisons he had found thirteen men, mostly Irish or Germans, who had received counterfeit money to buy bread, and were seized upon in the act of passing it by the police. These iniquitous rewards were at length abolished in 1818 by an act 58 George III., c. 70; but the abuse respecting counterfeit bank notes, for the convicted utterance of which banks pay £30, remained.

populous cities, for the necessary protection of the community, to make use of crime and vice itself to obtain hints and clues of the criminal doings in the community, for instance by pardoning criminals on condition of their informing the proper authority in future of the procedures of their former comrades. I am too well acquainted with the fact that criminals in large cities act upon most extensive and ingenious plans, and carry on crime upon systems ramified in a thousand directions, including distant agents to dispose of goods, and men who know the law to defend them with perjured witnesses and for rewards which are a share of the criminal plunder. Constables of large cities and experienced agents of prisons are the only ones who have a sufficient knowledge of these often frightfully extensive ramifications, necessarily hidden from the honest part of the community. So much, however, is certain, that although the protection of the honest may render these operations of the police excusable, they are wholly incompatible with right, justice, and sound government, so soon as they are made use of for anything farther than to obtain clues of crimes afterwards fully to be proved upon regular evidence and not on that of the criminal informer alone, or so soon as they are carried to such an extent as to foment and prosper crime.

XXXIII. I have referred so far to common crimes only; but when a government keeps spies, or establishes what is called "a secret police," to report upon the doings and the disposition of the honest part of the community, especially upon their political sentiments, it is engaged in a ruinous and criminal course of measures. To watch and mislead men under false pretences has at all times been considered so dishonorable and shameful an occupation, even by the employers of the spies, that none but the worthless and abandoned will enter upon so disgraceful a trade. All the dangers mentioned in the previous section are in this case increased, for here the question is of dispositions which cannot be strictly defined, and the innocent may be affected; the citizen has no remedy against such espionage, because the reports are made secretly, and therefore may, and generally do, vastly differ from truth; it is of itself an unlawful proceeding of government, which is established to protect and to acknowledge, pronounce and maintain right and law, not to pry into the thoughts and dispositions of the citizens; and the knowledge of the existence of spies and secret police, besides destroying candor, frankness, and the spirit of mutual reliance, engenders immorality by the conviction which the people have that the government consider themselves separate from and opposite to the people. Of all the unfortunate features of that institution which, view it in whatever light we may, appears as one of the worst, most immoral and demoralizing, if indeed there is another equally unjust one in history —the Inquisition, the most deplorable perhaps was that it rendered an extensive system of spies — called familiars — necessary, and, by the help of fanaticism, made espionage and informing honorable among all classes; for there were familiars among the highest nobility and poorest pedlars. And, ruinous as this whole institution has been for Spain, this part of its operation had probably the most mischievous effect upon the national character of the Spaniard, who thereby became distrustful. If we are told that by a system of informers many offences may be discovered which otherwise might never be brought to light, we shall place the whole question at once on its proper ground, by asking that question which we are bound to ask whenever we wish to judge correctly of an institution: What is among other effects its moral operation, always of greater importance than the physical? The many sacrifices which have been offered by the Inquisition are doubtless a grave subject, but it is of little importance that the various writers differ by many thousands. It is the moral effect which this baleful institution has had, which is infinitely greater than all the physical pain which it inflicted with fiendish zeal. Those who were burnt would at any rate slumber now in the grave, but the nation where it flourished continues to be ruined.

The history of every despotic government is replete with

proofs of the misery entailed by informers and a secret police. The informers during the Roman empire form one of its worst features; they grew out of the pestilence of demoralization, and flourished by the public ruin. All that Tacitus says of the delatores, the vermin and pests of human society, and whom he calls " genus hominum publico exitio repertum," is but too true. The secret informations· and summary actions upon them in the former republic of Venice were often awful.[1] All the imprecations in France against the "mouchards" were but too well founded.[2] The secret police under Napoleon in France and all the countries he conquered, in all classes from the highest to the lowest, and the counter secret police to observe the first, were some of the most melancholy traits in that grave period. To the shame of our advanced race, we find that the Chinese penal code makes all anonymous information against a penal offence punishable with death, whether the information be true or not, and any officer who takes upon

---

[1] The brass lion hollow and with open mouth in front of the doge's palace received the anonymous informations.

[2] Within our own times a case has occurred which shows the effects of such a system in all its horror. The elder branch of the Bourbons, after their restoration, soon found that they were not the race of the people,—not national. Their government became uneasy. Conspiracies were suspected; a desire to punish soon grew up. Carron, an officer residing at Colmar, in Alsace, was in 1822 abused by a diabolical intrigue of the ultra-party to commit himself so that a show of an intended insurrection in Alsace might be made. Köchlin, deputy from that part of France, intrepidly published in 1823 the whole plot, for which he was punished. A court-martial sentenced Carron to death; letters to bring the sentence before the court of cassation at Paris, to which Carron had a right by law, were retained by the post-office for some days, and an application to the keeper of the seals for staying the execution until the court of cassation should decide, received answer from Mr. Peyronnet, then keeper of the seals, that he would consider it after a few days, on October 4. In the mean time a telegraphic despatch had ordered the execution of Carron on the 2d October, when it actually took place. And now for the "mouchards." Two of them, sergeants, were made officers; a captain was made chef d'escadron; the two former and another sergeant received each one hundred and fifty francs, and others still the cross of the legion of honor. The French dictionary says, ad verbum Mouchard, with much naïveté, " Those who have the misfortune to employ these abject persons think to disguise their contemptibleness by calling them observers."

himself to proceed upon such anonymous information shall receive one hundred blows, while no individual shall be punishable upon evidence thus obtained. I do not even find that high treason makes in this case an exception, though the code exempts cases of treason from almost every advantage granted to the accused.[1] In Spain the Inquisition proceeded not only upon secret information, but the accused could not learn the accuser and informer—a right frequently though unsuccessfully asked for by the descendants of the Jews and Moors, who were willing to pay for it a high sum.

Governments are frequently desirous either to get rid of individuals against whom they have not sufficient evidence to justify any serious procedures, or to obtain more power by a show of danger. For this purpose they ensnare their victims in pretended conspiracies, or induce them to utter unlawful cries, and the like. This diabolical procedure, to which all despotisms resort if convenient, was technically termed trepanning, under Charles II. and James II. The public trials for treason at the time are full of evidence of this infamous measure, and the diaries and correspondence of the times show us the use of the term. Any free people who omit promptly to impeach a minister guilty or strongly suspected of this crime of trepanning, or even of establishing a system of mouchards, omit one of their most urgent public duties.

The Greeks had probably no systematic secret police, except under the tyrannis. There we find perfect models of it. Hiero I. used to send listeners to the banquets of citizens. The Greeks have various names for these instruments of tyranny.[2] But the absolute democracy of Athens had, if not a regularly organized secret police, its sycophants or informers, a shameless class of men, who were as mischievous in the passionate, wavering, and arbitrary administration of justice of the times of democratic absolutism as the demagogues

---

[1] Sir G. T. Staunton's translation, p. 360.

[2] Aristotle, Pol., v. ix. 3, speaks of them. They were called Ποταγωγίδες at Syracuse. Προσαγωγεύς was another term for a *mouchard*.

were in its politics. The sycophants were considered by the ancients as a natural and unavoidable consequence of absolute democracy, and in this as in many other instances we see the great similarity which all absolute governments, of whatever form, bear to each other, a fact on which we have dwelt already in the first volume.[1] The worst period of the French revolution shows the same.

It is a different question whether governments have a moral right to allow a crime, of which they have knowledge, to mature to a certain degree. Undoubtedly it is a principle of justice as well as of policy rather to prevent crime than to punish it when committed, as has been stated already; but it is not unfrequently of great importance for the public service to punish or otherwise extinguish a criminal act, for instance a conspiracy, of which government may have evidence sufficient for moral but not for legal conviction. Were a government in these cases to proceed in the prosecution at too early a stage of the crime, it would only turn public opinion against itself, by showing itself unable to sustain its charges, and would thus in many cases strengthen the offenders. A government has certainly not an absolute obligation to stay crime of which as yet there exists no legally convincing proof; but it has no right to allow the crime to mature to such a point that citizens suffer thereby, if it have any convincing proof; still less to favor the consummation of crime in any way whatsoever.

XXXIV. Most codes of civilized nations make it a punishable act to omit informing either the proper police authority or the endangered person of an intended crime against the safety of society or the life, health, honor, reputation, or property of an individual, if it can be done without endangering one's self or any third person. The English law does not acknowledge this obligation except in cases of conspiracies against the community or state. The former codes on the

---

[1] See, for instance, Athen., iii., 74; Schol. Aristoph., Plut., 31; Simonides, apud Plutarch., Timol., 37.

continent of Europe made informing after the fact likewise a legal obligation; but all inflicted only a very slight punishment for the omission, because the informer, if not bound by his office, has at all times been held "in universal and natural abhorrence, which the legislator has reasons to esteem."[1] The lightness of the penalty shows that, even in countries where informing is obligatory, the penalty for the omission may be fairly considered as belonging to those which I have a right to consider as an equivalent for the offence, to which I may willingly expose myself if I have reason to disobey the law. Informing, therefore, becomes everywhere an act wholly or nearly wholly one which we must strictly consider as falling within the sphere of political ethics.

On the one hand, a frank and honorable intercourse among the members of society is so necessary for its whole well-being, and informing, without urgent reasons, has been always so much abhorred by honorable men, and, on the other hand, the condign punishment of crime is so necessary for the physical and moral welfare of society, that the rules for an upright citizen need to take both these considerations into account. The establishment of a government in itself in a very great measure relieves the private citizen from the obligation of informing; for all the sacrifices of time, property, and other things made to the government, and the restrictions to which he submits are, for the very purpose, among others, that the government shall protect him and shall find out, prosecute, and punish offences. This is its business. The more a government circumscribes individual action, the less obliged is the citizen freely to assist. This has always been felt. The more restricted a government is, on the other hand, the more it becomes the affair of the people, and the greater ought also to be, and generally will be, the people's readiness to assist the government. Now, I hold it to be a sound rule that a citizen has a fair right to leave it

---

[1] Remarks on the Penal Code of Bavaria, Munich, 1813, published by authority, vol. i p. 221, also p. 211.

wholly to his government to look after all minor offences, for otherwise a citizen might lose his whole time. Police offences, except those of a generally dangerous character, for instance against general health, belong to this class. The citizen, however, ought freely to inform against grave offences or crimes, unless the information would militate against other sacred duties or ties, for instance those of near consanguinity. Yet it must be observed that the citizen is not bound to ferret out the crime if he suspects it only upon rumor or insufficient indications, nor will he find himself obliged or at liberty to inform of offences the apportioned punishment for which he holds to be wholly out of proportion. No honorable man would have felt himself at liberty to inform against a shop-lifter while the English law existed which punished even the first offence with death.[1] Or who would inform, except in cases of utmost extremity, against near relations? The family ties are so sacred and of such primary necessity for society that they must be respected. The Chinese code makes information against superior relations a punishable act. (Staunton's transl., p. 371.) But it is pusillanimous not to inform against, or, where the law allows of individual prosecution, to prosecute crimes or offences which endanger society, its safety or liberty, and the penalties for which are in due proportion to reason and justice. The citizen who omits to take the proper step to bring a murderer, a public defaulter, a conspirator against public liberty, or a traitor, to his just punishment, or who allows a fellow-creature whom he knows to be innocent to be prosecuted or his reputation unjustly injured, loads his conscience with a great offence, and promotes the disregard of public morality, without which society cannot obtain its

---

[1] According to the Spanish law, the descendants of a convict in the first and second degrees are incapable of holding office. What Spaniard would not have condemned a person who should have informed against such a person who might have succeeded in obtaining an office, the crime of the father being forgotten? What must every man think of Lord Bristol, himself a Catholic, when he impeached Lord Clarendon, in 1663, among other things, for having endeavored to bring in popery? Compare Pepys's Diary under July 10, 1663.

highest and noblest ends. He gravely offends against the general moral law. Public spirit and patriotism require him to act even at the price of his own inconvenience.[1] Informing becomes an especial duty when the committed offence continues to affect the rights or essential interests of others, for instance, as observed above, if an innocent person is considered guilty or even only prosecuted, if a slur remains upon the reputation of a man, if he continues to be deprived of lawful property, as by documents we know to be falsified, if the committed crime is an indication that similar ones will be committed, such as theft or the fabrication of false documents, and if the offence is against the liberty and protection of the people, like that of unlawful voting, or falsified returns of polls. Of course it must depend upon the citizen whether he thinks it more advisable to inform the authority or the interested individual.[2]

These rules relate to offences already committed. Respecting inchoate crimes, or any offences of a graver sort, with which an honest citizen may become acquainted, it is too clear upon all grounds of morality, and the love of our neigh-

---

[1] There existed a short time ago, and probably still exists, in one of the American cities, a society of gentlemen mutually pledged to inform against the committing of a certain offence which they considered of great injury to society. That division of responsibility, if I can so call it, so frequently used for iniquitous purposes, was applied here for a good end. The obligation was entered into upon general grounds. The odium attached to individual information, therefore, did not exist; and when the individual case occurred, the odium or reluctance caused by the individual case and by the temporary office of prosecutor vanished and was merged in the general and distinct obligation into which many had previously entered. We have only to glance at history to observe how frequently a similar division has served for the same reason, namely on account of the apparent extinction of personality in the case, for evil ends. I have spoken of this in the Legal and Political Hermeneutics.

[2] The Motives of the Penal Code for the Kingdom of Würtemberg, 1835, say (page 92) that the new code abolishes the general obligation of denunciation existing according to the old laws, because informing is against the general sentiment. Exceptions, however, are made respecting crimes of general danger or if innocent persons are under trial, from which, again, are excepted cases where the accused is by blood or marriage a relative of the individual who might inform, or where knowledge of the fact has been obtained by religious confession.

bor, both in relation to the party who intends to offend and that against whom the offence is intended, that the citizen acquainted with the projected evil is bound to prevent the offence, as far as in him lies, either by dissuading the evil-disposed party, or, if this be impossible or promise no success, by informing the endangered party.

# CHAPTER III.

Associations.—Associated Means, Endeavors.—Associations for the Promotion of Morals.—Pledges.—Trades-Unions.—Ancient Guilds.—Unlawful Combinations for Purposes lawful if pursued by the Individual. — Evil Effects of Trades-Unions.—Disclosures respecting them in Scotland and England.

XXXV. DIVISION and combination of labor, of energy, or of means, and the tendency to association, are, as we have seen, two of the main elements of all civilization. Both develop themselves more distinctly and forcibly with each step of the progress of society, and associated endeavors in a great variety multiply with every advance of civil liberty. Despotism naturally dislikes association; yet each association, if not carefully regulated, bears within it the germ of more or less despotism, either towards others or its own individual members, for the simple reason that it increases intensity of action, separates in some degree at least the associated members from the rest of the community, and subjects them to separate rules of action. We have associations for the promotion of mutual industrial interest, such as insurance companies, for public convenience[1] or objects of public spirit, or, as is frequently the case, for both ends united; associations for the promotion of knowledge in the higher spheres, as academies of sciences, or for the diffusion of general knowledge, common schools, etc.; associations for the promotion of charity or other moral ends, such as societies to promote prison discipline, temperance, or vaccination; religious associations, such as the monastic

---

[1] General insecurity as well as the religious spirit produced innumerable fraternities and associations, sometimes of a purely devotional character, at others for the purposes of public utility and safety, yet connected with religious usages. Such were, for instance, the fratres pontifices, or bridge-brethren, in the south of France, from the thirteenth to the fifteenth century, for the building and supporting of bridges, roads, ferries, hospices, and their safety and police. They degenerated, and were abolished by Pope Julius II.

orders and Bible societies; and political associations. These may be either for mutual protection, as in times of great danger or feebleness of a government, when it is unable to perform certain acts which are nevertheless necessary for men, like administering justice, or common protection in general; or for the obtaining of certain rights or privileges; or, finally, for opposing and ultimately changing a government. These are generally and necessarily for a time secret societies.

It is evident that there are societies which combine several of these objects at once. In 1584 an association was formed in England the object of which was to protect Queen Elizabeth against every attack upon her or her government; a similar one, it is well known, was formed under William III. in 1696, and in a degree made compulsory.[1] The Spanish Hermandad was a league of numerous cities to protect their liberties in seasons of civil war—so common in the feudal times.[2] But these associations of cities, of great importance in the middle ages, and which did the greatest service in the advance of civilization and of the civil liberty of the commons, may be more properly called leagues. The Carbonari were a secret Italian society for the promotion of certain political ends. Ireland has seen of late many political associations, among the rest the so-called precursor society, formed by Mr. O'Connell. The clubs in France at the time of the first French revolution were political associations, which have acquired great notoriety.

Not unfrequently associations, temporary or permanent, have been formed to carry elections, defray their expenses, or pay counsel at disputed elections. We shall find a more convenient place to consider all these strictly political associations, after having spoken of the subject of parties. At this opportunity we shall consider associations in a moral point, and such as exist in the regular state of society, when government is in full operation and neither anarchy nor revolution

---

[1] Trevor, William III., vol. ii. p. 291.
[2] See, for instance, Prescott, History of Ferdinand and Isabella, Introduction.

demands peculiar protection. Finally, we may mention those societies which preserve some religious, moral, or other mystery. In the early stages of society it can be easily imagined that the ignorance and vehement superstition of the whole people at large should make it necessary to make of some great religious truth, for instance the belief in one God, perhaps introduced from some distant and more advanced region, a mystery, for fear that if not kept as such it would soon be entirely eradicated. So likewise may certain scientific truths, militating with the common belief, be exposed to total extirpation by fanaticism, if not kept within a circle of initiated persons; but it seems that knowledge and religion with the white race have become so diffused that no such mysteries are any longer necessary, and that we are thus likewise spared the dangers to which these societies must always expose themselves as well as others.

XXXVI. The law must determine what are lawful combinations and associations and what are not; but there are many which the law cannot and ought not to prohibit, which nevertheless, being either dangerous or injurious, ought to be avoided by the conscientious citizen. The law of all countries says in general that every combination is unlawful which interferes with the just and fair rights of others or of society; but political ethics demands that we should avoid not only all associations which interfere directly with the rights of others, or in a manner that it may be cognizable by law, but also those which have a tendency indirectly to do so, or which in the nature of things lead to that indirect persecution which although not cognizable by law may nevertheless be very oppressive.

The first rule, then, is that we should inquire, Does the association directly or indirectly abridge the free exercise of any fair right of those who do not belong to it? Such associations will in general be the most harmless as have a simple clearly-defined object, openly stated; and especially if they are for mutual industrial interest or the promotion of arts or sciences only. But when the moral conduct becomes the object of associations, it must be remembered that they easily superinduce a spirit of exclusiveness, of supposed superiority, of indirect injury to others by advancing the members of the association only, in the various ways of mutual assistance, and of hypocrisy in some, who, seeing that they are in need of the aid of such an association for worldly purposes, accommodate themselves outwardly to it. Nor must it be forgotten that no moral phenomenon is more common than that the more compact an association becomes, the more its members are apt, be it by the common esprit de corps or by an erroneous feeling of honor, to value the interest of the association higher than any other, and sometimes, as has but too frequently happened, to end in adopting a moral code or standard of their own, to be judged of only by the promotion of the interests of that association. In a free country there is this additional danger, that such associations once formed, and having obtained a strong hold upon the affections and sympathies of its members, most easily become channels and vessels of political agitations and dissensions. Political unions, however, in themselves, have always been so interesting to all members of free states that they alone, without any additional aid, have a sufficient tendency to create divisions and separations, frequently disturbing the plain and easy intercourse of society. Nor can it be denied that experience amply proves that, whenever mixed up with extraneous matters, such clubs become injurious and may easily end in fanaticism of one sort or another. Morality is a general obligation, and every individual ought to promote it as much as in him lies, and keep himself as much untrammelled respecting all moral action as possible. Speaking in a general way, specific pledges will not easily improve the state of society at large, which is promoted by general improvement, instruction, and general diffusion of morality. Yet it cannot be denied that there is a great moral power in mutually countenancing one another by association, and vices may have become so general or have obtained such strong hold upon society at large that the individual, such as most men naturally are, will be too weak or frail to make a bold stand against them. Suppose, for instance, that the vice of gaming has become so general in some or all classes that it actually has infused itself into the whole intercourse of society, and that a man who should make a bold stand against it would not only be derided, but actually cut off in a great measure from that intercourse which is nevertheless necessary for him. Such a state of things has existed. Even then I believe it is far more thoroughly beneficial for society, in most cases, for the individual to take his stand boldly, prevail on others to join his endeavors and promote their common views, than to form a specific society for that purpose. The operation may be at first slower, but will be safer and more radical, without exposing us to the inconveniences or dangers indicated before. Dissension, hypocrisy, pride, the error of seeking the essence of virtue and distinction of goodness in a few definite outward actions only, and indirect oppression are evils carefully to be avoided. Still, it will be admitted that cases of extremity make here as everywhere exceptions. Intemperance has been to this day a national calamity in our country. Innumerable other vices and crimes as well as great misery arise out of it. Temperance societies have had, in many parts of our country, a beneficial effect. Yet even a society with so simple an object has led in some instances to dissension and indirect oppression. It is safe to say, then, that all associations formed for the avowed purpose of regulating the moral conduct of its members by means of pledges should be resorted to by way of exception only. We might otherwise dissolve society into numberless associations of a similar kind, and coercion and violence instead of freedom of conscience would be the consequence.

XXXVII. A species of association which has lately acquired great importance requires to be mentioned here in particular; I mean the trades-unions, or those associations of mechanics which have for their purposes the regulation of wages and time of labor, as well as the turns in which the members of the union shall find employment, or the proportion in which the employment of the unskilled shall stand to that of the skilled.

In former times there existed all over Europe corporations or guilds of mechanics, with monopolies and political privileges. They were necessary for the protection of the humble burgher and infant industry against an unruly aristocracy, as well as in some cases for the transmission of knowledge and skill. Moreover, it was the prominent feature of the times that every mass of men in any way whatever associated was also incorporated. Without them the cities would never have performed their high service in the promotion of civilization and the acknowledgment of the burgher's rights. The various trades were separated by these guilds, but within them the employer and employed had a common interest. The French revolution abolished these corporations, which in turn had, in many cases, become oppressive in the highest degree. Many other countries, for instance Prussia, followed the example, and in England their political influence was totally overthrown by the late reform act. The administration of justice has become general, governments have become national, and skill and knowledge are so diffused that no special protection by way of monopolizing corporations is any longer deemed necessary. The more enlightened countries acknowledge it as one of the most substantial blessings of civil liberty and order that labor, skill, and industry find their proportionate reward in the market open to all. But now associations were formed for the above-named purposes; they divided the employed as a class distinct from and opposite to the employer. Trades-unions may be considered in their relations to law, morals, political economy, and politics in general, as to their general influence upon the safety of society.

Not a few persons believe that all lawful acts may likewise be lawfully done in regulated combination with others; yet it is a principle of the law of all civilized nations that not only unlawful acts become the more criminal if done by combination of many, but also that lawful acts may become unlawful by combination, if the just exercise of the rights of others or the lawful operation and necessary intercourse of society is thereby infringed. Such combination is called conspiracy, and the conspiracy is committed when such a combination has been entered into, though no further combined act may have taken place. An officer may throw up his commission whenever he likes, but if a number of officers combine to throw up their commissions at the same time it justly becomes a punishable act.[1] All this has been repeatedly decided in England and America,[2] and Mr. Livingston in his projected code defines conspiracy, in Art. 683, thus: " Conspiracy is an agreement between two or more persons to do any unlawful act, or any of those designated acts which become by combinations injurious to others." In Art. 689 he says that the agreement " stipulating that the parties to it will not give more than a certain price for any particular species of service or property, or that they will not furnish or render any such property or service for less than a stipulated price, is injurious to that free competition necessary to commerce. And if such agreement be made between two or more persons, not being partners, it is a conspiracy, and shall be punished," etc. It is needless to quote other codes. All, I believe, agree in considering a combination to extort higher prices as unlawful; few, however, declare it with sufficient distinctness equally unlawful for employers to extort by combination lower wages; although the cases do not differ for the political economist, who well knows that the latter combination falls entirely within the sphere of the first; for if the employer extorts lower wages he only extorts a higher price (that is, demands more labor done) for the money which he pays, as in the reversed case the workman wants more money for his labor. That simple

---

[1] It was decided by Lord Mansfield, Burr. 2472, Vertue *vs.* Lord Clive; Ib. 2419, Parker *vs.* Lord Clive.

[2] Mod. R. 10; Ib. 320, The King *vs.* Edwards et al.; 2 Mass. R. 329, The Commonwealth *vs.* Dryden and others. So in New York, by the Supreme Court, in the case of the People *vs.* George M Fisher, Stephen Fowler, and Anthony C. Hoyt.

principle of political economy, that if I buy a barrel of flour for six dollars from A B, A B likewise buys six dollars for a barrel of flour from me, is, though so evident and of primary importance in judging of a thousand relations both of exchange and of right, continually forgotten; in other words, it is always forgotten that money is nothing but a commodity, although the most desired by all. Justice therefore demands as a matter of course that a combination among employers for the purpose of denying higher wages or of lowering the same is as unlawful as that of the employed not to take anything less than a certain amount. Indeed, the act is morally more unlawful, inasmuch as it is easier for the employers to combine than for the day-laborers, and they can generally hold out longer.

XXXVIII. The evil effects of these trades-unions, as they have appeared of late, in many countries, may perhaps be summed up thus: They are oppressive to the employer, who cannot freely choose the workmen he prefers; they interfere with society at large, by interrupting the free course of demand and supply, create unnatural prices, or wholly interrupt entire branches of industry; they necessarily therefore drive capital to other regions, where it will find its natural market, and thus the workman is injured; they promote idleness by procuring for the unskilled the same chance of labor, and, when once established, are oppressive to apprentices, of whom they admit but a small number in order not to increase the number of workmen and consequently the chance of labor; they intimidate and oppress masters and those workmen who are not members; they promote expense and immorality among the members by the strikes, and have it always in their power to injure grievously their employers by selecting periods for their strikes when they are under heavy engagements; they hurt themselves by actually raising wages in many cases above the natural price, and thus make industry flow to other countries; they are the more apt to adopt and follow their own code of morals, the more secret and unlawful they know their proceedings to be; they impose heavy taxes upon the intimidated and fearfully support the guilty of their association. In brief, they form a most oppressive, flagrant, and unrighteous aristocracy, knowing no interest or moral code but their own.

According to our principle, that we ought always to pay proper attention to those cases in which the principle of the subject under consideration has most strongly, distinctly, and consistently shown itself, I will give here a few facts respecting the trades-unions in England and Scotland elicited by several trials and statements before parliamentary committees.[1] Of course it is not meant that all have committed the same outrages, but these are the evils to which they may lead. Trades-unions are originally voluntary associations, but they easily intimidate those workmen who will not join them; they force the masters to employ men of their union only; they fix the proportion of the number of the skilful workmen to the apprentices to be employed; they elect their overseer; they regulate wages and time of labor; and woe to him who disobeys. In many cases refractory workmen have been murdered, or were made blind by vitriol being thrown into their eyes. The colliers of Lanarkshire, taking advantage of the great demand for iron in 1835 and 1836, issued a mandate that no colliers should work more than three days or four in the week, and at the utmost five hours in each day. The order was implicitly obeyed, not only there but in many other counties. They held out several months, and the price of coal was immeasurably raised, so that the total loss from coal monopoly and strike caused by the colliers' combination in eighteen months amounted to £678,000 sterling. The master is forced to employ those whose turn it is on the list: thus the main inducement to industry and skill is annihilated, and the inferior workmen, always more numerous

---

[1] Report of the Trial of Thomas Hunter, Peter Hacket, etc., Operative Cotton Spinners in Glasgow, before the High Court of Justiciary at Edinburgh, January, 1838, for the crimes of illegal conspiracy and murder. By Archibald Swinton, Edinburgh, 1838.

than the skilful, are encouraged. To keep the union from increasing too much, a very large entrance-fee is demanded, and the time of apprenticeship made very long. High rewards are paid for discovering any disobedience, or even for "unshopping," that is, throwing out of employment, highly skilful hands. Secret oaths were taken to keep the first oath itself secret, to inform against refractory workmen, and even to commit assassination of obnoxious masters, if commanded by the secret committee elected by intermediate elections. High sums were paid for assassination, the defence of the assassins carried on by common expense, and false alibis easily sworn to. In single cases the unions must be almost always successful; because, as was stated already, they select for their strikes those periods, if possible, when the employers are most embarrassed and heavy bills are running against them, while those that strike are supported from the common fund. The trades-unions wean the members from their families, and crimes, as is exhibited by statistical tables, have increased lamentably with their increase. The enormous losses which the community at large has suffered during the fifteen years when the unions have been in most vigorous action, and which were ultimately likewise sustained as a matter of course by the working classes, are almost inconceivable. Never has aristocratic monopoly been probably carried out more sternly, ruinously, and barbarously than by the Scottish trades' unions.[1] If it should be objected that the abuse here stated, and undeniably proved by judicial and patient trials as well as by minute statistical inquiries, proves no more against trades-unions in general than murders would prove the unlawfulness of keeping arms in general, we must observe that the cases

---

[1] With regard to Ireland, see Mr. O'Connell's speech, Mirror of Parliament, February 4, 1838.

I would refer the reader to an article on Trades-Unions and Strikes, in the Edinburgh Review for April, 1838, replete with most interesting facts and statistics.

See also Miss Martineau's Tale of the Manchester Strike.

Respecting combinations in general, see Hansard's Parliamentary Debates, 1825. Also, T. Gibson's opinion, in Hall's Journal of Jurisprudence, 226.

are not the same, for trades-unions, if they are for the purpose of extorting higher wages, are in their principle unlawful as well as unjust on moral grounds; that according to the natural course of things, according to the universal character of man, they must lead to oppression and great abuse, as they have done everywhere, though they need indeed not lead to assassination; but that with regard to this latter point we ought also to remember that these awful effects of trades-unions took place not in nations where murder is common, but among the Scotch—a people not prone by any means to violent crimes.

It is not necessary here to mention that unions among the working classes for charitable purposes and mutual support in distress are lawful and highly laudable.

## CHAPTER IV.

Liberty of the Press. — Primordial Right of Communion. — Journalism.— High moral Obligations of Editors. — Temptations in the way of Editors. — Power of Leaders, good or bad, rests upon their seizing upon that principle which is the moving Agent of the Mass. — In what the Power of leading Papers consists. — Conditions which give great power to single Papers. — Populous Capitals in Connection with the Influence of Papers. — Obligation of Veracity peculiarly strong for Editors.—Political Importance of gentlemanlike Tone.— Publishing private Letters.—Dangers of Newspaper Flippancy.—The Political Position of the Clergyman. — Opinion of ancient Theologians. — How far the Clergyman ought to share in the Politics of his Country.

XXXIX. It has been seen that the liberty of the press, or communion by print, belongs properly to the general and primordial right of communion, and ought to be abridged, among those nations which under the developing influence of civilization have arrived at a distinct perception of rights, only in exceptional cases, for instance in a besieged fortress. Communion is absolutely necessary for men, and the free intercommunion of minds by means of print is as necessary for the existence of civilized society as the word of mouth for the daily intercourse of men. The story reported by Ælian is too pointed a caricature of the restriction of communion not to be mentioned here.[1] A certain tyrant Tryzus prohibited talking, in order to prevent dangerous combinations among the citizens. They resorted to communion by gestures; these too were prohibited. The citizens obeyed; but it so happened that some general misfortune touched all of them so deeply that they were on the point of breaking forth in tears. These symptoms of their feelings would likewise have been a sort of communion, and Tryzus ordered his police to prevent and prohibit weeping in the market. Upon this, at

---

[1] Ælian, Var. Hist., xiv. 22.

length, some idea of individual and primordial right, above the government—and that of sighing or crying, it would appear, must be acknowledged to be one—occurred to the patient burghers: they revolted, and the tyrant was slain.[1]

The press is a power, a gigantic power; and can it not in turn become tyrannical, as well as other powers can? The press, and especially the newspaper press, which with its whole organization and all its qualities and powers is now termed journalism, has been mentioned already as one of the mightiest agents in all that interests society, and especially in politics, peculiar to our own times, of which neither the ancients nor the middle ages knew anything. It not only gives increased rapidity, and, in many cases, greater vigor, at least for a time, to political action for better or worse, but it gives to public opinion a new intensity as well as rapidity of action, and even where it is best regulated draws before the public a thousand transactions or events which without it would have remained strictly private, and by the force of public sentiment submits individuals to some sort of public trial. I do not speak here of common cases of slander, but of cases which, however private in their origin, oblige the individual to pay regard to public opinion simply because the case has once been touched upon by the papers and the reputation of an individual is at stake, or in which it is otherwise necessary to disabuse the community. For instance, a London physician of eminence was lately suspected not to have rendered that speedy and humane assistance to a friend travelling in his company on the railroad and suddenly falling sick, which it was believed he ought to have rendered. A long controversy and several statements by the physician and his friends, exculpating him by proof of facts, were the consequence. It would have availed the physician little to go to law, for some-

---

[1] * The Spanish government published an order by beat of drum, at Madrid, prohibiting all persons from speaking of the destruction of the Spanish fleet off Sicily by Admiral Byng (Viscount Torrington) on the 11th of August, 1718. Dispatch of St. Aignan to the Regent of France, Mémoires de Noailles, vol. v. p. 96. I quote from Lord Mahon's History of England, i. 477 (i. 331).

thing was at stake which never could have been fully established by a legal trial, bound as it necessarily is to fixed forms within a fixed sphere. Here the press subjected a private individual to a trial of its own. Similar instances are daily occurring. It is not maintained that this is to be deplored. I merely speak for the present of the fact as showing the new and great power of the press. Very frequently, indeed, it re-establishes reputation, however bitter the trial may be to which the individual must submit in being unceremoniously handled by just and unjust, honorable and malignant editors. But for the press, rankling slander would go on, without being openly inquired into or satisfactorily contradicted, and would be taken for truth in that circle in which it became known, or would leave sinister suspicion.[1]

Whenever a vast new agent of society is brought into play, it takes some time before it and the laws become mutually adapted; it was so when Christianity became a vast social agent, when the commons or third estate rose in importance, power, and political consciousness, when the Reformation became a great agent and diffused knowledge: hence it appears to me that upon examination it will be found that one of the main problems of our times is, and for a long time to come will continue to be, how this agent of the public press, unequalled perhaps in power, at any rate in movability, by any previous one, is properly to co-exist with the rights of the individual, of society, and of the state at once. The struggle through which all great problems must necessarily pass has only begun, and we find on the one hand as much tyrannical abuse of this mighty power as on the other hand we find fruitless or ruinous endeavors to disown its naturalness and

---

[1] The recent case of Lady Flora Hastings is strikingly in point. Bitter indeed as for her this public trial must have been, is it not upon the whole better for her that all has thus become known than that infamy should carry on covert slander? The above was written and going to press when the news of the death of this lady arrived. What was stated in the previous lines has been still more strikingly illustrated. The injured maiden made a dying request that her innocence should be proved by a post-mortem examination. It has been done, and the papers are carrying the certificate of the physicians in/ ᴐ all parts of the reading world.

its necessary place in the course of civilization, as indeed has always been the case when new agents come into existence and play. Crowns have been lost because those who wore them shut their eyes against the press or attempted to strangle it; and societies have been convulsed because the press would act as though it were an agent which justly possessed absolute power. The ministers of Charles X., in their report of July 26, 1830, which preceded the fatal decree that "The liberty of the periodical press is suspended," had this passage: "At all periods, indeed, has the periodical press been only, and it is in its nature to be only, an instrument of disorder and sedition."[1] The same has been said at times, for similar reasons, against printing in general, against the claim of the people freely to read the Bible, against natural philosophy, the study of which was actually abolished in the Spanish universities by a decree of Ferdinand VII., and indeed against all inquiry. The press is like a thousand other things; the question is not, shall we rule without it? It may be interesting by way of speculation to inquire whether it would be better for mankind were there no press; but this is a wholly fruitless inquiry in politics, for the press is a *fact*, a given condition of our period, just as much as the soil forms one of the given conditions for each country, or the clime for each region. The statesman has not to speculate about them, but his laws must take them as facts, and be shaped accordingly. The only question is, how shall we regulate and preserve liberty,

---

[1] This report, signed by seven French cabinet ministers, is a valuable document, which I would recommend for perusal, not to satisfy curiosity respecting what a party considered tyrannical has to say,—this is not the true use which we ought to make of historical documents of such importance,—but because it probably embodies the most important views of one of the two contending parties on that subject in our times. We must never forget that the true principle respecting subjects of magnitude develops itself out of the struggle, and is never produced at once in an absolute and finished manner. United with this report and the subsequent ordonnances must be the spirited protest of the Paris journals and that of the deputies. I believe we do not venture too far if we say that the liberty of the press and consequently the journals had become the pledge and symbol of civil liberty.

public and private, with the press? It is as natural and necessary now as crying was to the subjects of Tryzus. The same question might be raised respecting large cities: do they or do they not promote crime, tumults, rebellions? this is not the question. We have them, we ought to have them, civilization requires them, there they are; the question can only be, how shall we maintain order and liberty with them? A distinguished writer of the last century discussed the subject whether, upon the whole, the disadvantages of easy intercommunication by good roads, especially in cases of invasion, did not overbalance their advantages? He is, upon the whole, against many good roads. But this is not the problem. Roads belong to the social agents of civilization; the question can only be, how shall we govern with them? It would be as rational to ask whether it would not be easier to govern a state composed of blind people. It is for the science of politics proper to indicate how this great agent is to be reconciled and amalgamated with all the other great and indispensable objects of the state or of society at large:[1] here our object can only be to consider the ethic points involved in the great subject.

XL. The whole periodical press, literary, religious, and political, is of vast importance to society; the diffusion of knowledge, truth, error, or falsehood is multiplied. The press at the same time is not unfrequently conducted, partly or wholly, by persons so unqualified and upon principles of moral responsibility so doubtful that it most assuredly deserves the closest and frankest attention. But the general

---

[1] Thus, it has been proposed in an article ascribed to one of the most eminent men of our age that protective societies should be formed against newspaper slander and all attacks upon reputation, partly to discourage subscription to slanderous papers, partly to prosecute them at law with the rigor of united means; and possibly such protective societies may become necessary in some parts of the world. If the press really becomes tyrannical, and the individual should be incapable of resisting it single-handed, societies of this kind would be as necessary as protective unions were necessary in the middle ages against feudal aristocracies.

subject of the present work requires that we should limit our inquiries to the political press. Of this the newspapers form of course the most prominent part, although it seems that history will point out the influence of some quarterly periodicals as very great, because they offer an opportunity for discussions extensive enough to be thorough or detailed, and yet too short to form a work; which discussions often would not have found half as many readers had they been issued as separate books. The periodical reappearance of these works, and therefore the periodical rediscussion of important subjects in their various aspects, increases greatly their power.

Newspapers have become the substitutes of the oral communion in the ancient market, when cities were states; but their action is in some respects greater and more lasting, because print lasts. Journalism is communion multiplied and of swifter action than oral communion; what orally would slowly travel from mouth to mouth, or drop before it had become extensive rumor, is now conveyed within a few hours to many thousands. All the moral obligations, therefore, of a man and citizen which refer to communion in general, hold likewise respecting this species of communion, with this additional characteristic, that in the same degree as this communion is vaster and more powerful, so do all the moral responsibilities connected with it increase in intensity. This appears to be evident: if a man says an untrue thing of his neighbor to a single person, it is an offence of which he ought to be ashamed, yet not so great an offence as if he says the same in an assembly; this again is not so great as if he writes it in a letter to be shown to many; this in turn is a less offence than when the same is coolly stated in a pamphlet. Yet party excitement seems to have almost established it as a principle that the wider and more rapid the action of communication, the less binding are the moral obligations of him who makes them. If there is a class of men upon whom it would be more binding to be good men, good citizens, and true gentlemen than upon any other, that class are editors. To me, the calling of an editor, be it as promulgator, instructor, guardian, or leader, seems a very grave one, however many of them may disregard it themselves; they have peculiar charges in the service of modern civilization, taking this word in its most comprehensive meaning.

Yet every fair observer will acknowledge that many difficulties are inherent in and peculiar to this branch of industry, such, for instance, as that a newspaper, while on the one hand it assumes the charge of informing if not always of instructing, is on the other hand an article of merchandise, and subject, as a matter of course, to all the laws which regulate every demand and supply; and that, owing to the multiplicity of papers, a certain strong language is necessary to effect only a hearing which by language far less strong is obtained in private intercourse, or in works in which arguments may be developed at their full length; or that when a newspaper belongs avowedly to a party it becomes in a degree its organ, and will be, therefore, more careful in not allowing advantages to the opposite party than the private citizen as member of a party feels called upon to grant, while this circumstance likewise is a strong temptation to trench upon the cause of truth. For these and many other reasons it becomes only the more necessary to consider the ethical obligations of conductors of papers. On the one hand we have seen that unshackled liberty of the press is not only a most valuable right of freemen, but society at large is deeply interested in seeing free discussion of all public measures and men protected in as wide a range as public security and morality as well as private rights admit; on the other hand, the licentiousness of the press and its tyranny is a great calamity, and it is exceedingly difficult to maintain the precise line between the two by positive law,— in many cases is absolutely impossible. The moral obligation of the conductors of the press, therefore, becomes the greater from whatever point of view we may consider it. For this purpose it is necessary to dwell on some particulars for a moment longer.

XLI. Some persons believe that the power of newspapers

to lead the public is far greater than it actually is; others undervalue their power. In general it may be observed, as has been alluded to already in a previous part of this work, that leaders, be they citizens in private or in official situations, editors, parliamentary leaders, legislators, reformers, or even monarchs, possess power only in so far as they have the penetration, intellectual or moral vigor, sagacity, instinct, greatness of soul, divination, or whatever else it may be, to seize upon the principal moving agent of the masses or times, to pronounce clearly what the masses feel, and to act out what all more or less consciously strive for or the circumstances of the times demand. This may be for better or worse according to the tendency of that body of men whose feelings or purposes the leader sagaciously pronounces or represents. The chief of a piratical expedition is in this respect as much a leader as the wisest statesman or purest patriot may be for a whole nation in its noblest and grandest efforts. It is true, therefore, that a leader can be such only and in so far as he follows the general impulse or acknowledges the common principle of movement; but it is likewise true that, this once done, a leader greatly concentrates, invigorates, propels, and accelerates. In a leader a party or society becomes conscious of its own wants, endeavors, and energies.

These remarks apply to newspapers according to the degree of leadership which they possess. A remarkable instance seems to be on record. It is confidently reported that when the question of British reform was on the eve of being seriously discussed in the commons, the proprietors of the London Times newspaper sent agents into various parts of England to ascertain how the great body of the people seemed actually disposed respecting this intended great measure. The report was that the people were in favor of it. This once done, no one, I believe, will deny that this paper, in conjunction with others, such as the London Chronicle and the Globe, were of decided and marked service in bringing about this measure. They acted like burning-glasses. Where there are no rays, the burning-glass cannot collect them; but where they are scattered about it, may collect them and direct them powerfully to one point. A paper, the Rhenish Mercury, edited in 1813 and 1814, when the allied powers warred against Napoleon, was, somewhat hyperbolically, yet not without truth, frequently called "the fifth ally,"[1] the other four being Great Britain, Prussia, Austria, and Russia.

The chief papers of the various countries occupy, in this respect, different positions. The more populous the capital of a country, and the more the political and social life of a whole nation is concentrated in such a capital, and at the same time the more the laws or other circumstances prevent a multitude of papers, the greater will be the specific influence of single ones; because the subscription-list of the papers will be greatly increased, which of itself would enhance their influence, and the income of the paper being so much larger, its proprietors have it in their power to unite higher and more varied talent in its service. Papers may thus acquire a power which may be very dangerous or salutary, according to circumstances. In no country, I believe, have papers within their respective countries a greater influence than in France, owing to the peculiar position which Paris as a capital enjoys. Subscription-lists of daily papers have amounted there to twenty thousand. Each paper is not only read by several persons, as is common everywhere, but there are "reading cabinets" in which people throng from morning to night to read them, and some places where a person reads the most important parts to audiences around them. In England, owing to the very different position which London, although much larger than Paris, as being the capital of a less numerous nation, occupies, and because the political life is far more diffused in all parts of the country, papers do not exercise such dictatorial power. In France likewise it is, as it seems, on the decrease in the same proportion as the communities at large acquire more and more distinct political life and action.[2]

---

[1] By Mr. Görres.
[2] An extensive view of the circulation, and remarks upon the influence, of the

In the United States, where there is no capital to be compared to Paris or London, where the political action which otherwise might become dictatorial is broken by the circumstance of the population being scattered over a vast country, by the numerous state legislatures, and by the great political action each community enjoys, the leading influence of the papers is comparatively small. Yet all papers, it will be allowed, possess a propelling power in their sphere. Even if we consider many papers as nothing more than letters written to subscribers, they receive an influence from their uniformity in writing the same to many, from their constant repetition, and, what is not the least, from the fact that anything in print, even although he who prints may not be held in universal esteem either for rectitude of conduct or capacity of mind, has for most men some sort of authority; at any rate, whatever stands before our eyes in print receives more attention than what is uttered by word of mouth, or pen and ink alone.

---

London papers and periodicals are to be found in a work entitled "The Great Metropolis," 1837, London and New York. The facts collected there are of high interest. The article "Newspapers" in McCulloch's Commercial Dictionary contains most valuable statistical information, especially respecting Great Britain. For remarks on the history of Newspapers, and their existence in the various countries in the world about ten years ago, see the article "Newspaper," in the Encyclopædia Americana. It is well known that within the last few years a government paper in Turkish has been established in Constantinople; while the Sandwich Islands as well as New South Wales have theirs. About eight years ago a weekly paper called the Cherokee Phœnix was established at New Echota, in the state of Georgia, printed partly in Cherokee, partly in English. Gradually, however, the Cherokee part in it seemed to diminish, and I am not aware whether it still exists. The newspaper has become so decided an accompaniment of our civilization that wherever it extends the newspaper likewise takes its root. Even the negro colonists at the infant colony of Liberia have their paper.—For a general estimate of the papers issued by the American press, see the American Almanac, annually issued in Boston.—The newspaper is emphatically a concomitant of modern European civilization. The Chinese have long possessed a paper in their capital; but it is only an official promulgator. [A number of newspapers now published in the United States (1874) for number of subscribers compare with the most popular European ones, and for enterprise in collecting news from various parts of the world far outstrip, it is believed, any published outside of England.]

XLII. Though daily or weekly papers are expected to give an account of all the most interesting facts which occur, to be in a degree the cast of actual life as it passes on, presented for the calm consideration of the beholder, it is advisable for every paper that it should have one branch of communication in which it is peculiarly strong and may be depended upon, of whatever sphere this may be. Thus alone it can calculate upon lasting and considerable influence. Steadiness and singleness of purpose have here as everywhere else a great effect. Let the editor clearly know himself, in what branch he is capable of being a guide, and in what he ought to attempt merely to be a reporter of what occurs.

It is not only allowable, but, I believe, desirable and necessary, that parties, societies, institutions, of importance and engaged in a decisive movement, should have their avowed organs, papers to which the community can at all times look for the particular view which that part of society takes of specific cases. But this in no way disengages such an organ either from the common and eternal obligation of truth or plain morality, which must ever regulate the intercourse of men, if society is to be maintained; still less does it allow any one actually to sell his talent or conscience either for specific reward or for the profit expected from subscription.[1] This would be a prostitution of mind and soul. In no case whatsoever can an editor be allowed to utter a known or suspected falsehood, or imprudently to assert anything against the reputation of individuals or societies. It is his bounden duty first to inquire. The assertion that if false it will be contradicted is of no avail. This would equally well apply to many falsehoods in private life, and the obligation of truth is general; but though falsehoods uttered in papers may in many cases be expected to be contradicted in large cities, where there are many opposite papers, or if vented against eminent men, it

---

[1] It has happened that an English paper wilfully slandered a respectable lady, merely to come into notice by the ensuing trial, which was worth more to the paper than it lost by the fine. Goede, if I recollect right, mentions a case in his England, Wales, etc., Dresden, 1806.

must not be forgotten that the contradiction does not necessarily flow in the same channel and to the same parts of the country. There cannot be any doubt that a man may be seriously injured by false assertions, leaving, even if contradicted, shades of suspicion, which all who are vain of their own peculiar sagacity are ever ready to adopt, especially if the attack be systematically repeated. Not only may contemporaries be deceived, but posterity likewise. A newspaper ought ever to keep in mind that it acts in a most unfair and ungentlemanly manner by using that advantage which it daily has over a private individual of uttering to many hearers whatever it pleases. If hints and insinuations are highly reprehensible in private intercourse, they are on this account far more so in newspapers.

It would be hardly necessary to mention that if in any situation the pampering of vitiated or criminal appetites is one of the greatest derelictions from duty, it becomes tenfold so in newspapers. It is no answer that the respectable or moral part of the community will not read them. Perhaps not; but many do read them who are vitiated by these accounts and become more and more confirmed in their disposition. Any person who has paid attention to the unfortunate portion of the other sex, and to criminals in general, well knows that lascivious papers as well as the constantly repeated detailed accounts of atrocious crimes do infinite mischief in all countries.[1] There is not the slightest testimony of competent

---

[1] Reports of trials are necessary; the public are deeply interested in them; but they differ from those accounts of crime and atrocity which depict merely to satisfy a vicious craving for atrocious stories, or represent vices and offences with levity. There are weekly papers which occupy a large part of their columns with these accounts, accompanied by disgusting wood-cuts. There exists an American weekly periodical, called the Terrific Register, etc., the title itself being a register of everything that is loathsome and criminal. Quite similar periodicals exist in England and France. There are several mentioned in "The Stranger in America." Many criminals have not only been originally familiarized with crime by such accounts, but, as they have confessed, their appetite was first excited by it. This is not a fit place to discuss the psychologic phenomenon—the fact may well be mentioned—that frequently the desire of incendiarism, and sometimes that of poisoning, is awakened by accounts of these crimes.

persons to the contrary, that I am aware of. But we need not speak of these two extremes only. There are many other injurious dispositions or inclinations which may be pampered, developed, sped to a ruinous extent, by the papers. Ridiculing whatever commands respect, with that zest which for many persons mere boldness or impudence ever has, and which is so often mistaken for wit; attacking directly or indirectly private character; seasoning with gross personalities excitement of all sorts arising from political and religious fanaticism, hypocrisy, or narrow-mindedness; making light of the laws of the land;—all these evils may be greatly promoted by newspapers. They may indeed be caused by any writing; but newspapers are more widely diffused and constantly renewed, hence if bad their danger is greater. Many papers act in times of excitement as though there were no danger in throwing brands at random among combustibles, as if their highest duty were to foment and disturb, and as if they were not conscious of the infinite concatenation of everything good or bad in the millions of elements constituting society, intercourse, and national life.

In continually making overstatements,[1] or, what is of course still worse, habitually employing misrepresentations, which generally are far worse than positive falsehoods, because so much more insinuating, language loses its proper value, and part of the community accustom themselves to look upon all similar assertions as not to be trusted, so that truth can no longer rouse from torpor or find entrance with those to whom it is not advantageous or palatable. This is a state of things which very frequently takes place in times of great excitement. The spirit of veracity and with it of honesty and courtesy flies, and a considerable part of the community becomes morally

---

[1] Instances are unnecessary: still, one may stand here for many, and is extraordinary enough. A London daily paper, one of the first of its party, said in August, 1838, that every true Englishman's blood must curdle at the idea that Lord Durham had proposed, at a public entertainment in Canada, the health of the President of the United States. Even merely as an entertaining anecdote I think it is not undeserving of a place in a note.

blunted. Society is not only interested in a general gentlemanlike intercourse on account of general convenience and refinement, but free states are, in my opinion, for political reasons deeply interested in a general esteem of gentlemanly propriety, founded upon a nice feeling of that honor which is ashamed of doing anything even slightly mean, upon mutual acknowledgment and readiness to serve, or absence of selfishness, and upon habitual avoidance of what may hurt one's neighbor, which elements are perhaps the most prominent in the character of the true gentleman. In this respect politeness, decorum, acquire political importance. Cicero and Washington fully acknowledge it in their writings. Newspapers, however, may very largely and essentially contribute to lower this sentiment by ungentlemanly personalities, and in general by discarding those rules which are universally acknowledged in well-bred society and from which they can never be absolved.[1] "Nothing is easier," wrote Erasmus (Jortin's Life of Erasmus, i. 257), " than to call Luther a blockhead; nothing more difficult than to prove him one." Editors ought to remember, likewise, that, as a uniformly gentlemanlike behavior gives, according to all experience, great influence in deliberative assemblies, so does a paper acquire a very powerful aid from a uniformly unruffled gentlemanlike tone. Its words will be taken in their full value; its arguments will be allowed more readily; its sincerity will find greater credence.

Is it necessary to mention here that editors sport with most sacred rights if they publish private letters without being authorized, and that in these cases they constitute themselves what we have seen to be one of the most hateful features of despotism—a secret police?[2] It is not unfrequently the case

---

[1] That scurrilous papers use all sorts of language is natural; but both in England and America leading papers forget themselves frequently. A distinguished citizen of the United States was frequently called, during one of the late most exciting discussions, by opprobrious names, that alluding to his name not excepted. A leading London paper of December 22, 1834, speaks of the "goosehead patriot of Charing Cross." The duke of Wellington was called "blockhead" during the reform excitement.

[2] * That to do this is against law unless permission of the writers [or their

that single editors, and among them many who have had no other preparation for their task than that of having been compositors, assume the task of judging of all subjects, of politics, literature, theology, or the fine arts. Leaving their presumption out of the case,—which must draw the ridicule of the considerate upon them,—they lower that tone of reverence which, whatever may be said to the contrary for the sake of flattering, is indispensable for the true life of every individual and of all society. Where skill, talent, industry, knowledge, learning, perseverance, proved rectitude, experience, professional reputation, no longer receive that due share of regard and influence which talent, virtue, and reputation ought to enjoy, to distinguish human society from animal herds, it cannot, it will not prosper. Folly must necessarily supersede wisdom, arrogance must outweigh worth. I cannot conclude this section without mentioning the disingenuousness of giving garbled reports. It is a mere subterfuge, unworthy of an age in which it is largely acknowledged that in all human interests common sense must aid us in ascertaining and maintaining truth, to say that in having given mutilated and garbled reports we have asserted nothing false. Such a report may be one of the worst, nay, most infamous, falsehoods.[1]

It does not lie within our scope to speak of the general advantages and disadvantages of an extensive news press, the diffusion of knowledge on the one hand which it undoubtedly promotes, and the superficiality and hastiness of argument on the other; or the unity of feeling which it creates in large countries by aiding that general sympathy and greater uniformity of feelings and desires, without which liberty cannot avoid constant exposure to partial and provincial com-

---

heirs or other representatives] be obtained was fully settled in the case of Pope *vs.* Curll, June 5, 1741, by Lord Hardwicke, quoted by Lord Mansfield in the famous case of Miller *vs.* Taylor, respecting the unauthorized print of Thomson's Seasons, 4 Burr. 2303. Holliday's Life of Mansfield, p. 216.

[1] An article, ascribed to Lord Brougham, on the Abuses of the Press, in the Edinburgh Review for April, 1838, deserves to be read: though the author appears to place some evils in too bold a light.

motions. Upon the whole, the good derived from newspapers is decided, and, though it were not, it is certain that they form one of the conditions of modern social life: we must endeavor, therefore, to have them as sound, respectable, and true to every good cause as possible. All are interested in this. Vicious papers should be frowned down and lose all support; active and good ones ought to meet with all possible fair support.

XLIII. It is desirable that we should consider the press in one more view. The state or a society cannot be supported by those three branches alone of which we have spoken on previous occasions; namely, the legislative, judiciary, and executive. A power is necessary which penetrates where those powers cannot reach: it is the censorial power, that power which watches over morality, private life, and industrial economy, so far as they form integrant elements of the commonwealth. The ancients embodied this power in institutions. In Rome it was the censorship, which Cicero calls the magistratus pudoris et modestiæ. But the sphere of the censor extended farther than merely to what we should strictly express by morals: the censor watched, for instance, over the agriculture and took official notice of a neglected farm. The areopagites in Athens, and the Spartan ephori, had a similar tutorial power. We moderns have not enacted this censorial principle into an institute, but our states are societies like theirs, and we cannot dispense with the principle any more than they could; that is, we too want a power which will impel the indolent and restrain the licentious. We do not constitute, however, this power into an institution; we leave the censorial action of society, with very few exceptions, which include as a matter of course public immorality, to the general action of public opinion. This public opinion, which we have acknowledged already as so mighty a power, appears, therefore, in this case likewise as an indispensable agent of society. It is not necessary to investigate here how far the press may be considered as leading public opinion: it suffices to consider that they are closely connected. We all know, moreover, that wherever there exists in cases like the present any connection at all, there is likewise a continual reciprocal action and reaction. The papers, therefore, stand in a close connection with this censorial power of the state—necessary, and yet so easily becoming tyrannical in its exercise; a power which it may be as wrong to weaken by making light of vice, as to use despotically to the discomfort of the individual.

XLIV. Owing to the peculiar relation in which the clergyman stands to his flock, it is necessary that we should consider for a moment his position with reference to political ethics. It is a question solely appertaining to politics proper, whether it be wise or necessary that the clergy should be represented as a separate body in the legislative assemblies, whether it ought not, or under what circumstances it ought, to be considered as forming a separate "estate" by itself. We can occupy ourselves only with the question whether there are any rules applicable peculiarly to the clergy to guide their action in matters relating to politics.

The sacred charge which a priest, clergyman, or minister has of instructing and guiding the people is so necessary and constant a one, that from the earliest to the latest times of Christianity there have been distinguished theologians who have maintained and urged that not only should the clergy nowise occupy themselves with politics, but that they should continue faithfully to discharge their sacred duties unconcerned about the government, even though a usurper swayed the supreme power. It is, so maintained those theologians, no matter of theirs.[1] I am well aware that in the earlier times

---

[1] Among the many passages which might be quoted I will instance but the following. See the History of the Gallican Church (in French), vol. i. 1, 2, year 383, respecting the conduct of the Spanish and Gallic bishops, and of St. Martin himself, towards the tyrant Maximian; the letter of St. Ambrosius (Ep. lvii., ad Eugen.) to the usurper Eugenius, who was placed on the throne by Arbogastes the Frank when Valentinian II. was strangled; the letter of Gregory the Great to Phocas, who had massacred the emperor Maurice and his family (lib. 13,

of Christianity this view was sometimes taken partly on the ground, or at least partly originated from the belief, that the clergy were too sacred to occupy themselves with the so-called merely worldly affairs of the laymen.[1] Such views were natural when an ascetic spirit was likewise natural; and, considering the turmoil and warring confusion of the times, it was a view not without its salutary effects. Nor am I ignorant that in not a few cases the Catholic church maintained this view to make the clergy, the church, the more independent and compact in itself. But these were not the only grounds, nor were they the lasting reasons, upon which the above view was supported.

XLV. Our times have arrived at different convictions. We believe that governments exist according to the decrees of God, which ordained man to be a social being, and to have reason that he might maintain right; we believe that civil freedom is as sacred and holy a cause as any on earth, and that every one ought cheerfully and conscientiously to contribute his aid for supporting it. A minister or priest, there-

---

Judic. vi., Ep. xxxi., ad Phocam); the protocols of the clerical assemblies of France (in French), vol. iii. p. 686, et seq.; and, on pages 90 and 91, the answer of pope Gregory XIII., which ever since has been considered as a rule of conduct. We all know very well that the church has but too frequently meddled with politics; but these were at least the professed and acknowledged principles. As to Protestant theologians, there have been some, indeed, who taught contrary principles, but far more professed the same. Quite recently, in 1839, the Methodist conference in New Jersey passed a resolution, if the papers have reported correctly, declaring that any clergyman who should hereafter become a candidate for the state legislature or congress would receive the general disapprobation of the conference.

[1] Eusebius says, "One description of Christians live a higher life than that of the founders of Greek and Roman freedom. . . . He who has chosen out this life to himself, who is dead to the lower life of mankind, who lingers on earth with his body only, and dwells in thought and with his soul in the heavens, looks down on this world as it were contemptuously, like a deity." In another passage the same author calls the laity the lower class, because they care for household concerns, engage in judicial business, carry on trade or agriculture, and for learning and hearing the word of God have appointed fixed days only.

fore, ought to give a good example in the performance of our civil duties. I think they ought to vote whenever called upon, if it does not interfere with their clerical duties, or if they have not otherwise specific reasons to abstain from it. But it seems that no one ought to guard himself more strictly against meddling, directly or indirectly, with politics, taking part with one or the other side, than the clergy. There are many powerful reasons, which perhaps may be comprehended under the following heads.

A minister will necessarily lessen his influence and the good he may do, as the messenger and fosterer of peace and love, in the same degree as he sides strongly for or against a measure or party. All are Christians, and to all he should be a friend, an unsuspected and unprejudiced friend.

The more ministers meddle with politics, the more, in the natural course of things, is religion carried over into politics, and the more we are, consequently, exposed to fanaticism and persecution, open and violent, or secret and indirect. We cannot be too careful of leaving these two elements separate. Shall history have recorded so innumerable and melancholy accounts in vain? so many proofs that religion, instead of being the balm of life, becomes, if once brought into contact with party strife, the fiercest of all excitements? The history of the Netherlands, when most of the ministers had become politicians, and persecutions and executions of the wisest and purest, such as Barneveldt, were the consequences, would alone suffice, if honestly and attentively perused, to check our rashness in this respect forever.

It is not only against the most essential interests of the minister and of the cause for which, if pure, he lives, when the pulpit is turned into a rostrum of political strife; it is also unfair in the highest degree. The minister has not been appointed nor is he supported for that purpose. Merely regarding him as a gentleman, he ought never to make use of that place where no one can answer him, to debate politics. Is he not, among gentlemen, considered peculiarly exempt from insults because he is known to be unable to answer them like other men? On a similar principle he ought to abstain from political discussions or allusions in the pulpit.

Ministers, like all other men whomsoever, from the president to the constable, are apt to mistake opposition to them personally, or to certain steps of theirs, for opposition to their whole cause and to the principles or systems which they defend. But as the cause of the ministers, for which they professionally live, is religion, they are, upon this principle common to all men, apt to mistake any opposition or resistance to them for an opposition to religion. Hence partly the great vehemence and inveteracy whenever religion is mixed up with politics.

The minister or priest has naturally much influence over part of his flock: on this ground it becomes dangerous to the people if they abuse this influence in making it serve for political ends. Civil liberty can nowhere exist where the clergy act thus against their own sacred calling. That the clergyman cannot observe these rules if he strives for or accepts of political offices, and must interfere by doing so with his own essential efficiency as a clergyman, is evident. The English revolution, as well as the history of the British court, furnishes ample proofs.

XLVI. I do not recommend political indifferentism. On the contrary, I believe that, generally speaking, the clergy in our times urge far too little the importance and sacredness of all civil duties and political virtues upon the people. Let them cultivate and expound the holiness of obedience to the laws of the land, of love of liberty, of the fruitfulness of public spirit for the community as well as for him who possesses it, of the inspiration of patriotism, of the instructive, invigorating, and tempering effect of the study of our own history; and if they make these virtues gush forth from the heart like pure and native streams to nourish and irrigate a thousand different plants, the ministers will not be idle as citizens, but will form, even in a political point of view, a most invaluable class of men. But so soon as they turn the Bible to support or attack one measure or the other, they cannot but diffuse mischief. In cases of extremity, when the land is in danger by invasion, when liberty is to be defended by war, then indeed let them mount the pulpit and inspire their hearers with all the life they can; when citizens, faithful to their country, suffer hunger and plague, besieged by the enemy, let them exhort and comfort and strengthen, as those of Leyden did against the Spaniards, as George Walker did in Londonderry in 1689.[1] Who that believed William III. a benefactor to England would not thank Walker for his conduct? On the other hand, we have the instance of the hermit Nicolas of Flüe, who, when the Swiss cantons in 1481 were on the point of disunion because they could not agree on a division of Burgundian booty, and when the danger had reached its highest point, darted forth from his solitude, went among the confederates, and called for peace in the name of that God who had given them so many victories. His words were penetrating, his admonition powerful; he saved his country. He could not have done it had he habitually or occasionally interfered with politics.[2] The Rev. Dr. Witherspoon was one of the signers of the American Act of Independence. Those times were of an extraordinary character; but even in those excited times he continued to exhort from the pulpit, to show a spirit strong in resisting any call to surrender the rights of freemen, yet ready for reconciliation upon the condition of the security of those rights.[3]

Nearly the same may be said of the ethico-political obligations of schoolmasters with reference to their pupils. Let them cultivate true and generous patriotism.

---

[1] Trevor, Life of William III., vol. ii. chap. 3.

[2] Johannes von Müller, Swiss History, vol. vi. p. 299. A very brief account may be found in the Swiss History forming part of Lardner's Cabinet of History.

[3] For instance, in his Pastoral Letter from the Presbyterian Synod of New York and Philadelphia, in 1775, written after the battles of Bunker Hill and Lexington.

# BOOK V.

## CHAPTER I.

Voting.—Principle of Unanimity; of Majority and Minority.—Deliberative Procedures.—All who have a right to vote ought to vote.—According to what Rules.—(Election Statistics.)—Voting for Officers.—When we ought to abstain from Voting.—Influencing Elections.—Canvassing.—Intimidation, individual and official.—Bribery.—Severe Laws against it at Athens.—Mutual Insurance Companies for Bribing at Athens.—Bribes of common Voters.—Bribing Judges; Legislators.—Bribes by a Government of its own Citizens.—Bribes by foreign Powers.—Betting on Elections.—Election Riots and Disturbance around the Poll.—Various other Election Malpractices.

I. VOTING is the usual way of ascertaining the disposition of any number of men or a society respecting the adoption or rejection of a certain measure or person. Whenever a number of men must come to a final conclusion and joint action, voting must be resorted to if there is not unanimity among them. By voting on a large scale, public opinion passes into public will. The ancients were acquainted with voting, and had largely introduced it into politics; they had majorities and minorities; but in the middle ages the principle of unanimity, and, in cases where mere rejection of some proposed measure did not suffice, of forced unanimity, a principle we act upon still in England and America in jury verdicts, was in many cases adopted. The election law of the German emperor, of 1356, called the Golden Bull, decrees that if the electors shall not have chosen an emperor within thirty days they shall have nothing but water and bread until choice be made, and that when the election has ultimately taken place it shall always be considered as unanimous.[1] A single voice

---

[1] Constitutio Aureæ Bullæ, tit. ii. 5 and 6.

against a bill at the diet of Poland was sufficient for its defeat. Any single member of the ancient Aragonese Cortes had the power to put a stop, by his dissent, to the progress of any measure during the whole session.[1] Many instances might be added. In other cases, for instance when the council of free cities voted, a majority of three-fourths was requisite for the passing of a proposition.[2] There were many reasons why procedures appearing to us so surprising were natural in those ages. In a future part of this work we shall recur to this subject, when we have to treat of the citizen as representative, and of Instruction. Here it may be observed that the deputies in the middle ages were agents sent from more or less independent bodies or corporations, not representatives of nations, which nations or states were not yet considered and felt to be one organic whole; people had not yet re-learned— for the experience of the ancients had been lost—that the excellence of a measure is not an absolute one, that people therefore may widely differ in their views respecting laws, even though passed; and parliamentary management and the laws of deliberative assemblies had not yet become settled and developed; nor is it so even to this day in many nations whose state is one of political infancy.[3]

---

[1] Prescott, Ferdinand and Isabella, 2d edit., Introd., xciii.; Schmidt, History of Aragon, Leipsic, 1828 (in German), 6th division, Constitution.

[2] Among other works, see Sismondi's History of the Italian Republics, vol. xiv. ch. 126.

[3] The American or English reader, brought up almost from early youth in an acquaintance with, and in many respects even under the influence of, the parliamentary law and usage—for it extends to our very schools—considers many things indeed most natural and hardly worth reflection which nevertheless required ages to become acknowledged, and for want of which civil liberty, or at least the expedition of the common business, could not prosper. All usages and laws which relate to debating, such as we know them, for instance as they are embodied in Hatsell's Precedents of Proceedings in the House of Commons or Jefferson's Manual of Parliamentary Practice for the Senate of the United States, are of essential importance to liberty itself, and they must be considered as one of the safeguards of liberty which we possess in advance of the ancients. Jeremy Bentham has systematically treated of this subject in his Tactics of Legislative Assemblies—a work which contains much that is excellent. To form an idea

The more civil liberty becomes acknowledged and protected, the more important also becomes the subject of voting. There is no subject connected with voting, that I can think of, which is not deserving of great attention, from the question who shall have a right to vote and for what, to the mere external conveniency and security of the poll and other measures of election police. The extent of the right of voting, as to citizens, and the subjects which shall depend upon voting, the expediency of frequent voting, of direct or mediate election, the age of voters, their registering, the open vote or the vote by ballot, the legal obligation of voting, the distribution of polls, their accommodation, what subjects shall depend upon mere majorities, what shall require two-thirds of the votes, the question of majorities and pluralities, of judges of elections, of their managers,—all these subjects are either in

---

how piteously people had formerly to struggle, for want of experience in this means of ascertaining and guarding deliberative truth, and how difficult it was for them, with the best wishes, to observe deliberation and come to any conclusion, the reader may peruse, for instance, the account given of the French diet in 1614, in Raumer's History of the Sixteenth and Seventeenth Centuries, illustrated by Original Documents, vol. i. p. 438, et seq. Well may Mr. Raumer end this communication with the words, "All these manuscript sources of information confirm the fact that fixed form and rights were wanting to these assemblies. There was much ado about nothing." The whole first French revolution is one continued melancholy instance of the want of this law and usage. For a whole week the members of the assembly would debate and inflame one another, without having even so much as a question before the house. Dumont, the well-known editor of Mr. Bentham's works, relates, in his Reminiscences of Mirabeau and the two first Assemblies, edited by J. L. Duval, an instructive anecdote. He says, "These primary assemblies [to elect deputies] were at a loss how to organize themselves and to make an election. During breakfast, at Montreuil-sur-Mer (if I recollect right), our landlord gave us an account of the tumult and embarrassment of their meetings: two or three hours had been lost already in palavering and disorder; a president, a secretary, ballots or votes, counting the votes, all this was unknown. Dumont and his friends, in mere joke, drew up some regulations. The host, delighted, took it, and when Dumont arrived at Paris the papers bestowed much praise on the commune of Montreuil, on account of the greater order with which the election had been carried on than anywhere else." In order to have a just idea of British constitutional history it is necessary likewise to follow up the history of parliamentary usage.

principle or practice of the greatest importance, and must be treated of in politics proper.

II. The question has been made, whether a citizen, possessing the right to vote, ought not to be legally bound to vote for general elections, as the citizen is obliged to serve on juries.[1] Why, it is asked, should those, for instance, who possess most property and receive the full benefit of the law, from indolence, superciliousness, or cowardice be allowed to refuse to join in that manner of expressing public opinion or of appointing law-makers which the law of the land establishes? It cannot be denied that affixing a penalty for unexcused omission of voting would have this advantage at least, that the public opinion respecting the obligation of every citizen lawfully to aid in the politics of his country, and the discountenance given to political indifferentism, would be fixedly pronounced by law. But there would also be difficulties in the way, deserving attention. If the penalty were imprisonment, it would be a very harsh measure in many cases; if it were a fine, it would be difficult either to make it expansive enough to strike the rich and poor with equal force, or to prevent tyrannical exaction, to which all extensive fines are but too liable. The case, in whatever light it may be viewed, however, differs essentially from that of the jury, as the slightest attention will show. The subject, as being one of right alone, belongs properly to politics; but it is for political ethics to consider the moral obligation of the citizen to go to the poll. We have treated already of the bad motives and mischievous tendency of political apathy or supercilious-

---

[1] The ancient Galli punished, according to Cæsar, B. G., v. 56, absence from or coming too tardy to armed popular assemblies, with death. This is somewhat strong. In Athens, those who attended received three oboli, called the ἐκκλησιαστικόν, except such as came too late, as the sans-culottes of Paris were paid for attendance when the first revolution was highest. This is dragging the suffrage into the mire at once. It draws the poorest, even the paupers, to the poll, and they, finding their account in elections, will increase their number. It makes of elections schools of idleness, which we have seen it is one of the first interests of society to repress, and extinguishes every spark of public spirit.

ness. A man who from indolence or blamable disdain does not go to the ballot-box knows little of the importance of the whole institution of the state, or must be animated by very little public spirit; or he deserves the mantle of lead which Dante apportions to cowards in the lower regions. There seem to me to be two rules of perfect soundness and elementary importance in popular politics.

1. There is no safer means of preventing factious movements of any kind, and the state from falling a gradual prey to calamitous disorders, wherever the franchise of voting is enjoyed on an extensive scale, than the habitual steady voting of all who have the votive right at all primary elections; and

2. The moral obligation of depositing without fail one's vote increases in the same ratio as the right of suffrage extends, which right will necessarily more and more extend with modern civilization, so that with increasing civilization this obligation of voting increases.

When democratic absolutism and fearful corruptions had reached their height in ancient Greece and several places of Lower Italy, it was natural that some philosophers laid it down as a maxim that a man who loved wisdom should not meddle with politics, and included in this meddling with politics the voting in the place of assembly. When the ascetic spirit of the middle ages, partly from misunderstood disregard of this world, and the transplanting of asceticism from Asia into Europe, and partly from the troubled state of Europe, was a natural effect of the state of things, we cannot be surprised at finding it again and again recommended that we should withdraw as far as possible from this wicked world and all its affairs. Our times, however, move on a different principle—that of substantial, practical, civil liberty, in conjunction with open, public civilization and knowledge, not merely contemplative knowledge retired within itself. There is no great principle which has ever actuated mankind that has not had likewise its inconvenience for the individual; so has the main moving principle of our times; but we are not on that account absolved from conscientiously acting upon it and acting it out. Therefore, if we have a mind honestly to join in the great duties of our period, we must act as conscientious citizens, and if we mean to do this we must go to the poll. It is, I repeat it to my young readers, of primary importance, and the more they read history the more they will feel convinced of it. The more extended the elective franchise is, the more it must likewise extend to those persons to whom time is of little value, to people who make a feast-day, perhaps a riotous day, of the election-time. They whose voting is the least desirable are the surest to be at the poll; but the industrious mechanic, the laborious farmer, the man of study, the merchant and professional man, in short all those who form the sinew and substance of the state, feel it a sacrifice of time to go to the place of voting, where they are not unfrequently delayed for a long time by the other class from depositing their vote, especially in populous places. They are, therefore, the more imperatively called upon to keep constantly before their minds how important it is that they should vote, and not leave the election to be decided by those who have the smallest stake in society. Let no man be prevented from voting by the consideration of the loss of a day's labor, or the inconvenience to which he may expose himself in going to the poll.[1]

---

[1] Election statistics are of much interest. Among other things, they show the interest taken in elections.

In Athens not more than 5000 votes were generally given on the most interesting questions. (Thucyd., viii. 72; Boeckh, Public Economy of Athens, Eng. trans., vol. i. page 309, note.) For ostracism 6000 votes were requisite. The whole number of citizens—that is, as I understand it, of voters, not the children included—amounted to about 20,000 or 25,000. (Boeckh, i. book i. 7.) So that about the fifth man made use of his franchise.

In France we find that in 1834 the number of electors was 171,015, the number of real voters 129,211. In 1837 there were 198,836 entitled to vote, and 151,720 did vote. That is, in 1834 there were 151 votes given out of 200, and in 1837, 153 out of 200. (Paris papers of September, 1837.) Thus, in France about three voted out of four who had the right.

The proportion greatly decreases with the extension of the franchise, as will be seen from the following statistics of the United States. The reason is probably twofold. First, the extension of the franchise itself is, unfortunately, a

III. If it is important for every one to vote who has this right, it is of course of great importance to know how the individual should be influenced in giving his suffrage. The object of primary elections is either the appointment of men, or the settlement of a law or measure which may come before the primary elective bodies directly, for instance when the final adoption of a constitution, or amendments, are proposed to them, or indirectly, when we know that the election of an individual mainly or solely turns upon the final adoption or rejection of a certain law.

---

cause of decrease in interest. The individual thinks his single vote will not make much difference. Secondly, where the franchise is universal many persons find it inconvenient to leave their work, or to move to a distant county poll, while in France the elective franchise is restricted to the class which lives in ease.

At the election for governor in Connecticut, in 1830, it will be found that the seventeenth person of the whole population voted. Yet where there is universal suffrage it is certainly not beyond truth if we suppose that every fifth or at least sixth person has a right to vote. Suppose that the many manufactories in Connecticut, employing a large number of females, increase the proportion, we may at least say, with perfect safety, that every seventh man has a right to vote. Hence less than half who had a right to vote did vote. In the same state there were given, in 1839, for governor, 43,578 votes, which, if the papers have reported correctly, would indicate a very highly increased interest. [In 1873 the votes for governor were 86,881, or more than 1 to $3\frac{1}{2}$ of all the males.]

In Pennsylvania I find that in 1830 (when the census was taken, and the population therefore is known) every tenth man voted. The late propositions in that state, first to hold a convention to amend the constitution, and afterwards upon the proposed amendments, excited of course much interest. According to the official journals, there were polled for a convention 86,670, against it 73,166, together, therefore, 159,836; and for the amendments to the constitution, proposed by the convention, 113,971, against them 112,759, together, therefore, 226,730. This would give about the sixth man of the whole population, and, if we take the fifth man entitled to vote, it shows a very intense interest indeed.

At the presidential election of 1828, the votes given throughout the Union amounted to 1,200,000; the white population, at the same time, amounted to 9,500,000: hence every eighth white man voted, which shows much interest in the election. In 1836 the votes polled for the presidential election amounted to 1,498,885, while the white population in 1830 amounted to 10,526,248. Considering the increase of the population from 1830 to 1836, we shall find that only one out of eleven white persons voted. In the above votes those of South Carolina are not counted, because the legislature then elected the presidential electors in that state. This circumstance would slightly alter the proportion in favor of the interest shown in the election.

Respecting the election to single offices it ought to be hardly necessary to mention that a citizen should give his vote for that individual only who unites with general worth and fitness the peculiar capacity requisite for the specific office in question. Yet it is unfortunately but too frequently the case that the citizens of free countries at large, as well as the appointing officers in free or unfree countries, are swayed by totally different considerations, and quiet their conscience by the consideration, "he will do well enough." The appointment of incapable officers, however, and the habitual appointment to offices on considerations wholly foreign to the office, be it family interest, court favor, party reward, or clannishness, is equally detrimental to free and to absolute states. It lowers the whole standard of morality, capacity, and activity in the public service, and with it the public morality of the community at large; it deprives the state of that necessary promotion of the public good which can be effected only by having sound and capable officers devoted to the public service, and makes them satisfied with barely coming up to the words of their patent in the fulfilment of their duties; it begets boldness in the incapable or dishonest. These remarks must appear almost superfluous, if thus stated; yet the importance of the subject invites attentive reflection in all its bearings. The history of Spain during the last century, and that of Athens after Pericles, give proper illustrations of the above remarks.

If a citizen has to vote for an individual in a more or less representative character, he ought to be influenced by the candidate's wisdom, probity, and general tenor of life respecting those principles which the voter holds to be essentially important. If there are other more or less strong additional guarantees, for instance that a candidate is bound to these principles by his connections, his family, or any strong interests of a worldly character or of reputation, so much the better. But neither single sayings nor single transient actions nor protestations ought to weigh much. (As to regular pledges, I shall speak of them in treating of representatives.)

We do not judge of a character in history by single anecdotes; we must take the whole man, and above all the tenor of his actions, unless the very character of a single act or saying is in itself sufficient to show the mind of the man.[1] "I ask," says Montesquieu in the preface to his Spirit of the Laws, "one favor of the reader, which I fear will not be granted, namely, not to judge by the perusal of a moment the work of twenty years; to approve or to condemn the whole book, and not some passages. If we are desirous of discovering the plan of the author, it is not possible to do it except in the plan of the entire work." No one can deny the reasonableness of this request; and may it not with equal force be applied to public characters and the whole lives of men? Have they not the very fair right of asking to be judged by "their work," that is, by their actions taken in connection? Has he who wishes to judge of the man, generally, anything else by which he could do it conscientiously? Is not many a man justly acquitted in court from apparently very strong charges, simply because it is impossible to imagine any connection between the single offence charged to him and the undeviating tenor of his life? Yet no blindness is recommended, nor can the principle of law that a man shall be considered innocent until proved to be the contrary be transferred to politics, so that a man shall be considered capable until proved the contrary. We want positive proofs and facts in order to elect a man. "Les gens de bon sens jugent des faits," said Napoleon, according to Las Cases.

IV. Absolute knowledge is possible in human life only in a few cases, and our judgment respecting our votes is subject to the same rules for forming an opinion to which our judgment is always subject. We judge directly where we can, mediately through those of whose sound judgment and agreement with our principles we have sufficient knowledge,

---

[1] See Legal and Political Hermeneutics, where I speak of the interpretation of spoken words.

or by strong probabilities, derived from past facts. If, however, a citizen is incapable of deciding respecting a man or a measure by his own knowledge or capacity, and if he finds that those he has most reason to trust are divided upon a measure or course of policy which nevertheless strongly affects his country, in that case, it seems to me, he ought not to be swayed by extraneous circumstances, but to abstain from voting; for this omission to vote in such a case seems to me to be even necessary for a substantial representation of public opinion upon such a measure. This is one of the very few and rare cases in which a citizen should consider himself absolved or even prohibited in his conscience from casting his vote.

If he must give his vote on a measure, directly or indirectly, as mentioned above, let him in no case whatsoever forget to ask himself, how will the law *operate* in given circumstances? The essence of the law, the reality of the law, consists neither in its wording nor in its professed principles of themselves, but in the action of those principles upon the material. If you read a proposed law, imagine it passed, and say to yourself, "And what then?" Try to see it operate in advance; represent it clearly and in a lively picture to yourself; but do not suffer yourself to be disposed one way or the other by party vanity—a very powerful agent—dislike, revenge, or merely the pronouncing of a favorite principle or political idea of yours. This question respecting the actual operation of a law becomes, perhaps, most important when we abolish institutions. Laws and institutions ought to be abolished, not with our faces turned backward to the principle from which we started, but with the principle in our mind turned forward to anticipate its operation; for surely we do not make laws for the pleasure of proclaiming them, but for their action. The wisest is he who, like Janus, may look at once back into history and forward at the future operation. Quacks or deceivers always deal most in general principles; honest and wise men know and feel their sacredness and prove them by facts.

V. All popular representation rests essentially upon election; everything, therefore, which in any way interferes with election, either by demoralization of the voters or by disturbance or falsification of the election, is a grave offence against public liberty; but in a representative republic, in which the whole government rests on representation and supreme power is in the people, we cannot but consider every such offence as a crime against the majesty of the people, a crimen læsæ majestatis. As it is treason in monarchies to falsify acts of the prince, or to control his actions by combination around him, as it has been punished as treason strongly to influence the prince to the detriment of the people's liberty, so we cannot but acknowledge that in principle every forcible or malicious influence upon elections, or their unlawful interruption or falsification,—by false votes or false returns,—is treason against the people in an elective and representative republic; for it is a hostile act against the fundamental principle of the body politic. I do not know that a greater political outrage can be committed than to surround the poll with a set of stout fellows and thus forcibly prevent all voters of the opposite side from depositing their vote. It is the use of brutal force in a place all the meaning and sense of which is that the opinion of the assembled citizens shall be ascertained. It amounts to waylaying and carrying off the monarch in order to extort his assent to certain acts. When Huskisson was candidate for Dover, in 1802, he was opposed by Mr. Spencer Smyth, whose brother, Sir Sidney, had got possession of the church in which the election was held with his boat's crew, and effectually prevented the approach of any voter for Huskisson. No year passes in which similar outrages are not committed in the largest cities of America and England. As to bribes, they are prostitution in the bribed, simony in the briber—a simony of the worst kind—and treason in both. We shall return to the subject of bribes.

Elections may be wrongfully influenced by unjustly influencing the voters before they give their votes. I do not speak here of maliciously publishing falsehoods—though every election in America and England exhibits instances of this political immorality, which is too clear in itself, nor of the grave offence of influence on elections by officers, as I shall return to this subject on another occasion. Canvassing may be unlawful, permitted, or desirable. How jealously the early Romans considered the abuse of canvassing appears from the origin of the word ambitus, from *ambire*, to "go about," though afterwards it was done most publicly and the crimen ambitus[1] included all electioneering offences, bribing, etc., and all ways of obtaining an office by unlawful means, except, as it would seem, the *ambire* itself. Canvassing is not only allowable but necessary in many cases. The people ought to know their candidates, and if these are young, or if a particular question is pending, they or their friends ought publicly to avow their views. In this respect hustings and speeches "on the stump," if unaccompanied by feasting and riot, are on occasions advisable in thinly-settled countries or where the people have not known their representative personally. Personal intercourse and political contact between representative and constituents are necessary in order that the representation shall be real. But I believe all individual canvassing by men or women—and the latter often takes place in England,—all individual canvassing in the houses of voters or elsewhere, to be objectionable, both in itself and because it leads but too naturally to the greatest of all evils in representative governments, bribery, whether direct or indirect. There are cases, it is readily allowed, of very little difference as to the choice between the candidates, for instance when both belong to the same party and are not in the least opposed to one another,

---

[1] The term crimen ambitus, in the French *brigue*, which is retained in the law of countries that have adopted the civil law, refers to the obtaining of an office by unlawfully influencing some person or persons, and signifies with reference to government officers something similar to simony respecting ecclesiastic appointments. The German word for ambitus is very significant, and means the obtaining of an office by fawning and creeping (*Amtserschleichung*). Simony, according to the canon law, embraces, in its widest signification, nineteen chief crimes, of which the ambitus ecclesiasticus is a species. Feuerbach, Manual of the Common German Penal Law, § 181, et seq., and note to § 184.

but merely try both their chance of election. It would seem that these cases are very rare in England. In America they occur occasionally, and not only when the election is for inferior places, for I have known two friends of the same party to run for the governorship of a state without opposing one another farther than by thus aiming at the same place. In these cases individual canvassing by the friends of one or the other candidate might be harmless; but such cases are rare, and if common would introduce a dangerous custom. Properly speaking, individual canvassing is the opposite of what it often pretends to be; it is saying to a citizen, We know or suspect that you care so little about giving your vote conscientiously that we come to beg you to throw it into our scale.[1]

---

[1] There is an interesting passage in a letter from Mr. Macaulay in reply to one from the secretary of the Leeds Political Union respecting certain questions previous to Mr. Macaulay's election. I quote from the Spectator of August 15, 1832:

"The practice of canvassing is quite reasonable under a system in which men are sent to parliament to serve themselves; it is the height of absurdity under a system in which men are sent to parliament to serve the public. While we had only a mock representation, it was natural enough that this practice should be carried to a great extent. I trust it will soon finish with the abuses from which it sprang. I trust that the great and intelligent body of people who have obtained the elective franchise will see that seats in the house of commons ought not to be given, like rooms in an almshouse, to urgency of solicitation; and that a man who surrenders his vote to caresses and supplications forgets his duty as much as if he sold it for a bank-note. I hope to see the day when an Englishman will think it as great an affront to be courted and fawned upon in his capacity of elector as in his capacity of juryman. In the polling-booth, as in the jury-box, he has a great trust confided to him—a sacred duty to discharge: he would be shocked at the thought of finding an unjust verdict because the plaintiff or the defendant had been very civil and pressing; and, if he would reflect, he would, I think, be equally shocked at the thought of voting for a candidate for whose public character he felt no esteem, merely because that candidate had called upon him and begged very hard and had shaken his hand very warmly. I am delighted, though not at all surprised, to find that the enlightened and public-spirited gentlemen in whose name you write agree with me on this subject. My conduct is before the electors of Leeds; my opinions shall on all occasions be stated to them with perfect frankness: if they approve that conduct, if they concur in those opinions, they ought, not for my sake but for their own, to choose me as their member. To be so chosen I should indeed consider as a high and enviable honor; but I should think it no honor to be returned to parliament by

All intimidation previous to an election, all personal or official bullying,[1] all threats, as for instance of withdrawing employment of workmen, which happens with us on account of the extended franchise, or of shopkeepers, which happens frequently in London, all intimidation of tenants, as often in England, or of government officers holding their appointment at the pleasure of some superior officer—are high political offences. The worst of all election offences, however, is bribery.

VI. Whatever offence or crime may be committed, it becomes doubly loathsome if committed for the consideration of money—if to the offence itself the meanness of doing it for gain or hire is added. At all periods have laws pronounced the public abhorrence of bribed voting, and all states where this evil has become common have been irretrievably lost. The laws of Athens were severe against bribing of any kind, both against the briber and the bribed.[2] But when Athens sank into licentious democratic absolutism, bribing became so common that bribing companies were formed, called synomosies (συνωμοσία, an association upon oath)—a sort of mutual immoral insurance companies to bribe the judges, the council, and popular assemblies, for the benefit of the members,[3] not unlike the companies formed towards the end of the thirteenth century in England to bribe judges, whose bribes had risen since the high penal laws passed against them under Edward I.[4]

---

persons who, thinking me destitute of the requisite qualifications, had yet been wrought upon by cajolery and importunity to poll for me in despite of their better judgment."

[1] I know of a case, which happened some fifteen years ago, when a notorious duellist of great courage carried numbered ballots to the voters, telling them that he would fight every one whose respective numbered vote should not appear on counting the votes.

[2] Δεκασμός, the office of bribing; δωροδοκία, of being bribed. [See Meier u. Schöm., Att. Prozess, p. 351.]

[3] Thucyd., viii. 54; Xenophon, de Republ. Ath., iii. 7; Pollux, viii. 121; Demost., Or. poster. in Steph., p. 1137.

[4] Hume, History of England, chap. 13.

[At Rome, in the worst times of the republic, bribery was even more common than at Athens. In the latter state there were public prosecutions (γραφαί) of both givers and receivers of bribes, and it lay with the judges to estimate the amount of the penalty, which, it is probable, might even be the loss of life. At Rome the multitude of laws concerning *ambitus* would be a proof of the frequency and inveteracy of the crime, if history did not furnish us with clearer proofs.] The Romans bribed in the way of giving festivals, as well as money directly on the largest scale, as soon as public offices were sought for the profit they afforded, and the sums previously spent to obtain them were looked on as a mere outlay, to be largely refunded by plunder and extortion after the office was obtained. This cancer had long been eating in the vitals of Rome, until at length it was with criminal shamelessness sanctioned in the case of the election of Vatinius, a partisan of Cæsar's, to the prætorship, to the exclusion of Cato. The consuls had largely bribed the people, and, to escape the danger of heavy penalties on account of the crimen ambitus, they moved in the assembly of the people a resolution, which passed, to the effect that the new prætors should not be liable to any punishment for illegally obtaining their election: "ne qui prætuream per ambitum cepisset ei propterea fraudi esset"![1]

The English laws are very severe against bribing,[2] but

---

[1] Cicero, pro Planc., §§ 15–19, Cœl., § 7, Sest., § 15, ad frat., ii. 3, iii. 1, 51; Plutarch, Vit. Cæs., §§ 21, 28, 29, Pomp., § 51, Cato Min., § 44; Sueton., Vit. Jul. Cæs., § 19; Appian, Bell. Civ., ii. 19.

[2] The following is an extract as they now stand:
First, as regards the bribed.
Every person having, or claiming to have, a right to vote,
Who shall take, or even ask for, any money or other reward, by way of gift, or loan, or any device;
Or who shall agree or contract for any money, gift, employment, or other reward whatsoever—
Either to vote, or to forbear from voting—is subject
First, to a penalty of £500, which may be recovered, together with all costs of suit, by any person who thinks proper to sue for the same.
Secondly, to indictment or information, and, upon conviction, to fine and imprisonment.

the crime is common, as it is in many large cities with us despite our laws against it. Livingston, in his code for

---

Thirdly, on judgment being obtained against him in any such action, or on any such indictment or information, he becomes at once forever disabled to vote in any future election ; as well as,

Fourthly, disabled to hold or exercise any office or franchise to which he may then or afterwards be entitled as a member of any city or borough, the same as though he were naturally dead. Thus, if a burgess of any city or borough, he loses his burgess right forever.—Statute 2 Geo. II., c. 24.

And any person who shall accept any money, gift, or reward, or any promise thereof, or who shall accept any office, place, or employment, upon any engagement to procure, or endeavor to procure, the return of any person to parliament, shall forfeit the value of any money so received to the queen, and he shall forfeit any such office, place, or employment:

And shall besides forfeit a penalty of £500, to be recovered, with full costs of suit, by any person who shall sue for the same.—Statute 49 Geo. III., c. 118.

Secondly, as regards the briber.

Any person who shall by any gift or reward, or by any promise or agreement for gift or reward, corrupt or procure any person to vote, or to forbear to vote, is subject—

First, to a penalty of £500, to be recovered, with full costs of suit, by any person who shall sue for the same.

Secondly, to fine and imprisonment.

Thirdly, to the loss of his vote forever.

Fourthly, to disability to hold any office or franchise, as member of any city or borough, as in the former case. Statute 2 Geo. II., c. 24, sec. 7.

And any person who shall give, directly or indirectly, or promise to give, any sum of money, gift, or reward, to any person, on an engagement to procure, or endeavor to procure, the return of any person to serve in parliament, shall—

If himself returned, be incapacitated to sit in parliament on such election.

If not returned, shall forfeit the sum of £1000, to be recovered, with full costs of suit, by any one who may sue for the same.—Statute 49 Geo. III., c. 118, sec. 1.

For a history of the laws against bribing, see Hallam, Constitutional History, vol. iii. p. 405, et seq., and other passages, for which see his index.—According to the English papers themselves, bribery at elections has increased much of late. The following is a case of interest, Rogers vs. Mills, tried at Lewes in 1837. The action was brought to recover the £500 penalty accorded by the Act of George III., and was instituted by Henry Rogers against James Mills (agent of Mr. Easthope, one of the proprietors of the Morning Chronicle) for having on 17th April last corrupted one James Baker at the election for Lewes, to give his vote for John Easthope, a candidate, by giving to him £15, which was given as a reward for his vote, whereby the defendant forfeited for his offence £500. The case was ably argued, and the trial lasted eighteen hours. In summing up, Mr. Justice Littledale said the matter charged was equally an offence whether the

Louisiana, is no less severe.[1] Yet it is but too true that if the people at large are so debased that bribing for elections becomes morally possible, laws against it will avail very little, simply because public opinion is already corrupt. If, then, history holds up such fearful examples; if the universal spirit of mankind, expressed in the laws of all ages, points out bribing as a shameless crime; if conscience tells us unequivocally that it is a crime; if we know that a representative government becomes a melancholy farce when we acknowledge the form and violate the principle; if we remember that all nations, Asiatic or European, however widely different the principles of their political and domestic life, have invariably felt or pretended to feel the same disgust at bribery,—for the pretence shows in this case as much the truth of the principle as the feeling itself—no citizen who values either his own honor or conscience, or the safety of the state, or the essence of civil liberty, or right, or virtue, ought on any account to offer or receive a direct or indirect bribe, however safe the latter might be against any punishment according to the letter

---

party to whom the money was given were corrupted or not. The question was, whether or not Baker was mistaken in saying that Mills was the man who gave him the £15; and the jury would decide whether the admission of Mills that he gave the money was spoken in a serious manner or merely as an interrogation.

The jury retired for about a quarter of an hour, and found a verdict for the plaintiff of £500; costs, 40s.

There exists probably far less bribery with us, owing to the greater extent of the franchise, and thinner population; on the other hand, we never prosecute a case of bribery.

Before a member of the Netherlandish chamber is admitted to the oath as representative, the constitution demands of him to take the following oath:

"I swear that I have neither promised nor given, neither shall I promise or give, any gift or present, direct or indirect, under whatsoever pretence, to any person in or out of office, in order to obtain my election as member of the second chamber of the States-General." Constitution of the Netherlands, ¿ 84.

[1] Code of Crimes and Punishments, Title vii. chap. i., "Of Bribery and undue Influence." The first article punishes offering or receiving bribes to influence votes at public elections with a fine not less than one hundred dollars nor more than five hundred dollars, forfeiture of all political rights (the Greek *atimia*), and imprisonment for not less than six months nor more than one year. The penalty for bribing judges is still higher, as might be supposed.

of the law. In monarchies it is held that the subject owes allegiance to the prince whether the latter be actually crowned or not, or the former have actually taken the oath of allegiance or not. Is there no natural allegiance to truth and liberty, whether we have taken our oath in court or not? We have called certain acts in voting, falsifications, treason against liberty; bribery is the worst of these treasons. It would amount to treason of the highest kind in a monarchy to substitute a changeling for the legitimate infant who is heir of the crown. Is it less criminal to substitute a counterfeit for a genuine public opinion, for what the true election *returns* ought to be—the foundations on which the fabric of civil liberty greatly rests? And do we not commit these substitutions if we allow ourselves in any way to be bribed,—that is, if we allow ourselves by any considerations of interest or favor to vote differently from what our judgment tells us we ought to do? Does it not amount to perjury if I solemnly deposit a vote—that vote which the most fundamental laws of the state carefully, jealously, and solemnly secure for me—which is against my conscience? Is this *act* not a guiltier lie than a false *word* in a mere account of an event? There are many lies infinitely worse than the lies in words—they are the lies of actions, of the tenor of our life. Since then laws cannot avail much in this particular, and ruin must inevitably follow, if bribery becomes common, it is for each citizen to hold himself bound by all that is true and holy and just and pure to crush this crime wherever he meets it, as infallibly as he would rush to arms should he discover a band of enemies in the midst of his own camp.[1]

---

[1] The *classical* age of Bribery is when the Roman empire was sold by the prætorians, and the zenith of this splendid period is when the prætorians sold it by auction to the highest bidder after the death of Pertinax; when Didius Julianus obtained it against the bidding of Sulpicianus, father-in-law of Pertinax. Still, the public would not, depraved as it was, brook this; and Severus made it the reason why he disbanded the prætorians.

A most startling instance of regular bribery reduced to a proper price current is given in Raumer's Europe from the End of the Seven Years' War to the American War, from Documentary Sources, vol. i., where he speaks of the in-

In writing this I am not unmindful of that trial of a good citizen, one of the severest he can be placed in, when he sees that the malignant and shameless are ruining his own beloved liberty by the infamy of bribery, and that would he but resort by way of defence to the same expedient he might, apparently, save it. Has he not the right to defend himself, as against a murderer or in war, by the same means that are employed against him? No, he has not. The difference is essential. Killing is in itself not criminal; bribing is. We might thus protect ourselves by perjury against perjury. If I kill a man who strives to murder me, I do not commit murder. Bribery remains bribery. Besides, what is gained? If bribe be opposed to bribe, general demoralization is only consummated the sooner, while one party's abstaining from it may become the germ of a better state of things, and may indeed save the country.

> "Corruption wins not more than honesty.
> Still in thy right hand carry gentle peace,
> To silence envious tongues. Be just, and fear not:
> Let all the ends thou aim'st at be thy country's,
> Thy God's, and truth's." SHAKSPEARE, Henry VIII.

---

trigues of France, England, Russia, etc., in Sweden, previous to the Revolution in 1771,—when the king, Gustavus III., upset the old constitution,—especially on pages 216, 222, and 234. The diplomatic dispatches say that the present diet will cost us so much, for we require so many votes: the votes of the nobility cost so much, those of the clergy so much, the election of the speaker of the cities so much, that of the speaker of the peasants so much. See this especially on page 235, where the British minister writes home, March 24, 1769. He makes a classification of votes, namely: 1, votes to be had by the highest bidder; 2, those who have taken their resolution but require pay to go to the diet to vote according to their resolution (that is Bacon's selling justice, but not injustice); 3, unbribable ones. Three thousand dollars were needed for a vote of the first class; two thousand dollars for a vote of the second. The election of the speaker of the citizens will cost one hundred thousand dollars, of the peasants thirty thousand. The whole diet will cost thirty-four thousand five hundred and forty pounds. Later dispatches say the clergy may be had for six thousand pounds. Russia had spent three hundred thousand rubles, Denmark one hundred thousand rix-dollars, and added later ninety thousand; France paid four million five hundred thousand livres. The bribing of the diet was estimated to cost the various powers three hundred and seventy thousand pounds

VII. The bribing of judges is so vile an outrage, and, thanks to the advances of society in the most civilized countries, so unheard-of a crime, at least with reference to direct bribes, that I abstain from dwelling upon it. It is like poisoning a well from which hundreds of beings must draw their water.[1] Bribing legislators, however, is not by any means so unheard of; and yet is it not a fearful crime? Legislators indeed have been known to consider themselves fairly "retained" by the receipt of a fee, and have argued that the retainer was received by them simply, as they said, that they should use their influence in expediting a measure, whether the result should prove favorable or unfavorable; thus cloaking over what cannot be and never has been otherwise considered than bribery. Such a case I believe was that of Sir John Trevor, speaker of the commons, who was expelled from the house in 1694 for having received one thousand guineas for expediting a very just and humane bill respecting certain property and privileges of the London orphans.[2] So we have seen that Bacon in his case of bribery made a distinction between "sale of justice," which he avowed he had done, "and of injustice," which he had not committed, in the which, Lord Nugent says,[3]—and let us mention it to rejoice at the improved state of things—he was "countenanced by long-prevailing practice in that court (the chancery court) and by such examples as it would be shameful to urge in excuse of such a man."

All bribes offered to members of legislative bodies, as in-

---

[1] That this crime may be still now and then committed in the United States, Germany, England, or France, in the most secret darkness, is possible; that even some trial of a judge for this crime may have occurred of late, without my knowledge, I will certainly not deny; but I consider it well worth stating as a fact, that, being no inconsiderable reader of the newspapers of various countries, I do not remember having met with such a case, or so much as the breathing of suspicion of bribery against a judge, in any paper, say for the last ten years. [Dr. Lieber could not have written this in 1874.]

[2] Trevor's Life of William III., vol. ii. c. 15.

[3] Lord Nugent, Some Memorials of John Hampden, his Party and Times, London, 2 vols., 1837, vol. i. p. 44.

deed all bribes, may be classed under the heads of direct, indirect, and unconscious bribes. Direct bribes given by private individuals to legislators are now exceedingly rare, or perhaps do not occur at all, owing chiefly, it is probable, to the Argus-like press, to the dread of inevitable ruin should it ever be divulged, and to the great probability that some day or other the evil deed will transpire, and, once transpiring, will be most extensively known through the papers. But bribes proceeding from the government are not of rare occurrence either in England, the United States, or France. They consist generally in the direct promise or intimation of preferment, or elevation of rank, either with reference to the general course on which a legislator shall proceed, or to his vote and influence respecting some specific, important measure. Direct money bribes offered by governments are probably now rare; they are difficult to be kept from detection, owing to the better state of the control of finances. Yet Lord Russell tells us in his History of England that the favorite ministerialists under Lord North's administration were permitted to take part in the loans, which they sold directly at ten per cent. advance, that Fox charged Lord North repeatedly with having sacrificed nine hundred thousand pounds sterling of a loan in order to buy votes, and that some members of parliament at that time received money directly for their votes. Indirect bribes occur frequently, though they are sufficiently open to be branded at once in the eye of every honest citizen with their true character, and though their shape can appease only those consciences which are ready to derive comfort from the forms and not the essence of transactions. The promise to legislators in America of the privilege of subscribing for a certain number of bank shares, and the guarantee of a fixed advance on the par price, provided a bank charter, yet pending, should pass, is no less than a direct bribe amounting to the sum thus guaranteed in advance, whatever the form of the bribe may be. According to the English papers, it appears that sometimes considerable sums are given to members of either house, but especially to lords, in order to induce them to vote for canals, roads, or railroads, if they pass through and injure the property of those members. It has been frankly maintained that this is fair, for it was certain that the person in question would not vote to his own injury if no equivalent were paid. If, however, we consider the case plainly, it will appear to be indirect, perhaps even direct, bribery; for the legislator ought not to vote in his private and interested capacity, but in his legislative. As the juryman must give his verdict according to evidence and nought else, so must the legislator vote for the general welfare to the best of his judgment, and for nought else.

I would call that person unconsciously bribed who unconsciously allows himself to be swayed in his judgment respecting his vote as legislator by advantages probably accruing to him or his friends from the passing or defeat of a bill. We are all exposed to this error, and must be the more careful to avoid it, the more easily it may steal upon us. But above all, let no legislator under any circumstances allow himself to be rewarded, directly or indirectly, in any way whatsoever, for his vote. It must needs ultimately lead to that system of pilfer and pillage of which we have spoken several times; it takes away from the representative or legislator all feeling of manly independence and bold reliance on his own honor, and diffuses a general depression of morals, substituting sordid selfishness for public spirit.

There is one species of bribes, of great importance in history, and happily likewise on the decline in our times— namely, the influence which foreign powers once exercised by gratifying the sordid interest or vanity of citizens, ministers, or even monarchs. The pensions paid by Louis XIV. to so many ministers of other states; the money he gave to Charles II. on condition that he should do what the latter knew to be unlawful; the regular presents, that is pensions, which the cardinals formerly received from the chief monarchs, especially from Spain and France, and according to which they were openly divided into French, Spanish, or other "factions," that is parties, which followed distinct leaders, acknowledged as such by the respective foreign monarch; the unhallowed gold which flowed so abundantly from Persia into Greece, that Boeckh considers it as an important source of the increase of gold in Europe, and which set Greek against Greek; the snuff-boxes with diamonds, portraits with brilliants,[1] the titles, orders, and estates offered to a foreign minister if a proposed peace should be brought about—all these belong to this species of international bribes, and ought not to be suffered in any shape.

VIII. A practice which affects elections in an immoral and mischievous manner, and which has become very widely spread in the United States, according to the proofs in the newspapers as well as the charges of various grand juries,[2] is betting on elections. The practice is not new: we meet with bets in Rome on papal elections, three centuries ago;[3] but

---

[1] The American Constitution prohibits every officer from taking any present whatsoever from foreign powers or in the course of any public transaction. In a very few cases it was believed necessary to accept them; but they have been invariably deposited with the United States. It was lately mentioned by the papers —it is to be hoped with truth—that the late signing of the treaty between the six powers relative to Belgium and Holland would be the second signing of an important treaty without the usual presents of snuff-boxes, rings, etc., to the respective diplomatists. The treaty when these presents were first dispensed with was said to have been the alliance between England, France, Spain, and Portugal, respecting the two latter countries.

[2] At a sitting of the court of common pleas, in Bucks county, Pennsylvania, in December, 1834, Judge Fox very properly called the attention of the grand jury to the prevailing practice of betting on elections, and to the law on that subject. The Bucks County Intelligencer says, "The judge said he intended hereafter to bring this subject to the attention of the respective grand juries: he believed it to be pregnant with the most pernicious consequences to society, and indirectly subversive of the purity and fairness of the elective franchise. He said, the law prohibitory of such practice ought to be known, and, being known, he should enjoin it upon grand juries, hereafter, to observe its letter and spirit. He referred to the election in Philadelphia, and said that betting, there, had become a complete system of gambling, and was the pursuit of many men, during the excitement which precedes elections."

[3] Odds, we are told, were very strong against cardinal Monte; yet he was elected pope, in 1550. Monte called himself Julius III. Ranke, History of the Popes, etc., vol. i. p. 177 (Eng. trans., i. 172).

the betting persons were not voters themselves. Everything is to be much dreaded which leads elections in any way whatever from their true and straight channel. By bets, persons frequently the most doubtful in character among the voters become deeply and passionately interested in the elections, and when high sums are at stake, as is frequently the case, use any illegal means to insure their winning. It is frightful indeed to behold—by the offers which many brokers publicly make in the papers or in their shop-windows, or by the clusters of persons who offer or accept election bets at certain places in some of our large cities previous to elections—an election turned into a lottery affair or the sport of gamesters. In many states the laws are against it; everywhere they ought to be enacted; for they would at least prevent public offers of bets, which cannot be considered other than a glaring political indecency.[1] In England a vote is invalidated if a man is

---

[1] I copy the following advertisement from the Albany Argus of October 17, 1832. These advertisements are quite common, and I merely select this because it happens to be at hand:

"Bets—To all persons who feel the least confidence in the success of the opposition tickets. The following bets, or hazards, have been left with the subscribers, for negotiation. Responsible persons, desirous to take them up, will please call at our office.

*First Bet.*

$500 That the Jackson electoral ticket will be elected in Pennsylvania.

$500 That Andrew Jackson, if he lives, will be elected president of the United States.

$500 That William L. Marcy will be elected governor of this state at the ensuing election.

$500 That the Jackson electoral ticket will be elected in the state of New York.

*Second Bet.*

$1000 That Andrew Jackson, if he lives, will be elected president of the United States.

$1000 That Martin Van Buren, if he lives, will be elected vice-president of the United States.

*Third Bet.*

$100 That the Jackson electoral ticket will be elected in Ohio.
$100 do. do. do. do. Kentucky.
$100 do. do. do. do. Louisiana.
$100 do. do. do. do. Pennsylvania

proved to have been interested in a bet.¹ This is right, but by no means sufficient. No good citizen ought to suffer himself to promote or be drawn into an evil by which an additional vicious and most active passion, that of gaming, is connected with politics; for to protect politics against passions which it naturally produces, without perplexing it by additional ones, has been at all times the most difficult problem of the wisest legislators and best citizens. What would the public think if it should become known that physicians of a hospital were in the habit of betting on the chances of recovery of the patients under their charge? The case seems to me very similar. We should feel disgusted if they, appointed to heal and save if possible, allowed frivolous ideas of gain, which might even influence their actions, to mix up with their calling.

IX. The process of election itself may be seriously disturbed by the riot and drunkenness which in many places accompany it. It is humiliating indeed to think, what is nevertheless a fact, that on election-days, the days when the

---

$100 That the Jackson electoral ticket will be elected in Illinois.
$100   do.   do.   do.   do.   Indiana.
$100   do.   do.   do.   do.   Missouri.
$100   do.   do.   do.   do.   Mississippi.
$100   do.   do.   do.   do.   Alabama.
$100   do.   do.   do.   do.   New Jersey."

Here follow the names of the brokers, with other lottery advertisements.

¹ In 1838, the Youghal election committee of the British commons was occupied a whole day with the following case:

"The petitioners objected to the vote of James Browne on the ground that he had betted a new hat on the result of the Youghal election, by which act it was contended that he had become interested in the event, and had consequently rendered himself utterly incompetent to exercise the franchise with which he had been intrusted. The case excited the deepest interest throughout the day, and so nicely were the arguments on both sides balanced, so equal the weight of authority adduced, that it was not till about three minutes before the speaker was at prayers that the committee were able to come to a decision, that as Browne was offered the bet with a fraudulent motive, his vote should be held good. It appeared that an unscrupulous non-elector had basely betrayed James Browne into the business expressly in order to invalidate his vote, which alone induced the committee to come to the above favorable decision." London papers of March, 1838.

people ought to appear in their most solemn capacity, that of manifesting their integral and substantial citizenship, more crime probably is committed than on any other. An English clergyman of late strongly denounced the corruption, the drunkenness, the poisoned state of the public mind, and the violation of truth at elections, and probably with good reason.[1] In many places in the United States we all know that drunkenness is frequent at elections.[2] A great evil is the disturbance of the poll, or the besieging it so that none except of one party can approach, or at least not without great difficulty: the falsification of elections by bringing electors of other wards or places, or people who have no right to vote at all, causing them perhaps to commit the additional crime of perjury; the falsification of returns by destroying the votes of one or more voters [ballot-stuffing, as it is called]; the annoyance of well-known citizens—these are all serious and deplorable offences. Every citizen ought to feel disposed to prosecute all of such offences that are at all punishable by law. To do this, however, he ought first of all to free himself of having directly or indirectly taken part in any election malpractice. The time may come—it has perhaps arrived—in which a society for the promotion and maintaining of fairness and justice at elections should be formed. As it is an object of political importance itself, yet in itself of no partisan color, there could be no objection against it; and a society of this sort would frequently make salutary agreements between two parties to give up some election abuses; while attention and discussion would be drawn to these important subjects, and better laws be promoted.

---

[1] A Sermon preached by a curate at Hounslow, in October, 1837.

[2] In some Swiss cantons all disturbance, noise, drinking, standing in large numbers around the election-house, are prohibited. According to a law of December 18, 1832, of the Pays de Vaud, against *Brigues*, that is *ambitus*, the electoral college (election judges) have the right to order any tavern, inn, or other public house to be closed during election-day, and to order all customers away if they see fit. The law, consisting of twenty-six chief points, contains some interesting features. Under William III. a statute was passed against giving beer at elections. Trevor's Life of William III., vol. ii. p. 255.

## CHAPTER II.

Parties.—Has any free Country existed without Parties?—Can a free Country possibly exist without Parties?—Is it desirable that a free Country should exist without Parties?—Historical Parties and passing ones.—Conservative and Movement Parties.—Characteristics of a sound Party.—Dangers of Party Zeal and factious Passion.—Party Signs.—Misunderstanding of Language in high Party Spirit.—Ought a conscientious Citizen to attach himself to a Party?—The Law of Solon.—Independents.—Trimmers.

X. IF I have felt upon some occasions, while writing this work, more deeply impressed with the solemnity and greatness of its subject, and more ardently desired that my pen might be guided by the spirit of truth, discernment, and the power of clothing my thoughts with accurate and appropriate language, than upon others, I have never felt more so than now that I propose to write upon the subject of parties. Cato, when he stood the last time in the presence of judges, exclaimed, How difficult it is to defend ourselves before persons with whom we have not lived! But it is more difficult still to be plainly understood by contemporaries upon matters which greatly agitate the times. To mould the result of our experience and reflection into words which convey all we are anxious to say and no more, and to avoid the danger of unbidden associations, is difficult indeed; yet when the word has been uttered with due consideration, how few are there who endeavor to understand it in any other sense than that with which accidental association in the individual reader happens to invest it! I premise these remarks for my younger readers, that they may bestow upon this subject all the attention which its urgent importance on the one hand, and its many dangers on the other, demand, and that before all they may avoid the drawing of hasty conclusions apparently justifying what indeed is to be carefully shunned as a wasting disease of the commonwealth.

XI. By a party we understand a number of citizens who, for some period and not momentarily, act in unison respecting some principles, interest, or measure, by lawful means, keeping therefore within the bounds of the fundamental law and for the real or sincerely supposed common good of the whole commonwealth. If either of these latter requisites be wanting; if that body of citizens act by unlawful means or for sordid, selfish ends, or strive, secretly or openly, beyond the fundamental law—that is, if they no longer strive for a change of the administration or of some laws, but for a change of the government itself—they are called a faction.[1] All parties are exposed to the danger of passing over into factions, which if carried still farther may become conspiracies.

Before we attentively consider the various bearings of this vast subject, it will be well briefly to answer three questions. First, has ever any free country, at any period of history, existed for any length of time without parties? Secondly, can we possibly expect any free country to exist without parties? And thirdly, is it desirable that a free country should exist without parties? Has there ever existed a free country for any length of time without parties? This is a question of fact, and can be decided by history alone; and, that no misunderstanding may exist, I will add that by a free country I mean here any country in which the citizen, according to the law or custom of the land, has a right to take, and does take, a more or less direct and positive, and not a mere indirect or negative, part in the acts of government; in short, a body politic in which there is a widely diffused political action among the citizens at large. After this explanation I avow that, as far as my knowledge goes, I know of no instance of a free state without parties. Forms may deceive; a state may have a republican form, for instance, yet be hemmed in by overwhelming power, like the republic of Cracow, and parties may indeed not exist; but does there exist there any free

---

[1] If they act overtly and physically, they become either insurgents or rebels, as the case may be.

political action? The history of many free countries exhibits brief periods, indeed, in which common and imminent danger, or a universal and pure enthusiasm produced by a happy combination of circumstances, quiets all existing differences for the time; but I believe that there never existed a free country actively developing within its bosom constitutional law, and feeling deeply interested in the great problems of right and public justice, in which there were not also parties. For neither in the physical world nor in the moral or intellectual is anything great to be obtained without struggle, and where there is struggle there must be two sides, two parties. Indeed, we must answer at once the second question, that it is impossible for civil liberty to exist without parties. Politics does not differ in this respect from any other sphere of untrammelled action whatsoever. Where there is free action of whatever sort, political, scientific, or in the fine arts, and especially where men thus situated strive to obtain some common end, to establish some principle, or to act out some idea, those who hold to the same principles will naturally and must necessarily unite in some degree and combine their endeavors, strength, and energy. Without such union it would be as impossible, in many cases, to remove some impediment in the course of civilization, or to introduce some truth into practical life, as it would be to remove a physical obstacle without a union of several forces. Parties exist not only where there is political liberty, but, as was just observed, wherever there is freedom of action. Thus, as soon as an absolute monarch, with a superior mind and iron will, ceases to force all around him to walk in his prescribed paths, we shall find divisions, parties, factions of the court. We may lay it down, then, as a principle, that in the same degree as there is room for combined and self-directing action in any sphere, so likewise must parties exist.

Thirdly, upon many grounds it is desirable that parties should exist. Without parties there could be no loyal, steady, lasting, and effective opposition, one of the surest safeguards of public peace, as we shall see hereafter, for the want of which parties became in antiquity and the middle ages so much more frequently factions than in modern times in those nations which best understand the practical operation of civil liberty. Without parties many of the wisest measures could never be carried, and many of the best intended measures would remain harsh, unmodified, absolute; the polity of a free commonwealth would greatly lose its proper character. Without parties well understood, restless, shallow, ambitious theorists, the mischievous appendages of modern liberty, would worry society in a manner which, in many cases, would lead to serious reactions. Every vain, loud, and inexperienced innovator would harass society far more than such persons are now capable of doing. Lastly, the freedom of action in which civil liberty consists must leave a great degree of combination at the option of the citizens, which liberty will naturally be made use of in many cases by men misguided either by error, evil design, or fanaticism. How then are we to counteract them otherwise than by counter-combination? how is it possible to displace a vicious administration except by a combination of efforts?

Yet let us always and at every stage of this inquiry remember that parties themselves are exposed and expose others to much danger. This consideration, and the fact that, on the other hand, they are both unavoidable and useful, must prompt us the more honestly, manfully, and practically to inquire into the very essence of the matter, so that the subject may become the more and more justly understood.'

XII. There are two great classes of parties—historical and passing ones. By historical parties I understand those which are founded in the history of their country through a long

---

' In this respect the subject of parties only resembles a thousand others, for instance that of power, of punishment, of all the primary impulses, such as the desire of property, the wish to convince others of what we hold to be true ourselves, the union of the sexes, the partiality for our kindred, the very love of our country, nay, the first physical impulses, of eating and drinking: all are unavoidably necessary, yet expose men to moral or physical danger.

series of years, parties which adhere to certain political ideas, which have been handed down from generation to generation, developed and modified by repeated practical application, and expanded into a certain system and doctrine, having taken root in the practical life of the nation. They become the more especial representatives of their respective ideas, and the nation at large becomes well acquainted with their actions and operations, not their professions only; the nation knows how to appreciate them. Such, for instance, are the Tories and Whigs in England. It is a great advantage for a free state if its history has been propitious to the growth of such parties. They greatly aid in the steady development of substantial liberty.

Passing parties, on the other hand, are those formed for momentary purposes only, as for the carrying of some single measure, or merely the displacing of an administration, to which species coalitions generally belong; or for the sole object of "getting in," not in order to obtain power for the purpose of carrying out some principles or plan, but only for the sake of the power and emolument itself. It is one of the worst political accidents if the parties are merely divided into "ins" and "outs." They can hardly ever escape becoming factions. There are, moreover, two traits which generally, and especially in modern times, although we can discern them very frequently in antiquity, particularly in Rome and Athens, distinguish one or the other party. There are those that adhere to what exists, who strive to maintain and preserve, who represent the necessary stability of the state, without which no society can exist; and those who look forward, desire to change, improve, and develop; they represent the movement, without which it is, on the other hand, impossible for any society to exist. The former frequently carry their endeavors too far, and wish to preserve indiscriminately, so that conservation alone becomes the watchword. But that which is bad, inconvenient, or mischievous ought not to be retained; and Raumer, the historian, justly observes that it has been frequently as revolutionary to preserve as to destroy. The others often go too far in their turn, disregarding the gradual nature of all development, that it is always necessary and unavoidable for one generation to grow out of a preceding one, and they desire change without experience or modification—change for its own sake. We do not observe these two distinctive traits in politics only: they appear in religion, in science, in philosophy, in taste; they appear more or less clearly everywhere.

XIII. A sound party, which the conscientious citizen may join, ought to have the following characteristics. Its principle, upon which it exists or claims to act, or its object, ought to be an enlarged and great one, a noble principle worthy of moving masses; its numbers ought to be, if possible, large, or at least the ground on which it is formed ought to be such that the party may have the power of becoming national; its consistency and mutual adherence ought to be chiefly a moral or mental one, and it should have its strength in physical organization; its members ought to feel, and act as if they felt, that before all they are citizens of their country, and that their position as such is not changed by the party, consequently that the party does not treat itself as if it were the country, or a sort of privileged aristocracy to which the others are to be made passive subjects only, and that it does not show a spirit of bitter persecution as soon as a member feels himself conscientiously bound to dissent on some measure from the prevailing opinion.

Without the first, an enlarged principle or worthy and great object, parties become only the supporters or promoters of meanness, intrigue, or cabals.[1] All paltriness in matters of

---

[1] The word cabal, as is well known, is now generally believed, according to Hume, ch. 65, to have been composed of the letters with which the names of the five dangerous ministers of the time began,—namely, Clifford, Ashley, Buckingham, Arlington, and Lauderdale. (Burnet, Own Times, an. 1672.) Others derive it from the Hebrew Cabala, denoting a mysterious philosophy brought from Egypt. [It is certain that cabal was used to denote a faction or junto before the time of Charles II. It was borrowed from the French, who derived it from Cabala.]

union among men lowers the mind, depresses the moral standard, and in politics leads to factiousness. The second is likewise important; it prevents, in a great degree, intriguing; for large masses cannot easily be intrigued with, and, as Napoleon said, "the really guilty ones are the intriguers of all colors and all doctrines."[1] Every party must act with some sort of uniformity, otherwise its object of united action would be lost; public meetings and the meeting of delegates, as well as a certain mutual support in what is considered of general advantage, and, in the case of members of legislatures, pre paratory meetings for the management of questions of great import, are indispensable, and have at all times been held, in ancient and in modern. In fact, without them very little business of importance or advantage would be transacted. But nothing is more to be shunned than regular party organizations, with lists of admission and erasures of expelled members, with regular party assessments and distinct party obligations, with absolutely dependent papers dictated to by a leading paper, which is servilely re-echoed by the other party organs. Parties so organized are factions, or stand at any moment on the point of becoming such, and gather strength from the two facts that they are removed out of the common politico-legal operation of the state, and yet are close societies, so that they easily supersede the government. They may easily become what the fearful French clubs were during the first revolution of France; and, although it will be readily admitted that much of the insane cruelty perpetrated by the Jacobin club was owing to a number of quite peculiar circumstances, yet no one can study well the history of those clubs, especially of the Jacobin club, without perceiving that the dangers of close parties or clubs are demonstrated there in fearful consistency and glaring light, and no change of circumstances could prevent great evils from growing out of similar institutions. To speak briefly, a party ought not to

---

[1] "Les vrais coupables sont les intrigans de toutes les couleurs et de toutes les doctrines." Mém. de Sainte-Hélene, vol. iii. p. 30, Paris edit. of 1824.

be a society, lest it expose its members to all the dangers which have been noticed when we treated of societies, more especially of trades-unions. At Athens there were many political clubs, ἑταιρεῖαι, not without sacramental obligations. When democratic madness raged in that city, we cannot wonder that some citizens fled to this last hope.[1] We cannot treat here of what may become necessary in cases of utmost extremity. No principle is truer than that, if a nation were in a state of dissolution, the best citizens might act wisely and rightly in forming societies to administer justice.

XIV. Let us now consider the danger to which all party combinations are exposed, so that we may the better avoid them.

Every individual pursuing with earnestness a certain object of importance is exposed to the error of pursuing it to the exclusion of other objects equally important, of becoming "one-sided." This is the case in all spheres, the sciences, the arts, religion, politics, the pursuit of wealth, in education, —in short, everywhere. The danger naturally increases both with the degree of power we may possess, and of opposition which may be offered; for the one stimulates our eagerness, the other lends the means to act it out. Parties, however, always meet with opposition, else they would not exist; and they combine the endeavors, energy, and powers of many, countenancing one another; so that they are more exposed to the error of one-sidedness than men who pursue their object individually, with whatever eagerness.

The next danger, equally great, if not greater, is that the individual will lose his moral independence, and the party become too close, when it is exposed to all the perils which we have viewed under the head of associations,—in short, that the party will become factions; that the parties foment the spirit of dissension, while it is the duty of every citizen to assuage discord and allay civil strife as much as possible;

---

[1] Thucydides, viii. 54.

that we shall deceive ourselves in taking the opinion of our party for that of our nation, or that of a fraction of our party or a mere political coterie[1] for the opinion of the whole party; that party spirit will run into a variety of channels, such as religious distinction, the various classes of society, or separate trades, while the health of a commonwealth consists greatly in the close and intimate union of all classes, professions, and employments; that our own judgment[2] and even moral feeling may become warped and distorted, and that we shall judge of those things *by* which alone parties can be truly measured, such as justice, the prosperity of the whole country, truth, right, which are indeed the first principles upon which all politics shall move, by the standard derived *from* the party, thus making that which ought to be the standard the thing to be measured, and that which ought to be measured the standard, as inflamed sects will sometimes measure the truth by their tenets, not their tenets by the truth. The danger is that we shall look upon the party as the end and object, striving to make the community subservient to it, while that only which can give sense and meaning to a party is the community, the commonwealth, the country. In this latter respect we are all apt to forget the primary end and object, as indeed all men in all pursuits, when earnestly striving for some object, are prone to forget the end and place instead of it that which originally was but the means to obtain it. Gen-

---

[1] There is hardly any danger which besets men in civilized life, and especially those in the higher classes, more constantly than the mistaking of coterie talk for public opinion, coterie opinion for public judgment. Private individuals, authors, politicians, statesmen, and monarchs are equally exposed to it, and Charles X. of France lost his crown by mistaking a court coterie for the national party. Few men, indeed, have sufficient sagacity and elevation of mind to withstand the power of repetition in their circle, or to rise above it and see life and reality untainted by it. Observe real life, and do not neglect signs and clear tokens or proofs because they disagree with what you hear around yourself.

[2] Even so considerate and calm a man as Newton, it would appear, did not withstand party acrimony in his transactions with Flamsteed. This is not mentioned to justify us, inferior to him, but to serve as a still more significant beacon.

erals forget the object of the war; lawyers, that the ultimate end is not the rescuing of a criminal but the doing of justice. Pope Paul IV. (Caraffa) desired assistance from the Protestants, and urged the Turks to attack Naples and Sicily.[1] In brief, the danger is that we forget for what the party struggle is, and liken it to a war, the end of which is victory in itself, by whatever means or stratagems. Lastly, this blinding party zeal may pass over into factious passion and fury. Dumont, in his Reminiscences of Mirabeau, ch. xviii., says of Brissot—it is indifferent for the present purpose whether with perfect correctness or not, for it is at any rate a correct picture of the malady of which we speak—"Brissot was one of those men in whom party spirit was much stronger than all morals, or rather who saw no morals except in the party; he had more of monastic zeal than any one else; as a Capuchin he would have loved his vermin; as a Dominican he would have burnt heretics; as a Roman he would have shown himself not unworthy of following Cato or Regulus; as a French republican he was bent on destroying the monarchy, and neither disdained to calumniate nor to persecute, nor himself to perish upon the scaffold, so that he obtained his object."

Considering the danger of fomenting dissension, we ought ever to be careful not to let party distinction and animosity pass over into private life. It is delightful to see men who rigorously oppose one another upon conscientious grounds remaining in a strictly gentlemanlike or perhaps friendly private intercourse, a circumstance which can take place only where there is great liberty. For liberty accustoms men to respect the opinion of others, while absolutism or want of freedom so thoroughly weans men from this noble mutual justice that if for some reason dissension does break out it is

---

[1] His confessions on this head are given in Bromato, Vita di Paolo IV., vol. ii. p. 369, cited by Ranke (History of the Popes, ii. 184, transl.). The pope called upon Suleiman I. to give up his wars in Hungary and to throw himself with all his power upon Naples and Sicily. This was done to strengthen himself against His Most Catholic Majesty of Spain.

invariably vehement and inveterate, and every opponent is at once considered as an enemy. While the party spirit between the Union men and States'-right party ran highest in Charleston, several of the most active leaders of the opposite parties remained on terms of amity, and showed themselves to be so in public.

All party signs are to be deprecated, except it comes to an extreme, when indeed the question touches no longer the subject of parties, and a sign is taken as the symbol and eloquent pledge of the struggle, such as the tricolor in France in 1830. The fool's cap and beggar's bag of the Gueux in the Netherlands did great service. Signs rouse the inert, and commit the active irreversibly; they pledge and compromise, and are therefore useful in insurrections, but not until then. So long as peace can be maintained, party signs are much to be dreaded, whether they consist in the color of the cap distinguishing the theological factions at Constantinople, or in the Guelf's wearing the plume on the right side and the Ghibelline's wearing it on the left,[1] or in the "blue and buff" of the Whigs in the times of Fox, or the orange opposed to the green in Ireland.

Party spirit may run so high that the greatest link and tie of humanity, language, loses its very essence, and people cease to understand one another, when even the best-intended words, as in the theological controversies of religiously excited times, are unintentionally yet passionately or wilfully wronged, misconstrued, wrung from their very sense; such as Thucydides says was the case in Greece during the Peloponnesian war, "when the received value of names imposed for the signification of things was changed in an arbitrary way; inconsiderate boldness being counted true-hearted manliness; provident deliberation, a specious fear; modesty, the cloak of

---

[1] The distinction of party signs showed itself in the cutting of bread, in the wearing of the girdle, etc. (Ranke, communicating it from a *relazione*, in his Popes, etc., vol. i. p. 250, of the translation, Amer. ed.) The Chronicle of Cologne says that the two parties distinguished themselves even by their manner of husbandry. Biographical Notices of B. G. Niebuhr, vol. ii. p. 381.

cowardice; to be cautious in everything, to be lazy in everything. A furious suddenness was reputed a point of valor. To re-advise for the better security was held to be a fair pretext for tergiversation. He that was fierce was always trusty; and he that was the opposite of such a one was suspected. He that laid a snare, if it took, was a wise man; he that could find out the trap was a cleverer man than he; but he that had been so provident as not to need to do one or the other was said to be a dissolver of fellowships, and one that stood in fear of his adversary. In brief, he that could outstrip another in the doing of an evil act, or that could persuade another thereto that never meant it, was commended." The vivid description of that excellent historian goes on much farther, exhibiting to us the ripe fruits of those seeds which all of us carry within us; and if I have previously referred to the history of the Jacobin club as instructive for every citizen, I do so with no less earnestness to this whole part of the Grecian history; I urgently refer to it my younger readers.[1] It is very true, indeed, that our danger is not so great as that of ancient times, because our states are vaster, our race is less apt to be moved by masses, we value individuality higher, our religion, so long as it is unsullied by fanaticism, is of a tempering character, and, above all, we act through representative governments. Where the democracy is absolute, and the state small,—the one indeed requires the other,—it is difficult

---

[1] Thucydides, iii. 70–85. I recollect having seen, in a Madrid paper of the year 1822, this passage in an account of some tumult in the Spanish capital: "The infamous cry, Long live our country! was heard." Archbishop Parker, "who had been reckoned moderate in his proceedings towards Catholics, complained of what he called 'a Machiavel government;' that is, of the queen's (Elizabeth's) lenity in not absolutely rooting them out." (Hallam, Constitutional History, vol. i. p. 191.) The note which Hallam appends to that page gives instances, if indeed they were needed, of the truth contained in the remarks of Thucydides respecting the perversion of language in times disordered by the fury of party, and which are but too applicable to all parties at the period of the Reformation. In the first French revolution the words virtue, patriotism, consistency, had received entirely new meanings, as the word Thorough had between archbishop Laud and Lord Strafford, and probably among their whole party.

to see how any party can be secure against breaking out into passion. Let us, then, upon this ground among so many others, value and foster the more earnestly our representative system. Yet, despite all difference, the danger still exists; and will exist so long as men on the one hand cherish freedom of action, and on the other are, and in their nature ought to be, according to God's will, mental and moral individuals, differing therefore in their dispositions, and so long as they pursue with zeal what they hold to be true or right.

XV. Ought a well-meaning citizen to attach himself to some party, and to act with it? If he joins a party, how far ought he to act with it? When ought he to leave his party? These are questions of great moment, as all know who have practical knowledge of the politics of liberty.

The law of Solon, according to which a man who stands neuter in time of sedition is punishable with "atimia," or loss of civic rights, has been called by Plutarch peculiar and surprising.[1] Solon, even though he may have erred in procuring the passage of this law, must nevertheless have had strong reasons. Undoubtedly he strove by this very law to

---

[1] Plutarch, Solon, 20; Cicero, ad Att., 10, 1; Aulus Gellius, Noctes Atticæ, i. 2, c. 12: "Solon capite sanxit, si qui in seditione non alterutrius partis fuisset." I own this seems to me to be one of those many laws which express a principle or theory, and may be repeated for centuries, but of which a man acquainted with the practical part of civil liberty cannot easily see the operation. One or the other party engaged in the sedition must be victorious. Suppose it is that party which was opposed to the administration in power. Can we imagine the successful party to begin their administration with indicting all citizens who did not take up arms against them, or punishing all who remained neutral, while they leave unpunished those who fought against them? But if it is expected that they will punish the neutrals, or passive, and all who fought against them, the law must needs work very mischievously. Indeed, it seems that the law of Solon would, if acted out, forestall every amnesty, with which peace must necessarily begin after civil commotions. I am not acquainted with a case of atimia having been inflicted for this offence of neutrality. When Emeric Tökeli was appointed commander of the Hungarian insurgents against the emperor Leopold I. in 1678, he proclaimed that he would suffer no neutrals. Since he fought against the imperialists, it is evident that he meant every one should be bound to take up arms with him. [Comp. Grote's History, vol. iii. p. 190.]

prevent broils and tumults, which, it has been observed already, must be frequent in small democracies if any excitement exists; on the other hand, he was probably aware of the fact that nothing favors strife and political turbulence more positively than when apathy or fear of mixing in the contest keeps the large mass of well-disposed citizens from taking part in politics. It surrenders the whole field to the restless and wicked, who certainly will try to occupy it, as they always have done. I do not know how it is now, but once the crime of murder was greatly promoted at Havana by the circumstance that as soon as the cry of murder was heard in a street, every one hurried away as fast as possible, that he might not become a witness and expose himself either to the revenge of the murderer's associates or the dangers and sufferings of the badly-conducted trials which were common in the Spanish colonies. We have spoken already of the general obligation of voting as resting on every one who has a right to vote. But the obligation of attaching one's self to a party is not so general, although I believe that in contests of great political importance it allows of but few exceptions. A man may be occupied with absorbing subjects lying wholly out of the sphere of politics, or he may, as actually will happen, expose himself and his family to danger or loss by decidedly joining a party. Yet, I repeat, these are but exceptions, and upon the whole it strikes me that the rule will hold, that a citizen ought, in times of great political danger, to attach himself to some party or other, if he can possibly find a party by taking part in which he does not do violence to his conscience, and if he has not very specific reasons for the contrary. There are, indeed, some men who are naturally timid, both in thought and in action. Their character is such that they may be useful members of society, if left alone; they are conscientious, and will not knowingly do wrong, but they become useless, and even dangerous, if they are forced out of their retired position, which is the element that the whole compound of their temperament requires. These two constitute exceptions.

XVI. Respecting the relation in which citizens may stand to parties, they may be classified, I think, under the following heads: apathists, neutrals or independents, party-members, partisans or zealots, factionists, and trimmers.

Of apathists, and their danger in free countries, we have spoken. If we understand by neutrals or independents those citizens who do not attach themselves to any existing and exacting party, and do not consider themselves pledged or in any way bound to vote with it on all those questions which in themselves are indifferent but become important on party grounds only, and who consider themselves perfectly free and disengaged to vote for whomever they think best—I speak of citizens at large—they form a highly valuable class of the community, and may contribute much to extricate their country from undue excitement and party action. But it must be well remembered that it is absolutely impossible for any person to have sufficient opportunity or grasp of mind to judge thoroughly and conscientiously upon every subject. Those who merely call themselves independent are not unfrequently influenced by ill-judging vanity; refusing to acknowledge that due influence which the opinion of friends and the aggregate opinion of that body of men whom one has reason to trust should always exercise over a rational man. The developments of events, of laws, and of institutions reflect themselves in parties, and we ought not to set up our stolid self-sufficiency against this fact. Of course, no man of self-esteem will consider himself so bound by his party as not fully to reserve his private judgment, to strike off from ballots, for instance, whatever names he thinks he ought conscientiously to leave out. Nor should he feel himself bound to stand up as a defender not only of all that the leaders of a party do, but of every single member, and of his private life as well as his political acts. Excited party-men not unfrequently make this demand; but this is party zealotism, and is as injurious to a sound state of the country at large as to a party itself. It weakens of necessity; while acts rising by way of justice, generosity, or truth above the party never fail to gain great strength for the party in the end; for they gain general confidence, which is power. Huskisson, when a member of the cabinet, went so far as to oppose, in 1822, a measure brought forward by the government through the leading minister in the commons; and he opposed it successfully. In the case of the East Retford Disfranchisement Bill he likewise opposed the government to which he belonged.[1] Very frequently, however, citizens call themselves independent in order to cover political vacillation, from weakness, inconsistency of temperament, or self-interest. They are the independent men whom Fox, if I mistake not, humorously defined when he said, an independent man is a man you can never depend upon. The latter, those who fluctuate between courses of action, are properly called trimmers, a term taken from nautical terminology, which has lost, I believe, much of its use since the times of Charles II. and James II., when everybody who was attached to the cause of royalty, and even ready to wink at much abuse, was stigmatized with the name of trimmer as soon as he showed himself unwilling to support and defend all the atrocities and corruptions of the court party. Real trimmers are to be shunned in politics as in every other sphere of action; for they are lacking in perseverance and manliness.

The remaining important questions respecting parties will be more conveniently treated of in the chapter on the opposition, which comes next in order.

---

[1] [Mr. Huskisson having in 1828 voted for transference of the franchise of East Retford to Birmingham, which the government opposed, resigned his seat in the cabinet on that account, with Lord Palmerston and others.]

# CHAPTER III.

Opposition. — Government. — Administration. — What is a lawful Opposition. — A well-understood Opposition the essential Safeguard of Liberty. — The Opposition a great Institution of Modern Times. — As such it dates from the Times of Walpole and Pulteney. — It is lawful to oppose the Majority, which is not always right. — (Order of Sitting in Legislative Assemblies.) — Public Opinion and General Opinion.—Ethical Rules relating to Opposition and to Parties in general. — How far ought a Citizen to go in his Opposition, especially in times of War?—Coalitions.—Parties formed on the Ground of foreign National Extraction.

XVII. GOVERNMENT, we have seen, is that establishment which has been agreed upon in order to obtain the ends of the state. It is the machinery of the state. We understand by government chiefly the characteristic and fundamental organism of the jural society, through which it acts as a jural society, including in monarchies the ruling family, inasmuch as the established dynasty is considered as one of the fundamental and, so long as that government exists, unchangeable features of the state machinery. The constitutional monarch is an institution. By administration we understand the application of those characteristic and fundamental principles to the occurrences of the day, and, more especially, the chief appliers of those fundamental principles; the chief officers— the cabinet ministers, who for the time have the application, the acting out, of the executive laws and government principles as they understand them, in their hands. Now, this administering of government, this application of the principles to practical cases, may not only be carried on in the spirit of wisdom, justice, conscientiousness, and soberness, or of folly, injustice, wickedness, and profligacy; but the best and calmest men may perfectly agree as to the principles of government but totally differ in opinion as to their application in specific and yet highly important cases. All those who desire a change of this spirit of application, and consequently of the chief persons—officers or law-makers—whose business it is to make this application, from whatever motive their desire may arise, and who unite in a party in order to prevent, by united efforts, the administration from the adopted course as much as possible, in order to dislodge those who occupy the chief places, so as to place in their stead persons of their own views, are called the opposition. An opposition is under and within the fundamental law, in England against the minister, for instance Walpole, in America against the president; but if in the former case the opposition went beyond Walpole and worked against George the First or the Second, as the Jacobites did, or if in the latter case an opposition should strive to subvert congress or the constitution, they cease to be oppositions, and become factions, treasonable bodies, or insurgents, as the case may be. Oppositions, therefore, are lawful; they are not only to be suffered, but they are, if not factions, of the greatest usefulness; and when the government itself becomes rebellious as to the fundamental law within and traitorous as to the relations of the country without, as for instance Charles II. became in the treaty of May 22, 1670,[1] with France, oppositions are the only safeguards to rescue a nation. Without well-understood, lawful, and loyal opposition, that support of all substantial civil liberty, namely, that the minority be protected and have every fair chance secured to them of converting the majority, would be either a mockery, or lead to continual violences; for opinion is like the air, harmless and easy if allowed freely to expand, but of tremendous power and danger if compressed.

XVIII. Without well-understood opposition, liberty cannot

---

[1] The treaty of Charles with France, after the conversion of Charles and James to Catholicism, in the second article of which it is declared that the king will make public his conversion, and receives the promise, from the king of France, of assistance by armed force in the carrying out of this design in Great Britain. For the copy of the original of this second article, see Life of William Lord Russell, i. 51, ed. 3. [Comp. Hallam, Const. Hist., ii. 518.]

co-exist with peace and order.[1] Hence the many sufferings of the republics in the middle ages. Nor is any state safe which excludes lawful opposition and treats all disagreement from the opinion of those in power as sedition or treason.[2] The fact is well known, that formerly the discharging of a minister from the divan of the Porte was always accompanied at least with banishment, and frequently with the silken cord: it was considered natural that he who is discontented must become, or thereby is already, a traitor. In most absolute monarchies, the displacement of a minister is called disgrace, and not unfrequently accompanied by a suggestion not to approach the capital within a certain circuit. So late as in 1610, when after the assassination of Henry IV. the imbecile French cabal had resolved to change all the political principles upon which that great king had conducted his government, Sully, his almost equally great minister, when informed of this change, said to his wife, "If I am wise, I shall quietly resign all my posts and employments, withdraw all my money, or as much as I can, with part of it purchase some strong castle in one of the most distant provinces, and keep the remainder for any exigencies that may happen."[3] So, absolute democracies or aristocracies could not endure opposition, not even the passive existence of those who were known to belong to the opposite side. Banishment followed banishment. Any administration in our modern representative states, which stigmatizes every opposition as factious, shows that it is either very weak or factious itself, and ought not to be borne with by the mass of substantial and good citizens.

---

[1] Mr. Ellice called Sir Robert Peel, in a speech relating to Lord Durham's mission to the Canadas, in January, 1838, if the papers be correct, the leader of her majesty's opposition. There is a deeper sense in this than that of mere pleasantry. The representative government of a free country is not complete without a lawful opposition. A proper lever is wanting.

[2] * In order to show the necessity and salutariness of opposition, I ought to have shown historically how often the principles of right and liberty have been insisted upon and carried by the way of excellent measures by the opposition, whether tory or whig. There must then be some classes of measures which can be more truly viewed by the opposition, simply because it is not in power.

[3] Memoirs of Sully, vol. iii. p. 260, Lond. edit. of 1761.

As to the history of this great institution, for thus I feel tempted to call it, I believe we cannot date its perfection farther back than under George II. against Walpole, after the Jacobites had given up the idea of restoring the Stuarts, and when Pulteney (afterwards Earl Bath) vigorously, yet not, at times, without the spirit of faction, led it. There existed, indeed, a regular opposition against William III., but it was generally more or less revolutionary; that is, it was in the interest of the Stuarts. The opposition in France mixes up frequently the two revolutionary parties of the legitimists and republicans, which is unavoidable so soon after the expulsion of a dynasty.[1]

---

[1] The manner in which members of legislative bodies place themselves is not a subject without importance in constitutional legislative police. It belongs to the external arrangements or police of parliamentary politics, hence to politics proper; yet I may be permitted to say a few words on it by way of note. The British commons sit on benches, close together, in rows on the right and left side of the speaker. On the right is the bench usually called the treasury bench, because the ministers take their seats there by custom, be they whig or tory. The administration party, therefore, sits always on the right, and the opposition opposite to them. In France the members, likewise at liberty to choose their places, arrange themselves according to party colors. The seats are disposed of in a semicircular form. The extreme right is always occupied by the party claiming to be the most royalist, or, as is the case now, super-royalist, that is, by the party who are for the old Bourbons; the extreme left, by those who claim to be the most liberal, or by republicans. Between them we have the right, the right centre, the centre, the left centre, and the left. Of whatever party the administration may be, these groups do not change their places. The ministers sit on distinct places appropriated to them. At one period during the first French revolution the Jacobins occupied the upper tiers, and were therefore called the Mountain party, while the Girondists occupied the lower seats, and were called the Valley. The American distribution of seats differs from both the present English and French arrangement. Each American member of a legislative assembly selects any one of the unappropriated seats which he likes, and keeps it throughout the session. I know of no exception in the various state legislatures. All party colors are mixed, administration and opposition are not represented to the eye. Each member has a desk, with writing-materials, drawers, etc., and the members sit in arm-chairs. This different arrangement may have originated from the fact that at the period when the like subjects were not yet settled by custom there was such unanimous spirit respecting the administration of General Washington that there existed no open, compact opposition. At present the disposal of the seats according to the choice of the first comer has been adopted in most of the standing rules of the legislatures. At first glance it might appear that the American method is prefer-

XIX. If there were any more truth in the pretended maxim that the majority is always right, and that it is the foundation of republican liberty, than in the monarchical, that the king can do no wrong, that is, if it were anything more than a political fiction to lay down rigid rules for the control of legislative bodies and citizens in their choice of measures, every opposition would be factious or treasonable as soon as the sense of the majority had been ascertained and an administration formed accordingly. We have seen in the case of the trades-unions that the majority may not only be grievously wrong, but they may naturally form the inferior body, and be disposed to oppress the superior—in that case the most skilled and most industrious. Republican liberty lies far deeper than in a maxim, such as that the majority is always right—a position a thousand times contradicted by history. Republican liberty consists, among other things, in the unrestrained right of the minority, of a fraction, nay, of an individual, to convert, if it can be done by lawful means, the majority; republican safety consists in the fact that the measures of those who have the power, even be they the representatives of an overwhelming majority, may become modified by opposition; for right, if we speak of any continued course of action, is never absolutely on one side. We may go farther: the more overwhelming a majority becomes, the more necessary, steady, yet lawful, opposition may become, and in most cases actually does become, lest government approach to the vortex of absolutism. The history of all civilization, and that of political is not excepted, presents hardly any other picture more frequently than that of an orderly succession of changes produced by minorities hardly visible in their origin, gradually

---

able, inasmuch as it might be supposed that it does not aid at least in increasing undue party spirit; but, upon the whole, the English arrangement strikes me as far the best, and the American as the least eligible. The sitting *close* together, according to parties, and especially without desks, is a decided preventive of those interminable speeches with which the smallest-minded always beset assemblies most, while the expediting of business is much promoted by sitting close and in parties together. The desks are objectionable, and ought to be abolished. [At present seats are taken more or less by lot.]

swelling in number and power, and enlarging in thought, modified by experience, and ultimately growing into a majority, supplanting a former one which has been gradually dwindling into a minority. A majority does not always even indicate public opinion, although it may show momentary general opinion, to which rumor belongs. By public opinion we must understand that opinion of the community which has been influenced either by the modifying correction of time, or the talent or knowledge of those who are peculiarly able to judge upon the subject in question. General opinion may be and very often has been egregiously mistaken. Error, want of information, fear, excitement, revenge, thirst for gain, pride, superstition, fanaticism, false shame—all these may be common to most or all members of a community, and consequently influence general opinion, and mislead entirely. Public opinion indicates always some settled more or less digested opinion respecting subjects which involve matters of right, the true appreciation of which consists in the due counterbalancing of a number of considerations. For this reason it is so important when it is turned towards these subjects; but as to matters of knowledge only a single individual may, and often has, justly set up his own thorough knowledge against the whole general opinion of his age and many antecedent centuries. It might perhaps be appropriately expressed thus, that by general opinion we mean simply the aggregate opinion of many individuals singly taken, an opinion which is general to many individuals; by public opinion we understand the opinion of the community as a connected and organized body, the ultimate result of mutually modifying or counterbalancing opinions of men who as the members of a community mutually influence and depend upon one another. But even well-settled and clearly-pronounced public opinion may be erroneous, and greatly so. It cannot be denied that it was public opinion at Athens that she should side with Philip. Yet Demosthenes was right. Public, at least general opinion, it was that cried out, Crucify, crucify.

On the other hand, it will have appeared, from the remarks

on public opinion in the first volume, that it is always entitled to the greatest respect, and that a citizen ought to follow it unless he have distinct and powerful reasons for not doing so; and that indeed he makes himself a very annoying member of the community, if he opposes it from supercilious vanity or wrong-headed arrogance, or a factious member, if he does so from sordid interest or sinister ambition. A means of judging with a degree of fairness between both parties is to consider them as if both were recorded on the pages of the past, as if you met with them in history; disentangle yourself from the meshes of self-interest, and before all apply the plain yet very powerful test of asking yourself, Would you frankly acknowledge your inmost motives—for which, however, you must diligently or honestly search—before posterity?

To return once more to public opinion. We have first to inquire whether the subject at issue is one on which there can exist any public opinion at all, so that we do not mistake general opinion for public. If millions believe certain statements touching matters of fact, of which I have undeniable evidence contrary to the general belief; if I live among people who yet judge by the mere appearance of the heavenly bodies, and who believe that the moon is larger than all the stars, or who pronounce a general for having lost a battle incapable, or perhaps a traitor, while I may have the undeniable knowledge to the contrary, or am perhaps acquainted with the opinion of a great captain who pronounces that general to have shown the greatest skill and talent in that very battle which he lost—in all these cases general opinion has no sort of weight, and I should prostitute my mind, perhaps my conscience, were I to follow it. The same is the case in many trials. There may be a very general opinion, loudly, clamorously expressed, respecting the guilt or innocence of the arraigned person, and yet the juryman before whom the facts are divulged in their successive order and in their true bearing ought to pay no regard to any opinion of any person or of the public except the judge only. Nevertheless, real public opinion is carefully and respectfully to be consulted, for the two reasons, first, that there is a very great chance that if it be settled, and, of course, touches a subject on which there can exist any public opinion, it is upon the main correct, and if not, that there is at any rate much to be learned from it; secondly, that it is the greatest, mightiest of all powers, and therefore not to be slighted. It must be observed, however, that it requires tact and honest observation to ascertain public opinion. Clamor is not public opinion. The organs of a nation, of whatever kind they be, for instance the members of legislatures, the public press, the courts, pronounce sometimes not only hastily, but repeatedly, one thing, while facts, carefully observed, show at the same time that public opinion, the settled sentiment of the people, takes its current in an entirely contrary direction. It is the discovery of the latter, and the acting boldly upon it, which has given some statesmen so great a power in executing vast designs, apparently in direct contradiction to public opinion, because opposed to what those organs, for some reason or other misrepresenting public opinion, pronounced. A common case of this sort is when parliamentary bodies opposed to an administration are dissolved, and an "appeal to the people" is made, who by their new elections show that they side with the administration, and that the former therefore misrepresented public opinion. Finally, a shrewd statesman may know that though this public opinion of the great mass, upon which he is desirous to found his strength against what he conceives to be the misrepresenters of public opinion, does not yet exist, the elements for it are there, and that it *will* rise and support him. This it was that Napoleon meant when he said that he was often obliged to act against all those who could express or represent public opinion, knowing that the masses would support him.

XX. If then a citizen is in the opposition—and indeed most of the ensuing remarks relate to parties in general, whether in or out—he ought to observe, it would seem, the following rules:

The moment that justice is sacrificed to party interests, the party or individual so doing becomes factious; for justice being the grand object of the law, of the constitution, of the state itself, the party sets itself above these, and makes itself its own object, while a party can have no right to exist except so far as it is formed for the public good. In denying justice the party turns into a faction. No party consideration, therefore, ought in any case to influence votes on private bills, especially not if the restitution of reputation or property be in question. If the old proverb, Fiat justitia et pereat mundus, has any meaning—and why else has it been handed down so many centuries?—it is certainly much truer still, fiat justitia et pereant partes.

There are many measures, for instance appointments for offices, which may be fairly and justly influenced by party considerations, provided always the honesty and fitness of the applicant be kept in view. We have seen already that it is ruinous to the whole state if persons are habitually appointed without regard to their fitness. As to appointments of broad utility for the people at large, and not merely for simple executive places, party considerations ought to have no sway, for it is the public service, not party service, which is the object. Appointments for critical transactions of great moment, for scientific tasks, for the administration of justice, ought to be influenced by party considerations only when there is actually a suitable choice left, which is not very frequently the case. It gives great strength to a party if it rises above itself and gives a frank vote on the mere consideration of public utility, nay, even of rewarding high individual worth, and sees only the honor and reputation of the nation at large reflected in such preference on account of talent and character.

There are measures which are of public utility, nay, of public necessity, and which an honest opposition may nevertheless oppose without becoming factious, because to adopt them would give new vigor to an administration which the opposition holds to be ruinous or vicious. One of these cases is the common one of supplies. A man in the opposition votes against supplies, not because he means to say that they ought

not to be passed, but simply because he desires to deprive
the administration of the means of getting on. But if the
proposed measure is one of broad and lasting utility to the
people, and would materially suffer, or even be only endangered, from not being passed now, it is factious to oppose it
though its passage would strengthen the administration. If
a citizen in the opposition were to oppose an advantageous
treaty, in order to prevent an administration which he considers vicious from gathering new popularity, it would be
highly factious. But the rule does not merely apply to the
more important class of measures. Suppose an opposition
member in the United States should be convinced that for the
essential benefit of the whole the decennial census ought to
be connected with an extensive collection of statistics, and
that this could not be executed without creating some new
offices, and yet, on the consideration that this would give new
strength to the administration, he should oppose it; such an
act would be reprehensible. The great question how far an
opposition ought not only to yield, after war has once been
declared, but to aid patriotically in carrying it to a glorious
end, belongs to this class of measures. Wars may be wicked,
nay, infamous or stupid; they may be undertaken for the
very purpose of distracting public opinion and turning it
against popular liberty; or they may be undertaken by a
large majority of the people, and yet against the decided
opinion of the opposition. Now, I believe that a rule, which
allows of but very few and peculiar exceptions, is this: If
your *nation* engages in the war, and not simply a preposter
ous *administration*, against your opinion, you may act in the
relations of a private citizen as you like, provided always you
do in no sort or manner aid directly or indirectly the enemy,
—although a patriotic citizen will not doubt what he has to
do; but if you are a representative or officer, you are bound
first of all to bring the war to a happy and glorious end, and
not to cripple the administration. The latter would be treasonable. Remember that it is your state, your nation, that
declares and fights out the war, not this or that minister;

remember that the honor and history of your country are engaged; that, however conscientious you may be in your opposition, you may err after all; that you cannot oppose the administration without strengthening the enemy who has unsheathed his sword against your kindred, and that, whatever your opinion was as to the beginning of the war, all considerations absolutely cease when the enemy approaches your own country.[1] A traitor is he who will not gladly defend his own country. If an opposition feels really and conscientiously convinced that the war is inexpedient, let them follow the old Roman rule: treat after victory, but fight until then. The English history from the times of Henry VIII. is full of instruction respecting all different sorts of war, but mean, imbecile as the government of Charles II. was, I suppose no one would call him a true Englishman who, however opposed to his corrupt court, should have embarrassed the administration after De Ruyter had swept the Thames with his broom on the quarter-deck. We must not forget that nations as a whole have their meaning and destiny; not the individual only.

In brief, if you are conscientiously in the opposition, annoy the administration as much as you think you can answer for, but do not harass the public or embarrass public service, and do not forget, while you make a distinction between the administration which you believe you may lawfully oppose, and public service on account of which you claim lawfully to oppose the administration, to make likewise the proper distinction between *your* opposition and the public; do not believe that everything which suits your party is on that account beneficial to the public because you believe the administration in the wrong.[2]

---

[1] * Fox went altogether beyond the proper line of lawful opposition when, in 1792, he sent Mr. Adair, as his representative and with his cipher, to St. Petersburg, there to frustrate the objects for which the minister from the crown was authorized to treat. He succeeded in this design, and did actually frustrate the king's minister in some of the objects of his negotiation. This was justly called treasonable misdemeanor at least. (Tomline, Mem. of Pitt, 2d edit., vol iii. p. 310, etc.) Fox did it on his own account. The party did not know it.

[2] [The author would doubtless limit these remarks to cases of expediency, as

XXI. As to our own judgment in party matters, we ought in all matters of expediency to yield fairly to the collected opinion of our friends, and not set up our self-sufficiency against them.[1] If it comes to principles, if, after careful examination, we believe that a compromise of principle is demanded, or that our party has become factious, we must either act for ourselves in the respective single case, or entirely abandon the party, all the clamor about deserters and traitors to the contrary;—though no good or prudent citizen will do this upon slight grounds.

The remark which was made, that a party ought always to take a broad national ground, as being the best preventive of pettishness or factiousness, applies especially to oppositions. In studying the times or history, we sometimes observe little oppositions which remind us of a dog tied behind a fast-rolling wagon. The animal opposes indeed, but, although its four feet are stiffly set against the wagon's motion, the four horses move on unconcerned about the opposer behind, who is obliged to follow, and, if he would but give up his opposi-

---

where there was just or lawful ground for war, but the war would be hurtful to national interests. An unjust war, like any other unjust transaction, must be opposed by all, whether in the opposition or on the side of the party in power.]

[1] Lord Durham said in 1837, "I have already, in parliament, proposed household suffrage and triennial parliaments, and my opinions are still the same. But at the same time I am not prepared to press them obstinately against those of other reformers; for, though I will not yield under any circumstances whatever to our enemies, yet I am not ashamed to say that when true and real reformers differ from me I give way to their particular views. As to vote by ballot, you are all aware, gentlemen, that considerable difference of opinion prevails upon this question. Some think it not advisable, and somewhat inconsistent with the practice of a free state; but I tell you that my opinion is decidedly in favor of the ballot. This is not a declaration made to serve a momentary purpose. Those who know me best know that I have long entertained that opinion, and that I have acted upon it. . . .

"Let me observe that when I alluded to the subject of compromise I meant compromise with an enemy, not that fair concession which may and must occasionally take place with a friend. There is no real reformer but will yield his opinion on minor points to those who are actuated by the same principles with himself; but what I object to is the system of mutilating and compromising to gain an enemy who cannot be conciliated."

tion, might trot comfortably enough between the wheels—nay, in the end might be taken up perhaps by the coachman, on the box. In short, if we do not oppose on broad grounds, we expose ourselves to that fault which we have called political grumbling, or—what is equally to be shunned—to spending the force of an opposition in merely harassing the other party. All broad, bold, open, straightforward, and persevering opposition earns esteem, but harassing embitters the opponent. By political harassing I mean all opposition for the sake of annoying. If the reduced party offers the annoyance, it will only irritate the other party still more and lead it on to violence; if the reduced party suffers the annoyance, it may be driven on to desperation; it is always embittered. In every political sphere, not only among parties, spite, annoyance, and wilful humiliation are as much to be shunned as in private intercourse, and they have ruined many a party, class, or government. They are forms of revenge, and therefore, with all kinds of revenge, totally to be discarded.

The question of coalitions of parties is not so important in an ethical point of view as in a merely prudential. If parties believe that they can conscientiously unite, without compromising principles which they hold and have ever proclaimed to be essential,—for without this they amount to factious conspiracies,—there is of course no objection on the score of morality. But it must be observed that although parties at variance as to essential principles may unite for some definite, well-understood, and publicly proclaimed end, as for the overthrow of an administration, after this each party is again to stand on its own ground. There is always great danger of contamination of principle, and that the broad moral principle of the party should be forgotten or overshadowed in the expediency of the case. Coalitions generally arouse distrust in the public mind against the coalescing parties, and if a coalition has been formed not only for attack, but also for continuance after the dislodgment of the administration, it is exceedingly difficult to give it that moral strength which a pure national party alone can have. Coalitions must, in their nature, be in most cases weak after they come into power: it is easy to oppose unitedly, as men of all different qualities may easily pull down a house, but their different opinion, taste, and skill would appear the moment that they came to rebuild it. In coalitions, one party is generally the dupe of the other. The coalition of Fox and Lord North was made to last, and not for opposition only; the coalition of part of the whigs and tories, the latter then generally Jacobites, against Walpole was such that a compromise of principle seemed evident, and the public very generally considered it as factious on that ground. The late coalition in France against Count Molé is perhaps the most interesting on record as for the mere purpose of opposition. It united, for the time, the extreme left with the extreme right, republicans with legitimists, with almost all intermediate shades, and nearly all the many ministers whom France had since the year 1830 and who supplanted one another in the various changes of administration. Of course, no one could believe that these many fragments could keep one moment together after their common object, the displacement of the administration, should have been obtained.[1]

XXII. I believe I ought not to conclude my remarks on this subject without adding a word on parties or fractions of parties formed on the ground of extraction or foreign nationality, a subject of importance in the United States. If a country is so happily situated as to be able to afford a ready reception to emigrants from distant countries, and the nation which inhabits it so liberally disposed as to offer their own citizenship, in its fullest and almost unlimited[2] extent, upon

---

[1] A remarkable coalition was that in Belgium preceding the revolution, by which the professed unbelievers united with the ultra-Catholic party. However, this has happened before, as for instance in England, even when persecutions were going on for heterodoxy.

[2] The foreigner by birth who has become a citizen of the United States is in every way whatsoever equal to the native citizen, except that the constitution does not allow him to become president of the United States unless he was a citizen at the time when the constitution was adopted.

easier terms than those of the naturalization of any other country, it appears to me, from whatever point of view we may take, even that of mere national courtesy not excepted, entirely inadmissible to form unions, of whatever consistency they may be, for political purposes on the avowed ground of different national extraction. Generally speaking, it is well, I believe, if an emigrant, after having become a citizen, abstains from all party matters proper, though he ought under the general obligation of the citizen conscientiously to vote, and thus may usually vote with a party. This, however, he must decide for himself; yet it strikes me that no choice is left him as to the other point, namely that of forming a party on the distinction of birth. He must decide for himself whether he will accept of the citizenship or prefer to remain an alien: when once, however, the oath is taken, he is bound by all moral and political considerations to be, act, and pass himself as a bonâ fide citizen of his adopted country, and not to abuse national hospitality in so glaring a manner as to throw the entirely extraneous element of foreign national feeling or animosity into the party movements and excitements of his adopted country. It strikes me as a very great dereliction of duty, and as a high-handed offence against true and conscientious allegiance—an ill return for liberal laws. There is nothing more dangerous to a country than the dissension of its citizens on the score of national extraction. We have the case of Canada before us. The Athenians and Romans would hardly have hesitated to treat such combinations as treasonable, if indeed they would not have spurned the idea of suffering them to grow into any sort of importance. The spirit of exclusiveness of the ancients, according to which all distant foreigners appeared as barbarians, would indeed have been sufficient to prevent the like affiliations on the basis of foreign nationality together with the enjoyment of full citizenship; but, though our religion as well as the diffusion of a common civilization over many nations teaches us far different sentiments regarding foreigners, I still believe that every citizen of a free country should cherish his own citizenship with sufficient patriotism, pride, and jealousy to prevent him from associating the names of foreign countries, however noble or endeared to him they may be, however sacred he may keep their names in the inmost recess of his soul, with affairs peculiarly those of his country. There is no just middle term, that I can think of, between an alien and a bonâ fide citizen joining heart and hand in the weal and woe of the country whose citizenship he has, by choice and not by force, received. If these remarks are founded in truth, it is clear that it is equally offensive in native citizens to foment this improper spirit, to make use of national inclinations and dislikes for party purposes, and to call upon those adopted citizens as the natives of foreign countries and according to their various nationalities. Is the citizenship of a free country so light a thing that it can be changed like a vestment and be put on temporarily only for convenience' sake, so that under it the foreigner remains a foreigner, unchanged, unaltered by the new oath of allegiance? We ought to change the ancient saying, "the sea washes off all evil," into "let the sea wash off all difference."[1] But what shall we say of those native citizens who make use of the ignorance or criminal levity of the lowest portion of emigrants, to bring them to the polls long before the law permits it, and who make these poor beings begin their career in the new country which they mean to adopt with a flagrant breach of its sacred laws, with a bribe and perjury? That they fully share in the guilt of this treble crime. If it is the fundamental law of a country that the majority of the lawful votes lawfully polled shall be the last decision, the final supreme authority, which decides and can be appealed to, it amounts to a contamination of the supreme authority when we corrupt it by the introduction of any foreign element. But enough was said on this subject when we treated of bribery.

---

[1] θάλαι τα κλύζει πάντα τὰνθρώπων κακά. Eurip., Iphig. in Taur., 1193.

# CHAPTER IV.

*Public Men.—Leaders.—Self-examination before a Citizen embarks in Public Life — Physical, Moral, and Mental Qualities desirable in a Public Man.— Necessary Knowledge for a Public Man.—Caution in entering upon Public Life.*

XXIII. In all free countries there are citizens who, owing to the influence they exercise over a portion of their fellow-citizens and in guiding or impelling the public mind, have left the sphere of the private citizen proper, and who may at times actually be charged with public offices, but need not be so, while yet they essentially influence the politics of their state. These men we call public men, and, according to their influence, leaders. Their influence depends upon themselves and upon circumstances. They may actually rule, and yet be not officers but simply public men. The most remarkable instance is probably afforded in the case of Pericles, who swayed the destiny of Athens for upwards of forty years, and yet was but a public man or leader. Where there is a real active political life, it is natural that there are public men, more or less influential, or important, according to the wider or narrower circle of the respective community in which they move. Every county, every village, even every ward in a large city, has its public men. From these, in the natural and salutary course of things, are generally taken those citizens whom the public of free states charges with offices, especially the representatives and all elective officers.

Now, whenever a man fails in his calling, mistakes his powers, and deceives himself as to his proper strength and natural vocation, bitter disappointment, perhaps an acrid temper, and, above all, the despairing consciousness of having failed in active usefulness and in gathering the harvest of a well-guided life, on the one hand, with a more or less direct injury to the community on the other, are the infallible consequences. How many men have learned with sorrow, in the middle of life, that they had wholly mistaken their powers, inclinations, or peculiar strength! All writers upon the various professions have endeavored to exhibit the characteristics necessary for the several callings, and the obstacles unavoidably met with in them, so that the aspirants may calmly examine themselves before they make so important a choice, which must very powerfully influence their peace and contentment through life. A proper self-examination of this sort, however, is more important before a citizen fairly embarks or suffers himself to be drawn into public life, than when he contemplates entering into other spheres of action. For of all the agents which may prompt a citizen to do this, a degree of ambition will almost always be one; and bitter indeed is the darkness of chill neglect which follows the bright dreams of ambition. The acquisition of wealth is but very rarely and by way of exception connected with politics in a free and comparatively pure country; yet though the citizen, when young, may have no desire of wealth, the years may come when he sees his former companions accumulating wealth and amply providing for their offspring, and when he regrets having pursued what now perhaps appears to him a bauble. Success in politics requires a peculiar compound of temperament, which is the free gift of nature and cannot be made at will; which does not, indeed, insure success, but without which success can rarely be calculated upon. Politics is an exciting pursuit, and whoever is accustomed to excitement finds without it an intolerable void, so that, once accustomed to excitement, the citizen will continually return to it, though he is conscious that he ought to give up a political career and that it is not his proper calling. And, finally, the freer a country, the more frequently are chances offered for embarking in politics. Yet a man who was not destined to be a public man, but nevertheless continually obtrudes himself into this sphere, is a great annoyance to a free community, and may, if he chances to obtain an influential employment, become a very dangerous and injurious member of a political society without even suspecting it himself, through his mistake of his own powers. We see, then, that a citizen owes it to himself, his family, and his community, not heedlessly to enter politics. Every man is a valuable member of the community if he is in his proper place, sphere, and utility; but a man who might have pursued the profession of medicine with real delight may feel himself daily disgusted with the profession of the law, and may do much harm to his fellow-citizens; and vice versa. A man that meets with constant disappointment as a merchant, or misses his true aim of life as a clergyman, might have made a contented, useful, active farmer, contributing his essential share to the common stock of national success. Philip III. of Spain, it is reported, exclaimed in anguish, on his death-bed, "Oh that I had never ruled! that I had rather been the poorest man!" Are there not many citizens who in the secret of their hearts feel something similar respecting their pursuit of politics?[1]

In order to see more clearly to what points this examination ought to be directed, it will be serviceable to inquire into the most necessary qualities of a public man, especially of a leader, as experience suggests them, or as we may learn what they are from the best leaders in history. Afterwards we may make the necessary and individual deductions from this image, when we look at the more reduced spheres of various classes of public men. I do not mean to say that no one can hope for success who does not combine all the qualities which will be exhibited. Genius, peculiar circumstances, may become powerful substitutes. Zisca commanded his army when blind. Nor do I say that the union of these qualities will insure

---

[1] * Many consider themselves, and are considered by others, most capable, until the real opportunity of showing it arrives, when at once it is seen that they seemed to be worthy of power only so long as they were out of it. "Omnium consensu capax imperii, nisi imperasset." (Tacit., Hist., i. 29, of Galba.) Out of power we may shine by speeches; in power action is necessary, not single actions, but substantial action throughout; that is, we must have sound fundamental or main ideas, of which the actions are but the *overt* facts.

success; but certain it is that without the conjunction of many or most of them a citizen cannot calculate upon or even hope for success. Nor is it sufficient to say that the freer a people the easier they will be the judges of the capacities required. No one who knows the least of the operation of politics in free countries will assert this. A man must have shown himself ready in some sort before they can choose him. Town meetings must lead to parliament or congress.

XXIV. A public man ought to be of a strong constitution, enjoy a free flow of health, and have naturally sound digestive organs; for the excitement and labor of public life, especially parliamentary excitement and long speaking, will affect even the best; but a deranged digestion is apt to deprive memory of its full retentiveness, the brain of its easy action, and to render a man nervous, and nervously sensitive. But a nervous man will ruin himself if he meddles with politics, unless, indeed, he confines himself to writing. He ought to have a fair and clear memory, or he will be continually defeated by surprise; exactness of mind, a natural tact of observation, of dissolving whatever appears around him into its elements and seizing upon what constitutes its vital principle; and that power of imagination which combines what is separated by time or space and grasps and seizes upon masses. He ought to have a ready eye for facts, for reality, and a keen mind to understand them thoroughly and to see beyond them—to divine. One of the greatest minds of the age has said, He who cannot read between the lines of a book cannot understand a great work. Well may it be said, He who cannot see between facts cannot understand a great nation or a great period, present or past, be he statesman or historian. A leader ought to have the native inventiveness of mind and elevation of soul which together produce that fecundity of which Cicero speaks when he says, " Periclem censet Socrates uberem et fecundum fuisse."[1] He ought to have that noble quality of

---

[1] [But Cicero, Or., 4, 15, attributes these qualities of Pericles to the instructions

communicating to others the moral sparks of his inmost activity, and the higher he rises the more he must trust in his own principles and purposes and freely leave to others their own respective departments in carrying them out. Defeat must not deject him; he must esteem his friends, and not reject their advice with obstinacy, yet be constant and firm. He must be cautious, yet have the courage finally and decisively to make up his mind and boldly to act accordingly, even where many reasons are for and against opposite measures. Let him be liberal in opinion and expense; a man of action, and of contemplative mind; love his kind, and be free from selfishness. He ought to be of a naturally confiding disposition, and not of a suspicious temper. We gain confidence by confiding. He will be deceived; yet if he trusts no one he will lose more, or rather gain nothing. He ought to be a firm friend, and be of that temper which can commune with minds in a sphere above the temporary questions which divide parties.

A leader ought to be a man of untarnished integrity and tried reputation; he must have sufficient ambition to impel him, and faith in those whom he leads. Men cannot for any length of time be led by mere imposition, nor can imposition sufficiently animate the leader. People soon find out whether he who wants their support despises them or has faith in them or his time. He ought to be a man of strong nerve, of elevation and purity of soul, rather than of delicate susceptibility; of tenacity of purpose, yet esteem for the opinion of others. He must know that his best-meant actions will be misrepresented, and that a thousand annoyances will be tried to disgust him. Let him disregard all attacks upon his motives and his character; his friends will take care of that. Pitt never answered a single one of the thousand slanders levelled against his motives; but when an editor accused him of speculating in the stocks while minister of the finances, he

---

of Anaxagoras, and refers to Plato (Phædr., 270, A.), where Socrates makes a similar remark. Inventiveness and elevation of soul are not referred to.]

promptly brought a suit of slander against him. A public man must not shrink from having his most private affairs scanned and misrepresented. As to his capacity, let him prove it by works and actions, not by words; it is the only effectual answer, the only convincing reply, in any sphere whatever. An ungrateful son represented Sophocles as in his dotage and unfit to manage his affairs; Sophocles read his Œdipus at Colonos, just finished, to the judges, and he was carried home in triumph. Aristophanes held up Socrates to ridicule in the theatre: the sage, after the conclusion of the satiric comedy, is said to have risen up out of his seat in the theatre, that strangers to him might have a view of his person.[1] When the fate of sacred music depended upon the sentence of the papal committee, of which the strict and devoted Charles Borromeo was a member, and much was urged to endanger it, Palestrina composed a work, on the manuscript of which are found the words, "O God, enlighten my eyes," and his work brought victory for his cause.

The public man must be a man of no timidity; he must be able to speak boldly before those who dislike his truth, and he must have courage to take his stand decidedly.[2] He ought

---

[1] [For the first anecdote see Plut., an seni ger., § 3, p. 785, c.; for the second, Æl., Var. Hist., ii. 13. Both need better vouchers.]

[2] As a striking instance of self-knowledge, not indeed otherwise to be imitated, I copy the following passage of one of the letters of Erasmus. "I see now," says he, "that the Germans are resolved at all adventures to engage me in the affair of Luther, whether I will or not. In this they have acted foolishly, and have taken the surest method to alienate me from them and their party. Wherein could I have assisted Luther, if I had declared myself for him and shared the danger along with him? Only thus far, that, instead of one man, two would have perished. I cannot conceive what he means by writing with such a spirit: one thing I know too well, that he hath brought great odium upon the lovers of literature. It is true that he hath given us many a wholesome doctrine and many a good counsel; and I wish he had not defeated the effect of them by his intolerable faults. But if he had written everything in the most unexceptionable manner, I had no inclination to die for the sake of truth. Every man hath not the courage requisite to make a martyr; and I am afraid that, if I were put to the trial, I should imitate St. Peter." Jortin's Life of Erasmus, London, 1808, vol. I. p. 250.

to be a man who can resolutely make up his mind, and, having made up his mind, promptly act; he must not be by natural constitution a man of timid hesitation or of that degree of scrupulosity which prevents one from finally making up his mind. When young, he ought to be careful before he compromises himself; at the same time he must know that he has no lever for whatever energy he may possess until fairly committed to some great principle.[1] No pilot can steer a vessel through a winding channel by orders from the shore; he must join his danger and hope with those of the crew. He must be frank, and his sympathies must be those of the people; without it they do not understand one another; he must be of enlarged liberality, yet keep out of debt, and command respect by all his domestic affairs; he must be calm, and in all the excitement around him be able to seize upon what is real and substantial, and separate it from what is but spray washing over the deck. He must be active, and a man of business. "Par negotiis nec supra," is a phrase of great import. Clarendon, no friend of Hampden, yet describes him

---

[1] Few things more strengthen the action of a man, whether in politics or any other sphere, than to be fairly and wholly committed to some great principle. It gives a steady direction and consistency to all the single actions, promotes self-respect and character, and gives efficiency to life, while in the public it inspires steady regard, and the important conviction, that the individual may be relied upon. That devotion to his principles alone, which the public can judge of only by a series of actions, will bring back to a man the public esteem that may have left him for a time. But a public man, as in truth any man who moves in any active life, cannot take too much care to avoid committing himself too easily in regard to minor points; for this must produce fluctuation. This danger is best avoided, not by subtlety or intrigue, but by silence—that silence, I mean, which is broken only when necessary. There are many garrulous men who daily commit themselves either upon points not sufficiently known or weighed, or farther than they intended; they then must retract, or modify—all which weakens. There is a great power in silence; a great manliness in suffering the actual cases to arrive, as the judge on the bench does, and decide when fully heard. Still, no man, of whatever genius in his respective sphere, can avoid committing errors. If such is the case, there is again great power in candor, in positively and frankly acknowledging a mistake. Only we must take heed, in this case again, to be calm and considerate, and not to be rash in pronouncing judgment upon our own error, as we were before in committing it.

as peculiarly made for a leader, and dwells repeatedly upon his calmness and activity, and on the fact that he was "not to be tired out." Alexander won his battles because he moved briskly about on horseback, while his stately enemy was enthroned on a scaffold or high wagon, that all soldiers might see him. Neither stately speeches nor senatorial mantles can lead; Napoleon was never so much himself as in his gray coat. It is action that gains respect and sways. Exactness and activity have given to many a citizen an influence far superior to that acquired by men of much greater capacity who were indolent. A public man must be a man of veracity; no arguments ever so conclusive will convince, if the hearers first of all do not believe that the speaker himself believes in them; he must be honest in money matters to a degree of minute scrupulosity; he must be ever ready to retire, content with his own merit, without grumbling; he must be prepared to meet with ingratitude, as every one must who follows him or serves those that have power. Let him be a man of fervent religious veneration; without it the busy life, practical turmoil, the immundicity through which he must wade, the thousand impurities with which he becomes acquainted, will infect him and make him sordid. His religion therefore must be of that true and genuine kind which enlivens and purifies, and rejoices in adoring and loving, and not that unhappy counterfeit of religion which benumbs the heart by encompassing it with dogmatic bitterness and narrow illiberality, or equally unjust and unholy fanatical excitement. His manners ought to be affable, yet never cringing; he ought at any moment to disregard his comfort, to revere justice, and love his country.

XXV. A public man ought always to know well the elements of his own society, be it small or large, its whole public and social economy. He must know how the things that are, the laws and customs, operate, and how they become such as they are. The history of the institutions of his country is indispensable for him, or he will commit a thousand errors or dangerous faults. He ought especially to study those periods in which the most important institutions rose to their highest action or showed their vigor in struggling into life. In brief, he ought to know the constitutional history of his country well, and if a nation has branched out from another at a time when the latter had already many settled and important institutions, as our nation from the British, he must connect the study of these latter with it. To these he ought to add the study of Greece, especially of Athens, and of Rome, because they were great nations, belong to the past, afford an undisturbed study, and unite with the glory of their rise and high civilization the pointed lessons of their decay and ruin.

A public man, acting in a wide or elevated sphere, will derive great benefit from the minute and deep study of some great man who with few means produced vast results, to whom he feels especial inclination. If he feels attracted by the peculiar character of a man such as Washington, Chatham, De Witt, Sully, and has the means of carefully tracing his character and actions, he will invigorate his soul and enlarge his mind by penetrating them and making them his own more and more. Fortunate will it be if, in addition to this, the literature of his own country furnishes him with a truly great poet, who has exercised a vast influence upon his nation and thereby shows that the vigor of his mind knew how to seize upon the vital principles of man's life in general and of his nation in particular. The English and Americans are peculiarly fortunate in their Shakspeare. A public man cannot read him too much. Not that he should learn particular lessons of public action in specific cases from this great poet, although even as to this point he furnishes golden passages which in times of need will suddenly rise up in the mind of one who is familiarized with his immortal works. But the reasons why I would recommend the ever-repeated perusal of his unrivalled poems are of greater extent. There is so vast a stage of action in his works, such a quintessence of all human life, such a vigorous delineation of character and such depth of observation, such an exuberance of thought, of subtle penetration, and endless variety of sentiment, all the differently combined motives of the infinite multitude of human individualities are so impartially viewed and given from a point so high above them, vulgarity is drawn so truly, and human greatness, joy, and misery are presented with such loftiness, that his works are like a concentration of all that is essential in the active life of men, of what ephemerally passes or historically lasts, so that no one can penetrate into his works without having his mind invigorated and enlarged and his vision made keener as well as loftier.[1]

XXVI. Every one, therefore, before he embarks voluntarily

---

[1] There is a remarkable passage in Las Cases, containing Napoleon's opinion of the poet Corneille and the influence which so great a poet exercises on a nation. Napoleon was then emperor, and ended with the words, " Yes, gentlemen, were he living now I should make him prince." Though he probably would not have done so, it sufficiently shows in what manner he viewed a great dramatic poet. Las Cases, vol. ii. p. 344, Paris ed. of 1824.

The passage of Mackintosh's pamphlet, A Discourse on the Study of the Law of Nature and Nations, in which he defends Grotius and speaks of his quoting poets and orators, deserves here to be mentioned. " He was not," says Sir James Mackintosh, " of such a stupid and servile cast of mind as to quote the opinions of poets and orators, of historians and philosophers, as those of judges from whose decision there is no appeal. He quotes them, as he tells us himself, as witnesses whose conspiring testimony, mightily strengthened by their discordance on almost every other subject, is a conclusive proof of the unanimity of the whole human race on the great rules of duty and the fundamental principles of morals. On such matters poets and orators are the most unexceptionable of all witnesses, for they address themselves to the general feeling and sympathies of mankind; they are neither warped by system nor perverted by sophistry; they can attain none of their objects, they can neither please nor persuade, if they dwell on moral sentiments not in unison with those of their reader: no system of moral philosophy can surely disregard the general feelings of human nature and the according judgments of all ages and nations. But where are those feelings and that judgment recorded and observed? In those very writings which Grotius is gravely blamed for having quoted. The usages and laws of nations, the events of history, the opinions of philosophers, the sentiments of orators and poets, as well as the observations of common life, are, in truth, the materials out of which the science of morality is formed; and those who neglect them are justly chargeable with a vain attempt to philosophize without regard to fact and experience, the sole foundations of all true philosophy.

in the rough and rolling vessel of politics, or suffers himself to be imperceptibly drawn into the currents of public life, ought to ask himself whether he be willing or able, according to his mental and bodily frame, to make all the sacrifices which he assuredly will be called upon to make, and whether public life might not become to him a continued chafing and disturbance of mind; whether other pursuits would not suit his particular temperament, constitution, and taste far better, and afford him that superior repose which our souls always derive from continued useful action blessed with success, or from mental activity which is peculiarly their own, and in which we feel we are completely what we were intended to be. There are some men so framed as to be strong, original, acute, and bold in the stillness of retirement, and to be capable of sending forth from thence many works of extensive and essential influence, affecting whole ages; or so organized that they are of substantial usefulness in all the varied social relations of their community, while unconnected with politics; but so soon as they are brought into contact with the concrete dealings political life involves, where things must needs be taken in mass, they shrink and lose their vigor.

Yet it may be asked, how is it possible to know before trial whether we are calculated for public life or not? The only rule, it seems, that can be given respecting this subject, is, first, that a citizen, doing all acts to which he thinks active public spirit should prompt him, should allow public opinion to concentrate upon him, that he should let public opinion seek him, and not himself seek public opinion for single employments or elevations, and that he should follow this rule throughout life, which guards even established public men against many errors; and, secondly, that having once begun his public career, he should be exceedingly cautious before he commits himself too much, while he has a fair earnest of public life and still is not yet so deeply affected by its peculiar character that a retreat would be too difficult.

# BOOK VI.

## CHAPTER I.

Extra-constitutional Meetings.—Their Necessity.—The Representative.—Summary of his Duties.—He is the guardian of the public Treasures.—When ought he to vote liberally?—The framing of Laws.—Legislation upon the Principle of mutual Accommodation.—Importance of a gentlemanly Character for the Representative.—Instruction.—History and the various Constitutions show that the Right of Instruction has been claimed and disclaimed as promoting and as injurious to Liberty, according to the Circumstances of the Times.—The Representative Government is not a mere Substitution for direct Democracy.—Essential character of the Representative Government.—The different characteristic Principles of Ancient States, the Middle Ages, and Modern States.—Nationalization of States; Socialization of Population.—National Representation the great Feature of Modern Times.—Difference between Deputative and Representative Systems.—Oath in New Jersey and the Netherlands to promote Public Welfare.—How does the Representative faithfully represent?—Advantages of Representative Government.—Objections to the doctrine of Instruction.—Instruction belongs to the Deputative System.

I. THE true and easy operation of a representative government, and, still more, the entire realization of national civil liberty, that is, of civil liberty as appertaining to a national state,—not to a city-state, of which presently more,—depends in a very great measure upon those many extra-constitutional, not unconstitutional, meetings, in which the citizens either unite their scattered means for the obtaining of some common end, social in general, or political in particular, or express their opinion in definite resolutions upon some important point before the people. These meetings may be entirely unofficial; sometimes they are semi-official, at others they are conventions of delegates, sent by the people, and yet they proceed altogether from the spontaneous action of society, without being called into existence by the prescribed rules of the constitutional law. No nation can hope for substantial civil liberty before it is well acquainted with this important social agent, so indispensable for modern, that is national, liberty. Many attempts at liberty have failed, because the people had no idea of these free extra-constitutional meetings, and expected constitutions to operate without them. In these meetings society frequently acts as such, separate from the state, for instance when they consist of members sent for industrial, or, as we have lately seen, for scientific purposes, from various countries; sometimes they are greatly abused and made the seat of party excitement; but, generally speaking, it is undeniable that they are at once the generators of that interior power which makes the machine of a constitutional government move and work in a national spirit, and the safety-valves through which the superabundant volume of that power escapes, when otherwise it would cause fearful explosions.

If we comprehend under these meetings all those which are composed either of the people themselves, or of delegates having an extra-constitutional character, we shall see at once that they are of great importance in order to direct public attention to subjects of magnitude, to test the opinion of the community, to inform persons at a distance, representatives or the administration, for instance, of the state of public opinion on certain measures, whether yet depending or adopted; to resolve upon and adopt petitions; to encourage individuals or bodies of men in arduous undertakings requiring the moral support of well-expressed public approbation; to effect a union with others, striving for the same ends; to disseminate knowledge by way of reports of committees; to form societies for charitable purposes or the melioration of laws or institutions; to sanction by the spontaneous expression of the opinion of the community measures not strictly agreeing with the letter of the law, but enforced by necessity; to call upon the services of individuals who otherwise would not feel warranted to appear before the public and invite its attention, or feel authorized to interfere with a subject not strictly lying within their proper sphere of action; to concert upon more or less extensive measures of public utility, and whatever else their object may be. It does not seem, however, necessary to dwell upon them particularly with reference to political ethics, except that, as they are necessary and salutary if freely and calmly operating, it becomes the greater dereliction of duty in influential men to use them for selfish ends, so that the country, instead of reaping the benefits of a steady operation of social agents from them, is exposed to all the feverish and withering effects of passionate, fluctuating, and wild agitation. A citizen of probity ought to remember two things: first, that he deceives himself who feels flattered by the exciting agitation which he has been able to produce—for it is frequently very easy to produce this effect, and the easier the less proud we should feel of those upon whom excitement has been produced. It is the calm and substantial action—action which bears within it the genial power of vivifying the seeds of action in others—of which alone a true man feels proud. Secondly, that the extra-constitutional meetings resemble in their necessity and usefulness, and at the same time in their possible abuse, other primary agents of society and of nature: they are salutary, if in their proper path; fearful, if in irregular licentiousness.

Those who are not personally acquainted with the practical operations and necessities of civil liberty are apt to consider all popular meetings as so many deviations and exceptions from the regular government, and ask, where is the guarantee against their abuse? The guarantees against the abuse are varied, manifold, and mutually connected; to a great extent they consist in mutual modification. An absolute guarantee exists against their abuse no more than against that of any primary vast principle. Great as the principle of modern hereditary monarchy is, and forming and having formed one of the agents of modern European civilization as it does, where is the final guarantee against the chances of birth, of contractedness of mind, or weakness of conscience, except in the mutual modification of a number of other political agents? The sun warms and enlivens, but we have no guarantee against all the injury he may do, and actually does in a thousand instances, in parching the soil or breeding fever.

The citizen ought to keep in mind that unnecessary meetings either excite and stir uselessly, and therefore injuriously, or lessen the interest in public meetings, which is equally undesirable, and may be injurious to public liberty; and that, on the other hand, it is unbecoming a free man, who values his liberty, to be prevented by civil indolence from taking those measures which through public meetings would produce demonstrations of public sentiment sufficient to arrest danger, pusillanimity, or civil immorality. If a citizen is sent as a delegate to a meeting for a specific end, especially political, he must be the more careful not to transgress the lines which we have endeavored to ascertain as the proper limits of party movements, the more definite the end is for which he has been sent, and the more decidedly he has been sent, perhaps, on party grounds; in brief, the more avowedly the end of the meeting is one of a party character, the more imperative becomes caution against being betrayed into factiousness.[1]

II. Before we proceed to consider the citizen in office, having viewed him in his capacity as an individual member of the state, we have to examine him in one of the most im-

---

[1] The pamphlet is one of the great agents of modern liberty, and of the greatest usefulness, in nations who value it. Some English pamphlets have acquired historical importance. They are excellent vehicles for certain communications, but they do not dispense with the public meeting. The public meeting is always necessary for *action*. Nations who neglect the public meeting and rely on the pamphlet alone for discussion of subjects of the deepest interest will not come to energetic action. Dumont goes so far as to express the opinion that the parties which multiply pamphlets weaken their power and hold on the public: they accustom themselves to talk instead of acting. I counted in the publishers' catalogue of 1838, sent me from Germany, one hundred and thirty writings, more or less voluminous, on the question of the archbishop of Cologne. In the United States there is a deluge of pamphlets, but on a thousand different and very frequently wholly uninteresting subjects. The unfortunate fashion of asking every one that delivers some public speech or other for a copy, and to print it—a fashion so common that it is no longer any honor, while its omission conveys a reflection—deprives the American public of all courage to look at anything issued in pamphlet form.

portant stations in which he can be placed, a position peculiarly belonging to modern civilization—namely, as a representative of his fellow-citizens, that is, as elected by a number of them to share in and contribute to the legislation of their jural society or state. On what he ought to legislate, and how he ought to do it, are questions to be answered by the science of politics, and involve in fact the whole subject of legislation, political society, social and public economy, and can of course not be expected to be developed here, nor indeed in any work, with specific reference to the representative. In general, it is his duty to make himself acquainted to the best of his ability with all the subjects essentially affecting public welfare, and especially affecting that portion of the society which he represents. On the other hand, it appears manifest that all the general rules given in the preceding pages as applying to the conduct of the citizens in general or of public men in particular receive additional force if viewed in connection with the representative; for he stands not for himself alone; his conduct, influenced by and reflecting in a great degree the general temper of the society which he represents, strongly influences it in turn. All his responsibilities as a man and citizen are infinitely multiplied, as are likewise, in many cases, his temptations—for instance, in party matters the temptation to transgress the proper line between party and faction. Yet it may not be without some profit if we reconsider or point out in particular a few principles of especial importance regarding the representative; after which I propose to inquire into the important question of instruction, which involves that of the essential character of the representative.

Perhaps we may sum up the most important points in the following manner:

Justice, truth, and disinterestedness are with him above every other consideration, and lend far greater strength than their dereliction ever can do.

The true representative is in the service of the public: he is sent neither for his own ambition or gain, nor for his party neither to serve exclusively a certain privileged class, nor a single division of the nation according to occupation or interest.

Liberty demands for him ample freedom of speech: hence his conscience alone must in most cases regulate the use which he makes of this great liberty of speaking before his nation, both as to the time which he occupies and takes from the furtherance of other business, and as regards either the principles or views he may thereby disseminate among the people at large, the standard of his respective assembly, which he may thus contribute to raise or lower, and the character of individuals which he may injure. No representative ought ever to speak except for the furtherance of that business which is actually before the house; and then always to the point.[1] There is no real, no masterly, eloquence except that which is strictly to the point. Demosthenes, Cicero, Chatham, Burke, Foy—I abstain from mentioning living orators—amply prove it,[2] and their best passages most so. Habitual, loose, prolix,

---

[1] * Simple as the following rule may be, it is of very great importance both to the community and to your own influence:

Speak never unless there is an especial reason for it, and this can consist only in this:

That you know the subject, or some part of it, thoroughly, or better than any one else;

That you are universally expected to speak, and silence would be misconstrued,

To justify your own vote, to the community;

To repel an attack upon yourself if very marked or peculiar, upon a particular friend, upon your constituents or part of country;

To explain;

If your constituents are the particular subject. At least, in such case, if all that is to be said has been said and well said, you ought to rise and say so, and that you mean to vote one way or the other. It is decent towards your constituents.

To talk against time may be an excusable artifice for some high purpose, but it is very rarely so.

If you are known to speak only if you have anything to say, you derive great influence from this fact alone.

But to speak for two or three hours solely to have your voice heard is folly.

[2] The more active men's thoughts are on a subject which engages their attention, and the better it is understood, the plainer, simpler, and more forcible are the discourses respecting it, in books as well as in speeches, on religious as well

and low speaking, without the nerve of thought and high sentiment, has a very decided and injurious effect upon the public at large. Every man who is really filled with his object, that is, whose soul and life belong to it, and who, therefore, acts for it, is brief-spoken. Soldiers, physicians, ministers, Christians, who are what they are wholly and thoroughly, act, and do not talk much of their action.

The honesty of the representative, applied to money matters, comprehends care with regard to himself individually that he propose or vote for or against no measure on account of any individual advantage, direct or indirect, out of the money of the people. According to the peculiar development which the representative system has taken in the European race since the middle ages, he is and ought to be the especial guardian of the public money. Waste in governments is not only oppressive to those from whom alone the money can come for any length of time and to any amount—the people; it is not only a great injustice, but wastefulness is immoral in its character. It leads the government from its true end and object, begets a desire for wealth without labor, and thus trains men in corruption, to the destruction of public spirit, independence, and virtue. Monarchies and republics are

---

as on political matters. Not that I undervalue, in any degree, true eloquence: I hold ready, striking, and elevated eloquence as one of the very noblest manifestations of the human mind; but it is this very eloquence which suffers and is stifled by a flowing style, tasteless disquisitions, or far-fetched comparisons. How simple are Demosthenes and Chatham! Any one who has read the speeches of the deputies composing the estates at the beginning of the modern age will have observed how unwieldy and pointless their words are, and—what is indeed a necessary consequence—how obscure they leave the main subject. To give but one instance, I would refer to the French diet of 1593, of which Raumer gives contemporary accounts in his already quoted History, etc., vol. i., towards the end. The Old Testament, and natural history and philosophy as then understood, are ransacked before an idea is expressed, such as that the third estate, though inferior to clergy and nobility, still forms part of the state. The history of British eloquence, as it may be gathered from various historical works, and on which it is high time that we should be furnished with a thorough and philosophical treatise, shows the same progress, namely, that the simplicity and truth of eloquence increase together.

equally bound to shun wastefulness. A nobility feeding and feasting upon the money of the people recklessly squandered away by a corrupt court, like that of Charles IV. of Spain, Charles II. of England, or Louis XV. of France, is as dangerous as the Athenian demagogue or Roman seducer of the people who distributed the public treasure among the populace.

Yet parsimony is not saving, but waste in disguise, in all human affairs, in public not less than in private. Jealous of all public expenditure to a degree of rigidness, the representative ought ever to be liberal first of all in every case of justice, which ranks above all things, and surely above the popularity of the representative and the disposition of his constituents. Indeed, giving every one his due cannot be called liberality. Therefore, the representative must readily vote for the discharge of all debts of the public to individuals, and punctiliously for the fulfilment of all engagements for which public faith stands pledged. The force of the law which binds the intercourse between citizen and citizen ought to be felt most imperatively when the question is one of engagements between the state or any part of it on the one hand, and individuals or other states on the other. Prudence, happily, coincides here with justice; for nothing opens greater resources for a state in a thousand different ways than undeviating justice and honesty in all its engagements. If representatives would consider how small the amount of the state's just dues become, when one compares the public means for paying them with the public gain obtained by the act of justice, they would never hesitate to vote frankly and readily for the discharge of any honest debt. History furnishes abundant examples both of encouragement and of warning.

The representative ought liberally to give his vote for all expenditures, commensurate to the means of his society, for the essential promotion of education, that is for the elevation and extension of knowledge, and for promoting the elevation of mind, be this by way of diffused knowledge or the promotion of discovery and of the arts. He ought liberally to vote for all improvement of intercommunication,[1] if it cannot be obtained by private means; for appropriations demanded by the needs of administration, public justice, and public security. The representative ought readily to vote for what is due to faithful and efficient service, according to the general standard of reward in the community at the period in which he lives. One of the main objects of all calm and settled governments must be to render justice as purely and effectually and to protect society within and without as powerfully as possible, and, in striving for these objects, to press as little upon the people as possible: these ends are accomplished, not by contriving that the citizens shall pay little or less than is necessary (which indeed makes a very expensive government), but that they shall receive the fullest possible equivalent for the justly decreed and levied taxes which they pay. There were few, and frequently no, systems of constant taxation in the middle ages; every free and elevated nation at present has many. Yet our present governments in the end are cheaper than those of the middle ages. If, for instance, the regular administration of justice by sufficiently paid judges demands a greater outlay than irregular justice dealt out occasionally by officers appointed likewise for other purposes, as for the executive and military command of a county, which was frequently the case in the middle ages, we must not forget the immense gain of the people in the rise of property and value of labor, effected by regular and systematic law courts.

In framing or voting for a law, the representative ought to consider well whether the law, intended as it is to be general, rests on a general principle and is not a mere expedient; and, on the other hand, how it will operate, together with its general principle upon, or by means of, the given circumstances of the society for which the law alone is calculated: yet he ought never to introduce a law for its supposed philosophical principle alone, which is but a misnomer; for no law is philo-

---

[1] [Qu. by incorporations only, or by money grants to private individuals or companies?]

sophical which does not grow out of the given circumstances —out of that society for which it is calculated. They are but the productions of the brain. Locke's constitution for South Carolina, and the first French republican constitution (the second in number of the many constitutions which that country has witnessed since the first revolution), are illustrations. A wise law must have these two requisites: it must be called for by the circumstances, and must consist in a just principle judiciously applied to these circumstances, which implies that it be harmoniously applied to the whole state system and do not jar with it. The representative ought to test the bill upon all imaginable adverse grounds; for he may rest assured that, in the endless variety of combined cases which practical life daily offers, all the weak or mischievous points of the law will some time or other come into play or develop themselves. In finally making up his mind as to all that is urged for and against a general law, it is average justice which must guide him. In this consists one of the great differences between the legislator and the judge, who must not decide by average justice but deal out specific justice. Finally, the representative ought on no account to change partially or entirely an organic law of the state in order to suit a particular and momentary end, whatever the excitement or strong desire of the moment may be. To do so is the worst of all legislation, even if not against the solemn oath of the law making department.

The representative, like every public man, must prove in all his acts that he is actuated by public spirit, by patriotism, leading him not only to self-denial, but also controlling him in all the wider circles of his political activity. He ought to obey the law which prevails throughout the universe, that the greater, wider interest prevail over the lesser and narrower. The interest of the country or of the state must be preferred to that of the province; that of the province to that of a county; that of a county to that of the town; that of the town to that of a street; that of the street to that of a house; that of the whole house to that of an individual in it; that of our whole family to that of ourselves individually.

The fact that every law ought to have the nerve of a general principle, that it ought to stand the test of general consideration, even though it be a private bill or a bill directly affecting but a part of the community, prevents, if conscientiously acted upon, that public calamity of legislation arising out of the mutual accommodation of separate and selfish interests, which on a gigantic and enormous scale was acted out when the Roman triumvirs made the grand compromise of their proscription-list, and which is always in principle equally immoral. It is, as we shall see more fully below, directly opposed to the true representative principle, and was one of the great difficulties in the way of safe politics in the states of the middle ages. In a limited degree it is unfortunately still acted upon in some legislatures, and has received in one of the American states the vulgar but not unmeaning name of log-rolling, because when the people clear the aboriginal forests they unite their labor in removing each other's heavy logs. The simile of this union of labor truly applies to the mutual support in the state, but the comparison of the log with a bill to be passed is seriously vicious. It was an awful log-rolling of this character indeed when, as alluded to, Antony, Octavius, and Lepidus united and gave up each other's friends and their common country. In principle, all political log-rolling amounts, more or less, to conspiracy.

The representatives are deeply interested in always supporting the character of the true gentleman. Whatever the apparent sacrifice for the moment may be, they will greatly gain in the end by it: their example strongly affects the manners and intercourse of the community, and large and gentlemanlike conduct in all transactions of life is of moral and political importance, as has been mentioned before. The whole character, efficiency, and wise action of a deliberative assembly depend in a very great degree upon the habitual gentlemanlike conduct and intercourse of its members. Decorum in the speech and manners of legislative assemblies has the same important bearing on their dignity, their self-respect, and, consequently, on the respect paid by others to their manly action and moral deportment, which universal decorous habits of a nation in dress and domestic life have on a universal feeling of independence, self-respect, and political dignity. Personalities, therefore, are usually against order in these assemblies;[1] nor will a member be apt to resort to them who values even his own influence. It is generally one of the greatest advantages which a member can throw into the hands of an opponent, if he deals in personalities and the other does not retort on him, but shows his respect to the assembly by an unruffled reply.

Lastly, the representative must be the true representative of his constituents. What is the entire meaning of this expression? It is the answer to this question which will occupy our attention on the following pages.

III. According to the natural order of the subject, I ought to treat first of pledges, and then of the right of instruction;

---

[1] Hence very properly it is out of order in the British parliament and in all American legislatures and congress to speak of a member by name. The rules of order can, however, carry decorum too far; especially if the order is that members must appear, or at least speak, in a particular dress. This is against all business-like debating, and leads to that unfortunate custom of reading prepared discourse after discourse without any reference of one to another. Louis XVIII. dwells on the importance of his prescription of the *robe* in which alone the deputies were allowed to speak. He was right from his point of view; it was to restrain genuine debate; but where real liberty and conformable legislation is the object, the matter assumes a different aspect. It is for business these assemblies meet, and not for parade; and no one can have seen the former French chamber of deputies—I do not know the precise character of their present transactions—and the British commons, without perceiving at once that legislative debating is wholly a natural, genuine thing with the latter, which it had not yet become with the former. As to the members keeping their hats on, as the British commons do, and the members of congress did until 1837, unless speaking, a certain taste of course can alone decide. I confess, I rather liked it; it showed the business style of the house; and there is history in it, as well in the case of the English parliament in particular, as that in general the cap, the hat, and to remain covered, have always been with the western race, from the times of the middle ages, the emblems and evidences of liberty and independence.

but the latter involves a discussion of the true character of representative governments, and many points which materially serve in solving the question of pledges, so that it will be advisable to treat of instruction first.

By instruction of a representative we understand, in the politics of representative governments, his being directed by his constituents, subsequent to his election, to vote on a question yet depending, in a manner pointed out to him; or the command over the vote of a representative by his constituents The relations of representatives to those who elect them are different, and the subject of instruction has been viewed accordingly. If a political body, organized and belonging itself to the government, elect representatives, as is the case with the senators of the United States, who are elected by the state legislatures, instructions are held by many to have mandatory power; that is, they must be obeyed. If the constituents, it is farther maintained by some, are the people themselves, and the convening of them, except at the election, is not regular or in forms prescribed by law, the instruction can have no mandatory power, but ought to be unreservedly obeyed as soon as the representative is convinced that the instruction expresses the opinion of the majority of his constituents.

I shall treat of the subject in as far as it relates to the United States senators separately, and first view the matter in general.

Before we proceed, however, it is necessary to divest the question of all the undue associations that generally cling to every subject which has strongly and in opposite directions interested large numbers. The most important of these is the belief of many persons that an adherence to the doctrine of instruction is naturally coupled with a warm affection for general liberty, and that those who disclaim the doctrine belong necessarily to that class of men who habitually distrust the masses or are shy of general liberty. It is easy to be explained why this view should be prevalent now on account of the late history of this doctrine; yet the view is unfounded, as can be shown from history. It was the very instructions received by the members of the mediæval estates which prevented the nations, with the exception of England, from rising to general civil liberty; and, on the other hand, the second republican constitution of France, of 1795, surely not wanting in democratic spirit, contains the following paragraph (§ 52): "The members of the legislative body are not representatives of the departments which have elected them, but of the whole nation, and no specific instruction shall be given them." The same expression is to be found almost verbatim in the constitution of the Cisalpine republic of 1797. In all the constitutions established under the dictatorship of Napoleon, the terms national representative and national representation are carefully avoided; and when he was greatly dissatisfied with the deputies, convoked, in consequence of his disastrous campaigns, in 1813, after they had been disregarded during his imperial reign, he said to a deputation of them, "And who are you? Not the representatives of the nation, but the deputies of the departments."[1] On the other hand, again, we find in article ninth of the constitution or "Edict" of the grand duchy of Hesse, of 1820—an instrument which no reader of Anglican views would consider liberal—that no member of the first or second chamber can exercise his vote by proxy, or receive instructions for his vote.[2] So has the constitution of the Batavian republic, of 1805, by which Na-

---

[1] It was on the same occasion, January 1, 1814, that Napoleon strikingly expressed the view he took of his whole position: "You strive, in your address, to sever the sovereign from the nation. I alone am the true representative of the nation, for who of you would be able to take upon himself this burden? The throne is a thing of wood covered with velvet; only he who occupies it gives meaning to it," etc. I have heretofore remarked that Napoleon was the French democracy grown into monarchy; his power rested, like that of the Roman emperors, upon popular absolutism. See the end of book second. How different from this avowal is the British expression, "The queen is an institution."

[2] The prescribed oath, taken by every deputy, runs thus: "I swear fidelity to the grand duke, obedience to the law, punctual observance of the constitution, and to further the common weal only, in the meeting of the deputies, according to my own best conviction, uninfluenced by any charge" (instruction).

poleon, having crowned himself as emperor of the French, made that state approach more nearly to monarchy, for which he had destined it, the following provision (Art. 23): "Their high mightinesses (that is, the representatives) vote singly according to their personal opinion, without mandate or instructions received from the departments. They are in no manner answerable to the departmental meetings for their conduct in the hall of their high mightinesses." The anxiety to sever the representative from his constituents is here evident. Lastly, I may mention here the bill of rights, preceding the constitution of North Carolina, adopted in 1776. Article eighteenth of that bill says, "That the people have a right to assemble together, to consult for the common good, to instruct their representatives, and to apply to the legislature for redress of grievances." But what, according to the public law of that state, this instruction precisely is is not clear; for the legislature of North Carolina passed, in 1838, certain resolutions with reference to the votes to be given by her senators in congress on a question of importance then pending; and when the senators asked whether they should consider these resolutions as instructions, the legislature passed a resolution declaring that they had spoken clearly enough, and declining any more distinct or mandatory instruction.

In short, if we peruse the one hundred and thirty or forty written constitutions, more especially so called, which the European race has produced, we shall find that instruction has been declared inadmissible sometimes because the powerholders granting the constitution were afraid of too direct a connection between the representative and his constituents, sometimes because the people establishing the constitution felt that it was impossible otherwise largely to protect civil liberty and give it that guarantee which advanced political civilization and national liberty demand. Adherence to the doctrine of instruction, therefore, is of itself in no way a sign of liberal politics. Instruction has been claimed and disclaimed on entirely opposite grounds, according to the peculiar circumstances of the time.

IV. The doctrine of instruction, as it is now presented by its advocates in the United States, may be stated thus: The representative ought, as far as he is able, truly to represent the wishes of his constituents, and if on any important question the views and desires of the majority of his constituents are made known to him in any manner which convinces him that it is really the voice of the majority, he ought either to obey, or, if he cannot conscientiously do so, to resign. An attempt is thus made to give to the representative a character between that of a representative and a deputy, the difference between whom we shall presently consider more accurately. The chief arguments urged in favor of the above doctrine, and in fact, as far as my knowledge extends, the only ones, are these: That, could the people meet, as in ancient times, in the market, they would act for themselves, each according to his interest and views, and that now, when the number of inhabitants or extent of country prevents them from meeting in a general and primary assembly, it is clear that those who are sent for the mere sake of expediting the business, instead of the people's convening themselves, must speak as the people themselves would have spoken. The representatives are the speaking-trumpets of their constituents, and nothing more. Secondly, which in fact is but the above in other terms, the representative is the servant of his constituents; and how can he be called a servant if he does not their will? See Tucker's Blackstone, Appendix, 192, et seq., where Judge Tucker quotes with entire approbation a passage from Burgh's Political Disquisitions, from which it appears that both of them had in mind, when speaking of popular liberty, what was called in the first part of this work democratic absolutism, seeking for the essence of liberty in the entirely unrestrained execution of the will of the people, which is in practice, as a matter of course, of the multitude or the majority; but not in guarantees, checks, and organic laws, controlling the will of the supreme power, whoever may be its holder. The question does not, indeed, seem to be solved, according to their own argument, in this manner; for the term people is in this case, as in so many others, taken in different meanings in the same argument. First, when it is maintained that the representative is the representative of the people, the word is used as meaning the aggregate of all men of a certain society; a groundwork is thus obtained for the right of instruction; but when it comes to the most important point of the right of instruction, namely the guidance of the individual representative, the word people does not mean any longer the aggregate of all the citizens as imagined in the agora, but the small part only who elected the particular representative. If the representative is merely a speaking-trumpet of the people who can no longer assemble, it appears to me perfectly clear that consistency would actually demand that he should speak say three hours for a measure and one against it, if he has been elected by six thousand votes against two thousand, for these two thousand would or might have spoken in the general assembly and laid their views before the assembly. I beg to observe that this is not advanced in a sportive sense but gravely. If we are to have absolute democracy with agents who do not speak for the minority, this minority loses all the right which it had in the primary assembly.

Those who build the theory of instruction upon the fact that the representatives are the servants of the people, do not inform us who are meant by the people, whether the voters only, that is the majority of the voters, or the people at large, of whom many may not have the right to vote but certainly are members of the state and ought to be represented, for instance where freeholders or householders alone possess the elective franchise.

Now, at no time has the doctrine been maintained that the laws of the assembled citizens should be adopted according to a balance and calculation of the individual and selfish interests of each individual; but, the frequent practice to the contrary notwithstanding, it has always been maintained that even when the citizens assembled in the agora they were expected to judge of general measures with reference to general welfare, according to the light which they might receive then and there. The contrary has always been considered as detestable meanness, or even selfish treason, and acts of egotism were positively punished in Athens on the ground of egotism. The more corrupt the times in those republics founded upon direct and absolute democracy were, the more frequent and loud we find the demagogues in their protestations that they act for the public benefit only. Where has there ever yet been a man who recommended a measure except on the real or pretended ground of public, that is general, benefit? If the Athenian citizen had not been expected to vote with reference to this public and general advantage, but with reference to his tribe, section, or street, I do not see where we can stop until we come down to the individual himself; and what becomes of public spirit, country, and all that is good and glorious in political life? No people ever were farther from such views than the ancients. But if the representative has to obey the so-called instruction of the people, that is the instruction of the majority of voters, which may indeed be a small minority of the people, the result would be far worse than the one resulting from absolute democracy founded upon mere individual selfishness; because in the ancient forum each voter heard at least what was urged for and against the subject in question, not indeed elicited by debate or deliberation proper, but at least in the various discourses delivered to them; while in our case, if instruction is believed to be absolute, the vote cannot be affected by the light which may be thrown upon the matter, and a representative instructed to vote against war, because it would ruin the wealth of his manufacturing or commercial constituents, would have no right to vote for war, though he had become convinced, since he met in the assembly of the representatives, that war alone might save the country from servitude or disgrace. The citizen in the agora of the ancient city-state would have had, in a corresponding case, the enviable privilege of voting patriotically for a war which he nevertheless knew would make him individually a poor man, or expose the quarter of the city in which he happened to live to fearful ravages.

V. If we resort to representatives only because we cannot any longer meet in the agora ourselves, the whole representative system amounts to nothing more than a second-hand contrivance, something which may be good enough and with which we must put up, since unfortunately we cannot any longer have the true and essential thing itself, the ancient pure, real, and visible market-democracy; a political *pis-aller* at best; something indirect and circuitous.

Yet in reality the representative system is a flower of civilization, such as neither antiquity nor the middle ages either enjoyed or conceived of, something direct and positive in itself, an institution having its own full, distinct, and independent character, the excellence of which is not to be measured by asking how closely it may approach to something beyond it, which would be the best thing could we but have it, but which for some reason or other we must needs resolve to give up forever. The representative system seems to me one of the very greatest of the political institutions that adorn the pages of the history of civilization, for through it alone can be obtained real civil liberty, broad, extensive national liberty, founded upon equally extensive political societies, and not on narrow city-communities.

We might ask, indeed, Why not return to the ancient state of things? Why not split into a number of city-states again? If direct democracy is the only political truth, and the other systems but approximations to it, more or less successful semblances of this truth, why do we not strive for this real good, and why are we satisfied with shadows? Increased population in modern times cannot be the chief reason which prevents us from doing so. Very few parts of the United States, for instance, are now as peopled as Etruria, Sicily, Greece, the Greek colonies, and Phœnicia were, when all these regions were divided into numberless independent states, working out in their way and according to the proper means of their time their own task of civilization. Perhaps we are answered, It might be done, but it cannot be done, because the people will not do it And why not? Why should they dread the idea of shivering their society into numerous parcels in the manner of the ancients, and why could they not do it, even should they attempt it? Because their feeling, sympathy, and very instinct prevent it; not the accidental taste of the time, but the very genius and character, the moving principle of modern times prevents it. Because the people have tasted the sweets and securities, the mutual support and mutual elevation, which modern political society, enlarged as it is yet forming one organized and united thing throughout,—the social guarantee which the modern state alone affords, and can afford; and because this political form, a *nationalized* society and *socialized* population, stands on an enlarged and broad foundation, is the essential form of our times independent of the denser or sparser population, and is the only form which can satisfy the many high, great, and noble demands which, in the course of civilization, men have come to urge in our present period— demands never made in ancient times or the middle ages.

The free ancient states have been spoken of in the first part of this work. We observed that their character designated them essentially as city-states, and that their liberty consisted mainly in the equal participation of each citizen in government, not in the broad protection of the individual and his peculiar individual rights. The ancients knew of no nations, in the modern acceptation of the term. There were tribes and races, coalesced or superinduced one upon the other; there existed vast empires, but they were only annexations of countries over which one victorious tribe—the Mede, the Persian, the Arab—ruled, without fusing the many discordant components into one society, one organized thing, one nation which should be animated and impelled, in some respect or other, by one moral agent, one vital social principle, or impulse extending through all parts and through a series of periods. [In fact, the Median, Persian, and Arabic political forms themselves arose out of some coalescence of earlier tribes of blood-relations under one government, and that not without the help of force.]

In the middle ages, again, we find no state, if we give to that

word the sense in which we generally take it, that is, a clearly
organized, enlarged political society, until after the time when
the free cities had raised themselves into existence. In the
earlier times of the middle ages there was but a concatenation,
and frequently hardly anything more than a co-existence, of
numberless almost independent communities, a feature which,
though gradually vanishing, continued to appear down to the
beginning of modern history. Everything in the middle ages
had a tendency to individual and isolated independence, a
condition of things most necessary in the course of civilization, but below our broad civil liberty. The castles, cities,
bishoprics, republics, communities, or whatever the character
of the various independent groups and clusters was, were not
strictly socialized with one another, that is, they had not
grown into one comprehensive society; one active political
system did not pervade and unite the whole, though in most
cases the various independent bodies were founded upon the
same principle. The various populations had not, properly
speaking, become nationalized.[1] This spirit of establishing
independent circles was not territorial, but any mass of men
united for some permanent purpose was forthwith incorporated, with rights and prescribed actions peculiarly its own.
Every trade, profession, or occupation, even dishonorable
occupations[2] formed separate corporations. I do not say that

---

[1] I beg the reader to keep in mind that I mean by nationalization of the populations the growing of *a people*, which did not exist in the strictly feudal times, and by nationalization of governments, something entirely different from mere centralization of government. Centralization is the convergence of all the rays of power into one central point; nationalization is the diffusion of the same life-blood through a system of arteries, throughout a body politic; indeed, it is the growing of the body politic as such, morally and thoroughly cemented, out of a mass otherwise uncemented. The following sections, I trust, will make the subject clearer than it will appear at the present stage to those unversed in the history of the periods touched upon.

[2] Prostitutes were frequently incorporated. There is a curious passage in Thourel's Histoire de Genève depuis son Origine jusqu'à nos Jours, 1833, relating to the women of the town before the Reformation : " Pour que suivant l'ancienne coustume ces pécheresses soyent mieux dirigées, elles pourront eslire et se con-stituer une reine, laquelle prestera serment en leurs mains, sur les saints évan-

these corporations are necessarily hostile to general liberty, nor that they have not been at times too much abandoned in the modern era. We have not to investigate this subject here. But such as the corporations show themselves in the middle ages, they evidently belong to the general spirit of forming little independent circles and appearing each to every other as one separate whole only—circles which are in a greater or less degree approximations to sovereignties.

These independent territories were indeed, in many cases, in contact with one another, but not joined; connected, but not united. It is the characteristic trait of the feudal times. Indeed, at one time there was such a total dissolution into unconnected baronies, jarring or in open hostility with one another, that an event like the crusades, animating and impelling once more whole masses with one and the same idea, became in the opinion of some great historians a real blessing to the Western world.[1]

---

giles, d'exercer le dit emploi bien et fidèlement de tout son pouvoir, sans affection ni haine."

[1] The crusades, though much deplored by some, for instance Sismondi, are nevertheless held by many of the calmest historians to have been one of the most powerful means by which Providence has rescued the Western world from barbarity and led it on in its amazing career of civilization. Heeren, the historian, places them in this light at the beginning of his essay on the Political Consequences of the Reformation (translation, Oxford, 1836), in dwelling on the new impulse they gave to the mental life of Europe, the great political changes which they produced in Europe itself; though their immediate object was no more obtained than that for which Columbus started into unknown seas. Abel Rémusat, the French Orientalist, among others, has well traced the intercourse of Europeans with Asiatic princes, which, relighting as it did the ardor for knowledge, was first of all brought about by the contact of the West and East during the crusades. (See Mémoires sur les Relations politiques des Princes chrétiens avec les Empereurs Mongols.) The discovery of America is doubly connected with the crusaders,—internally and externally : the first, because that indomitable desire of discovery, adventure, enlargement of knowledge, and of striving physically and mentally beyond the known limits, that peculiar longing for the distant, which characterizes the period of maritime discoveries, standing in close connection with the information continually brought from the East, was first of all caused by the crusades; the latter, because the great Columbus was actually in search of the Zipangi of Marco Polo, when he stumbled on America because it lay across his way.

While these many separate districts, in the course of civilization, could not withstand the gradual and growing socialization, and were forced into closer contact, they met together, nevertheless, in a very great degree as separate elements, with separate interests and desires, separate rights, privileges, chartes. The estates of the middle ages consisted of deputies, strictly instructed, limited, and fettered; sending for new instru tions on each new question which might turn up; jealously, often hostilely, extorting from one another; granting and demanding, like separate sovereigns; little concerned about the advantage of the other parties or general justice and universal fairness; treating as now a congress of plenipotentiaries, sent from various independent nations would do, but upon no broad or social and mutual principle: thus, Guizot observes that "the cortes, like the states-general of France, have been an accident in history, and never a system, never a political organization or regular means of government;"—only we must give a correct sense to the term "accident in history." [1] In the feudal times we have many independent

---

[1] The term Accident is so totally denied by some, and, again, superficial observers please themselves so much in ascribing the vastest historical phenomena to accident, that I believe an explanation of this term is not undeserving the brief space of a note.

If we call accident a fact which has been produced by causes wholly extraneous to a subject but which materially influence the latter, we may certainly say that a man died by accident if his skull was broken by a tile which the violence of the wind tore from a roof, in contradistinction to a death which is the necessary consequence of causes in the system of man in general or of this individual in particular. In the highest point of view there are no accidents, inasmuch as we imagine Providence overruling the universe in all its elements. In a historical point of view there are few accidents, far less than many superficial observers imagine, who ascribe wars to momentary indispositions of monarchs and the like. Yet there are certainly accidents of momentous importance. That Gustavus Adolphus was shot in the battle at Lützen was, historically speaking, an accident; for it was a fact brought about by causes not founded in or growing out of the necessary development of society. There was no connection between the social state of Europe and the pistol from which the ball was fired. Yet this accident was [seemingly] of the most momentous consequences for all civilized mankind. How differently, in all probability, would history have turned out had Gustavus Adolphus lived to make himself Protestant emperor of Germany! But

authorities, but not public authorities; royal power itself is, down to the times of Louis XI. in France, and of Isabella in Spain, but an isolated feudal power. There were in France *pays d'obéissance-le-roi, pays des barons,* and *pays hors l'obéissance-le-roi.* Much of this is, doubtless, to be ascribed to baronial arrogance and lawlessness, but this very baronial arrogance is a thing peculiar to those times, at least in its extent and prevalence. We find in the middle ages power enough, but not public power; an infinity of institutions, but not public institutions; numberless chartered and frequently highly valuable privileges, but not what we now term public law. We have, in brief, as indicated already, separate yet clustered independence, not individual yet public liberty.

Civil liberty, something very different from feudal independence, became established only in the same degree in which these many separate groups united into a society, these isolated parts into nations, and in which the deputies of the separate estates were transformed into national representatives — a career in the history of civilization in which England long preceded all other nations, and for the want of which other countries, such as Germany, Italy, France, and Spain, failed so long to obtain liberty, or fail to this day to enjoy it. For, though the British parliament, having grown into a national body, a body that belonged to and represented political society at large, was also for that reason, in periods when civil liberty was yet but indistinctly felt and seen, more subservient to the

---

when some superficial writers tell us that the Reformation was caused by the accident that a bungling seller of indulgences, Tetzel, happened to meet with so fiery a man as Luther, they show how little they know of mankind, society, and the connection of social phenomena. The Reformation must have not only taken place, but pretty much at that period, though neither a Tetzel nor a Luther had ever lived. The estates, therefore, were very far from being accidents; they were most necessary and natural phenomena in the course of the social development of civilized mankind; but we might call them accidents with reference to the effects which some of them had in producing national representation, because they arose out of causes which had nothing to do directly with a national representation, but on the contrary were founded upon an opposite principle, that of chartered, insulated independence.

monarch, as for instance under Henry VIII., than the deputies of estates in other countries, for instance in Spain, might have proved, still the broad foundation of civil liberty was laid; and when the period of absorbing centralization of power arrived for the continent of Europe, the British alone of all were able to withstand it, though they had monarchs as wise, and wiser, and as much disposed for centralization, for instance Elizabeth, as much so as Ferdinand the Catholic or Philip II. in Spain, or Louis XI. and Louis XIV. in France. Prescott even distinctly says that the extraordinary power committed to the commons in Castile was unfavorable to their liberties.[1] The reason is, as I said before, these independent territories prevented the growth of a foundation for national representation, and that broad, mutual support in the cause of liberty, which cannot be built upon any other foundation; and when the time came that the many loosely connected political parcels grew into one real body politic, a firmly knit political *society*,—which process all nations had to follow, because their languages, laws, literatures, and, with many, their churches, necessarily became national,—there was no other large power left but the general government, the monarch. It will always remain a characteristic and peculiar feature of British liberty that England passed over from the feudal independence of estates or single communities to national and public liberty, without the intermediate process of entire concentration of power; or that, at any rate, the attempt at it—under the Tudors, who did it judiciously, and under the Stuarts, who did it injudiciously—did not succeed, but led at once to determined resistance. On the continent of Europe power was firmly concentrated, or where this did not take place, on account of

---

[1] History of Ferdinand and Isabella, page 50, Introduction. I would likewise refer to pages 60 and 80 of the same Introduction, as in fact to the whole of it. The reader finds there repeated proofs of the important fact that it was owing to the want of nationalization of the deputies that Castile and Aragon, whose estates enjoyed greater liberties than those of any other extensive countries in the middle ages, did not obtain modern civil liberty, and are now in such painful travail to give birth to it.

the imbecility of government, not of the resistance of the people, as in Spain, a state of things still worse, that of planless interference, a restless and aimless despotism, was the consequence.

It was, therefore, an immense step made in the cause of French liberty, and indeed the one from which it dates, that in 1789, at the convocation of the estates under Necker, after very protracted debates on the question whether the "cahiers" (instructions) of the deputies should be considered absolutely binding,—while many of the nobility desired to join the third estate, but scrupulously doubted whether they were not bound to adhere to their instructions as members of another estate, —at length the deputies declared themselves representatives, and the estates changed into a national representation.

It does not belong to our present inquiry to show how truly fortunate England was, that amid circumstances frequently disastrous in their immediate effect, yet beneficial in breaking the power of the barons and producing national representation, this prodigious civil change did not fuse all estates into one chamber, but suffered the idea of estates so far to continue as to assign a separate house to the high nobility, from which fact the highly important political institution of two houses, or the bi-cameral system, arose. Any one who wishes to convince himself of the actual misery—we cannot call it otherwise—attending all the debates, if such they can be termed, of the feudal estates, where the necessity of a national system began strongly to be felt, but was prevented by the relations of the deputies to their principals, must read the detailed accounts of the French estates, or of the diets of the German empire.

The great change of the British deputy into a national representative was consummated in the sixteenth century, especially when the old law, requiring members of parliament to be resident burgesses to make the elections valid, fell into entire disuse. Hallam (Constitutional History, i. 362) says, of a debate on the proposed abolition of the law in 1571, "This is a remarkable and perhaps the earliest assertion of an important constitutional principle, that each member of the house of commons is deputed to serve not only for his constituents, but for the whole kingdom; a principle which marks the distinction between a modern English parliament and such deputations of the estates as were assembled in several continental kingdoms; a principle to which the house of commons is indebted for its weight and dignity, as well as its beneficial efficiency, and which none but the servile worshippers of the populace are ever found to gainsay." Here I have only to observe that not only worshippers of the populace gainsay it, but persons of the opposite character likewise, because opposed in their whole view to modern popular liberty, which they see well is so closely connected with broad, national representation. Niebuhr, in one of his letters, written in 1808, says of Mirabeau, of whom he has just spoken in high terms, "Assuredly he is likewise innocent of the terrible idea of a general representation" (" schreckliche Idee der allgemeinen Repräsentation." Biographical Notices, vol. ii. p. 72.) Both the licentious demagogue and he who fondly clings to the past age of corporative separation and the consequent systems of mere deputations are right, each in his way, in opposing the vast principle of national representation.[1]

VI. It appears then, and I confidently state, that every page of history will furnish to the student ample evidence of the fact that ancient politics was characteristically city politics; that a leading political trait of the feudal times was a number of almost independent power-holders under a suzerain, defying, and extorting from, one another; and that the prominent

---

[1] With reference to various subjects touched upon in the previous section, as well as in several antecedent passages of this work, I would recommend to the reader the perusal or reperusal of the concluding chapters of Sismondi's History of the Italian Republics in the Middle Ages, beginning with chapter 126. The historian gives in them so lucid a view of his opinions upon a variety of subjects connected with ancient and modern liberty, and his opinions are entitled to so much respect, that attentive reflection upon them must be fruitful to the reader, even though he should differ in some points, as in fact the writer of these lines does, from the philosophical historian.

feature of political activity in modern times consists in the endeavors to establish broad civil liberty, guarantees, checks, and justice, on extensive national grounds, not on accidental specific grants. Hence the universal establishment of constitutions so peculiar to our times. The European race has only stepped over the threshold of this third period, having in many cases as yet to struggle against centralization of power, which frequently was nevertheless necessary in order to annihilate feudal baronies. Our modern civil liberty demands justice broadly diffused throughout a state, not chartered or wrung from some one contesting it, obtained separately and in a variety of degrees by the different communities; it demands the broad guarantee of society, not the specific and chartered ones of essentially independent corporations. An instance will serve as illustration. Where do we expect a firmer guarantee of the free exercise of religion, or for Protestantism in particular?—in modern France, where society at large has pronounced by the constitution that every man shall be allowed peaceably to exercise his religion, or after the wars of the League, when the edict of Nantes granted to the Protestants a number of fortified places exclusively, and the right to keep armed men? Where do we expect less hardship and burden? from a general taxation as in our states, or from the separate and tenaciously contested grants or even immunities and exemptions in the middle ages? In short, where is there more justice, more knowledge, more action, and higher activity, and greater impulse—in our bodies politic or socialized states, or in the many smaller or larger circles in the middle ages?

These enlarged societies, however, cannot obtain or guarantee liberty, except by representation, and their representation must be social, national, that is, it must represent not only the separate component parts but the totality of society as one organized whole. The representation itself must form a faithful organ of the entire and unbroken society, which, to repeat, is not an agglomeration of severed atoms, but a union of parts belonging to one organic whole.

It is by this representative system alone that mutual support, mutual reliance, mutual protection, and mutual elevation can be effected, which, as we have seen, constitute the enviable trait of modern times. The representatives must, in order to be the true representatives of society, which is one organized, living thing, with nerves and arteries of life ramified throughout, represent this whole society as such; they again form one whole organ, and though there are only a few constitutions which actually impose an oath upon every representative "not to assent to any law, vote, or proceeding which shall appear to him injurious to the public welfare" (Constitution of New Jersey, adopted in 1777, par. 23), or that "to the best of his power he will contribute to the advancement of the public welfare, without swerving from it on account of individual or provincial interest" (Constitution of the Netherlands, of 1815, par. 84), yet is not this oath written in every man's heart, is it not actually imposed in our times upon every honest man by plain common sense?

And here it ought to be observed that the above oath quoted from the Constitution of the Netherlands is imposed upon the members of the states-general, who are nevertheless elected by the provincial estates, corresponding to the former sovereign provinces[1] of the United Provinces.

VII. The representative of modern times, therefore, differs materially from the deputy of the feudal estates. Yet shall he not represent the sense and sentiment of his constituents?

---

[1] The United Provinces formed, as is well known, a confederacy of sovereign states, which sent deputations, not representatives, to the States-General, not very unlike the Swiss confederacy of the present day, though even less cemented, I believe, than these, according to the law. The confederacy of the Netherlands, which furnishes such a noble chapter to the history of the world, could not act with enough of social organic power, because it did not abandon the feudal idea of deputies and rise to a representation. The confederacy rapidly sank in power and consideration. On the restoration of the independence of the Low Countries, after having formed part of the French empire, we find, therefore, in the constitution, the following paragraph as the first of the division on the States-General: "The States-General represent the nation." Par. 77.

He must emphatically do so, not as a deputy of a separate feudal body, representing their limited or perhaps selfish desires, but representing them as part and parcel of the state, as a living limb of the whole body politic. That the body of representatives may form a real representation of the whole, it is necessary that the wishes and views of all parts shall have an organ. The representative is not appointed by a few, as a deputy, or minister to carry certain points, but he is elected by the concurrence of voices of his fellow-citizens for the pledges which his constituents find in his whole life: he is elected because his constituents believe that his views, principles, and sympathies are identified with their own, and because he will speak and act as the organ of their public opinion, not as the instructed deputy who shall wring advantages from the others. If it were so, he should receive instructions beforehand. But he represents his constituents fully and wholly, that is, as a body connected with the whole, whose entire public opinion, thus brought together from various parts, mutually modifying one another, and insuring the prevalence or general justice and fairness, passes over through these various organs into the public will of the whole, which is into law.

It is evident, therefore, that the representative is bound by these two great duties, arising out of the essence of the representative system itself. On the one hand he must represent as closely and as conscientiously as possible the interests and opinion of the whole district which sends him. He does not only represent the majority of his voters, but the minority likewise; otherwise insufferable party aristocracy would be at once established; and if the election has chiefly turned upon some prominent measure, and he be elected by a very small majority of a large number of voters, he is in conscience bound to allow to the views of his minority a very different weight in his judgment from what he would be called upon to do had he been elected by an overwhelming majority. He is farther the representative of the more especial interests of all the non-voters of his district, of the men without votes, of the women, the children, for they are all component and essential parts of the community which he represents for the purpose of finally making up public opinion, and law. On the other hand, he is bound to represent his community, not as a detached part, independent in the feudal sense, but as a living limb of his state or nation, and hence bound to allow the public opinion of the whole its due influence in modifying the opinion which he has brought from his particular section. Else why should he be sent to commune with the other representatives? Why should debates precede the passing of bills? Why, in particular, should, in cases of joint appointment, a difference of opinion be permitted? If they are the deputies of their respective constituent circle only, this would amount to absurdity. In France the elective franchise is comparatively much restricted. On an average each department has but two thousand two hundred electors, each commune but five. Is the representative sent to represent these five men in each commune only, or all men, women, children. and even property? The French representative, the moment that he is elected, is the national representative, whether he be elected by many or by few.

That in all the business which has exclusive reference to his section, or to individuals in it, the representative is the peculiar and proper servant of the public, and must give his whole time and exertion to their benefit, and serve them, to the best of his ability, and conscientiously, in endeavoring to obtain all that is right and fair, is evident.

We see, then, that all that is sacred in civil liberty makes political society equally interested in the two following points: The representative ought frequently to give his trust back to the people, and pass the trial of election, so that he may remain the true representative of his constituents and of his community. The word frequent is of course a relative term, and must receive its true meaning from a variety of circumstances; for there are as many evils in unnecessarily frequent elections as there are in those which occur at too long intervals. Secondly, the true character of a representative government does not admit of mandatory instructions to the representative, for it makes at once of the representative a mere deputy, who ought to have his instructions from the beginning. But in this case he ceases to be the representative of the people, and becomes a mere plenipotentiary either of a party or corporation. Yet it is true, again, that real public opinion and public will can only be elicited by the closest possible attention of each representative to the interests and desires of his constituents and community; he therefore will cheerfully be influenced by petitions, resolutions, or any other information from his constituents, a circumstance of the greatest and especial importance in monarchies, in which the influence of the crown must always be great and the representative is easily seduced from the people. But it would be a serious mistake to believe that special instructions are the best guarantee of the people against the seductions of the crown. Special instructions fetter as often as they lend power, and the crown, or indeed any powerful executive, of whatever name, can be effectually opposed only by free, united, broad, national opposition. The history of England, on the one hand, and that of the continental estates, on the other, prove this fact most abundantly. There are several other considerations against binding representatives by instructions, especially in states where there exist written constitutions, which will presently be given.

For the present I would sum up the previous remarks thus: The true representative is bound to represent his constituents closely, honestly, and patriotically: closely, so that by the union and mutual modification of the opinion of all parts strictly represented a true opinion of the whole may be formed; honestly, so that he neither meanly nor weakly desert his constituents, nor basely obey the dictates of passing passion or excitement in the district from which he comes; and, lastly, patriotically, so that he can sacrifice his own advantage or that of any part of the state to the benefit and advancement of the whole state.

These principles will lead to the rule, which I believe will be admitted to be correct, that the representative, constitutionally elected for a fixed term, as he is bound to maintain the fundamental law in every way, is also, in his own case, not to infringe it by receiving specific mandatory instructions, since the constitution does not acknowledge them; but, on the other hand, he will feel obliged, in order to maintain close representation inviolate, to resign as soon as he is convinced that the public opinion of his district decidedly differs from his, not on a single measure, but on a continued course of actions and series of views respecting important political subjects, and that they would differ had they all the knowledge which he has acquired in the necessary contact with the other organs of the public opinion of his state. The representative must feel convinced that he differs seriously and permanently, and that the difference does not arise from any sudden and excited change in his constituents; for in the latter case it is one of the very objects of the constitution, which says that he shall be elected for such a term, to avoid sudden and passionate changes. If one or the other be neglected, it seems to me that the essential character of a representative government is seriously impaired.

VIII. The meaning of a representative government, it appears, then, is very different from and far nobler than a mere approach to something we cannot obtain, the government of the people in the forum, or the ecclesia, to use the Athenian term. It has a great, a deep meaning of its own, and from what has been observed in the first part of this work, when we considered the nature of power and the necessity of its restriction, in whose hands soever it may be lodged, as well as from the remarks just made, it will sufficiently appear that the following are among the vast advantages which we obtain by this institution which the historian, it may be ventured to affirm, will always consider with reverence and rejoicing.

Masses are always impetuous. I do not speak of the rabble or mob; I speak of every mass, high, low, or mixed, as such. Every one of us is impetuous as soon as he belongs to a mass. The reason is simple: so long as we belong to a mass, brought together by the same impulse, desire, or interest, each individual has but that one object in view, else he would not have joined or been drawn into that mass which strives for it.[1] The moment we are singled out to act for the mass, that moment one of two things must happen: either responsibility is lawfully thrown upon us by the process of some appointment or election, when we feel at once the necessity of circumspection and moderation, because we act for others, and are answerable for the consequences; or some reason or other, arising out of the impulse or excitement of the agitated mass itself, devolves the duty of leader upon us. The leadership, thus acquired, depends upon the impulse itself, and we feel naturally tempted to lead on the mass in this impulse, for every one is careful to maintain that foundation upon which his power or authority rests. Now, as masses cannot in most cases act directly, but must have leaders of some sort or other, these become, in the natural course of things, the rulers or leaders of the unmitigated masses. But by the representative system we obtain these two advantages: we restrict the impulse which is inherent in the mass as such, and must be restricted, because every power-holder needs a check; and we avoid being ruled by one leader, as the Athenians always were in the later portion of their history. We, the people, therefore, are not absent from the legislative halls only because, for local reasons, we cannot be there, but because we ought not to be there as a people, as a mass, for the same reason that in monarchies the king is not allowed to be present in the halls of justice, or as the legislators cannot debate in the presence of the monarch. In both cases the reason is the same. The prince, that is, the power-holder (be he the people or the monarch), must be limited and circumscribed by law, especially in republics, because, as we have

---

[1] [In a note Dr. Lieber corrects what he says in the text, adding that " masses are impetuous for two reasons. 1. They feel they are not organized, and their action therefore is insecure; they are hasty, anxious. 2. Masses cannot be reasoned with, nor can the members reason with one another. That which is bold, violent, striking, alone can obtain attention and command."]

seen in Part First, the power of the people is never a theory, as that of a monarch frequently is, but irresistible reality; that is, for the same reason that the power-holder must not sit in judgment, his presence must not overawe the legislature.

It was right that all the commons were silent when Charles I. went to them on January 4th, 1642, to demand Pym and the four other members from among them ; and it was right for the British judge to tell the king that he must not come into court.

The government of a free state must act out public opinion. To do this, two things are necessary : first, it must know public opinion, and, secondly, its action must be the regular action of society, not an irregular series of accidental impulses. Public opinion, however, can be ascertained by the sifting process of a representative system only. Otherwise, general, momentary opinion, rumor, even whim, will rule, instead of true, settled public opinion. The representative must truly obey public opinion, not momentary impulse, excitement, panic, fear, revenge, spite, or fanaticism—all of which may seize and have seized masses because they seize upon the individuals composing them.[1] The representative, standing at a distance, being separated from the crowd, feels, in many cases at least, the necessity of calm reflection and of opposition to the sweeping current of excitement.

---

[1] "I did not obey your instructions: No. I conformed to the instructions of truth and nature, and maintained your interest, against your opinions, with a constancy that became me. A representative worthy of you ought to be a person of stability. I am to look, indeed, to your opinions; but to such opinions as you and I must have five years hence. I was not to look to the flash of the day. I knew that you chose me, in my place, along with others, to be a pillar of the state, and not a weathercock on the top of the edifice, exalted for my levity and versatility, and of no use but to indicate the shiftings of every fashionable gale. Would to God the value of my sentiments on Ireland and on America had been at this day a subject of doubt and discussion! No matter what my sufferings had been, so that this kingdom had kept the authority I wished to maintain by a grave foresight and by an equitable temperance in the use of its power." Burke, in his Speech to the Electors of Bristol in 1780. It will be well for the *American* reader to consider what the instructions were he considerately disregarded.

All unmeditated action in politics is dangerous, because it is power, for unrestricted power, be it physical, mental, or moral, is hazardous and dangerous. But not only this; impetuous and direct action, mischievous as it may be at the moment, is apt suddenly to lose its hold again. It is the gradual but well-directed action, in almost all cases, which is certain. The British house of commons, which at present has in reality the appointment of ministers, acts much more safely and powerfully than when in 1641, and on some other occasions, it aimed at direct appointment. It may safely be said that upon the whole the commons have an infinitely stronger influence over the ministers now than they would have were the appointment thrown upon them.

Masses are swayed by gratitude or the imposing pageantry of power, and, enraptured or bewildered, grant away their rights; the representative acts for others, and is cautious, provided only there are sufficient means to make him always a true representative.

By a representative government alone we can arrive at political truth.

By it alone, deliberation, debate, which neither absolute democracy on the one hand nor instructed deputations on the other admit of, becomes possible; and debate, whatever its frequent abuses may be, is of the utmost importance for civil liberty. Frequently, indeed, precious time is wasted by pointless speeches of unreasonable length; but we must not forget the mass of political information which thus is daily thrown among the public. Frequently members will be infatuated by party spirit, so that they will not listen to truth; but we ought to remember that debate also, in many cases, prevents them from becoming so infatuated. Debate, well guided, is an indispensable palladium of civil liberty. Instruction would make, and unfortunately has made, out of deliberative assemblies, assemblies without freedom of deliberation and without freedom of thought, which is a tyranny with painful consequences. Indeed, directing men to vote one way or the other, in a case in which it is nevertheless maintained that previous inquiry ought to guide, is repugnant to all respect for truth and for conscience. Napoleon, so it is said, directed at times courts-martial to find persons guilty before the trial had commenced. It may not be true; but what does every reader feel in reading it?

By the representative system alone we can act upon the salutary principle of the majority, the social principle, to the exclusion of the unanimity principle or principle of feudal independency. On this point presently more.

By the representative system, that is, by a representation gathered from the whole society, upon uniform and extensive principles *proportionally* applied to that society, we alone are able to gather public opinion. The deputy system does not aim at arriving at the public opinion of the state; it merely strives to redress single " grievances." Hence it could happen and be tolerated that the deputation from one city represented many cities, that of Salamanca, for instance, about a hundred places, from which it received their various instructions and acted accordingly. To have the " grievances" redressed was the main business of the deputy; to have public opinion gathered and acted out is the essence of representation.

By the representative system alone can be secured publicity of governmental action, which cannot be done in absolute unrepresented democracies, because there cannot be there real debates. By the representative government alone the extension of a political society can be united with substantial public liberty; the necessary energy of a government with its equally necessary control; and by it alone we can safely steer between the fanaticism of theorists and unprincipled expediency —one of the great objects of good government.

IX. From the foregoing remarks it will appear, therefore, how little those writers on politics have penetrated into the essence and real meaning of the representative principle, who consider it as the main problem to unite the extension of states with the ultimate rule and sway of the multitude alone, as ascertained by a census. The true and difficult object in politics, as everywhere where men have to act, is to secure by wise, that is by safe and appropriate, means, the discovery of truth and the empire of mind over matter, chance, force, and bulk. The mere number of itself does no more guarantee truth than the chance of birth. There can be no doubt that an overwhelming majority of all the inhabitants of the earth believe that the sun moves and not the earth, or that the chief object in punishing offenders is to deter others by the acuteness of suffering inflicted upon the former. Yet both opinions are equally wrong: and we justly prefer to adopt the opinion of those comparatively few whom we have good reason to believe well acquainted with the truth, the opinion of countless millions to the contrary. Few, indeed, of all the men that people our globe believe in one God, spiritual, omnipotent, and omniscient; yet we hold fast to the belief in him. Suppose, however, that we had agreed that the opinion of the mere number should sway, that is, as we termed it, the general opinion, and not the public opinion, which is, I repeat, the opinion of society as an organized thing, settled and influenced by the knowledge of those who best understand the respective subject, their views and conclusions having been likewise influenced and modified both by the action of society upon them in forming their views and in receiving them—suppose we had agreed to this abstract principle, we should be still as far from the ultimate object as before. For if the mere theorist says that each man shall vote, and that nothing shall be law unless directly voted for by the majority of all the individual men composing the respective political society, the question arises at once, Who are these men that must have the right? Shall women vote? and if not, why? Shall children vote? and if not, upon what abstract ground do we decide that the twenty-first year, for instance, shall mark the distinction between the mature and the immature intellect? Many a youth is wiser at twenty than other persons at fifty years of age, as our daily experience proves. Nay, more, how is it that the principle of maturity of mind is suddenly added to the theory which nevertheless was originally founded upon the principle of number alone?

James Harrington, the celebrated author of the Oceana, which was published during the protectorate and intended to be the image of a pure republic, provides in that work that the people shall elect a senate, and this senate the highest officers with a strategus at the head. The senate alone has the right of proposing laws, on each of which the people vote and adopt or reject it accordingly. This is the idea upon which the right of direct and binding instruction is demanded, carried out consistently. Not to regard, however, the utter impracticability of this constitution, it would nowise guarantee the ascertaining of true public opinion, for reasons given above.

It is a universal law, pervading all physical and intellectual creation, so far as human observation and experience reach, without one exception, that the higher or nobler the thing, being, or object to be produced or obtained, the longer and more varied is the chain of processes, and the more organic are these processes, by which it has been matured; and the lower the thing or creature, the more it is determined by agents from without; the higher it is, the more active becomes its own organization within. A mushroom starts into existence perfect, within a few hours, so soon as the necessary agents from without exist, but it takes a long time and requires a variety of processes, one connected with the other, before the flower of the magnolia adorns the rich foliage of its noble tree. The infusory animal detaches part of its body, and a new being moves quickly for itself, but it requires a long time before man's body and mind arrive at maturity; and before he comes into existence as a detached individual he has undergone a long series of the most wonderful processes and transformations in order to become sufficiently matured for parturition. The same principle obtains in the intellectual and political world. For a gross nation, gross despotism, perhaps determined by gross chance or the equally gross principle of mere force, may suffice. The little

of opinion which exists in a tribe on the pampas of America
or the steppes of the East is easily ascertained. The signal
is given, the men assemble, a proposition is made, assent or
dissent is expressed, and the whole process is at an end; but
the public opinion of an extensive, civilized, and organized
society is neither so rapidly generated nor so rapidly ascertained. The farther society advances, the higher it rises, the
more organic must be the process by which it is ascertained,
and stripped of casual adhesion due to prejudice, interest, or
excitement; and this organic process for producing the flower
of public opinion upon the many-branched tree of society is
effected, so it seems to me, by the representative system. In
this consists its highest meaning, and as such it has a high
value of its own, not a mere relative one by way of approxi-
mation to something beyond our reach—a value which we
shall honor and cherish the more, the better we become
acquainted with the true spirit of past ages and the occurrences of the day, and which will the more inspire us with
an ardent desire to cultivate, perfect, and expand, not to stint
and cripple it, the more we penetrate its essence.

X. If the doctrine of instruction be right, I hold it to be
evident that it is entirely inconsistent to allow an instructed
member, who disagrees with his instruction, to resign before
he has voted. He who acts the part of a deputy or plenipotentiary is bound first to vote according to instruction, and
then he may ask leave to resign; otherwise his constituents
lose unjustly their vote or share of influence upon final action.
Such action would have been expected of every deputy in the
middle ages, and to this day would be expected of an ambassador, who may conscientiously do thus because he is nothing
but an agent sent for the very purpose of voting, if any voting
is to be done, in a prescribed way; but who is a representative
in no real sense of the word, and is only so called because he
resembles one in the outward form. But what honorable and
independent man would degrade himself so low as to defile
his lips by a vote against his conscience and judgment, when

he was sent—under oath—to vote according to truth, to the fulness of conscience and the best of his judgment? If representatives are nothing but deputed officers, why would it be considered an outrageous act of immorality if a representative coming from a manufacturing or agricultural district were to take money for defending the interests committed to him, as the lawyer does, and as the deputies in the middle ages frequently did, or as to this day advocates do when sent by some corporation or society to the bar of the commons? No one finds fault with them. If we have the right bindingly to instruct after the election, we have likewise a right to elect on condition of certain instructions, and may exact "elective capitulations," as the conditions were called upon which the German electors used to elect the emperor. Suppose our electors of the President of the United States were either to agree upon such an elective capitulation before the election, or to send him instructions after election: would not the whole people scorn the idea, or consider it as a most arrant conspiracy? Yet this is quite imaginable, and there is not one argument brought in favor of instruction of representatives which would not apply to the assumed case. If the doctrine of instruction is sound, it is but the legitimate inference that the constituents should have also the right to recall their representative, as the deputies of the former estates were frequently recalled. Yet why do the constitutions of representative governments nowhere give this very important power, but universally prescribe the term for which a representative is to be elected, which was rarely done in the ancient estates and only where they approached the representative system? Because it has been universally felt that a representative differs in character from the deputy.[1] We may go farther: if the

---

[1] One of the senators of the United States, from Virginia, who was instructed to vote for the well-known expunging resolution, says, indeed, in his letter of February 27, 1836, to the legislature of Virginia, when declining to comply with their behest, " I do not hesitate to declare that if you had, as the accredited organs of the people, addressed me a request to vacate my seat in the senate, your request would have had with me the force of law: not a day or an hour

representative is the mere agent acting under instruction of those who unfortunately cannot be present themselves, I maintain that not only ought the constituents to have a right to recall him, but they ought to have the undeniable right of vetoing his vote, as was actually proposed by some theorizing politician in the French constituent assembly. He was perfectly consistent, if he believed the representatives to be assembled there merely because all France could not be present. The veto of the supreme executive upon any treaty signed by a plenipotentiary is now universally acknowledged, and the same ought to hold good if our representatives are but plenipotentiaries.[1]

It is said the representative is elected by his constituents, he is their servant, and must do their bidding, "otherwise it is a confined aristocracy, in which the people have nothing more to do than to choose their rulers, over whose proceedings, however despotic and repugnant to the nature and principles of the fundamental laws of the state, they have no control."[2] If this be true, the Americans live most assuredly under a confined monarchy, for no president would obey an instruction; nor would this absence of all confidence be in the slightest degree a guarantee against despotic proceedings.

A mere term has considerably misled in this inquiry, as in so many others. The representative is called a servant of the people; so is the president of the United States called, and he frequently calls himself, a servant of the people; but the word "servant," from the servus servorum, as the pope signs himself, down to the menial negro, is used in very different

---

could I desire to remain in the senate beyond that hour wherein I came to be informed that it was the settled wish of the people of Virginia that I should retire from their service." This is introducing a very extraordinary and serious power, of which the constitution knows nothing, if it mean that in instructing the legislature really expresses the "settled wish of the people." How can we know that they do? They were not elected, according to the constitution, to express such an opinion.

[1] [For this, which is not universally acknowledged in regard to treaties concluded according to full powers and secret instructions both, see Wheaton, Elements, part iii. 2, §§ 257–263.]

[2] Tucker's Blackstone, Appendix, p. 193.

meanings. It may signify one that serves another, labors for him, or one that mechanically does as he is bid to do. It is always considered an honor to be a representative, but there is no honor in doing the bidding of any one, people or monarch, without individual independence. The representative system requires not only men of talent, but of manly independence; liberty is not efficiently served by menials, or by men who do not think independently and who shrink from speaking and voting in candor and conscience. The doctrine of instruction greatly favors hypocrisy, for cases have occurred when representatives, seeing that measures upon which they stood compromised were fast losing ground, sent home to be instructed to vote contrary to the votes formerly given by them.[1] Where there is a constitution—and properly speaking there is a constitution that is fundamental law wherever there are representatives—but especially where there is a written constitution, upon which the representative takes his oath, the right of instruction becomes especially incongruous, for the representative is a guardian and trustee of and under the constitution upon oath—that constitution which is far above him and his constituents. It cannot be maintained that if he is instructed to do what he holds to be contrary to the constitution—as when the Virginia senators were instructed by their legislature to vote for the renowned expunging resolution—the very fact that his own constituents, the very makers of his authority, view it differently, shows him that he must yield. The legislature of South Carolina elects the supreme judges of the state; the judge takes the oath upon the constitution, and may be called upon not only to act dissentingly from the legislature which actually made him, but as judge may declare a law which it has passed unconstitutional. How is this, if the relation of the electors and the elected necessarily creates the relation of master and servant, ordainer and

---

[1] It is a well-known anecdote, that John Wilkes, with whom the modern history of the instruction question may be said to begin, when asked how it was possible to allow his judgment to be fettered by such a rabble as had instructed him, answered, "Oh, as to that, I always take care to write my own instructions."

obeyer? How is it in the militia, where officers are elected by the rank and file?

The advocates of the right of instruction appear to forget one fact, which seems to me very weighty. Among other political guarantees we have constitutions, fundamental laws, we have representatives, and fixed periods for renewed elections, for the purpose of protecting the community, for the continuity of views and opinions for a certain space of time in the legislation of the country; and we have laws to secure that manner of election by which the state hopes to secure best the rights of all citizens,—that is, impartial elections and certainty of election. Whatever the representative, thus elected by the organic law of the state, does, he does constitutionally, so long as he remains within the strict sphere of the constitution. But suddenly we have an extra-constitutional interference; men hold a meeting unappointed by law, unguaranteed as to its regularity, and they assume not to select an organ of legislation but something far more, to bid this organ already elected to legislate one way or the other. In Virginia, cases have actually occurred when papers were carried to the constituents to sign their names whether for or against the proposed instruction. The minority may be deeply interested in not having the member instructed thus extra-constitutionally; they are wronged out of their right; it becomes tyrannical ex parte legislation. The right of instruction may be easily made use of by skilfully seizing upon some excitement to "instruct a representative out of his seat," who may be disagreeable to some of his party. And, in general, it is highly dangerous to allow any man or any number of men or any authority to arrogate power not strictly laid down by the law. It is incompatible with all civil liberty. Binding and commanding instruction seems to me to loosen the very foundation-stones of true essential modern liberty in its broad, noble, and elevated character, because it defeats one of the essential features of the representative system, without which modern liberty cannot exist. Washington was averse to positive instruction. (Sparks's Writings of Washington, i. 491.)

## CHAPTER II.

**The Subject of Instruction with particular Reference to the United States.**—The ancient Articles of Confederation founded upon the Deputative System.—The Articles of Confederation compared to the Constitution of the former United Provinces of the Netherlands, the Swiss Act of Mediation, the present Constitution of the Swiss Confederation, and the Germanic Confederacy.—The Constitution of the United States boldly changed the former deputative character of the Confederacy into a representative one.—Senators are not Ambassadors.—In Leagues the strongest Member of these on terms of parity according to the letter must sway.—Hegemony in Greece, Phœnicia, the Low Countries, etc.—Relation of the State Legislatures to the respective Senator elected by them.—The History of Instruction in modern times, as connected with the Representative System.

XI. In order to show completely the relation of moral responsibility in which I hold a representative to stand to his constituents, it will be necessary to treat of the subject of Pledges. Before we proceed to it, however, I must say a few words on the right of instruction, with peculiar reference to the relation in which the senators of the United States stand to the several legislatures by which they are elected.

Very rarely indeed has the doctrine of instruction been acted upon in the United States by the primitive constituents of a representative in congress. The whole discussion as a practical question seems to have reference to the senators exclusively, and the reason can easily be perceived. As to the representatives the case is too clear; they are real representatives of the people, not deputies, forming a national representation, not states-general; and whatever the theory may be, or jealousy or love of power may prompt some to assert, sound instinct, produced by long valuable political tradition in the Anglican race, and good common sense require the people at large to view their representative only in the light of a representative and not in that of a circumscribed or fettered deputy. It is different with regard to the senators; their election, as well as the formation of the senate, differs materially from that of the representatives, and it is necessary, therefore, that we should ascertain the precise character of the senate of the United States. Thus alone we shall be able to judge correctly of the right of instructing its members.

The confederacy of the United States under the ancient Articles of Confederation of 1778 was nothing more than a league of entirely independent states (politically independent though united by feeling and sympathy), connected only by whatever might be agreed upon by their deputations, according to certain principles primarily adopted by the states; without any system or government proper; resembling the union of the former United Provinces of the Netherlands, or of the Swiss Cantons [under the Constitution of 1815]. In some respects the American Confederacy was a closer union, in others it was a looser one, but, if I mistake not, congress had the nature and character of states-general, and nothing else. The members of congress were deputies, and no more. This appears clearly from the Articles of Confederation themselves, and, among other points, from these: The states appoint the delegates as they think best, and may recall them in order to send others (art. 5, 1); their number is left to the option of the states, although for the sake of expedition of business and for other reasons the minimum of two, which became the prototype for the later number of senators under our present constitution, and the maximum of seven, were fixed (5, 2); each state was to maintain her delegation, because she alone was interested in it (5, 3); each state was to have but one vote, as a matter of course, according to the common principle in the feudal estates applicable to communities, professions, provinces, classes, and estates, because the deputies represented their respective primaries as a whole, and only them. If the deputies of any state were equally divided, the state lost the vote. Upon all the material points of the confederacy nine assenting states were necessary (9, § 6).

Let us compare these features with the corresponding ones in the most prominent confederacies of modern times. The

Netherlands, as I mentioned before, never elevated themselves to broad social or national representation; their governments, provincial or general, never became enlarged social governments, but remained chains of more or less connected independent communities; even the single cities had supreme or "sovereign rights," of which it was a natural consequence on the one hand that no resolution of the provincial states was considered binding unless it passed by unanimous concurrence, and on the other hand that the utmost inequality of representation existed : the cities formed the powerful aristocracy, the farmers were almost entirely disregarded.[1] The reader will remember an instance I mentioned, when speaking of the love of power, in the first part of this work. We must always keep in mind that the principle of the feudal times was mutual exaction of liberty, or at least separate conquest of liberty; the motto, get as much as you can, without reference to proportion, to general fairness, to common welfare. The principle of modern liberty, of socialized states, is *public* liberty, public, that is, common and mutual guarantee, public check, universal justice. The oath of fidelity by the stadtholder and soldiers was taken to the "confederate states of the Low Countries, that is, to the higher and the inferior orders of nobles, and to the magistrates of the towns of Holland," etc. Nothing can show more clearly the difference which I have endeavored to ex-

---

[1] In addition to the striking instance alluded to, I will mention here that in the province of Holland the independent communities of the province were represented by nineteen deputies chosen out of the nobility, the senators, and magistrates (that is, city authorities); the nobles having but one voice, the cities eighteen. The farmers, who bore the heaviest public burden, were neglected. Amsterdam had but one single voice in the states, and the smallest city in the province likewise. I believe the constitutional history of no state after that of Great Britain is so instructive to an American as that of the United Provinces, such as we may learn it from Basnage, Annales des Provinces Unies depuis la Negotiation pour la Paix de Munster, avec la Description historique de leur Gouvernement. The ancient cortes of Castile excluded many old cities, and would not readmit their deputies, after they had omitted to send them, and Prescott justly says they "imprudently" excluded the old cities, because, as I observed before, it was an additional obstacle in the way of the formation of a rational or social representation.

hibit between the feudal principle of independence, with the consequent deputative system, on the one hand, and the modern social states-principle of civil liberty and civil guarantee, with the consequent representative system, on the other. The effects of this system were consistent; the states-general of the United Provinces could decide upon war and peace, treaties of commerce, and all taxes and impost, by unanimous concurrence only.

I have on a former occasion briefly touched upon the principle of unanimity and majority in voting; we shall now be able to understand what otherwise appears so absurd, that a single man should have had the right of vetoing the procedure of an assembly, as it is frequently expressed, in the old estates. The expression is not accurate. The term veto expresses the idea of nullifying the action of some united body; but the old deputies were not such; unanimity was with them as natural, according to the principle which gave them existence, as it is now with a congress of ambassadors; each party is bound only so far as it has assented, because entirely independent; so that defeating a general result by a single dissent was as little a veto with those ancient estates as it would be with ambassadors at present. If the principle of unanimity was, nevertheless, in many minor cases abandoned, it was because the mere furtherance of business required it. But the principle appears more or less in all the most important estates (cortes, diets, etc.) in the middle ages, strongly at first, and the less so the more the various countries became nationalized and the interest of the different parts began more and more to affect one another. The salutary majority principle could only become known and well introduced with the complete victory of representation over deputation.

The Grand Pensionary of Holland, the chief officer of the chief province, and, indeed, virtually, the executive and chief magistrate of the whole United Provinces, took place after the deputies, because the latter represented independences, corporations with "sovereign rights." The members of the states-general came to no resolution without instruction and specific authorization from home; the provinces sent two or more members at pleasure, but the votes were given by provinces, not by the single voices of members; the time of service for deputies was differently regulated in the various provinces, as if it were a matter of utter indifference to the states-general; some were chosen even for life.[1] I have mentioned already the amended constitution of the Netherlands of 1815, which declares each member of the states-general to be a national representative, and gives him, consequently, a vote belonging to his moral, individual self as representative, not to his deputed authority as a mere deputy, nor depending on instructions, and settles their number, though they are elected, as formerly, by the provincial states. (Constitution of the Netherlands, § 83.)

The Swiss Act of Mediation (of February 19, 1803), digested under the direct influence of Napoleon,[2] in order to abolish the democratic concentrated government then lately established in imitation of France, ordains that each canton shall send one deputy to the general congress (Tagsatzung), that they shall have definite instructions and powers of attorney, and shall not vote against their instructions. (Ch. 20, tit. 1, §§ 25, 26.) And by the Swiss Act of Union of August 7, 1815, it is ordained that congress (Tagsatzung) shall consist of "ambassadors from the sovereign estates," meaning the cantons. They are the ambassadors of the twenty-two cantons and are bound to vote by their instructions. Each canton has one voice. Three-fourths of the votes are necessary for war or peace, treaties, and some important internal affairs. (Act of Union, § 8.) Lastly, let us throw a glance at the

---

[1] The deputy is the special agent or ambassador of the body which sends him; he has no general character as a member of one common system, as the representative has. What did it matter to the powers assembled in the congress of Vienna whether the minister of one or the other was recalled and another sent? The case of the deputy is similar.

[2] Napoleon, in the days of his greatest power, called himself emperor of the French, king of Italy (not of the Italians), protector of the Rhenish Confederacy, and Mediator of Switzerland.

present Germanic confederacy [1838]. If ever a government unfolded itself under most unfortunate circumstances, it was the former Germanic empire, which had all the vices and organic defects of an elective monarchy, with this evil superadded, that while in other countries the nobles were reduced and national monarchy rose, the nobles in Germany reduced the emperor and made themselves independent, while the subjects lost the advantages which they would have derived from a national government. The imperial monarchy had the effect of producing the independence of all the princes and petty states of the empire, and the consequent exposure and humiliation of Germany. Napoleon consolidated them considerably; and when he fell, the German princes felt that a union of some sort or other was deeply founded in the spirit of the nation and called for upon the score of common safety; consequently the Germanic Act of Union of 1815 was adopted at the Congress of Vienna. The Germanic confederacy is a league of princes and states, who send ambassadors to the diet, which ambassadors, of course, act by regular instruction; the members vote in two different ways, either in the "closer meeting," in which the larger Germanic powers have each one vote, but three, four, or five together of the petty states only one; or they vote in "plenum," some states, as Austria, Prussia, etc., having four votes, others three, two, and each member of the Union at least one. Austria has the permanent precedency. This brief exhibition alone will suffice to show its unnational, unrepresentative character, in which the people at large have indeed little interest, as to their advantage. The Act of Confederation of the Rhine (of July 12, 1806), under the protectorship of Napoleon, needs not to be mentioned here: it was a mere league of princes.[1]

---

[1] [The present constitution of the latest German empire, framed in 1870, says of the Reichstag, or house elected by direct vote of the people, that the members "are representatives of the people as a whole, and not bound to commissions and instructions." (Art. 29.) It is otherwise with the Bundesrath, or Federal Council. Art. 7.]

XII. How much superior, how lofty and great, appears our federal constitution, the very first in history in which the bold attempt has been made of substituting the representative system for the deputative in a confederation, thus adapting it to the necessary tendency of modern public liberty, and securing those advantages which such a system alone can possibly guarantee! As a federal charter, it is a matchless monument in history—matchless, indeed, despite the faults which it may be supposed to have on general grounds, for it is the work of men, and some of which it is not difficult now to discover; yet the historian, without blind or slavish idolatry, cannot help frequently gazing with reverence at this grand fabric, built upon such simple principles and on so vast a scale.

That the deputative character of the ancient congress was boldly and grandly transformed into a representative, we see from the constitution of the United States; and especially I beg the reader to compare the following points with those of the Act of Confederation which I cited above in order to prove the deputative character of the ancient congress.

First of all the constitution establishes an entire government with separate and regular branches, and it establishes not only a separate legislative branch, but this branch on the principle of two chambers which belongs to the representative system; it separates from "congress" the executive, elected by the people of all the states at large, and unlike an executive committee of deputies chosen from among themselves, such as the former "committee of the states." (Articles of Confederation, § 5.)

The first paragraph of the "constitution" (no longer called articles of confederation) establishes a house of representatives (no longer mere delegates). (Art. 1, sect. 1, § 1.)

The time for which the senators and representatives are elected is fixed. (Art. 1, sect. 2, § 1, sect. 3, § 1.)

The number of senators to be sent from each state is fixed, yet one individual vote is constitutionally secured to each senator. They vote personally or individually, not deputatively [and an organic character is given to the senate as a whole by the provision that one-third is renewed every second year]. (Ibid.)

Congress may make all elective regulations, except as to the places of choosing senators. (Art. 1, sect. 4, § 1.)

Each house is to judge of the election returns and qualifications of its own members, which is incompatible with deputations. (Art. 1, sect. 5, § 1.)

A majority of each house forms a quorum. (Ibid.)

Each house may punish its members for disorderly behavior, and even expel a member by two-thirds of the votes. (Art. 1, sect. 5, § 2.)

The yeas and nays may be easily demanded, that is, it is in the power of one-fifth of those present to throw each member upon his individual responsibility and representative character (Art. 1, sect. 5, § 3.)

Senators and representatives are compensated out of the treasury of the United States (Art. 1, sect. 6, § 1), and not paid by the bodies who send them.

Congress legislates for the people of the United States, not for the states separately. If a tax is levied it is upon the people; the quotas are not sent to the state legislatures; which must have been done upon the feudal deputative principle.

Let us now see what is the true respective character of the senate and the house of representatives, according to the constitution. What is their difference? The senators have frequently been called the ambassadors or ministers of the states. It is an unbefitting term. He would be but a poor ambassador who is not instructed beforehand, and cannot be recalled at any moment, but is appointed for a definite period of six years, and who joins a body of co-ambassadors, presided over, not by a member elected from among themselves and by rapid rotation, as was the case in the freest of the former estates, but by an officer in the origin of his authority wholly extraneous to the senate—an officer who does not come from a particular state, but from the people at large, like the president of the United States. The constitution thus links the senate, coming from the states as such, to the general system of government, of which it forms a part. But a body of ambassadors must be wholly independent, or it has no meaning. How could a body of independent ambassadors possibly form, not the supreme body of some confederation, but an integrant and permanent part of a continuous regular government of a union? The constitution gives one separate vote to each senator, even though the two senators from one state disagree, which is inconsistent with the function of a deputy and an ambassador, being strictly and wholly representative. For, besides the moral importance and influence upon society of seeing the two senatorial colleagues vote openly, even if opposed to one another, the subject becomes still more important in those cases in which two-thirds of the votes are required, as in impeachments of the president of the United States or of any other officer, or in cases when treaties with foreign powers are submitted to the senate (Art. 1, sect. 3, § 6, Art. 2, sect. 2, § 2), or in all cases where pluralities only and not majorities are required, and finally in all cases in which the two respective senators are opposed to each other and one happens to be absent, which of course must frequently happen.

The senate, moreover, is a deliberative assembly in its very nature; but ambassadors do not freely deliberate, they only negotiate; they try to persuade others to agree to subjects already settled in their mind, and for which they are particularly sent.

The representative character of the senators, therefore, is incontrovertible, yet they differ from the members of the house of representatives. The problem of the framers was to unite the representative system, without which, as I shall presently show, we must have been exposed to great disorder, with the system of a confederacy. If I do not misunderstand the history of our constitution, the true character of the senator and representative of the United States is that the senator is the representative, but not the deputy, of his state as such, that is as a political society of itself, yet a member of a union, in which capacity of course all members, that is, states, are equal, and for which reason an equal number of these state representatives is fixed for all; and the members of the house of representatives are the direct representatives of the people, hence they are, in justice, apportioned according to the population all over the land. That those from one state will act in many instances unitedly is natural, for the interest and public opinion of their constituents will lead them to do so; yet that they do not do so in a thousand cases, and ought not to do so, we all know. I hold it to be a principle of the last importance, that the representative in congress is a national representative, not only for the general reasons urged in previous passages, but also for one which relates to confederacies in particular. If this position of ours is correct, it appears that it is not acting upon the true principle of the constitution of the United States if members of the house of representatives of congress are elected by general state tickets, as [was formerly] done in four states, and not by separate district tickets. The states as states are already represented by the senators.[1]

XIII. Wherever mere leagues or confederations on the deputative principle are formed, and where the states meet as absolutely equal, or on terms of parity according to the letter of the compact, without the mediating representative principle, inequality in fact, notwithstanding parity in terms, must exist; that is, in the natural course of things the most powerful must necessarily sway where individuals as separate individuals meet. He that is the strongest governs. There is not one exception in history. The Greeks could not help leaguing together; their whole national spirit, always more powerful than single institutions or laws, led them to it; common language, religion, extraction, recollections, and similar laws, were so many ties counteracting governmental separations. But, as they had no representative system ramifying like

---

[1] [Since Dr. Lieber wrote this, a general law passed by congress in 1842 provided for a common plan of election in all the states. This requires that election shall be by districts, choosing one congressman each, and it overthrew the general ticket system of five states.]

a nervous system through the whole, one state or the other, Athens, Lacedæmon, or Thebes, must needs have the sway, or supremacy—the hegemony, as they called it. The Amphictyonic council was a general institution indeed, and not without some occasional influence, but it consisted of ambassadors or deputies only; it was a general institution in which most of the Greeks—as tribes and not as city-states—had a share, but, strictly speaking, not a national one,[1]—frailer still than the American confederacy under the ancient Articles. A large part of Greek national history, therefore, is one continued struggle of this inward yearning for union, or impulse of native national sympathy, on the one hand, and the struggle for and against the preponderance—the hegemony—on the other; a struggle of great bitterness. For tribes and states follow in this respect the same law which regulates the intercourse of private individuals; that is, the more sympathy or natural relations tend towards union, the more bitter will be the conflict if this inner urgency is counteracted by external separation. In the confederacy of the independent Phœnician cities, Tyre, Sidon, or some one of the richest and most powerful had the hegemony. A similar phenomenon is observable in the ancient Hansa, in the old city-union in the South of Germany and in Northern Italy, in Catalonia, and wherever we may direct our attention. When the Low Countries separated from Spain, the seven provinces, each independent and sovereign, confederated, and Holland, the strongest, necessarily obtained the hegemony—so decidedly indeed that a citizen like De Witt, pensioner of Holland, became the virtual regent and ruler of the United Provinces, and one of the most influential European statesmen of his age. The Swiss cantons have formed a confederacy in the ancient style, and Bern sways in a considerable degree; while the Germanic states formed a confederacy, in which Austria and Prussia had the controlling influence; and however daring and fruitless it may

---

[1] F. W. Tittmann on the Union of the Amphictyons (in German), Berlin, 1812. [E. A. Freeman, History of Federal Governments, vol. i., London and Cambridge, 1863.]

generally be in politics to deal in suppositions as to that which might or would have been the case, I believe that there can be no manner of doubt that, if our former confederation had continued to exist upon its ancient articles, New York must by this time have been in possession of the American hegemony, or, what is more likely, repeated wars for the American hegemony between such states as Virginia, which was indeed wellnigh obtaining it or may be said to have possessed it already in a degree, Pennsylvania, and New York, must have disturbed our social system. We have only to imagine the election of representatives for congress all over the Union to proceed by a "general ticket" throughout each respective state, to see at once the consequences. Pennsylvania and New York, or New York and Ohio, leagued together, would almost infallibly sway the whole congress.

It is on this point in particular that our constitution appears to me deserving of our deepest veneration and gratitude. By introducing the representative system, that is, *proportional* and *social* representation, and not representation of the states as corporate bodies alone, by nationalizing the house of representatives, all struggle for the hegemony which drowned the glory of Greece in the torrents of the Peloponnesian war was avoided. Am I not justified, then, in calling the framing and adoption of the constitution a great historical act?

XIV. It will now be easy for us to view the question of senatorial instruction in its true light. The legislatures of the different states elect the senators of their respective states. This is admitted; the constitution commands it. But we have seen already, in the case of the presidential election and in that of judges or militia officers, that election alone constitutes no sort of foundation for the right of instruction. This right, if it exists, must be proved on distinct grounds. The different state legislatures elect the senators in virtue of a common constitution. The constitution does not say that the senators are their ambassadors; and the legislatures have no more right to issue mandatory instructions than the electors of the president of the United States have to instruct the president, or than a state governor has who may have appointed a senator to fill a sudden vacancy. If he is elected directly by the people, as he is in all the states at present, such a governor stands in the relation of an intermediate party between the people and the senator whom he thus appoints. But who would tolerate it if the governor should undertake to instruct?

The legislatures are bound to elect for six years; they have no right given them to recall the senators, which at the time of the adoption of the constitution was demanded in one or two cases, but largely overruled. We all know perfectly well, however, that the right of instruction amounts in almost all cases of real importance, that is, when the instructed differs in opinion from his instructors, to a virtual recall; for if both parties agree, the instruction can have value only by way of moral weight. The legislatures have sworn to maintain the constitution, and must not arrogate so important a power as to interfere with and virtually to abrogate one of its most important provisions—nay, to blot out one of its leading features. The constitution gives no right to recall the resisting senator; but what does the right of instruction amount to, if there be no means of enforcing it? It is answered, the instructed senator is morally bound to obey or to resign. If he is morally bound, and not constitutionally, it follows that *he* likewise has to judge of the case. The right of instruction is said to be implied in the idea of representation. Does implication differ in this case from construction? Is, not, then the right which the state legislatures assume in instructing a constructive right, and dangerous to civil liberty? That according to my view it does not follow from the general principles of representation has been seen. Below are instances to show that this feature—election of senators for six years,—would be totally erased from the constitution if mandatory instruction were introduced¹

---

¹ The following is a passage of the speech of Senator Southard [of New Jersey] in the senate of the United States on February 22, 1835:

The constitution of the United States has introduced the system of two houses, so justly dear to the whole Anglican race as one of the happiest expedients which has been adopted by all nations that follow in their path of political civilization. But what is the true meaning of this system of two houses? It is a political guarantee, a check, and one of peculiarly beautiful operation. Masses, we observed, are impetuous; houses of representatives likewise as masses become impetuous. It is important, therefore, to have two houses so organized that they will not be easily swayed by the same impetuosity,—in other words, that the two houses be founded upon different principles. If not, as is the case in the present Belgian constitution, according to which the senate is elected by the representatives from among themselves, little more than the

---

" It may, it often does, happen that the political character of the legislature is frequently changed. Upon this theory there must be a new senator upon every change. In Rhode Island, if I recollect correctly, the changes have been such that she might have had, nay, ought to have had, six senators in two years. So in Ohio: last year she instructed her senators : one of them disobeyed; if he had resigned, the present legislature, which is of a different political aspect, would have instructed his successor, and we should have had two new senators upon the floor, and the state had five in a little more than one year. The rebellious one of last year might have been restored; unless indeed the legislature should, as they ought under such circumstances, spurn him from their confidence for his servility, as destitute of that moral courage and independence of character without which a public agent is a public curse. The history of my own state is not destitute of facts to illustrate this doctrine. The changes which have taken place in the political parties there since 1824 would have given to us some six or eight different members, and this resulting from no versatility or changeableness in the character of her people. The number of our counties is small—only fourteen. The parties throughout the state have long been nearly balanced. In several of the counties the change of a few votes, or the neglect of a small number to attend the polls, would not only give a new representative in the legislature, but change its political character; a little more than one hundred votes, in one or two of several counties, would have changed the late instructions. There are, I believe, about twenty members of the majority who hold their seats by an average of not more than one hundred and twenty votes; some of them by less than one hundred. Suppose there should be a small alteration of opinion, resulting from some general or local cause; the political aspect will be changed. Shall the legislature again instruct, drive the recently elected senator from his seat before he has had time to become familiar with it, and restore the one whose office is about expiring?"

outward form of the bicameral system is obtained. Now, if our representatives come fresh from the people at short intervals, and the state legislatures, coming from the same people at equally short intervals, undertake to instruct the senators, who are elected for six years, the system of two houses as a guarantee, most wisely established, is evidently destroyed, and we have upon all important questions but one house, though sitting in two different places; only two *bureaux*, as the French would call it, of the same body.

It has been objected, however, Suppose that the representatives or senators should really vote against the dearest interests of their constituents; in fact, I have heard it asked, what should we do if our representatives should vote for a law directly in contradiction to the fundamental law? All I would answer is, Suppose, on the other hand, the representatives will not vote for such a law but should be instructed to do so? One is as imaginable as the other. These are extravagant suppositions, against which no human system can provide, and the victorious power of public opinion, under which the representative emphatically stands, is altogether forgotten. A thousand similar suppositions might be made respecting the ultimate point of any constitutional institution. The British monarch can make an unlimited number of peers, and when, under Walpole's ministry, the earl of Sunderland proposed to close the list of peers forever, the commons most strenuously opposed depriving the crown of this prerogative, and to the objection that the crown might make a hundred peers in one creation, gave answer that the responsible minister stands under public opinion—that many things which *might* be done nevertheless cannot be done. Our congress has the right of expelling any member by two-thirds of the votes: suppose the members should league together to expel in the regular way the representatives of a certain district. All this might be done, but it cannot be done unless public opinion sinks so low as to permit it. There is no form, no guarantee, which can protect a degraded people; no senate could protect under a Tiberius, for all were degraded.

Another objection is, that although it be admitted that a constant recurrence to the right of instruction would deprive a parliamentary body of its deliberative character, yet it will be resorted to only in cases of extremity. This, however, is by no means so very certain; custom and repetition might soon reduce the representative system to one of mere deputies. But let us admit even that this would not probably be the case, all guarantees and checks are most important when cases of magnitude arrive; they exist for that very purpose. The most varied and even opposite forms are frequently indifferent in the common run of cases; but when the periods of difficulty arrive it is the very time they must show their essence. We try the wisdom of a political law of importance not by common cases but by great emergencies. The trial by jury is not of so great importance for the punishment of petty thefts; other forms of trial might sometimes be even preferable; but when difficulties arrive, when power of office and public opinion, resentment of the judge and unbiassed fairness, struggle with one another, then the trial by jury must show whether it is justly held dear by the Anglican race or not.

I know full well that it would be trying to see a senator perseveringly vote against what, according to the existing opinion, seems to be decidedly the general opinion of the state, without having the power to correct him according to the doctrine of instruction adopted by some states. But let us weigh well whether it is not one of the very objects of the constitution which orders him to be elected for six years, that upon occasions he should not quickly follow a sudden turn in the opinion at home; and, above all, whether, however wrong or obstinate he may be, it is not upon the whole infinitely better to suffer this passing and specific evil than to suffer the subversion of the representative character of the senate—of the constitution itself. Is there no such necessity in politics as moral restriction, and manly suffering of an evil in order to avoid a still greater one? We must ask again, has public opinion no ultimate force in a free country? I believe that no senator could possibly withstand for any length of time the course of settled public opinion if opposed to his course of action; though he may, as has often happened, oppose the drift of general opinion on specific, single measures. He has, in my opinion, received his peculiar authority by the constitution, among other reasons, for the very reason that he may do so. When is it that a senator is generally instructed, or that this whole subject becomes important? Not when he agrees with the instructions, nor when he flagrantly abandons his former course upon which he was elected. He cannot, in the nature of things, frequently dare to do so. He knows too well that his character would be gone forever. Instruction, then, becomes important generally in those cases in which not the senator but the opinion at home has suddenly changed since his election. Is it not for these very cases that the constitution grants him a term of six years, while it grants only the brief period of two years to the representatives? Is not the claim to the right of instruction by the state legislatures the old desire of power for more power, which steals so easily upon all of us, and to check which is one of the objects of fixed fundamental laws?

I do not believe that it has ever been maintained, even in impassioned controversy, that the legislatures would have the right to instruct when the senate was sitting as a high court of impeachment. There seems to be something so revolting in the case, reminding so directly of the worst cases under the Stuarts, when the judges were distinctly told by the court how to sentence, that I do not believe the right of instruction has ever been claimed for these cases. But why not? Because the senators sit as judges, and because to judge without trial, that is, to judge without conscientious conformity of the judgment to what appears upon trial and with regard to something else, is felt at once by every one to be the highest iniquity. But is it less unwise to legislate on any other grounds except the information brought to us by the debate, than it is iniquitous to judge except upon the information brought to us by the trial? Does not a single legislature by instruction assume to legislate for the Union, because it directs the vote of one who still continues to enjoy by the constitution the character and influence of a legislative representative; —thus assuming to decide the case, while the other uninstructed senators continue to be influenced by the debate and the opinion of society at large as elicited by the deliberation? Upon the general ground upon which the state legislatures claim to instruct senators in legislative business the respective governors might claim, and, in my opinion, with much more plausible right, to instruct the senators upon executive business; for the governors, especially where they are elected by the people directly, are the true representatives of the people for all executive business. Yet this has never been claimed.

In giving these my views, I am well aware that I have expressed myself directly against what some distinguished men have stated as their deliberate opinion, men in intellect and experience much superior to me. Yet the opinions of other great men support the views here given, and I believe it is not difficult to see that the former may have erred, as every one is apt to err, by regarding the opposite of wrong to be right.[1] If we have to combat one evil we are apt to go too far on the other side. If there were not a corrective process in the course of time, and if succeeding generations should not take deeper and more enlarged views, no advance of civilization would be possible, and we should become Chinese, looking back to their Confucius and Mencius as unalterable types. Not Plato, but Truth.

XV. It is evident from the previous remarks that the subject of instruction could not become matter of discussion so long as the system of deputation existed; for this was founded upon it. But when the deputies had changed into representa-

---

[1] * The great, although natural, mistake of continental liberals towards the end of the eighteenth century, and of Americans after them, was this, that they thought that the establishment of liberty consisted in the transmission of the assumed powers and rights of the despot to the people. Liberty consists in something essentially different.

tives, and the British parliament had gradually become more and more distinctly acknowledged as the national representation, it was natural likewise that the precise relation in which a representative, though national, still continues to stand to his particular constituency, and his obligation to represent their especial wishes, should become matter of earnest discussion. I believe the beginning of the history of this more earnest discussion must be dated, as already mentioned, from the time when John Wilkes was elected by the Westminster constituents, and more especially from Mr. Burke's speeches to the electors at Bristol in November, 1774. Mr. Burke, as we have seen, maintains that the imperative duty of the British representative requires him to attend to all the interests and desires of his constituents to his utmost power, but likewise to vote to the utmost of his conscience as the broad national interest demands, even should he go against the supposed or actually expressed wishes of the majority of his constituent-voters. The war between Great Britain and America, as well as the whole spirit of the eighteenth century, led many reflecting men to inquire, among other subjects, into the precise character of a representative. The British commons were, as is well known, under the almost total sway of the aristocracy of the land, and far from representing in many cases the people at large. In addition to this sway, the powerful influence of the crown, and the protracted period of seven years for which a member of the commons is elected, since the passing of the septennial bill in 1716, were causes tending to separate the interests of the members of the house of commons from the great mass of the people. These considerations, and the erroneous idea that the whole meaning of the representative government was that of an expedient and substitute for the meeting in the forum, made necessary by increased population, prevailing among most liberally educated men towards the end of the last century, led many of the prominent English advocates of parliamentary reform to the opposite of the evil of which they complained, as is nearly always the case during the first period of opposition to a deep-rooted error or other evil. Men like Burgh, in his Political Disquisitions, and Major John Cartwright asserted that the representative is (and they actually called him so) "the legislatorial attorney" of his constituents: at least this is the expression of Cartwright—thus reducing the representative to a mere deputy of the feudal ages. The cause of this error is now easily seen. These men, whenever they spoke of liberty, had in mind what was called in the first part of the present work democratic absolutism. Their error, which was natural in the course of this discussion, has, I hope, been exhibited. A collection of "legislatorial attorneys" would be far worse than an "ecclesia" of the ancient absolute democracy, as we have seen, because in the latter the individual voting for himself alone may be influenced by the demands of the public welfare, which the former cannot be, bound, mind and conscience, as he is by his instruction and power of attorney. Indeed, there is some contradiction in the term legislatorial attorney, for a legislator must needs weigh and reflect, and shape his course according to weighty considerations, even were he to legislate merely according to interested views. In the middle ages the instructions were no contradiction, for in most cases the deputies were not legislators proper, not at all so if we compare their functions with those of our representative bodies; they assembled chiefly for the granting of subsidies, *acknowledging* laws or persons, or exacting franchises. It is now amply settled that the British member of parliament is the representative of the nation.[1]

---

[1] As late as 1837, the radical member for Leeds, being applied to by the secretary of the Leeds Committee for giving relief to certain people of Leeds, said in his answer—if the papers reported correctly—that he was the representative of England, Scotland, and Ireland, and not of the borough of Leeds, and that he could not provide for all the needy of the realm. (London Ledger, October, 1837.) Hume gives a few remarks on instruction, with particular reference to the then existing British system of representation, in a note appended to Essay IV. of his Moral, Political, and Literary Essays. The fourth Essay is on the Principles of Government. These Essays were published in 1792, after Mr. Burke, therefore, had treated of the subject. Hume's remarks, however, are quite passing only.

In France, as we have seen already, the opposite course took place: liberty became closely allied with the defeat of specific instructions and the elevation of the deputy to the dignity of a national representative; and in the many phases through which the cause of liberty has passed in that country during the last half-century the representative was always repressed into a deputy whenever the cause of absolute power was in the ascendant. When Louis XVIII. returned to France in 1814 the name of deputy was retained, as it well agreed with the general spirit of the charter promulgated by him—an instrument which cautiously granted the least degree of liberty compatible with the urgent demands of the nation, and with the necessity on the part of the Bourbons of creating some sort of support for themselves. When in 1830 the charter was amended, and the power of the chamber of deputies greatly increased, the name was not changed; but the present French deputy is essentially and avowedly a national representative, not a departmental deputy.

In the United States the subject of instruction has become especially interesting on account of the senators. Many state legislatures have passed resolutions "to instruct the senators and request the representatives" to oppose or promote certain measures; but many senators have likewise resisted, and of course, as there is no power conferred by the constitution to remove a non-complying senator, have done so successfully. Indeed, instruction by legislatures cannot be said to have as yet assumed any higher authority than that of very distinct and implicit information, to which of course the senator is bound in strict conscience to pay the highest regard, as a governor, elected by the people, would pay due regard to powerful petitions or resolutions of powerful and respectable meetings in cases of great emergency, but would not receive instructions. In the state of Virginia alone it is considered by many that the right of instruction has, in a sort, become common law of the state; that is, a citizen accepting the senatorial chair might be considered as having accepted it on the implied condition of acknowledging instruction, provided always this citizen have not during his previous life candidly and openly expressed his opinion, or distinctly, previously to his election, to the contrary. Yet even in Virginia the difficulty is by no means removed which must forever arise out of the contradiction which necessarily lies in instruction in America, for the two simple reasons that the so-called right of instruction, though of organic and fundamental importance, is merely implied, nowhere granted, hence is without means for its enforcement, and consequently unsubstantial; and that a senator, who must be supposed to be a conscientious man and hence feel the sacred obligations of oaths, takes a solemn oath upon a distinct law and instrument, called the constitution, which is above him, legislature, and all, as much as the law of nature and God is above king and subject. This plainly appeared in the case of Mr. Watkins Leigh, in 1836, as mentioned above. The argument of his letter is this: " I fully acknowledge the right of instruction, but only within the constitution, by which all of us are primitively bound. If, therefore, you instruct me against the constitution, I cannot obey without perjuring myself." Mr. Leigh did not resign, yet, as he himself informs us in his letter, he was the citizen who in 1812 drew up the resolutions by which the legislature of Virginia endeavored to establish the right of instruction, and he endeavors to show that those resolutions do not apply to his case in 1836.[1] The legislature in such cases of course

---

[1] It is not easy to say what is the precise doctrine at present of Virginia, however simple the subject may appear at first glance. Mr. Leigh says in the letter above cited that "the resolutions of the legislature in 1812 were the work of his own hands without assistance from any other person whatever, and drawn up (as he but too well remembers) with a haste which in his own apprehension at the time materially impaired its value." However, he says that upon a recent and careful review he finds no reason to retract or modify anything. Yet these very resolutions were assumed and quoted in 1836 as the rules upon which Mr. Leigh was instructed, and by him as supporting him in not obeying the instructions. The instructions of 1836 state that they merely " reassert" the right, which " surprises" Mr. Leigh. No one who knows the high integrity of this gentleman will entertain for a moment any doubt that he expresses his real sentiments. I will subjoin one of the resolutions of 1836, because it seems to me very strongly to

answers, What is instruction, if not to guide you when we differ? When we agree, there is no necessity for it; now, this is a case of disagreement because we do not believe that what we demand is against the constitution. It amounts in these cases, indeed, precisely to the same dispute which has frequently occurred in the Catholic church, when a person acknowledged the infallibility of the pope upon all matters upon which the decision belonged to him, matters of doctrine under the dogma of the church, but denied that the specific subject under question belonged to this class; while, on the other hand, the pope declared that his infallibility would amount to nothing if it was not he himself who should determine whether this was a case within his competence to decide or not. The dispute of the Roman curia and the Jansenists turned upon this very point. It is worthy of observation that if the Virginia theory of instruction were adopted the senate would be a more changeable body than the house of representatives, because many state legislatures are changed every year, at least in their lower branch; and if they instruct accordingly the senate is also changed yearly, and thus one of the most fundamental features of our constitution would be annihilated.

From what has been stated before, it must clearly appear that the author, in his humble judgment, considers the Virginia doctrine unwarranted, inconsistent, and unconstitutional. Yet it is necessary for the reader to inform himself thoroughly upon the subject; and I believe that the chief periods during which the subject of instruction was most discussed and became more and more settled in Virginia are when the Bank

---

show how boldly men must always act in politics if they abandon the safe rule of law and constitution. It runs thus: "That after the solemn and now repeated expression of the opinion of the general assembly on the right of instruction and the duty of obedience thereto, no man ought henceforth to accept or retain the appointment of senator of the United States from Virginia who does not hold himself bound to obey such instructions or to resign the trust with which he is clothed." If all legislatures make similar proclamations, an entirely new provision is evidently added to the constitution of the United States, without pursuing the constitutionally prescribed course. Power, and nothing but arrogated power, would in that case have changed the constitution.

of the United States was chartered in 1791, when the renewal
of the charter was discussed in congress in 1811,[1] and when
the Virginia senators in 1836 were instructed to vote for the
before-mentioned expunging resolution, upon which occasion
one of the senators declined to give the vote required, but resigned, while the other declined both the vote and the resignation, on the ground, as we have seen, that the instruction
was against the constitution. I must refer to the debates,
resolutions, and letters relating to the subject.

---

[1] See Mr. Giles, senator from Virginia, on this occasion, against instruction, in the Legislative and Documentary History of the Bank of the United States, Clarke and Hall, Washington, 1832; and the resolutions of the Virginia legislature, passed in February, 1812, drawn up, March 2, 1836, by Mr. Leigh. There is no point at which arrogation of power can stop. Although Mr. Watkins Leigh is the author of these resolutions, he quoted them in his own defence for not complying with the instruction in 1836, but without effect upon the legislature: on the contrary, they passed very strong resolutions against "the two several letters of Benjamin Watkins Leigh," in December, 1836. (See Niles's Register.) Several of the debates on the adoption of the constitution of the United States, as published by congress, contain interesting passages respecting this subject. There is a series of articles against instruction by Mr. Hopkinson, of Philadelphia, Circuit Judge of the United States, of great merit, and for instructions, by an author with whose name I am unacquainted, in several numbers of the Literary Messenger, published at Richmond, Virginia, of the year 1837. The judge delivered likewise a speech against instruction on the floor of congress, in 1812. The Federalist (especially the remarks of Mr. Madison) is of course to be consulted. It will sound, I allow, strange if an author refers his reader to a work which is not yet published and with the contents of which he is entirely unacquainted, and yet I cannot but refer to the Madison Papers, now printing by congress; for I cannot doubt that they must contain much valuable matter bearing upon the point of our discussion, since they contain the debates of the constituent congress on the constitution then forming, and I humbly yet confidently hope that they will support the arguments of the text, especially the chief one, that it was the very intention of the constituent congress to superinduce the representative system upon the former deputative, as established in the Articles of Confederation.

# CHAPTER III.

Responsibility of the Representative.—Pledges.—Implied and positive, general and specific Pledges.—Are Pledges moral, and consistent with general Liberty and Justice?—When are they so?—Pledges originated with the Court Party and Aristocracy.—Strong Power of Implied Pledges.—Breaking Implied Pledges, and throwing one's self upon the Constituents by Resignation.—Duties of Presiding Officers of deliberative Assemblies; Speakers.

XVI. We have found that one of the most essential results of a well-regulated and truly representative government is the security and protection of public liberty, that is, of civil liberty as appertaining to and extending over the whole state, the whole jural society as one organic thing, and not as a loosely connected chain of separate independences. This broad, extensive public liberty consists, together with the protection of all essential individual—or, as we have called them previously, primordial—rights, in the sway of public opinion, and its regular passing over, by a safe and organic process, into public will—that is, law. This public opinion which becomes public will is the well-ascertained and clearly-settled opinion of the whole jural society or state, sifted and freed from the adhesions of momentary excitement, of sordid and local selfishness, and of the tyrannical dictation of one part of society over the rest. The elements of which this supreme public opinion is formed are the opinions of the several parts of that society, closely and truly represented or enunciated by their respective representatives, gathered according to an even, fair, and proportionate distribution over the whole of the society, upon principles which appear to that particular society the best adapted for collecting the opinion of the whole, and modified by mutual influence according to the main and fundamental principle upon which all legislation and execution rest, that is, general justice and public welfare. An additional and equally important feature of the representative government is that civil liberty requires that no one should finally act in any matters of the state without responsibility: where this principle is abandoned, there is absolutism. As the prince, therefore, in constitutional or representative monarchies cannot dictate laws at will, although he be, within the constitution and as long as it lasts, personally irresponsible, so does public liberty on the other hand, and especially in republics, where the people are the acknowledged power-holders, require that they do not dictate directly their laws upon no responsibility, which would constitute democratic absolutism, but through responsible intermediate persons—the representatives; although the people, as the monarch in the previous case, are irresponsible in their suffrage for representatives. The representative who has received these constitutionally—not morally—irresponsible suffrages is bound in all his actions, so soon as elected, by the constitution of the land, and is responsible to the people, who pronounce upon him by their next election, but not in each single case in which he votes; for this last would establish at once direct dictation of the power-holder and defeat one of the main objects of representative government.

The representative, then, must represent his constituents closely, under the mediating and uniting influence of general welfare, and hold himself responsible to the people. These considerations, I think, will lead us safely in discussing the subject of pledges.

XVII. Representative pledges are assurances or gages given by a candidate respecting his future course as a representative, should he be elected. They may be implied or positive, and the latter may be general or specific. Frequently it is impossible for the electors to have a sufficiently accurate knowledge of the candidate's views respecting subjects of great importance in their estimation. Meetings therefore will propound, through committees, certain questions, which the candidate is required to answer, and on which the suffrages of the querist are made to depend. Since the representative is bound in duty to discharge his office with strict honesty, a perfect understanding between the constituents and himself is important, and, in order to give him the necessary weight in his elevated position, indispensable. So long, therefore, as the pledges touch principles and views they are right; but the sacred duty of the representative—and he has none so sacred as this—to do all he can for the public benefit according to his best judgment, which consists of the opinion of his constituents brought along with him, but enlightened and regulated by the contact with that of other parts, represented and pronounced by his fellow-representatives, must prevent him from giving pledges as to any definite measures or laws, for in this case he robs other citizens of their undoubted right to state their opinion through their representative and ask a proper share of influence upon the opinion of the legislative body for it before the law be finally passed.

There are times of the utmost exigency in which everything seems to turn upon one measure which for years has been discussed by the nation at large and as to which a candidate is undoubtedly authorized to give a more definite pledge than is compatible with his duty in common cases. Such a one I take to have existed when, in 1832, the question in England was reform or not reform. Yet here again it would have been very presumptuous in a candidate to promise that he would only vote for such or such minute details as might be laid before him on the hustings. Every one sees that pledges of detailed laws are nothing less than antecedent instruction, so that they would amount to a bargaining for votes, and would raise party power and exclusion very high; because a voter might desire to vote for a candidate on account of one pledge, but not of others. Definite pledges, therefore, either beyond principles or great outlines of important broad measures which had long been before the people and had formed perhaps for periods broad party distinctions, would at once defeat the object of representative government, and cannot be given by an honest citizen who religiously loves his country; but they are as a matter of course very readily proffered by demagogues, the fawning courtiers of the people, just as some judges were ever ready to inform James I. how they would give judgment in such or such a case should it be brought before them.

Pledges, like instructions, have often been believed to be necessarily connected with the popular or liberal cause, but history shows the fact to be very different. Pledges to the court and ministers were formerly common, and Lord Brougham showed in parliament that ministerial and aristocratic pledges were common and customary at the time when one lord would return ten or fifteen members, and that no pledges were exacted on the popular side, but that they did not originate, as had been stated, with the reform of parliament in 1832.[1] Lord Brougham is decidedly opposed to pledges, as highly injurious to the cause of liberty and the necessary character of a member of the commons as a representative of the nation. I subjoin the opinion of a gentleman who has distinguished himself alike for sound thought and liberal feeling, and who was foremost in the cause of reform.[2] There are

---

[1] Hansard, xxx., page 590, debate of August 17, 1835.—James II., desirous to have his decreed "liberty of conscience" sanctioned by the parliament to be assembled, sent, in 1687, military officers, civil officers, priests, and laymen of influence, into various counties, to obtain pledges of certain persons that if elected they would vote for the king's measure. "The most general answer appears to have been that, if chosen to serve in parliament, the individuals to whom the questions were put would vote according to their consciences, after hearing the reasons on both sides; that they could not promise to vote in a manner which their own judgment after discussion might condemn; that if they entered into so unbecoming an engagement they might incur the displeasure of the house of commons for betraying its privileges; and that they would justly merit condemnation from all good men for disabling themselves from performing the duty of faithful subjects by the honest declaration of their judgment on those arduous affairs on which they were to advise and aid the king." Mackintosh, Review of the Causes of the Revolution in 1688, chapter vi.

[2] Mr. Macaulay, in the Letter to the Secretary of the Leeds Political Union, in August, 1832, quoted in a previous passage, where I treated of Canvassing, says, "I wish to add a few words touching a question which has lately been much canvassed,—I mean the question of the Pledges. In this letter, and in every letter which I have written to my friends at Leeds, I have plainly declared my *opinions*. But I think it, at this juncture, my duty to declare that I will give NO

several striking instances of manly resistance against pledges. A near connection of Lord Brougham's resigned his place

1 LEDGES. I will not bind myself to make or to support any particular motion. I will state as shortly as I can some of the reasons which have induced me to form this determination. The great beauty of the representative system is that it unites the advantages of popular control with the advantage arising from a division of labor: just as a physician understands medicine better than an ordinary man —just as a shoemaker makes shoes better than an ordinary man—a person whose life is passed in transacting affairs of state becomes a better statesman than an ordinary man. In politics, as well as every other department of life, the public ought to have the means of checking those who serve it. If a man finds that he derives no benefit from the prescription of his physician, he calls in another; if his shoes do not fit him, he changes his shoemaker; if his representatives misgovern him, he can discard them at the next election: but when he has called in a physician of whom he hears a good report, and whose general practice he believes to be judicious, it would be absurd in him to tie down that physician to order particular pills and particular draughts; while he continues to be a customer of a shoemaker, it would be absurd in him to sit by and meet every motion of that shoemaker's hand; and in the same manner it would, I think, be absurd in him to require positive pledges and to exact daily and hourly obedience from his representative. My opinion is that electors ought at first to choose cautiously, then to confide liberally; and when the term for which they have selected their member has expired, to review his conduct equitably and to pronounce on the whole taken together.

"Consider, too, that the business of a member of parliament is the pursuit, not of speculative truth, but of practical good; and that though, in speculation, every truth is consistent with every other truth, yet in practice one good measure may be incompatible with another. It is often absolutely necessary to bear with a lesser evil in order to get rid of a greater. For example, I think the corn-laws an evil; but if there had been in this parliament a hundred or a hundred and fifty members absolutely bound by pledges to attempt the abolition of the corn-laws, there would have been a division in the ranks of the reformers; the tories would have triumphed; and I verily believe that, at the moment at which I am writing, Lord John Russell's bill would have been lost, and the duke of Wellington would have been prime minister. Such cases may and will occur again. Some such cases I can, I think, distinctly foresee. I conceive, therefore, that it is the true wisdom of electors to choose a representative whom they believe to be honest and enlightened, and, having chosen him, to leave him a large discretion. When his term expires—when he again presents himself before them—it will be their duty to take a general survey of his conduct, and to consider whether he have or have not pursued that course which has, under all the circumstances, most tended to promote the public good.

"If the people of Leeds think fit to repose in me that confidence which is necessary to the proper discharge of the duties of a representative, I hope that I

because he would give no pledges, though he agreed with his constituents on all points on which they asked pledges [1]

XVIII. Implied pledges, for the reason that they are implied, have a very strong power, as they necessarily have everywhere with a gentleman. Implied pledges are derived from the life of the individual, his professed principles, his habitual siding with one or the other party, or from some definite action which may justly induce the voters to believe that it indicates some distinct view or other. The implied party pledge can never go farther, as must clearly appear from what was stated on parties as well as on the general character of pledges, than the broad civil principles and views upon which the party is avowedly built; they cannot bind the individual to vote on all important occasions blindly with the party. On the contrary, it is just these highly important occasions on which the citizen may feel himself conscientiously bound to leave the party. Suppose a member has been elected as a member of one party, and after his election the question of war or peace, and, as he believes, dishonor and misfortune, comes up. His party votes against war, which he conscientiously believes to be necessary for the country. In this case he cannot be considered as being bound by an implied or moral pledge to his constituents to vote against the war, for the great pledge of public welfare

---

shall not abuse it. If it be their pleasure to fetter their members by positive promises, it is in their power to do so. I can only say that on such terms I cannot conscientiously serve them."

I ought to refer the reader back to the passage previously quoted, because part of it very strongly bears upon the present point.

[1] The scene which happened when Mr. Poulett Thomson was nominated at Manchester, England, in 1835, as reported in the London papers of the time, is sufficiently characteristic and instructive. The candidate underwent a long and detailed public examination which he sustained with dignity and apparent honesty, without binding his conscience by absolute pledges. The account was copied into the American papers, for instance the National Gazette, Philadelphia, of June, 1835.

stands first; nor ought he to resign before voting, for it may be very important in his conscientious opinion for the country that he should give his vote. In these cases, however, in which he changes but his constituents do not, it will be honorable, honest, and gentlemanlike to throw himself upon the judgment of his constituents by a resignation, as of course also it will be in those cases in which the representative has knowingly broken the implied pledge on grounds of unavoidable urgency. Sir Robert Peel justly resigned his seat for the university of Oxford, February 4, 1829, because he had determined to introduce measures for the relief of the Roman Catholics, while previously, and before matters assumed so dark an aspect of threatening civil war in Ireland—as Lord Wellington at least confessed in the lords—he had always strenuously opposed Catholic emancipation, and he knew perfectly well that of all bodies in the world the university of Oxford would probably be the very last to send a member who should profess liberal principles towards the Catholics.[1] The implied pledge seems to me to require the tenderest regard.

XIX. A subject which demands the faithful attention of the representative, wherever the modern representative system exists, is the interpretation of the fundamental law, and its construction in those cases for which it does not specifically provide, but which nevertheless must be judged by that instrument. In the ancient deputative system, the deputy being directly occupied with the advantage of his corporation and of the estate to which it belonged, the case was not so difficult. Charters or other fundamental laws might be inter

---

[1] When Sir Francis Burdett, elected as a whig, openly became a tory in 1837, he resigned his seat, at the request of some of his constituents, to stand a new election at Westminster, and, by the great exertion of the tories, was re-elected against Mr. Leader. Had he not done so, it is evident that he must have lost all power, influence, and consideration, for it would have been a palpable desertion and betrayal of his constituents.

preted with much ease by them, as by special attorneys, by lawyers in their special pleading. The case is very different, however, where public liberty is sought for with a legislation based upon public spirit, and where the representative is bound to understand and interpret—for whatever consists in human words must be interpreted—the constitution, as the conscientious representative of the whole society. It was at this stage of my work that I originally intended to give my views of interpretation and construction, but, as I have indicated in the preface, my remarks increased to such an extent, without the possibility of curtailing them so as not to injure the clearness of the subject, that I resolved to follow the advice of publishing them separately.[1] I consider, however, the subject of interpretation so closely connected with political ethics, not indeed in its distinct rules, but in their faithful application, that I feel bound to refer the reader to the work alluded to, as to a complement of this work.

XX. The experience of all constitutional countries has amply shown—what every one who has ever been a member of a deliberative assembly with power to decree is fully convinced of—that no such assembly can in the least degree approach the object for which it meets, if considerable power be not given to its presiding officer, especially when it consists of many members, like the British commons or the French deputies, who amount to nearly six hundred. The history of the first French revolution proves the lamentable consequences of a want of knowledge in managing the debates and rules of order, as I have stated before; and Dumont, tch judicious and experienced author of the Reminiscences of Mirabeau and of the two first legislative assemblies, enumerates among the nine chief causes of the unfortunate turn taken by the French revolution as the third, "the bad mode

---

[1] Legal and Political Hermeneutics, or Principles of Interpretation and Construction in Law and Politics, with Remarks on Precedents and Authorities.' 2d edition, Boston, 1839.

of deliberating;"[1] in which opinion every one who knows the details must readily agree with him. The importance of judicious parliamentary debating has been spoken of: here it must be observed that the chief part of this vitally important subject is formed by the rules to be enforced by the speaker, to which many other important duties are generally added, especially that of appointing committees. Even if a speaker had no other duty and power than that of granting the floor by " catching the eye of a risen member, "—and he or some individual must needs have this power,—and that of appointing committees, his power must be very great indeed, and may be very outrageously abused to the detriment of all fairness and free representation. The presiding member who has the power held by the American and English speakers—that of the presiding lord on the woolsack is considerably less—must always remember that he holds one of the most exalted stations; he presides over and in a measure guides the representation of the whole nation; to whatever party he may have belonged, the moment he is elected he ought to remember the words of Louis XII., who had been duke of Orleans, when he became king: " The king of France must not revenge the injuries done to the duke of Orleans;" for as the whole representative organism is the nation's, so is the speaker emphatically a national officer; upon him rests in a great measure the whole operation of the representative system; he may promote a free hearing of all parties, for which they are sent there, if he do his duty, or debar it by injustice. A speaker ought to remember that he is speaker of the whole house, that is, of the whole representation of the whole nation, and not of a party; that in giving an opportunity of speaking, therefore, and in appointing upon committees, justice and fairness ought always to guide him, as in all other acts done by the authority of his chair. The more necessary the great and discretionary power is which he exercises, the more is he

---

[1] Souvenirs sur Mirabeau, ouvrage posthume publié par J. L. Duval, Brussels, 1822, chapter xvii.

bound morally to exercise as a true citizen, justly, judiciously, and patriotically.[1]

---

[1] The *règlements* of the various legislative bodies on the continent, as the French call all that part of our parliamentary law and usage which relates to the internal management of the house itself, are interesting on this account. It is by far the best règlement, here as in so many other cases, if public opinion is so strong that it prevents the speaker from widely swerving from his duties. Long custom and the conviction that strict justice in the speaker is to the advantage of all cause the speaker of the British commons to act, upon the whole, with great justice and high-minded impartiality.

# BOOK VII.

## CHAPTER I.

Executive Officers.—Difficulty of controlling them.—Their Interference with Elections: in Athens, Rome, France, England, the United States.—Plato's Opinion of the Duties of Officers.—Post-Office.—The Chief Executive Officer.—Confidential Officers.—Official Interpretation of Constitutions and Laws.—The Veto.—Ancient and Modern Veto.—Absolute, suspensive, and conditional Vetoes.—Privilege of Pardoning in Monarchies; in Republics.—Danger and Difficulty in Republics.—For what purpose is it granted?—Rules which ought to be observed in making use of the Power of Pardoning.

I. "How can a man serve the public? When out of office, his sole object is to attain it; and when he has attained it, his only anxiety is to keep it. In his unprincipled dread of losing his place he will readily go all lengths." These words sound as if they were taken from a modern debate or a discussion in our papers of recent date, yet they were spoken two thousand five hundred years ago by the greatest sage of a people at the other end of the world, utterly independent in its whole civilization upon the western, Caucasian race to which we belong; they are the words of the Chinese sage Confucius,[1] in which I have substituted only the word public for that of prince,—not an illegitimate substitution; for even the Chinese acknowledge in their laws, their classical works, and in the prayers offered up by the emperor, that he is the vicegerent of heaven for the maintaining of justice, order, morality; in short, for the benefit of the people.

The Greeks found the same difficulty of controlling their executive officers. Their whole history testifies to the fact. It is shown also by the constant, generally annual, rotation

---

[1] Lun-yu, Conversations and Sayings of Confucius, recorded by his Disciples, chap. 17, sect. 16, quoted from Davis's "The Chinese." [Lün-yü has been translated by Schott, 1830.]

in office, and the drawing of lots in some cities for offices and magistracies; by the very extensive system of checks, which, in Athens for instance, was carried out into the minutest details, as the reader may see in Boeckh's Public Economy, book ii. 8; by the repeated and periodical inquiry not only into the accounts of officers, but into the whole administration of their office—the εὐθύνη, which the Greeks valued very highly, and upon the absence of which in the Lacedæmonian council Aristotle animadverts (Politics, ii. 9;)—and by the Athenian nomophylakes, the office intended for the purpose of controlling the officers. And to mention no other of the many laws, institutions, and events which prove the fact, we actually meet with insurrections of the people against the officers, who, it was believed, had established themselves as a party and become an unlawful oligarchy, such as that of the Thespians mentioned in Thucydides, book vi. 95. Comp. also Aristot., Pol. vi. 7, 19.

The whole Roman history is one continued commentary on the difficulty and danger to be encountered in the solution of the grave political problem, how to give sufficient power to the officers, and at the same time to prevent them from arrogating more, and uniting into a formidable aristocracy of placemen.

Modern monarchies and republics offer no different spectacle. The crown or executive has the command over the legion of executive officers, and must have it in a high degree, for otherwise no government would be able to obtain its end; and, on the other hand, this influence is abused for purposes separate from the interests of the state, or directly hostile to the liberties of the people, and to the very objects for which alone the whole government is established, and for which the different officers have received authority under and within the same. Every chief executive officer of whatever name, king, president, or consul, and every subaltern under them,—indeed, every one that has power,—feels, when opposed, the desire rise in his bosom to carry his point and to interrupt the steady course of law by the "per speciale mandatum regis," by which the Stuarts would have set at nought all British liberty, had they been suffered to do it. The whole struggle for civil liberty in England turns upon what the commons thought undue influence of the executive in setting aside acts of parliaments, despite special acts of parliaments against this license and against the boldly arrogated influence and direction of elections on the part of the executive, which forms a peculiar difficulty in all representative governments.[1]

In France, to speak but of the latest times, we find that the first charge against Polignac, when impeached after the July revolution of 1830, was that of having unconstitutionally interfered with the freedom of election, by sending circulars to all public functionaries, requiring them to vote for the ministerial candidates, in addition to which, written evidence was exhibited showing that places and offices had been promised in return for votes.[2]

In the United States we find in the report made by a committee sent in 1839 by congress to the city of New York, to inquire into certain affairs connected with the custom officers of that city, that they had been assessed, not indeed by authority, in proportion to their salaries to furnish contributions towards election expenses. Nor is it possible here to pass over in silence the open interference of the office-holders with the election laws of the state, which occurred in the state of Maryland in the year 1836.

II. The difficulty then has been felt at all times and in all governments, but in some respects it greatly increases with the establishment and firmer securing of modern liberty, such as it has been characterized in the previous book. A government whose only object is security and justice, not liberty,

---

[1] It is perhaps not useless for me to refer here, among the many authors and collections relating to this point, to Brodie's British Empire, vol. i. p. 113, et seq., and, indeed, to the whole of his Introduction; the reader will find there and in Hallam's Constitutional History all the necessary references carefully collected.

[2] English Annual Register of 1830, published in 1831, p. 224.

has to watch over the honesty, efficiency, and obedience of the officers only; but where the additional and highly important object of government is the security and protection of liberty, the people have a right to watch over the officers that they do not interfere with it, especially with the elections, the primary means by which we endeavor to secure it. If the officers paid by the state to serve as agents of the government interfere with it, this virtually amounts to conspiring against one of the greatest of state objects: it is a capital usurpation. We have seen that the very idea of modern liberty—state-liberty as contradistinguished to feudal corporation liberty—requires enlarged societies and continuous and systematic governments. These again require a large number of officers well united into one coherent system, and thus, of course, expose society in the same degree to the danger of seeing those who were intended to be the mere agents of the law and government becoming the masters or leaders, secure in their places, from which it may become the highest interest of society to dislodge them. There is no single and absolute principle, however, by strict adherence to which we may be sure to avoid all difficulty, as by the fixed operation of a machine. The contrary has been often erroneously supposed. The Greeks at length threw aside all consideration of talent and peculiar moral fitness, and resorted to the lot.[1] The state, as was natural, rapidly declined, and bribery and dishonesty became the order of the day. Incessant rotation begets evils as great as the danger intended to be avoided by it. It prevents any one from making himself thoroughly acquainted with his official duties, deprives society of the service of many most qualified persons, and, by holding out a hope to the least qualified to have their turn of office, begets a general greediness and thirst for it, and a mean anxiety for salary among those who either are unfit or indisposed for any steady, regular, and laborious trade or profession,—to the exclusion of

---

[1] [The author seems to think the lot universal in Greece, but it belonged to extreme democracy, and became more common with time; but even at Athens sundry officers were chosen by *chirotonia*.]

those to whom an office no longer affords any inducement, either by way of remuneration or honor, to interrupt their own proper pursuits. Thus the government sinks gradually more and more, and becomes the most expensive of all; for t' ere is nothing more expensive than to feed indolence and incapacity, while a state loses just so much in nerve and healthiness as the desire to obtain money without labor increases, and as offices are bestowed for other reasons than merit and capacity. The more an officer knows that he does not stand upon his own merit and capacity, so much the more dependent he feels himself to be upon his employers, and considers himself their tool and servant, not the public's, a mere party follower whom good luck has thrown into a good berth, of which, therefore, he must make the best while the time lasts. Want of high-toned honor, genuine love of liberty and country, ready devotion to her best interests, whole and entire, and pride of his citizenship, must give way to a spirit of dishonor and dishonesty; he sinks from a citizen of his country to a lackey of his party; from a deserving citizen who is conscious that the workman is worthy of his hire, to a pilfering or blood-sucking slave. The system of throwing all appointments into the hands of the people affords no certain guarantee in itself; for if the general spirit of honor and liberty is depressed, this system will only make of every idler a petty demagogue, hurrying on general decay. The system of mutual check and periodical inquiry—of the last importance, and far too much neglected in many modern states—is still not sufficient alone to guard against the danger; witness its little utility in Athens. We must acknowledge, then, that in addition to wise laws relating to the tenure of offices, to the real responsibility of those who hold them, and to the power of appointment and removal, conscientious discharge of official duties and jealous watching over them on the part of the people are of the highest importance, and cannot be dispensed with, whatever laws or principles we may resort to. It is the error of those who fail in experience, or take but superficial views of the affairs of men, to believe that a sort of government machine can be possibly invented, or some principle be discovered, which must operate exactly, independently of the character of its agents. Were it so, man would no longer be the moral being which his Creator made him. The science of politics has to treat of the laws and principles by which men will be most likely to secure a discharge of official actions consentaneous to the constitution and the objects of the state; it is for political ethics to consider the duties of official men, and impress them upon the citizen. Let us keep strictly in our mind that as the great problem of our times is to unite civil liberty with extensive, socialized states, which as we have seen is to be obtained by the representative system, so it is one of the more important of our problems to make a large number of officers compatible with civil liberty—a problem the solution of which we can hardly say has as yet fairly begun, and which, like every great political problem, cannot be solved by merely proclaiming and inconsiderately carrying through some apparently very simple and symmetrical theory, but must be solved by results obtained by lofty views applied with careful observation, conscientious love of truth, and wise consideration of all the given circumstances, and of the gradual development of the many relations which constitute the state.[1]

III. All those duties and principles which are most important respecting executive officers are so simple, so clear and

---

[1] If we study history with that spirit of truth which alone makes it a wise instructor, we shall find that no men have been greater benefactors to their countries or times than those whose moral and intellectual loftiness led them to adopt great and elevated principles, and whose comprehensive and penetrating mind enabled them to apply them wisely for the whole of society, who, therefore, even while they struggled actively and zealously against obstacles, comprehended, nevertheless, in their true and ultimate object the *whole;* and that none have done more injury than those men who, possessed of a narrow mind, were nevertheless placed in high stations, either by birth or circumstances, and whose confined intellect made them settle upon some general theses and adore them with obstinate idolatry without regard to reality. Some of the prominent actors in the French revolution, and James II. of England, are instances of the latter; Henry IV. of France, and Washington, of the former.

evident, that they are hardly ever denied by word of mouth; yet it is very different if we consider men's actions. We must pay, then, some attention to points which otherwise it would be gratuitous in an author to touch. Though truisms, they must be repeated.

Cicero says in his Offices, "Those who design to be partakers in the government should be sure to remember those two precepts of Plato: first, to make the safety and interest of their citizens the great aim and design of all their thoughts and endeavors, without ever considering their own personal advantage; and secondly, to take care of the whole collective body of the republic so as not to serve the interest of any one party to the prejudice or neglect of all the rest: for the government of a state is much like the office of a guardian or trustee, which should always be managed for the good of the pupil, and not of the persons to whom he is intrusted; and those men who, whilst they take care of one part of the citizens, neglect or disregard another, do but occasion sedition and discord." (Offices, i. 25.) No one dares to deny the truth of these words, yet thousands act in opposition to them.

The officer is the officer of the government which is for the benefit of the people, and "by the word people is signified a community taken as a whole; but an oligarchy means only a party." (Athenagoras in Thucydides, vi. 39.)

From this fundamental truth it naturally follows that the officer must not abuse his position for his own interest or that of his friends or party, nor to the injury or detriment of the people, and he must conscientiously strive to obtain the object for which he is appointed, that is, first, to act according to the true spirit of the laws, and secondly, to do as much essential service to the public as he can. Respecting the first point, dishonesty, as well as the pampering of any passion or lust, is wholly and essentially against the oath, nay, the very sense, of office. No charge has ever been held more odious than that of official filching or robbing on a large scale. We have sufficiently considered this subject under the head of Honesty. The officer acts equally against this fundamental principle when he supports matters personal to himself by official power, be this on a small scale in an underling, or on a large scale by designating those who oppose him as opponents to the public welfare. Parties are very apt to confound these two points which are yet distinct: they frequently go so far as to stigmatize every one who is not the open, active friend of their leader as not only hostile to him but to the public at large. The ministerialists under George III. of England and Charles X. of France called themselves the king's friends, and Mr. O'Connell, on the accession of Victoria, wrote a letter to Ireland to form a party to be called the queen's friends. In the United States those who oppose the administration, or only a single measure, have been repeatedly termed enemies of the constitution.

As an officer is grossly dishonest who uses official information for his own pecuniary advantage, or furnishes early information to his personal or political friends, so is he likewise grossly dishonest who uses the power and influence, or even the means which he obtains through his well-earned salary, for party purposes, especially for elections. This the laws and political procedures of all free nations corroborate. Of all usurpations one of the most odious and unwarranted is an oligarchy of place-holders, men who use the very means granted them by the people against them—for they use their power against the people as soon as they interfere with the free operation of elections, whether this be by influence beforehand, or by making themselves active at the polls. I have seen in the United States sheriffs, who have no official business at the polls as they have in England, taking a most offensive part in "bringing up" voters, and other procedures. It is surprising that all the world agrees to set down a man as an offender who uses a power of attorney for his own benefit or against his employer, and yet that the officer, under oath to keep the laws of the land, and having received his office, directly or indirectly, only for the intended benefit of his employers, should not be considered such when he does the same thing. All political deliberations in the army or navy are justly looked upon by free nations with a jealous eye, and in most nations are punishable acts; but so ought likewise the executive officer to be disfranchised as long as he holds his office, and where this is not the law he ought in common decency to abstain from such arrant political interference. Still more odious and intolerable it becomes if whole institutions, established for the convenience or protection of the people, are made use of to serve the partial interests of those who happen to have authority over them. There is no institution more necessary for modern civilization, more directly for the convenience and necessary wants of the people, and the officers of which ought to consider the performance of its duties more religiously sacred, because it exists by trust and confidence alone, than the post-office. And yet this offers a most wide-spread means of usurped influence, and of seriously injuring some of the most essential interests of the citizen. In several countries this sacred agent of European and American civilization has been shamelessly abused by its officers for prying into the political sentiments or plans of the citizens; and the large and peculiarly well organized, affiliated, and diffused body of postmasters has been made subservient to the administration, thus superinducing a usurping government upon that granted by law, which it is exceedingly difficult for the citizens to shake off.[1]

IV. The duties of a superior or chief executive officer necessarily embrace those of the citizen and of the subordinate officers in general, but the higher he stands, the more imperious are the claims of duty upon him: especially is this true of the chief magistrate, for he must be in many cases the last resort, upon whom the ultimate decision depends. As regards his more particular actions I propose to consider

---

[1] * It is to be considered whether the post-office ought not to be made independent. What has the postmaster to do with the cabinet? I have written an article for the New York Review on the subject, at the suggestion of Senator Preston. May, 1841.

them in the following order:—his appointment of officers, and discharging them, the use he makes of his personal influence and power in the legislation of the country, before a bill comes fairly before him for approval, and the conformity of his actions to the spirit of the laws and their interpretation, which is closely connected with the legitimate use which he ought to make of peculiar privileges, for instance of the power of pardoning.

As to the pervading and general principle of his conduct, he, before all, ought to realize in his actions the great end and object of the state, that is, justice; truth and justice on the one hand, prudence and wisdom on the other, ought to be to him what the light and heat of the sun on the one hand, and care and foresight on the other, are to the husbandman. When Charles V. had cited Luther before the diet at Worms, and many high prelates importuned the emperor not to keep his promise of safe-conduct to the heretic, the youthful monarch exclaimed, " If faith and truth are banished from all the world, they must find with me a refuge."

The chief magistrate is the magistrate of the state, of the whole. He cannot too frequently represent this to his mind; not only in order to avoid acts of injustice and low partiality (do we not expect the same of every mayor, captain, schoolmaster, or father of a family?), but also in order to shape his course and guide the government. All the science of ruling, in whatever narrow or extensive sphere, resolves itself into aiding the society over which we rule, and not part of that society merely, in obtaining its greatest and highest end; all the art of ruling resolves itself into reconciling, through lofty principles, the opposites, mediating contrasts, and making all parts, however opposed to one another, move towards the same great and common goal. We rule, when we seize upon the principle of life in each component part and make it aid and support every other part; we only conquer or destroy when we oppress or suppress one part by the help of another.

It has been mentioned several times how baneful it is for a country if, in the appointment of officers, no regard is paid to capacity; still worse if moral unfitness is disregarded, and men with tainted or actually wrecked reputation, disowned by the society of the honest, are seen clothed with public office, to the detriment of that public moral feeling without which political vigor and the necessary buoyancy of civic spirit cannot exist. Republics and monarchies are equally interested in the appointment of fit and honorable persons.[1] If capacity for office no longer constitutes a title for office, general corruption and universal public robbery follow, while the affairs of the commonwealth, conducted by imbecile men, are neglected, and a state of things is produced against which excited party passion may be blind at the time, but which never fails to produce melancholy and universally felt consequences for the next generation.

That a chief officer will prefer a citizen of his own party if he has the choice, is clear; he is in many cases bound to do so; but, as has been remarked already, to appoint a less fit person because he is one of our party, when a fit person might have been found of different political opinions,—only he must not be a zealot of his party,—is placing the party above the public. Those officers who have to advise the chief magistrate, or who fill offices the faithful execution of which requires an

---

[1] General Washington's views respecting appointments are given in his own words in Sparks's Writings of George Washington, vol. i. p. 455. It is true that Washington had to contend with no party; but there would have been parties under almost any other mortal. I cannot forbear giving here Montesquieu's impressive words respecting the court-government of Louis XV., for the French government, after the injudicious total severance of the government from the people, destroyed institutions and was embodied in the personality of the monarch. Montesquieu's words apply likewise to the Roman history, and partially, mutatis mutandis, to some existing states as well : " L'ambition dans l'oisivité, la bassesse dans l'orgueil, le désir de s'enrichir sans travail, l'aversion pour la vérité, la flatterie, la trahison, la perfidie, l'abandon de tous ses engagements, le mépris des devoirs du citoyen, la crainte de la vertu du prince, l'espérance de ses faiblesses, et plus que tout cela, le ridicule perpetuel jetté sur la vertu, forment, je crois, le caractère du plus grand nombre des courtisans. Or il est très-malaisé que la plupart des principaux d'un état soient mal-honnêtes gens, et que les inférieurs soient gens de bien ; que ceux-là soient trompeurs, et que ceux-ci consentent à n'être que dupes."

indispensable agreement of political principles as well as of views and dispositions with those of the chief executive officer, in short, confidential officers, must, as a matter of course, change with a change of the administration; but it produces very evil consequences if it comes to be considered that a change of the administration is the signal of a universal turning out of office, and if every minor officer is declared to be a confidential one. Such a procedure produces a general thirst for office and consequent subserviency in the party that is to come in; it engenders a spirit of spoliation, and makes the office to be considered a spoil won by victory, so that the public service, the people, are forgotten; and when the party is in, it makes the office-holders fearful to act openly as just citizens in their simple and primary civil duties. A degree of political recklessness is necessarily diffused in the state, and if it is not low sordidness which prompts to these actions, it is the political bigotry which declares every one dissenting in opinion to be opposed to public welfare, or even destitute of honesty. James II., when heedlessly rushing on in his mad career of projected absolutism, after the fashion of Louis XIV., declared (in 1686, to Lord Rochester, Clarendon Correspondence, ii. 117, and other works) that no one should retain an office who was not "of his (the king's) opinion." He must have no other interest but what he acknowledges, supports, and promotes. A compact and subservient body with official subordination is thus formed; an aristocracy of officers, far worse than an aristocracy of birth, is thus produced, and a number of citizens are led meanly to betray their best rights for fear of losing their posts; in short, the saying of Confucius placed at the head of this chapter becomes amply verified. The French lately felt it with the greatest indignation that some of the officers were turned out because they had voted against the Molé ministry in 1839. I repeat, all confidential officers ought to be changed if a different party comes into the administration; but it is vicious to make all subaltern officers, for instance, those of the custom-house, confidential, that is, to compel them to assist the administration, beyond what the public service demands of them in their respective places.[1]

---

[1] There are some passages of interest with reference to this subject in the late speeches of Lord Russell and Sir Robert Peel on the vote of confidence respecting the administration of Ireland, in April, 1839. I ought to add that the whole question of discharging officers, which is important already but will grow in magnitude with the increased demand of liberty and increased extent of states, is very differently viewed on the continent of Europe and by the Anglican race. In Germany and France there is such an immense number of government officers, and government employment offers so regular and steady a career, that numbers choose it as their regular profession, for which in not a few countries regular preparatory studies are demanded. The officers form a hierarchy, and calculate upon regular promotion as the reward of honesty and talent, precisely in the same way that with us or in England an individual chooses the army or navy for his profession. It is evident that where this state of things exists, the question of the power of discharge is of vital interest to thousands, and it has been held that no officer ought to be discharged without inquiry and giving reasons; especially is it so where there is no public liberty. In these latter countries honor, title, consequence, support, and future promotion depend upon the office. To be discharged is disgrace and ruin, as it is for the mandarin to be struck from the list. In brief, in those countries discharge without reason or sufficient inquiry is considered as exceedingly tyrannical. With the Anglican race the question assumes a totally different aspect, for two reasons: first, the number of general government officers is comparatively small, and many officers have retained their civil character; citizens fill the office for a time and leave it again; secondly, since civil liberty exists with them on a large scale, changes of administrations have happened more frequently. These changes, however, have required several further changes in the officers, so that on the one hand it is no disgrace to be turned out, on the other hand the offices, being few in number and insecure, are not calculated upon as a regular profession—there is no officer-hierarchy. The latter is a necessary effect of centralization of government power, the prominent feature of the European continental history of the last century, and will and must vanish again with it. Yet I do not say that the question is solved; it will form one of the most interesting questions of politics to ascertain how a sufficiently free power of discharging in the executive—which in free countries must exist—is to be united with that degree of security for the officer which shall protect him against executive tyranny. It forms a very different question. In monarchies, which are not free, the security of the officer against being turned out without some legal procedure is, not without reason, considered as a sort of guarantee against ministerial and monarchical despotism. Free nations want far different guarantees, and, though the question of appointment and discharge always remains an important one, it never can acquire with them that grave importance which, to judge from various works, it has acquired on the European continent, where, as I have said already, the only remnant of public life is the service in government office.

Since the above was written, the speeches of Sir Robert Peel and the duke of

The executive has repeatedly endeavored to influence the votes of the legislative body by open declaration of his sentiments, or he has beforehand declared that he would use his authority of non-approval if such or such a bill should be passed. The constitution cannot prohibit such declarations, or, if it did, could effect nothing, because there would be always means enough to evade the prohibition; but such acts of an executive are certainly directly against the spirit of a truly constitutional country, where legislation must be as free and unfettered as possible until it comes to be connected with the executive by his approval or rejection. The English are at present peculiarly jealous of perfectly untrammelled debate, and it would lead to very serious consequences should now a member of either house make a declaration similar to that of earl Temple in the lords, that the king would consider every one his enemy who would vote for the East India Company bill brought in by the coalition ministry.[1]

---

Wellington, on May 13 and 14, 1839, to explain their proposed change of some ladies of the court of Victoria which led to a failure of Sir Robert's attempt to construct an administration, have reached us. They are not without interest respecting one of the most important points in constitutional monarchy. They touch upon a question which will become more important every year.

[1] * This was in December, 1783. Fox and his friends were vehement against "secret influence," "secret cabal;" and Mr. Baker, seconded by Lord Maitland, proposed the following motion in the commons: "That it is now necessary to declare that to report any opinion or pretended opinion of his majesty upon any bill or other proceeding depending in either house of parliament, with a view to influence the votes of the members, is a high crime and misdemeanor, derogatory to the honor of the crown, a breach of the fundamental privileges of parliament, and subversive of the constitution of the country." William Pitt warded it off. (Tomline, Memoirs of Pitt, vol. ii. p. 225.) The clamor against the use of the king's name in this affair was, however, so great that Lord Temple gave back the seals he had received three days before. (Tomline, as above, p. 231.) The letter which George III. wrote on March 20, 1785, to Pitt, after he had laid his plan of a reform of parliament before the king, who was unfriendly to the measure, is worthy of the reflection of any chief magistrate. George states that he should think it very base in him to influence members upon so momentous a question, and that he should think very ill of any man who would vote on such a question biassed by friendship. He moreover declares that he never had given his opinion, nor should he do so before parliament had discussed it. (Tomline, as above, vol. ii. p. 40.)

The earliest period when the principle that the executive should not influence debates by declaring his decision beforehand came to be more particularly discussed, or at least when it was stated that despite such a declaration debate on the respective subject is not useless, because the executive may be induced by that very debate on the strength of the vote to yield, is probably that period when Charles II. opened several parliaments by declaring that he would grant all reasonable demands, but that they must not touch the hereditary succession (that is, exclude his brother James), and the tories told the whigs that all their attempts to exclude James were useless, since the king would never concur; whereupon the whigs answered that kings had often yielded, and that at any rate the houses must do what they consider their duty, and leave it to others to do theirs. They justly observed that constitutionally no person can know the king's mind or be charged to declare it upon a subject which has not yet been brought constitutionally before him; that, therefore, all these declarations of his intended veto are but surmises or suspicions, not sufficient to be made by the houses the foundations of actions of the highest magnitude.

Declarations not unlike this have been made in congress; at least, members believed, and in fact known, to be personal friends of the executive have declared that it was useless to debate on a certain subject, because the executive would veto the bill if it should pass. This is as much against parliamentary dignity and decorum as against true constitutional spirit. One of the great objects of constitutions is to secure independent action to various branches, and to produce by a union of all a well-poised result. These gentlemen could not have considered what frightful consequences might ensue from this incipient abuse. If it were carried out with any degree of consistency, it would soon virtually deprive the legislature of its initiative power, and make it a body which has only to confirm or reject measures proposed by the administration; and in whatever degree it might be acknowledged, it would effectually forestall all necessary reforms, to which, for the time being, the majority as well as the executive were known to be opposed—all those "annual motions" which have in most cases succeeded by dint of unconquerable perseverance. Who does not know that it is frequently of the greatest importance first of all to start the discussion on a subject at large in the country by a debate in the house? Those who made that unconstitutional declaration forgot that a house of representatives is very different from a body of mere deputies. The house of representatives is, as we have seen, the organ of public opinion, with the power of making it public law, and it is one of its most important functions that it represents public opinion also in this, that the incipient nucleus of a minority, nay, individual opinion, may grow into the opinion of a majority, if it have the internal strength of truth and be supported by perseverance. Whether the executive shall veto or not must remain to be seen, after he is acquainted with the arguments and with the greater or smaller majority which carried a bill. Still worse is it if the chief officer endeavors personally to influence elections by requests or threats. Charles X. sent letters signed by himself to the various officers to inform them how to vote, and that the ministers were acting in his spirit. If this were suffered, it would of course destroy all constitutional responsibility of ministers and all check upon the monarch. It is held that the British monarch cannot give personal instructions. If it is inadmissible in the subaltern officer to influence elections, it is evidently a far greater dereliction of duty in a chief magistrate. Nor does it add to his strength, for every movement beyond the limits of constitutional law and propriety betrays weakness, lowers him in the eye of the people, and will ultimately recoil upon him.

V. I have shown on another occasion[1] that it is absolutely

---

[1] Legal and Political Hermeneutics, where the reader will find also some remarks on the subject of Precedents, which is of much interest in executive questions.

impossible for the human mind to devise any written law which can possibly provide for all cases, or the sense of which may not be stretched or narrowed according to the interpreter's disposition. As the interpretation of the chief magistrate is of the last importance, it is equally important that he should never abandon the two main props of all sound interpretation, without which the most liberal constitution may be made to mean the most servile things, and the wisest provision may be made to cover the most selfish designs;—I mean good faith and common sense. These must be the main guides in the interpretation of the constitution, of the laws which he is charged to execute, and of the privileges bestowed by the former upon him: he must fairly interpret according to the spirit of the law and constitution, of constitutional and representative liberty in general, and of the genius and history of his people in particular. The constitution of the United States gives the right of nominating officers to the president, but the senate of the United States must confirm the nomination, except in the case of inferior officers, where by law the full appointment is vested in the president or some other chief officer. The president, several years ago, nominated a person to a certain office, but the senate declined approving the appointment. The moment the senate had adjourned, the same person was re-nominated, and when the senate met again the new nomination was laid before them. This was certainly not in the spirit of the constitution, which can have no other meaning than that there shall be a check upon the presidential nominations, and that if some nominated person is rejected some other should be chosen; else of what use could be the whole provision? Yet the act of the president was in conformity with the letter or form of the law. The constituent people of Texas, who adopted their constitution soon after this event, seem to have taken counsel in it, for they added a provision to their constitution that the chief magistrate shall have no power to re-appoint a person rejected by the senate.

The executive veto, absolute, conditional, or suspensive,[1] that is the necessity of concurrence on the part of the chief executive or monarch in a bill before it becomes law, and consequently his power to deny his concurrence, is a point of much importance in political law. It has misled many writers and politicians, that they treated of the veto as a separate privilege, a prerogative which seemed to be given directly to interfere with the acts of another branch, as the veto of the Roman tribunes in many cases actually was, for their specific sanction was not necessary to make a bill a law; they had the power of the intercession or veto as such; they were not asked to approve, but they had the prerogative of interposing in other cases as well as with reference to laws; they could veto, that is, stop the farther procedure in the comitia, they could suspend the administration of justice, the execution of a sentence, and could interfere even with the procedures of the consuls. Indeed, the origin and essence of the tribunitial power was an interference with a particular act of a consul for the purpose of protecting a man of the *plebs* or common people. It is different with us: according to modern constitutional law, it is believed necessary that the executive should have a concurrent authority in making laws, partly in order to prevent the absolute tyranny of the legislature, of which history gives many instances, partly to pledge the executive to the execution of the laws by securing his consent to their enactment; to prevent him also from becoming a mere committee, as it were, of the legislature, and for various

---

[1] An absolute veto is possessed, in theory, by the king of England; a suspensive veto by the king of Norway. If he declines concurring, the same bill may be proposed by the next storthing (parliament); if the king declines again, and if the next storthing after passes the same bill, it becomes thereby a law without the concurrence of the king. This provision belongs to the constitution of 1814: in 1824 the king desired such an alteration of the constitution as would give him an absolute veto, but the Norwegians repeatedly declined. The president of the United States has a conditional veto: if he declines concurring, the senate and representatives may repass the bill by a majority of two-thirds, whereby the bill becomes law; but whatever has happened in one congress, which lasts two years, can in no wise affect the next.

other reasons. This constitutional concurrence will be found, upon thorough inquiry, to belong to those main constitutional discoveries characteristic of modern times, and to those political guarantees which are peculiar to civil liberty. For it is very clear that without it the executive either loses all energy or is at war with the legislature; in either case factions must decide, and the sway of public opinion is impaired or annihilated. But while this privilege of the chief magistrate's concurrence allows public opinion to acquire a greater degree of power, his frequent use of his power of non-concurrence meets with an obstacle in the same public opinion. Still, this concurrence or non-concurrence is quite different from the vast, absolute Roman veto. That our veto is no original privilege of itself is clear, among other things, from the fact that most modern constitutions of any degree of liberality settle the form in which the chief executive shall withhold his approval or sanction; in most constitutions it is expressed in a courteous form, such as, the king will think about it, or will examine. The veto question, in modern political law, can never be properly treated, except as part of the greater question of executive concurrence in the great political act of making laws. This concurrence is the primary question, the veto a consequence only. The concurrence, however, is, as it appears to me, one of those necessary *conciliatory* principles so indispensable in politics. But it must appear, likewise, plain that the veto, being but incident to the concurrence, while the concurrence is the last finish given to a law, not the essential production and generation of it, which is the province proper of the legislature, ought to be used with the utmost caution and only when it appears to the executive that insurmountable obstacles are in the way of his sanctioning the proposed measure. The veto question is more important in governments like that of the United States, where a disagreement between the executive and legislature may exist not only in theory but practically, since there is no practical means of enforcing harmony at the instant, no constitutional conciliatory principle until new elections take place. At least no such means has as yet worked itself out in practice. Congress has no means indirectly to coerce the executive into compliance, as parliament has by refusing supplies, which would not have the same effect in the United States; nor has the executive any power to produce compliance if it should be diametrically opposed.

In constitutional monarchies, where the monarch is above and outside of the administration, we all know the practical operation of the conciliatory principle, which has worked itself out of the supplies on the one hand, and out of the constitutional impossibility of regal action without ministerial co-operation on the other. Hence the king of England has not declined concurring for above a century, except, indeed, by anticipating the necessity of non-concurrence by proroguing parliament. The president of the United States may veto, and has often done so. It becomes therefore the more urgently necessary for him to do so faithfully, conscientiously, and cautiously, in the constitutional spirit of his country; not in the narrow limit of a party.

VI. In most countries in which there exist constitutions, the privilege of pardoning and reprieving is conferred upon the chief executive, with few or no limitations, if we speak of the punishment for common offences only. The restrictions relate in almost all states exclusively to impeachments and political offences, to protect which the executive might feel tempted or which may involve the executive itself. The question of pardoning has not received by any means that degree of attention which it deserves, since the time of the essential change which has taken place in the spirit of penal laws on the one hand, and the more decidedly acknowledged sway of the law as indissolubly connected with substantial civil liberty on the other. Montesquieu says that pardoning is the most beautiful attribute of sovereignty;[1] a recent writer on constitutional law[2] calls it the most precious right of the

---

[1] Esprit des Lois, vi. 5.
[2] Aretin, Staatsr. d. constitutioneller Monarchie, i. 205.

monarch. Whether these assertions are exaggerated or not it is not necessary to examine here. Certain it is that when Montesquieu wrote, and when the penal law bore the imprint of a spirit of revenge and indignation at rebellious disobedience against the will of the power-holder, mercy in pardoning justly appeared to be a most beautiful attribute; and we can understand the meaning of pardoning hundreds and thousands at a time, on some joyous occasions, though there was also a wrong idea always connected with it. In our times it becomes flagrant violation of the law if whole numbers of common criminals—not of political offenders—are pardoned, and the community is thus exposed again to all the dangers to life and property, as was for instance lately the case when a son was born to the king of Naples. If it was unnecessary to keep the criminals imprisoned, it was shocking to retain them at all; if it was right and necessary to retain them, it was shocking to let them loose upon the community. To make either dependent upon the birth of a prince, a wholly extra-judicial and extra-legal event, is contrary to the spirit of the law and the duty of the executive. The king might have pardoned all whom he conceived to have offended him or his authority more individually; but he evidently abused his prerogative in pardoning common criminals. It may be very consonant to a father's heart bounding with joy to give joy to hundreds, in a moment of happy exultation, but it is no pleasure to the honest to have criminals turned upon them by the hundred, most of whom, there is not the slightest doubt, committed new crimes before three days had passed.

Yet the incalculable mischief caused by unwarranted and injudicious pardons in monarchies hardly deserves mention if we compare it to the evil caused by this interruption of the proper course of law in the United States, already so mild in many parts, and yet so often set aside upon the most frivolous grounds, indeed very frequently upon no grounds at all, except that some persons, who allow their zeal to be stirred more by sympathy with the guilty than with the honest obtain a number of signatures to a petition. "Forcasmuch as many doe offend in hope of pardon that pardons be very rarely granted," has been said already by Lord Coke.[1] In some of the United States pardon almost amounts to certainty; and, were we not warranted in drawing the conclusion from statistics, we have the confession of the criminals themselves, to the effect that the impunity held out by constant pardons has influenced them greatly, either in a direct way, or indirectly by lessening the fear of the law in general. Yet this is not the greatest of the evils caused by injudicious pardoning. Clergymen who injudiciously collect signatures for pardons little think of the incalculable injury they do to many young persons by aiding the propagation of crime, by returning unpunished and hardened criminals upon the community, and to society by loosening the necessary framework of the law. This, however, is not the place fully to expose all these many evils. It belongs to criminal statistics, and to the whole science of punishment, and I must refer the reader for further discussion of the subject to works relating to those branches especially.[2] But one remark I wish to make for charitably disposed persons, who see in the punishment of a sentenced criminal some evil or other befalling an individual only, and forget his previous crime, the welfare of society, and the will of God that we should have laws, and that therefore we should obey and not interfere with them. My remark to such persons is this, that if they knew the affiliation and what might be called the whole economy of crime, they would know among other things that an immense number of offences remain untried, and an immense number of tried offences unpunished, and that the common offender stands already, in all countries in which the summary process is

---

[1] 3d Institute, 243.

[2] Beaumont and Tocqueville, The Penitentiary System in the United States, translated and provided with Notes by myself, Philadelphia, 1833, in the Introduction to which, p. xxix., I have given my views on pardoning; and my Letter on Subjects of Penal Law, published by the Philadelphia Prison Society, 1838. The repeated Reports of the Agents of Penitentiaries, and many persons in high employ in prison-matters in Europe, all concur that injudicious pardoning is a very great dereliction of duty in him who has the power. [Cf. Civil Liberty, App. II.]

justly abandoned, a great chance of escape, without holding out to him this additional hope of ultimate impunity, after tiresome proof and conviction.

VII. Nevertheless, it is necessary that the pardoning power exist somewhere, even where the laws are conformable to the spirit of the age, and imprisonment is not of a kind to expose the prisoner to contamination and greater corruption. For it is impossible for any legislator to frame his laws in such a manner that their application to some complex cases should not operate against their own spirit or object. Other considerations, such as imperative demands of public welfare, may exist, which make the suspension of the rigorous course of the law advisable or necessary; or actual mistakes may happen, so that the execution of the sentence would be no longer the execution of the law, but unlawful barbarity. A Frenchwoman, Elizabeth Colliaux, was sentenced, in consequence of an error which the jury themselves had noticed, to five years' imprisonment. The jury, who expected her acquittal, were surprised at her sentence, and prayed at once for pardon. Strange to say, she was not pardoned on the day of St. Charles, when many real criminals were; she was put in the pillory and branded.[1]

On the other hand, a pardon or reprieve, being an interruption of the law, is of itself dangerous in all states in which the supremacy of the law is justly considered the main shield of civil liberty. This difficulty is much increased in republics, because in them the supremacy of the law is of the very last importance, and at the same time the chief magistrate is so easily accessible that resistance against solicitations for pardon becomes the more difficult. By what principles ought those magistrates, then, to whom this prerogative is confided, or the ministers of the crown who propose pardons, to be guided? I believe by the following:

---

[1] All France was deeply affected at this heart-rending event. Gazette des Tribunaux, No. 1347 of 1829.

Pardoning power has been granted by the state to an individual only for the better obtaining of the true ends of the law, or the better fulfilment of its true spirit and not of its mere form. The contrary would imply an absurdity. It would be absurd, indeed, first to make laws with great expense and trouble, then to make offenders amenable to these laws with still greater expense, and finally to invest an officer with a privilege to set at naught all these ends, unless it were meant that this privilege should aid in obtaining the general end of all law, that is, right and justice. There ought always to exist peculiar and strong reasons, not why the law ought to be adhered to, but why its regular course ought to be interrupted. A case actually occurred a few years ago, when the governor of one of the largest western states of the Union respited a criminal sentenced for murder in open daylight, " in order that the sentiments and wishes of the people of [a certain] county might be known," declaring "that if at the expiration of the time he could be satisfied that it is the wish of the citizens of [said] county generally that this sentence should be commuted to that of imprisonment for life, their wishes could then be complied with." Thus the governor introduced on his own responsibility the entirely new system of making the *execution* of the sentence, after having been delivered in due course of law, dependent upon the " wishes" of the majority of that county to which the criminal happened to belong. What a view of general law and general justice!

If, therefore, a case is brought before the chief magistrate who has the power of pardoning, he ought to inquire whether there are any strong palliating circumstances of which the law could not take notice, or circumstances which render the sentence, although in strict conformity with the law, severer than the intention of the law-makers themselves can fairly be supposed to have been. If such be the case, a partial or entire pardon is proper.

If the law is manifestly and offensively against the more humane spirit of the age, especially if old laws demand cruel punishments and tortures, a pardon is right; for it is fair and just to suppose that this is one of the cases for which the privilege was granted, namely, to temper the law by equity and mercy. The code of Prussia decrees for some crimes the punishment of breaking on the wheel; the judges are bound to award it; but the king invariably issues an order to strangle the criminal before his body be broken on the wheel, or commutes the punishment into simple beheading.

The more recently, therefore, the laws have been revised, and the more the process of revision has been such that we may suppose it to have been fairly influenced by the spirit of society, the more rarely pardon ought to be exercised.

It is dangerous, however, in the highest degree, if pardons are granted from a merely private compassion for the offender, or from any other motive unconnected with the welfare of the state or the peculiar hardship of the single case. The enormous abuse of pardoning in the United States has contributed to undermine political morality, and has seriously interfered with the greatest safeguard of right and liberty, the government of law. If a case presents circumstances which can leave no feeling heart without regret, which yet are the necessary consequences of the law, known perfectly well by the lawmakers at the time of making the law,—for instance, the affliction of a respectable family by the committal of a degenerate son to prison, or the want and poverty of a mother with her children in consequence of her husband's having been sentenced for a crime,—the pardon must necessarily be refused; for the magistrate is not charged to consider these circumstances.[1]

---

[1] I cannot forbear transcribing here a passage from Beccaria's Essay on Crimes and Punishments, Engl. transl., Edinburgh, 1807, chap. xlvi. Beccaria will be allowed to be the best authority for a lenient spirit:

"As punishments become more mild, clemency and pardon are less necessary. Happy the nation in which they will be considered as dangerous! Clemency, which has often been deemed a sufficient substitute for every other virtue in sovereigns, should be excluded in a perfect legislation, where punishments are mild and the proceedings in criminal cases regular and expeditious. This truth will seem cruel to those who live in countries where, from the absurdity of the laws and the severity of punishments, pardons and the clemency of the prince are

Every pardon granted upon insufficient grounds becomes a serious offence against society, and he that grants it is, in justice, answerable for the offences which the offender may commit, and for the general injury done to political morality by undue interference with the law. The pardoning magistrate ought never to forget that society and the criminal form two parties, the one invisible as a whole and unrepresented, the other under sufferance before him and hence engaging his feelings very differently; and that, moreover, while it is but natural that our feelings should turn somewhat in favor of the prisoner the moment that sentence is actually pronounced, because he appears as the vanquished party, these feelings must not sway him in whose hands society has in part intrusted the maintenance not the subversion of law, the protection not the undermining of society. Still more objectionable is it if considerations such as the female sex of the offender are urged in favor of a pardon. Is then woman not a moral and a responsible being, and shall we again disgrace her by holding her unaccountable after she has been raised by positive laws to moral accountability? The Chinese wife is not morally emancipated to this day. They have a maxim to this day that a "married woman can commit no crime; the responsibility rests with the husband." How degrading for the woman! I have cited on another occasion the Swedish law of 1335 by which the woman of that country was made amenable to the laws in her own individuality.[1] Lately, some respectable British papers expressed the hope that an atro-

---

necessary. It is, indeed, one of the noblest prerogatives of the throne, but, at the same time, a tacit disapprobation of the laws. Clemency is a virtue which belongs to the legislator and not to the executor of the laws; a virtue which ought to shine in the code, and not in private judgment. To show mankind that crimes are sometimes pardoned, and that punishment is not the necessary consequence, is to nourish the flattering hope of impunity, and is the cause of their considering every punishment inflicted as an act of injustice and oppression. The prince, in pardoning, gives up the public security in favor of an individual, and, by ill-judged benevolence, proclaims a public act of impunity. Let, then, the legislator be tender, indulgent, and humane.

[1] My letter to the Philadelphia Prison Society, p. 39.

cious murderess would be pardoned, because she was a woman and the monarch was of the same sex! Nor do those who so readily claim pardons for women because they are women seem to be aware that a woman once a criminal generally belongs to the very worst and most dangerous class of offenders. "What use is there in dragging a weak woman to prison?" is current cant assuming the garb of generosity, while it is in fact the effect of an unfortunate laxity in all views of public morals, of right, and the most sacred principles of society and mankind.

If doubts are proved as to the correctness of the verdict or of the sentence, pardon ought to be granted.

If for whatever reason the punishment becomes severer than the sentence intended it to be, for instance by the prisoner's becoming consumptive in a prison in which proper medical aid or care cannot be obtained by him, pardon may be granted under certain circumstances, although it is not necessary that it should be.

If the offence has been committed in the opinion that it was a right or perhaps a praiseworthy act and no danger accrues from pardoning, pardon ought certainly to be granted on all fair grounds, for instance in cases of political offences.

If the law is cruel or obviously against the spirit of the whole society, there is no harm if the magistrate forms a rule for himself to grant conditional or entire pardons in all such cases, for instance if no children are ever executed in England although they are sentenced to die. But it becomes highly dangerous if by this privilege a chief magistrate sets himself up against a law which he individually considers inexpedient; for instance if he should be opposed to capital punishment and on that ground were to pardon all convicts sentenced to die. He would legislate in a very important sphere alone and uncontrolled by society, for he would evidently change the law, which he was acquainted with before entering office, and to maintain which he took a sacred oath.

The reported reformation of the convict must in no case form the sole ground for pardoning. This is acknowledged,

I believe, by almost all penologists of note and practical knowledge; and where it has been tried to hold out an abridgment of the punishment as a reward for good behavior, the consequences have been found to be bad, as for instance in France, where the officer who drew up the law holding out that reward petitioned, after having observed its operation, for its abolition.[1] I speak here always of revised laws, and proper systems of punishments, for nothing can be given as a rule for bad laws and worse punishments. The hope of pardon for good behavior, which of course can never be absolutely known, leads to hypocrisy, and prevents the very reformation sought for, because it does not allow the prisoner to enter into that state of calm resignation which, according to all experience in criminal psychology, is an indispensable requisite for reformation. If the punishment is mild, and the penitentiary system sound, the truly reformed convict himself will hardly desire a pardon.

The pardoning magistrate ought to be influenced, in conjunction with other considerations, by the nature of the guarantees the individual to be pardoned can offer, such as whether he knows a trade, has received some education, has honest relations who acknowledge him or not, and can give other pledges of a probably steady life.

---

[1] Mr. de la Ville de Mirmont, Inspector-General of the Central Prisons, says in his work, Observations sur les Maisons Centrales de Détention à l'Occasion de l'Ouvrage de Beaumont et Tocqueville, Paris, 1833, p. 55, et seq., that he was the one who obtained the law in 1818, and that he often repented of it. The Bavarian code offers pardon after three-fourths of the time of imprisonment have elapsed, if the conduct has been correct. Of course the apportionment of punishments is made accordingly. I do not know how the law operates.

## CHAPTER II.

Judge, Juror, Advocate, and Witness.—Official, external, and moral Independence of the Judge.—Sanctissimus Judex of the Romans.—The Judge, where there is doubt, must interpret in Mercy, in Penal Cases; in Favor of civil Liberty, in all.—The Institution of the Jury.—The sacred Office of the Juryman.—What is he to do when the Law is contrary to the universal Conscience?—The Institution of the Advocate.—Moral Obligation of the Advocate.—Political Relations of Lawyers in Free Countries.—Duties of the Witness.

VIII. From all that has been said of justice as the main and broad foundation of the state, of the superior sway of law as an indispensable requisite of civil liberty and the necessary independence of the judiciary, it must appear that there is no member of the state or officer of government superior in importance to the judge, and indeed very few of equal importance with him. All mankind, if at all advanced in political civilization, have agreed that an unjust judge defiles the very altar for the service of which he was ordained a priest. The religious codes of the most remote antiquity, the law-books of the absolute governments of the East, fettered by hereditary castes, pronounce this universal feeling as distinctly as the religions, laws, or poetry of the modern or freest nations—the Vedas as well as Shakspeare. A truckling judge fawning on power, whoever may possess it, whether monarch or people, is one of the most offensive and humiliating sights, and a demoralizing example to a nation. If it be shameful or criminal for a citizen, to whom no peculiar charge has been confided, to betray his country, it is doubly so in a judge to betray justice and liberty by yielding to power, and swerving from what is just, true, and right, because to him in particular has their custody been confided, and in forsaking justice and liberty he betrays his country. It is painful to peruse the bad periods of monarchies or republics, when judges are found ready to bend the law according to the desire of the monarch or ruling party, and it is comforting indeed when we find, on the other hand, men who comprehended the lofty character of the judge, and had sufficient firmness to stand as the independent interpreters or pronouncers of the law, for or against whomsoever this might be. The names of judges great in their views, calm in their decisions, and pure in all their life, who are known by the whole people to have distinguished themselves by unswerving honesty and stout hearts, judges whose grasp, penetration, and blandness of mind were equally great, form a moral element in the history of a nation; they constitute a most valuable part of the inherited and traditional stock of national virtue, and give a moral tone and stability to the community, for which nothing else of equally great effect can be substituted. Those great judges whom England counts in her history have done more of good than the infamous ones who have disgraced the British bench have been able to do of evil. The greater the liberty the greater likewise, as is natural, the necessity of unbiassed, clear, learned, and strong-minded judges—that is, oracles of the law. This truth of general import has fully appeared from all the preceding parts of this work; but it is necessary to mention here in particular that the moral independence of the judge is of most particular importance in republics founded upon an extensive popular principle: this is owing to the fact which has been touched several times, that resistance against the crown has something heroical in it and will seldom fail to awaken the sympathy of the multitude, while resistance to popular clamor, passion, or interest appears in the eye of the excited many as sin and heresy. The American history offers instances of judges who either have been overawed by the clamor of the people, or, which is equally to be shunned, have participated in the general excitement.

The idea which the Romans entertained of the judge, the Sanctissimus Judex (Cic. pro Planc., xiii. 32), and indeed the very origin of the word Judex,[1] are characteristic, and distin-

---

[1] Judex from jus-dicere, as vindex from vim-dicere. The judex, therefore, was not in the eye of the Roman the avenger, as he is called in several languages. So

guish them strikingly, and in this particular favorably, from the Greeks. The latter likewise acknowledged the law, not only as infinitely superior to the individual charged to execute it, but also as that which alone should have true supremacy. Yet this was the case with respect to law in general only. The Greeks never sufficiently separated judicial law from political and administrative; the judge, therefore, with them never appeared in so sacred a light as with the practical and honest Romans.[1] It might, indeed, be observed here as a general remark that the Sacrosancta Auctoritas inherent in the highest offices is quite peculiar to Rome, and indicates one of the most essential features by which that republic so remarkably differed from the Grecian states.

If the judge, then, ought to be independent in every way, he ought to be, as we have seen in the first part of this work, independent of the executive and power-holder, unswayed by prince or people;[2] he ought to be made independent in his situation; his salary ought to be sufficient both to elevate him above want and its influences and to command the highest talent; for in every well-regulated commonwealth a judgeship should always be the last and highest goal the lawyer looks for: his salary, again, ought to be fixed, not dependent upon fees,[3] and so not dependent, in appearance at least, upon those whom

---

are Justice and Revenge or Retribution in many idioms one and the same word; but Judex meant the pronouncer, declarer of right. [But *jus* denoted originally id quod populus jubet. The moral sense came into it.]

[1] [The Romans lost this feeling of the sacredness of the judge at length. For instance, the question between senate and equites, as to the order from which the judices should be drawn, had for its motive in part to screen persons under accusation for peculation, maladministration, etc.]

[2] This applies in a great measure to all law-officers whose ultimate end is the administration of justice. Erskine calls Lord Coke—even Coke—" the infamous prosecutor of Raleigh." (Defence of Thomas Hardy, for High Treason.) The dereliction of duty is equally great if the sovereign is not the monarch but the people, though it may not appear so at the time.

[3] There is a strange anomaly in the British high court of admiralty. The judge has no salary, and consequently very little indeed in peace, but in times of war his salary amounts to about eight thousand pounds. Nothing is more directly against all true principles of government than to give part of confiscations to the judges

he judges, nor diminished whilst he holds his seat, lest he become or be suspected of being dependent upon his employers, the legislature or executive. His independence implies, as we have seen previously, his immovability from office, except by impeachment. Finally, it is not sufficient that the judge be placed in a state of independence: he must place himself so as much as in him lies. Lord Brougham lately pronounced himself against judges having any seat as members of elective legislatures, so as not to be influenced by their constituencies.[1] It is of course impossible to draw with any distinction the line beyond which a judge ought not to go in his participation in public political meetings; but certain it is that he injures the sacredness of his office in the same degree in which he becomes a partisan, and that he ought ever to be mindful that his moral power in pronouncing judgment according to the law already made will be impaired, if he mixes in the excitement which may be connected with the making of it. His moral weight, of the greatest importance in every free country, is derived greatly from the fact that he can say, "Not I, directly or indirectly in any way whatever, but the law, which is given to me and is my master, says thus."

As it is a rule that where a law leaves any doubt it shall be interpreted in mercy for the prisoner, so ought the judges in a wider sphere to consider themselves as the perpetual servants of civil liberty and of strict government by law, and never to join either the executive or any party, political or religious, in persecutions, in injurious interpretations or distortions of law, or in any even the slightest oppression. Where there is doubt at all on points of public or constitutional law, the judge ought always to interpret in favor of civil liberty; and, in fine, he ought not in penal cases to consider the mere disobedience to the law in itself an additional offence besides the crime or offence committed—a view which

---

as reward for their alacrity in prosecuting, as we give a small piece of the hunted game to the hounds who pursue it, to incite their future zeal.

[1] In the Lords, February 12, 1839.

formerly led but too frequently to harsh punishments, and afforded a basis for the inadmissible penal theory which derives the punitory power of the state from public vengeance.

IX. By the institution of the jury two great ends, the one of liberty, the other of the administration of justice, have been united—namely, direct participation of the people in the dispensing of justice and the preventing of it from falling entirely into the hands of the executive or of a separate and closed caste. From whatever point of view we may examine this peculiar institution as it has developed itself in the Anglican race—and it may be viewed in a great many, all equally important—it will always appear that the citizen cannot act in any more solemn capacity than that of a juror: in my opinion, in no capacity so solemn and important. Society requires the state; the state acts through laws; the laws are the great organs of human society, of combined reason; and now, when the very moment ultimately arrives for which the law was made, when it is finally to be applied as a general rule to a practical and concrete case, when, in short, the abstract principle is to be realized in practical life, for weal or woe, for the protection of some or the punishment of others, all this is in a great measure left to the juror, to the citizen taken fresh from the people. The jurors, therefore, are justly called by the British law the country.[1] There is a deep meaning in this expression, as it has grown in the course of centuries; for the jury truly and practically represent the country to the person that is to be tried. The law is the expression of public will, and the jury represent the jural society, in judging whether in the given case the facts warrant the application of the law. The jury represent the country, not the government; they judge of facts according to rules and laws indeed, but also with the feelings of living men, and not merely as if they repre-

---

[1] For instance, when the clerk, reading the indictment, concludes thus: "Upon this indictment, gentlemen, the prisoner has been arraigned; upon his arraignment he pleaded not guilty; and for trial hath put himself upon God and his country; which country you are," etc.

sented the abstract law as it is written down. To represent this a learned judge would be sufficient. The jury represents, or rather is, whenever faithful, the living, operating law. In deed, it may justly be said that though for a brief time, yet, for this brief time, a jury represents more fully and entirely human society as formed into a state, with its great objects, than any other person or body of men, even the monarch's person not excepted. Not that I mean to intimate the idea as if on this account the jury were released either from strict obedience to law or proper advice. Even though they were the very sovereign, we have seen on a previous occasion that sovereignty and absolute power are very different. On the contrary, the jury according to the essence of their character are strictly bound by the law, yet by the law as their country requires it or must be supposed to require it, applied to the particular and, probably, complex case before them.

A juryman, therefore, ought to serve with the deepest impression of the grave responsibility which his oath has imposed upon him : he sits there for his country, he acts for the country; the laws must be applied through him, they must strike or protect through him. The foundation of the state is justice; the country asks it at his hands for the prisoner. The just object of the state is protection; the country demands it against crime at his hands. The juryman therefore must not trifle with his duty, either by discharging it lightly or indolently;[1] he does not sit there to dispense with the laws, or set them at naught by ill-advised and weak compassion for guilt, but to *apply* the law; and he is bound by sacred ties to his country and mankind to receive the law at the hands

---

[1] I have seen a juryman asleep during a trial for murder. It is true it was hot, and in the afternoon. Feuerbach, in Considerations on Public and Oral Administration of Justice, Giessen, 1825, vol. ii. p. 221, says that he has seen the judges in Paris repeatedly sleep on the bench ; but it ought to be observed that there are several judges, and that Feuerbach does not speak of the presiding judge or president; as, indeed, in the above case it was not the foreman who slept. The author adds in a note an extract from a French Dictionary, published in 1778, according to which sleeping and talking about the news of the day was then not uncommon for judges when in audience.

of the judge, wherever necessary. No consideration, private favor or disfavor, no political bias, must influence his judgment. All this indeed amounts to embracery on an enlarged scale: although it cannot be made indictable, yet it has all the guilt of embracery, which is the offence of improperly influencing the jury. The juror, as he is always instructed to do, must judge by the evidence which is brought before him, and nowise by the capricious impression which he may have received elsewhere. Respecting this point, he must remember that the words of the verdict "not guilty" are not of absolute import, but have a legal meaning; that is, the jury, in delivering the verdict, do not mean to say, We absolutely declare the prisoner at the bar not guilty, nor even that they are morally convinced of his innocence. All that a verdict of not guilty can mean is this, that according to the distinct rules of law and the evidence as now laid before us in the course of the trial, the prisoner cannot in the sense of the law, according to such application of it as society demands, be called guilty; or, in other words, according to those rules which society wills us strictly to obey in judging of the prisoner, he has not been proved guilty.

X. Here I have arrived at a question of a peculiarly serious and delicate character, which it is nevertheless necessary candidly to discuss in a work that occupies itself professedly with ethics in connection with the state, or the subject of right. The question is, Can a jury, under any circumstances, bring a verdict of Not Guilty, if, according to evidence as well as the letter of the law, their verdict ought to be Guilty, without perjuring themselves? Many distinguished jurists have unqualifiedly answered that, whatever the law may be, the jury are bound to go by its letter: it is no province of theirs to judge of the law and its mild or severe effects. This is undoubtedly true in all cases except those of extremity, and these are the very ones which constitute the difficulty. So it is not for the soldier to judge whether what his officer bids him to do is right; yet in cases of extremity he will and must do so. Mankind will not and cannot be reasoned out of their original and natural sentiments; and so, as obedience to the laws is a general duty, while resistance adopted as a general principle would necessarily dissolve human society, we disobey and resist in the extreme case when a government openly, directly, and repeatedly acts against the very objects for which it was established. So it is absolutely impossible to force mankind into an obedience to laws which directly and palpably militate with the conscience of every one, whatever learned men may have said to the contrary. If an ancient law punishes the pilfering of a trifle with death, it is absolutely impossible to force a jury who, with the whole age in which they live, consider the law murderous, into what they would feel to be directly opposite to the ends of all law, that is justice and protection. If the law-maker neglects to adapt the law to the altered circumstances and the spirit of the whole age, the law may indeed remain undisturbedly upon the books, but the inevitable difficulty of applying that law to real cases is not thereby avoided. The jury will not bring a victim to so barbarous a law, nor load their consciences with having contributed in destroying him. Some of the most eminent judges have evidently entertained the same opinion. Lord Mansfield, as I have mentioned already, instructed a jury to find a verdict for theft of less than twenty shillings, when the amount of stolen goods had been proved to be worth far more; because the case was of a very peculiar character and the prisoner would otherwise have been hanged. Now, on what ground could the judge instruct thus or the jury bring a verdict against the truth before them? Were they then not perjured? They could, it seems to me, bring this verdict, which was clearly at variance with the real state of things before their eyes, on the ground that the words of the verdict have a meaning relatively to the law, the case, etc. If a jury formerly, although the crime was proved, brought a verdict of not guilty for a prisoner, say twelve years old, charged with shoplifting, for which the law said that he should be hanged, the words of the verdict mean, I take it, Not Guilty in the sense in which the country wills the law to be understood ("in mitiori sensu," as it were)—the law which has a sense and meaning only in so far as it is for the benefit and not the ruin of society, and the letter of the law, which in this case, when a boy of tender years would be hanged for an offence arising out of juvenile thoughtlessness, palpably militates against the very objects of the state. I am well aware that nothing is more dangerous than to look habitually towards the effect of the law, for a jury who ought in common cases to decide only on what is submitted to them. But I speak of extraordinary cases, which do occur in some instances, and, despite their danger, must be decided one way or the other. Nor do we gain anything by deciding them theoretically, against the universal conscience of mankind. For the practice will prove too powerful for the theory. Where the laws, however, are mild, perhaps already too mild, where many pardons are injudiciously granted, a jury ought to consider nothing but the peculiar questions before them, and consider neither condition, sex,[1] nor any such circumstance in making up their verdict.[2] The jury ought never to forget that the cases spoken of above remain exceptions.[3]

---

[1] It is lowering the character of the woman, if juries are influenced by the fact that the arraigned prisoner is a female, or by her beauty; though this has frequently happened.

[2] The utmost attention and care are necessary in juries; sad mistakes have taken place, and are on the records of legal history. I would refer the reader to Blackstone, iii. pp. 378–385; Kent's Commentaries in the proper places. The Guides for Jurymen, with which I am acquainted, relate more to the business than to the ethical relations of the juryman.

[3] [The author here substantially invests the jury with a pardoning power. This ground is a dangerous one: his extreme cases must multiply, if all persons admitted that the jury had anything to do besides saying that the facts were proved. One man would never find guilty in cases where the punishment was capital; another, where it seemed to him of great general evil to society. All biasses which prevent a juryman from looking at the question of fact, of guilty or not guilty, are wrong. All meanings given to guilty or not guilty, relatively to the benefit of society, are false meanings. The jury could recommend for mercy, they could even protest against the law; but they must not take their oath in a non-natural sense.]

XI. Wherever nations have arrived at any high degree of political civilization, so as to value the protection of individual rights, we find the institution of the advocate, which, such as we know it, we may consider as peculiarly belonging to Western or European life. We find, indeed, attorneys and "the borrowing of another's mouth" in Sumatra,[1] among some of the Hindoo nations, and in Morocco;[2] but neither Turkey, Siam, Persia, nor China has advocates proper, whose order the venerable D'Aguesseau calls "as ancient as the office of the judge, as noble as virtue, and as necessary as justice."[3] This is certainly a little French, and, whatever we may think of the second position in particular, it is nevertheless true that the institution is absolutely necessary for the true empire of the law. Despotism sees very little or no difference between civil and penal actions; all actions become penal, they are trials, and all trials are conducted upon the principle of inquisition on the part of the judge;[4] and the trials are by no means conducted on the principle of the greatest possible protection under the law so far as the ends of the law and justice admit.

XII. That it is dishonorable for a lawyer to foment disputes—as there are those who do in all countries—is too clear to need any consideration. It amounts to actual robbing of the clients. Physicians might as well first promote sickness in order to have afterwards the benefit of curing. Nor does

---

[1] "Pinjam mulut;" Marsden, History and Description of Sumatra.

[2] Höst, Information of Morocco.

[3] D'Aguesseau, Discours sur l'Indépendance de l'Avocat. Œuvres, tom. ii. p. 4, Yverdun edit.

[4] In despotic empires exists what Montesquieu calls "la magistrature unique," that is, there is but one judge, and not a number of judges. Feuerbach, in his Considerations on Public and Oral Administration of Justice (in German), vol. i. p. 354 et seq., has many pertinent remarks on the subject. He there exhibits also the great error of Montesquieu, who asserts that "in despotic governments there is no law; the judge is his own rule" (Esprit des Lois, vi., ch. i. 3), when in fact the body of Turkish, Chinese, and Hindoo established and collected laws equal or exceed in bulk those of Rome or England.

it require our attention to consider how much more honorable it is if he who knows the law uses his knowledge in giving advice to prevent rather than profit by litigation. In this respect, honorable lawyers of extensive practice are real blessings to a community. Let us proceed at once to the consideration of some of the prominent duties of the advocate during trial, as they interest political society at large, leaving all the other duties to the consideration of those who may make hereafter legal ethics the peculiar subject of their studies. It certainly deserves the fullest attention; and many points would then be examined by reflecting men which at present have in some countries hardly attracted any notice, while in others they are considered with great rigidness.

The advocate, wherever the institution exists, enjoys various privileges. In some countries he is actually considered an officer. For what purpose are those privileges granted him?

The state, on the one hand, must needs act upon the principle that the law is known to every one, or may be known to every one, if he chooses to know it; while on the other hand it knows full well that in every civilized society it is impossible that the law in its whole extent can be actually known to every citizen. The advocates, therefore, as a class, are favored by society, that they may freely give advice before a lawsuit has commenced, and may freely speak for the client, with all their knowledge of the law, during the trial. Secondly, the state, desiring to extend to every one full protection and civil liberty, is as much interested in seeing the full protection of the law realized in each case, that is, that no more be demanded than what the law does demand, and that all the advantage granted by the law be actually enjoyed, as it is in seeing every wrong suppressed and right secured or re-established wherever it has been interrupted.

To obtain these various equally important objects, the institution of the advocate is established; and from these premises we shall be able to derive some very important ethical conclusions.

The advocate exists for the better obtaining of justice and protection. It would be absurd to imagine that human society first makes laws with great pains and expense, and then suffers or charters a whole class of skilful men to defeat them. All the conclusions, therefore, which people have drawn from the analogy between warfare and a lawsuit are utterly inadmissible. It has been even asserted that the counsel are permitted to state what is not true, just as the soldier is permitted to deceive the enemy. Nothing can be more erroneous. That which characterizes war is the fact that the belligerents appeal from reasoning to the use of force; the lawsuit, however, and the whole administration of justice, are founded upon the very ideas of truth, justice, and reasoning, according to sound rules of judgment and proof. The lawsuit is part and parcel of the intercourse of the citizen in peace and *within* the sphere of law: it is, in short, the very opposite to war in every respect. So it has been said that the lawyer has nothing whatsoever to do with the morality of the case which he defends, and that he lets out his talent and knowledge to his client, who, if he himself possessed it, would use it in every way for his advantage. This again is erroneous; for, first, no man can divest himself of his moral individuality, as we have seen before: else the hired assassin would be right, who says, My employer hires me; he has not sufficient physical strength or courage; these I lend him for money; but I have nothing to do with the morality of the murder. Secondly, even if it were so, it would be wrong in the client to state falsehoods; and, finally, if it were actually so, the state could do nothing better than speedily to abolish so dangerous a class of men. If it means that the lawyer should defend every case if called upon, that he ought to do everything consistent with law and morality which may be advantageous to his client, this is correct, as we shall see presently more fully.

Lastly, it has been said that the lawyer has no more to do with the morality of the case offered to him than the physician who may be called upon to save a man whom he knows to be an injury or dishonor to his country. Thus, though the lawyer fully knows that the case which he defends is founded upon fraud, and that if he succeeds he will rob others of their property, say an orphan in defending the case of a fraudulent guardian, he has nothing to do with the causes and possible effects of the case, but merely to handle it according to the best knowledge of the law and the skill which he possesses, as the physician, called upon to attend the patient who when in health ill-treats his wife and children, has nothing whatever to do with any other consideration than how, with his experience, he can soonest cure his patient. But the sole object of the whole healing art is the re-establishment of physical health, or, where this cannot be done, the greatest possible diminution of physical suffering. The object of all administration of justice is Right; and the vocation of the advocate has a sensible meaning only as forming part of this administration of justice. He is allowed to speak for another on so solemn an occasion as that of a trial, for the very purpose that truth may be better known and justice better done, but not to veil the one or to defeat the other, knowingly and purposely. It would be, as was said before, absurd.

It is believed that the ends of justice are best promoted, among other things, if every person charged with an offence have counsel, versed in the law, both to protect him against unlawful oppression and to obtain all the advantages for him which the law may offer; but the state cannot sanction immorality or the infringement of the rights of others. That my remarks do not apply to suspicions and rumors must be clear;. I speak here of wrong only that is positively known by the advocate.

XIII. The rules of action for the counsel are twofold, as appears to me—the common ethical rules, and those which are peculiar to his profession.

As to the first, the advocate does not cease to be a human being with all his ethical and religious obligations, a citizen with all his political obligations to his country and her laws, and a gentleman with all the obligations of honor and civil intercourse. He is no morally privileged person, as no man can be. The more justice and due protection of the citizen require that he should have great freedom of speech and action in court, the more he is bound to regulate his conduct towards a witness by genuine courtesy, and towards the court by due deference to the cause of justice partly represented by the bench. Yet a true advocate will never forget that in defending a citizen he is as much the representative of the law of the land, which wills protection to every one, as is the judge, and, with all proper respect for the bench, he will, if the case calls for it, stand for his client's rights as Erskine did in the trial of the dean of St. Asaph.[1]

As to the second class of rules, he must abide by the rules agreed upon among the members of the bar as best calculated to promote professional intercourse and the advantages of the profession, so far as they agree with the advantages of the community.

As it is the object of the institution of the advocate that every person should have all the advantage which the law affords, and that final sentence be given only after all that may be urged on both sides is said and sifted, there is no case in which a person charged with an offence should not be defended. Many codes enact this principle as law. There are not a few persons who revolt at this idea, conceiving of a case in which the guilt of the offender is known to every one. Defending, however, does not necessarily mean representing the prisoner as innocent, but merely, first, seeing that the guilt be actually proved,—for every man, as is well known, must be held innocent until proved guilty,—and, secondly, that no more than what is strictly warranted by the law should be awarded. Nothing is more common than that counsel give up a case as absolutely hopeless; but still they must continue

---

[1] In the trial of Shipley, the dean of St. Asaph, for libel, Justice Buller said, "Sit down, sir; remember your duty, or I shall be obliged to proceed in another manner." Mr. Erskine answered, "Your lordship may proceed in what manner you think fit: I know my duty as well as your lordship knows yours. I shall not alter my conduct."

to protect the client against a privation of any advantage which the law warrants, for instance that the sentence be not too severe.

I do not know that anything redounds more to the honor of the Americans than the readiness with which in 1770 the British soldiers who had fired upon the people in Boston found counsel even during that great excitement which preceded the Revolution, and that counsel, too, men who, as American citizens, were enthusiastic for the popular cause. There is a remarkable letter in the Life of Josiah Quincy, jun., of Massachusetts (written by his son, Josiah Quincy, Boston, 1825). He had been engaged for one of those soldiers, and his father inquired with great anxiety whether it was true that his son had become "an advocate for those criminals who are charged with the murder of their fellow-citizens. Good God!" he continues, "is it possible? I will not believe it." The son answered, in a noble letter, that they had not yet been found guilty, but were only charged with the guilt.[1]

Cicero says that the judge must always follow out the truth, but that the advocate may defend what is but the semblance of truth, though it be short of truth. I think the truth on this point is that the advocate has no more right to abandon truth than any one else in the whole world, but he is bound to represent his case in the best possible light consistent with the truth; so that if there be any substantially good point it may be found out. Cicero is not altogether very distinct or precise in this passage: thus, he says, "we need not, on the other hand, make any scruple of speaking sometimes in be-

---

[1] The work is written by the son of its subject, Josiah Quincy, President of Harvard University, Boston, 1825. The letter of the father is of March 22, 1770, that of the son, of March 26 of the same year. It is historically important and highly honorable to the people then on the eve of a revolution, that the most prominent men in the community where blood had been spilt, such as Adams, Hancock, Warren, Cooper, Henshaw, Cushing, Molineux, Pemberton, Philipps, strongly advised and urged Quincy to undertake the defence of the indicted soldiers. It is the evident manifestation of the Anglican veneration for the law, even in the midst of much excitement, and in the face of much popular odium which might have visited a zealous advocate with bitter hostility.

half of the guilty, provided he be not wholly villanous and abominable." But what is wholly villanous and abominable? Every one ought to be defended, that is, be it repeated, he ought to be so protected that he may receive all the advantage which the law justly and wisely affords and which his peculiar case allows. Escape of the client is not the ultimate object, but justice alone.

An advocate has not the right of injuring knowingly and willingly another person, either in reputation or property, in order to save or serve his client. It is evident that he cannot have the right knowingly to rob another for his client, or make aspersions upon the honor and reputation of an innocent man. He would certainly load his conscience with heavy guilt were he to exert his skill in defending, for instance, what he actually knew to be a forged will,—and such a case may be imagined; or were he to defend a criminal for a fee consisting, to his knowledge, of the very goods for stealing which the prisoner is indicted. This may not only be imagined, but has taken place. Nor is this surprising, for where the profession of the law is extensive—and it will always be extensive where civil liberty is enjoyed in a high degree—it is but natural that many of the best and some of the meanest citizens should belong to it. Every person charged with an offence ought to be defended, that is, duly protected; but this differs widely from aiding a client in committing a crime by gaining a fraudulent lawsuit, for instance by making use for his defence of documents most strongly suspected by the advocate to be forged. There may be many cases of this sort imagined in which no honorable lawyer would be willing to engage.

The advocate ought on no occasion to misstate the law, or endeavor to mislead the judge, or to misstate a fact in order to deceive the jury. This of course does not exclude the endeavor to make the best of the law for his client, or to present the more favorable points of the law or facts with peculiar force. Morality and prudence coincide here, as they so often do; for an advocate will but little advance his reputation as a lawyer, and consequently as little his worldly interest, by habitual disingenuous handling of the law or the fact.[1] It lends considerable power to a lawyer if judge and jury listen to him with the belief in his honesty.

There is a consideration which I submit to the peculiar reflection of those who intend to become members of the profession, because it is of grave importance to society, and yet perhaps but little known to lawyers themselves. From frequent and free conversations with convicts in the penitentiaries I know it to be a fact that many criminals have been led on in the path of crime by the circumstance that when young and indicted for the first offence, perhaps for a petty theft, and when they were deeply impressed with the consequences to which their guilty thoughtlessness had brought them, they became reassured when hearing their counsel boldly utter things in their defence which the young offenders knew that their counsel well knew not to be true. If, in particular, a verdict of not guilty was the effect, the young criminal came out of the trial with his previous rashness confirmed into conscious and settled purpose.

It is a serious evil which is necessarily connected with all public trials and defences in the presence of the criminal, both that he learns many ways and means intended by the law as

---

[1] "An honorable barrister will never misstate either law or facts within his own knowledge; but he is justified in urging any argument, whatever may be his own opinion of the solidity or justness of it, which he may think will promote the interests of his client, for reasoning in courts of justice and in the ordinary affairs of life seldom admits of geometrical demonstration: but it happens not unfrequently that the same argument which appears sophistry to one is sound logic in the mind of another, and every day's experience proves that the opinions of a judge and an advocate are often diametrically opposite. Many circumstances may occur which will justify or compel an individual member of the profession to refuse the defence of a particular client, but a cause can hardly be conceived which ought to be rejected by all the bar, for such a conduct in the profession would excite so strong a prejudice against the party as to render him in a great degree condemned before his trial." (Christian's note to 4th Blackstone, 356.) But there are cases, as mentioned before, in which the aid of the advocate is required, in order that with his knowledge fraud *may* be committed; which of course must be declined by all honest men.

the protection of innocence, but, of course, used also by the guilty as a screen for nefarious doings, and that he becomes more hardened by hearing the counsel speak so confidently and openly in his favor. The necessary assurance of the advocate becomes shamelessness in the offender. He accustoms himself to consider the whole trial a game of skill and cleverness, and no more. This evil, great as it is, cannot possibly be separated from public and oral trial, the many and substantial advantages of which, and, indeed, the necessity of which for civil liberty, make us endure it. Still, we ought to remember that the evil exists, and that it is a great one. The advocate, for this very reason, ought not to increase the evil by adding his authority, in the mind of the criminal, to his own disregard of right and wrong.

From all that I have been able to learn from convicts as well as the most intelligent superintendents in the penitentiaries, I cannot but consider the circumstance just spoken of as an active cause in the diffusion and propagation of crime, and deserving, therefore, I feel sure, the fullest attention of every honorable advocate.

Few things are more important for the upright advocate than to scrutinize with the utmost delicacy of honor and tenderness of conscience all opportunities of increasing his wealth which may accrue out of his legal transactions, except those of receiving fees in the strictest sense of the term; nor must he ever be unmindful of the object for which he is employed by his client, that is, the client's advantage, which includes the quickest possible termination of the particular case, or, in other words, that he is in the service of the client and that his client is not his prey.

If the advocate is a prosecutor for the public, or, as it is called in monarchies, for the king, it is very necessary for him never to forget that, although it is the advocate's bounden duty to represent a case in the best possible light when he is counsel for the private party, it by no means follows that it is his duty, when he prosecutes for the public, to represent the case in the worst possible light, or to aim always at the highest damage or penalty which the case may allow. This would amount to reasoning backwards, and is therefore wrong. The defending counsel must represent the case in the best possible light, for the very reason that he defends a being prosecuted by public power; he defends the individual against the society. But to draw from this fact the conclusion that because the case of the accused person is presented by his counsel in the best possible way, the first and originating party, that is, the state, ought therefore to present it in the worst possible light, would be turning the effect of the original danger, that power may be too strong for the individual, into a new cause of its own increase. And, be it observed, this remark holds equally good where the criminally indicted prisoner has no counsel allowed to him: the prosecuting officer in such a case is in conscience bound to consider himself the protector of the prisoner,[1] the impartial substitute for the counsel who ought to be

---

[1] Christian, in his note to 4th Blackstone, 356, says, " Hence, in all criminal prosecutions, especially where the prisoner can have no counsel to plead for him [the writer therefore includes all cases, and says indeed as fully as I have said in the text, that a prosecuting officer is not allowed to make the case as black as his ingenuity will permit], a barrister is as much bound to disclose all those circumstances to the jury, and to reason upon them as fully, which are favorable to the prisoner, as those which are likely to support the prosecution." It is right to give this as a rule, but it is likewise right to consider man's nature, and that few are willing and still fewer capable of thus willing a thing (the accusation and representation of guilt of a man) and at the same time of throwing all possible obstacles (the reasons for the prisoner) in the way. Indeed, the theoretical junction of the British prosecutor and defensor in penal cases is contradictory in itself, and, speaking in reference to legal philosophy, as absurd as the threefold person " as which we are told we must consider the judge in the inquisitorial process (the one in practice in most countries in which the civil law has been adopted), namely " as representative of the offended state, inasmuch as he is bound, in its place, to see right done according to the penal law; as representative of the accused, inasmuch as he is bound at the same time to find out and represent everything on which the innocence or a less degree of criminality can be founded; and, finally, as judge, inasmuch as he must judge of and decide upon the given facts." (Feuerbach's Manual of the Common German Penal Law, 10th edit., § 623.) I know of no higher authority than Feuerbach; I know of no passage ever written by the adversaries of the inquisitorial process which sets forth half so well its general badness and its utter incompatibility with civil liberty as the quoted one. One mortal man shall be at once accuser, defender, and judge!

assigned to him. Nor ought a citizen ever to be placed in a state of accusation on insufficient grounds, for the reason that the state has provided for him ample means of defence and barriers of security. An individual is to be defended because accused, but not to be accused because he will be defended.[1]

Although we do not suffer the evils of an inquisition, whose mere accusation is blasting although acquittal follows, still the prosecuting officer should never forget that he cannot calculate or know how much suspicion may deface a man's character even after a fair acquittal. Since the only true object of society in prosecuting is justice, he has no manner of business to involve the accused in greater difficulty, or to throw a heavier cloak of suspicion over him, than the simple facts of the case warrant and the objects of political society demand. A penal case is not a case between two equal parties, nor a trial of skill and ingenuity between two advocates, nor a matter of legal reputation for the respective lawyers, but it is a very grave case between the state and an individual charged with—that is, until proved, strongly suspected of—an offence; it is the case of Justice one and indivisible alone, not a tournament of legal dialectics.[2]

---

In cases where affection is not the foundation, as in the family, but where right forms the sole basis! There are some advantages connected with the inquisitorial process, indeed, which the process of accusation lacks; but what are these advantages, compared to this startling jumble of the most opposite characters? Where is there the slightest guarantee for times of usurpation? To prevent misconceptions, however, I ought to mention that, though the judge is also defender, a separate defender is assigned to the indicted person, and, what is remarkable, in most countries a person cannot be sentenced for any high offence without having been defended, even though the defender should plead guilty. Yet the defences by such a defender sound to us, accustomed as we are to the freest and often boldest scope of counsel, very tame indeed, and the court frequently rebukes where we should not see any boldness in his words or arguments.

[1] [Dr. Lieber, in a manuscript note, here discusses malicious prosecution and prosecution on insufficient grounds. The substance of his remarks is inserted in his Civil Liberty, chap. vii. p. 77.]

[2] I must refer the reader for some more remarks on the ethical relations of a barrister, especially with respect to his obligations connected with interpretation, and the important question whether he may feel himself at liberty, as a strictly

XIV. Where there is enduring civil liberty, the supremacy of the law must be acknowledged; where the supremacy of the law is acknowledged, the lawyers must necessarily possess much influence. It is so at present with all free nations, who are not merely enjoying a transient period of liberty, but have founded it on lasting institutions; and it was so in ancient times, in which the freest republics have probably never suffered so much from professional lawyers as from demagogues who were not members of their profession.[1] Their constant occupation with the laws of the land and questions of right, and their habit of consecutive reasoning, as well as the necessity in which they constantly find themselves of viewing a subject in its different lights, make them more fit to grapple with many questions which involve the rights and interests of many and opposite parties, than other people, as well as more liberal, upon the whole, towards those who dissent from their opinion, and bolder in asserting rights where there is danger in doing so, because they are better able to find out the firm ground of positive law and of well-acknowledged precedent. These advantages, however, have also their counterbalancing evils. The professional lawyer, accustomed to seek the best arguments for any side on which he may be engaged, not unfrequently loses the original impulse of the first principle from which matters of state derive their value or want of value. The professional lawyer carries at times the habit of special pleading into the halls, where subjects are to be treated of on the broad principles of general good; and this may be the cause that we find few of the greatest British statesmen and great parliamentary leaders to have

---

moral man, to make use of "artful interpretation," to my Legal and Political Hermeneutics. Mr. Justice Story speaks of the general duties and elevated position of the advocate in his inaugural address as Dane professor in the law school of the University at Cambridge, Massachusetts (Miscellaneous Writings, p. 452). He likewise touches upon the subject in his Law of Agency, Boston, 1839, page 25. [Comp. Dr. Lieber's Civil Liberty, chap. xx. p. 239, et seq.]

[1] [In free Greece there were rhetoricians and teachers of rhetoric, but no lawyers. In Rome the profession was but in its infancy when the republic fell. That lawyers thrive in a country is no proof of free institutions.]

been professional lawyers, or, if they had entered the bar, like Pitt, they can hardly be called virtual lawyers. Impulses towards great reforms in legislation have rarely, I believe, proceeded from the profession.[1]

The lawyer, always looking up to the law as his great authority, which, as was mentioned, makes him frequently the bolder in asserting right, becomes generally rather the representative of that which exists than the advocate of that which ought to be; still farther, he is not unfrequently blinded by existing laws and institutions, and resists improvements which must be judged of upon strict principle and consist in a change of what exists. For this reason it is always desirable that the lawyers take an active part in the legislation of a country; for it is most necessary that the existing state of things be fairly represented, and that the legislators of a state do not precipitate the state into heedless speculation or untried experiments, appearing brilliant to the unexperienced; but their number

---

[1] * There is a very excellent passage on this subject in the reflections of Sir Samuel Romilly on himself and the good he might do should he be appointed lord chancellor, page 384 et seq. of vol. iii. of his Memoirs, 2d edit., Lond., 1840. He says, "It is not from such [men as have for a long period been appointed to the chancellorship] that we should expect comprehensive reforms or important alterations in the law. His education, his inveterate habits, the society he has lived in, the policy by which he has always regulated his conduct, have all tended to inspire him with a blind reverence for every part of that system of law which he has found established. When we reflect on this, when we trace the former lives of all the chancellors of modern times,—when we see them, from the moment when they quitted college, giving up their whole time to the study of one positive science and cultivating no faculty of the mind but memory, the talent of discovering and pursuing nice and subtle distinctions and forced analogies, and the art of amplifying and disguising truth,—when we see them stunned, as it were, during the best years of their lives, by the continual hurry of business, reading nothing but what relates to the particular cases before them, shutting out all liberal knowledge from their minds, and contracting their views to the little objects with which they are continually occupied," etc.

The passage must be read much farther.

With reference to America, however, we must observe that the lawyers as a class form the most liberal part of the people, and withal the only large class who attain anything like a *gradual* political education and represent more than mere momentary excitements and measures.

must not overbalance the other portion of the legislators, who view the existing law without that charm with which it is invested to the eye of the lawyer, and without that fond pertinacity which arises from the pains the lawyer has taken to learn the law with all the intricate difficulties attending it. The greatest part of the most important, radical, and salutary reforms have not originated with lawyers, as was mentioned already: still, we must not forget that Pym was probably as great a man as Hampden, and quite as indispensable to his great party.

When power struggles with liberty, and yet is forced to derive an appearance of support from law, as is the case when the crown or a despotically disposed party endeavors to arrogate undue power over a people still cherishing their rights and the endeared tradition of liberty, it is natural that the party of power should always find many valuable aids among lawyers, because there are men in all professions who desire their advancement at any price, and it is the willing lawyer who, in the cases alluded to, is of the greatest value on account of his peculiar species of knowledge. When the state of things is such that clergymen can better or equally well give their aid to existing power, there are never members of that profession wanting that are ready to degrade their skill, knowledge, and influence in a like manner. Indeed, the clergy have more frequently and more extensively sided with power and authority, in states where government can offer any preferment, than the lawyers. Though the British prerogative-lawyers have prostituted their knowledge to the essential injury of the people, we must also remember that liberty owes to the aid afforded by the profession of the advocate some of the greatest achievements in the cause of national progress. Laud and Strafford hated the lawyers most cordially: their instinct taught them rightly. How much has not Erskine done for the assertion and clearer representation of many valuable constitutional points! Does not our whole race owe much, in the cause of freedom, to such judges as Lords Somers and Camden?

If a lawyer then becomes a member of legislating assemblies, he must carefully strive to elevate his mind above the level of special pleading, so as not to be the mere advocate of his party or of power, and to view subjects on the ground of broad national interest. That in smaller matters he must not carry the dust of the courts adhering to his vestments, with all the petty manœuvring to which a circumscribed practice frequently leads, into the halls of the legislature, need not be mentioned.

XV. The importance of the pure administration of justice for the state in general, as well as for individuals, lends of course proportionate importance and solemnity to every part and element of this administration, whether it consist in applying the law and giving every one his due after the truth is known, or in aiding to find out this truth. Among the elements of the administration of justice belonging to the latter class the witness is the most important. A witness upon the stand, whoever may have called him there, whether the government or a private party, ought ever to consider himself as being for the time in the service of Justice herself, and unbiassed truth becomes his binding, solemn, and sole obligation. The oath or affirmation to tell "the truth, the whole truth, and nothing but the truth," puts a very serious, solemn, and great obligation upon the witness; for it is necessary that as witnesses we abstain first from every falsehood, even the smallest; secondly, from everything which in one sense may be true, but in the sense in which it will be probably taken by the adverse party or the court is not true; thirdly, from all omissions which materially interfere with the whole truth; and fourthly also that we solemnly bind ourselves to state nothing in rashness, nothing which we believe to be true but which nevertheless is only a framework of facts filled up with the productions of a lively imagination, so often repeated in our mind that they appear to us perfect truth—an evil to which women in particular are subject. Nor must we allow our feelings to be wrought up so that something may appear to us true at the moment we are testifying, which nevertheless is not true or not precisely as we state it. The holy cause of justice depends in a degree upon every word that drops from the lips of a witness; and the oath he takes, which to his fellow-men becomes the most solemn of all pledges of truth, ought to be within him a fervent prayer that his memory may be correct and his mind calm and clear, so that he himself mistake not semblance for truth and that he be in a frame of mind to choose the proper words precisely to express what he wishes to express. A witness must take care, therefore, not to suffer his temper to be ruffled, even though the questioning advocate should forget his duty by impertinence and arrogance. In all such cases it is by far the best for the witness to appeal at once to the court for protection, and not to enter by pert repartees into a contest with an insolent lawyer. A witness ought to prepare himself for the discharge of his duty, especially when he has to testify to facts either long gone by, or observed by him when he himself was excited, or which happened surrounded by tumultuous agitation. Few who have not made some careful experiments upon themselves have any idea how far we allow ourselves to be deceived by our constantly working and combining, picturing and deceiving imagination, and in what degree we may succeed in undeceiving ourselves and unravelling the mazes of our own fancy. Persons of a lively imagination are especially bound to review facts well and to endeavor to sift and prune what the imagination may busily have added, before they asseverate anything as witnesses for or against any man. The law makes a considerable difference between questions which may or may not be put to a witness under different circumstances; but whatever the law does allow to be asked—over which the court watches—must be answered in the spirit of absolute veracity. There is in the oath or affirmation of witnesses no different kind or degree of obligation to state the truth; all witnesses, whether for or against the prisoner (virtually they are all for Justice), solemnly pledge themselves to tell the truth, the whole truth, and nothing but the truth.

# CHAPTER III.

War.—Definitions.—Present Exaggerations against War.—Christian Religi n does not prohibit just War; neither the Bible, nor the early Writers of the Church.—Objections against War on the Score of Morality; of Reason; of Political Economy.—Just and Patriotic Wars have morally raised Nations.—Eternal Peace.—Arbitration by a Congress of Nations.—Just Wars.—National Debasing Effect of suffering national Insult and Injustice without Resistance. —The Age of Louis XIV.—Wars do not absolve from Obligations to the Enemy.—Who is the Enemy?—Are Citizens of the hostile State Enemies?—What means of injuring the Enemy are admissible?—Treaties containing Provisions for the Case of War between the Contracting Powers.—Shall Confidence be abused in War?—Does War allow Deception?—Capitulations are sacred. —Destruction in War.—Carrying off Works of Art, Archives, etc.—Duties of the individual Soldier.

XVI. In this last chapter it is proposed to give a few remarks on War, as connected with our subject. I am well aware that the whole subject of war belongs properly to the so-called law of nations and international ethics; yet so much has been advanced of late regarding war as affecting the morality of the individual, and so many cases which are to be decided on ethical grounds by the individual necessarily occur in every war, that I feel obliged to add this chapter to the present work, although international ethics in general have been excluded from it. I shall confine myself, however, to some remarks touching in general the admissibility of war among rational and moral beings, and some respecting the conduct of the individual who takes part in a war, excluding from our inquiry the whole important field of the law of war proper.

War is a state of enmity between two parties, in which each is known by the other to be ready to obtain its ends by other means besides intellectual ones, especially by force and stratagem. We generally use the word War as applied to *considerable* masses, and of a *protracted* contest; hence partly the term "state of enmity" has been used; for the word protracted is not sufficiently definite. Otherwise the following might be the simplest and most comprehensive definition: War is protracted and active enmity.

That it has been found difficult to give an exact definition of war is owing to the fact that the term is used for almost all shades of contest and continued enmity, more or less metaphorically. Most definitions which have been given of war would apply equally well to mere battles, or they exclude the various means besides force which we make use of in war in order to obtain our object, for instance, cunning, intimidation, the devastation of one's own country to deprive the enemy of sustenance, etc.[1]

---

[1] Cicero, in saying in his Offices that "there are two kinds of contests between men, the one by argument and the other by force," though undoubtedly meaning by the latter war, cannot have meant to give a strict definition, for this would apply to single battles likewise. But a war generally comprehends battles, on the one hand, and on the other there have been wars without battles. Grotius saw this deficiency distinctly. Albericus Gentilis, in his work De Jure Belli, Oxon., 1588, says, " War is a just contention of the public force." Surely, in that case, Ferdinand of Aragon and Louis XII. could never have been at war, despite all the blood with which their captains drenched the fields of Italy. Or, if Aragon pretended to be right in spoliating her poor kinsman, how should we call wars professedly undertaken for robbing? [Albericus means *just in idea*, as a judge may give an unjust decision in a court of justice.] Hugo Grotius says, " War is the state of contending parties, considered as such" (bellum status per vim certantium, qua tales sunt). (De Jure Belli et Pacis, cap. i. 2.) Puffendorf calls war the state in which those are who in turn harm one another and repel the harm by force, or who strive to obtain their due by force. (Law of Nature and Nations, i. ch. 1, 8.) Bynkershoek, in his excellent treatise on the Law of War, says, " War is a contest carried on between independent persons, by force or fraud, for the sake of asserting their rights." This would exclude civil wars, and apply to the single battle as well as the whole war. Vattel says, " War is that state in which we prosecute our right by force." (Book 3, ch. i.) There have been wars in which actually the possession of no rights was pretended. I have mentioned one in Book I. § xxxix.—But was this no war? See also Wheaton's Elements of International Law, 8th edition, 1866, § 295, et seq.— General Clausewitz, in his work On War (Vom Kriege), Berlin, 2 vols., 1835, says, " War is the act of compelling an opponent to submit to one's will. Thus, force is the medium, and submission the object, and the latter can only be obtained by the development of the former. In order to effect this, the enemy

XVII. War may be considered in various points of view, for instance, that of religion, of pure morality and right, of utility, and with regard to its effects. On all these and other grounds war has, at times, been represented as entirely inadmissible among rational beings, and, as is usually the case in discussions of this sort, men have gone all sorts of lengths, some from sincere zeal, others from vanity, and still others from sinister views. While some political economists and pulpit orators have maintained, in contradiction to facts and history, that nations in no case gain by wars anything to be compared to the loss sustained thereby, or that war may be the interest of one man but can never be that of the people, others have gone still farther in their exaggeration, and denied that greatness of intellect is shown and proved by great generalship; as if we could without paradox possibly deny energy and independence of thought, elevation and firmness of character, intensity of action, vastness of combination, inventive fertility, penetration into the simple elements of what is complicated, confused, and hidden, and that peculiar attribute of greatness of intellect by which it communicates the spark of moral electricity to others and obtains mental dominion over them, the command of souls, to men like Hannibal, Cæsar, Gonsalvo of Córdova, William I. of Orange, Gustavus Adolphus, De Ruy-

---

must be rendered powerless. This is the grand aim of all hostilities." This definition does not include the defence of small states against attacks of large ones, whom they cannot intend, because they cannot hope, to render powerless. Have not small communities, when attacked, gone into war, resolved to sacrifice themselves, and knowing that this would be the end? Yet this was, nevertheless, war.

The word War is radically the same with the German Wehr, meaning arms and protection, defence; Wehren, the verb, means defending and interfering with something, and is, radically, the same word with the Anglo-Saxon Weran, Swedish Värja, Icelandic Veria; which we have still in Beware, which means to take care, guard one's self; as the German Bewahren means to preserve and keep properly. The French Guerre, Spanish Guerra, and the corresponding terms in the other Romanic languages are all derived from the Teutonic War or Wehr, the $w$ changing into $gu$, as it does frequently, for instance in the names of Witt, Vitus, into Guido, Guy. [War, Anglo-Saxon Werra, is more naturally connected by philologists with Werran = Wirren, German, to confound, disturb.]

ter, Frederic, Napoleon, Nelson, or Wellington.[1] If some of
these men have committed acts which we disapprove, or are
supposed to have used the greatness of their intellect altogether for evil ends, it does not invalidate the position that
the fact of their having been truly great generals shows also
the greatness of their intellect, any more than the fact of
Bacon's soiling his pages with unworthy flattery of a puerile
monarch proves him not to have been a great philosopher, or
of Lord Coke's having disgraced himself by some of the most
servile arguments in favor of the crown and to the ruin of the
persecuted disproves his having been a capacious and penetrating lawyer. Views like these have generally been maintained by persons who have an inadequate idea of what war
actually is, what a general has to do, and into what parts war
resolves itself. They see troops moving by command on the
drilling ground, and think armies are commanded in a like
manner and as easily, and that moral vigor is altogether out
of the question. Others have pushed the argument so far as
boldly to assert that soldiers never fight from patriotism, and
that, if they did, it would not be worth much, patriotism being
altogether worth little to a Christian! Verily, it is seen that

---

[1] * ["A nation's external life, then, is displayed in its wars, and here history has been sufficiently busy: the wars of the human race have been recorded when the memory of everything else has perished. Nor is this to be wondered at; for the external life of nations, as of individuals, is at once the most easily known and the most generally interesting. Action, in the common sense of the word, is intelligible to every one; its effects are visible and sensible; in itself, from its necessary connection with outward nature, it is often highly picturesque, while the qualities displayed in it are some of those which by an irresistible instinct we are most led to admire. Ability is the adaptation of means to ends, courage, endurance, and perseverance, the complete conquest over some of the most universal weaknesses of our nature, the victory over some of its most powerful temptations: these are qualities displayed in action, and particularly in war. And it is our deep sympathy with these qualities, much more than any fondness for scenes of horror and blood, which has made descriptions of battles, whether in poetry or history, so generally attractive. He who can read these without interest differs, I am inclined to think, from the mass of mankind rather for the worse than for the better: he rather wants some noble qualities which other men have, than possesses some which other men want."—*Inaugural Lecture, Lectures of Modern History*, by T. Arnold, D.D.]

these writers can never have taken up arms in defence of their country, or have been ready to shed their blood for it without earthly reward. How much are those to be pitied whose hearts remain cold at some of the choicest pages of history that testify to every glowing bosom the nobleness of human nature! A devoted, humble citizen bleeding and dying for his beloved country, her laws and liberty, the freedom of his children, their religion, their language, for their very intellectual existence, is nothing to them.[1]

It is not difficult to see why men at our time should urge the inadmissibility of war, or assert the extravagant extremes just mentioned, more loudly than perhaps at any previous period. Europe had seen most melancholy and unrighteous wars during the seventeenth century. Most governments strove for concentration, and military service was the best rewarded and most honored of professions. While thus good and pious as well as judicious men naturally began to raise their voices against war, it was likewise an inducement for the bold and witty to speak against great generals as if no better than common robbers either in capacity or morality, and a Shaftes-

---

[1] Mr. J. Dymond, in his Inquiry into the Accordancy of War with the Principles of Christianity, etc., 3d edition, Philadelphia, 1834—a work which would seem to embody all the objections that have been raised on the ground of the Christian religion against war, and on this account is to be consulted by the student—declares that soldiers do not die for their country, and seeks to prove it by asserting that no one of them would be willing quietly to be executed for his country in a distant land: hence, he thinks, it is clear that glory alone prompts him to fight for his country. As to the first point, it must be observed that no doubt there are some who would willingly lay down their lives for their country. If his own heart does not tell him that there are some such, let him look at history, which will give him instances of men who willingly died for their country but could not have expected their names ever to be known. Why not deny the same respecting religion? Regarding the second, I do not know how glory can be the all-powerful agent in a national war such as the Dutch war of independence was against the Spaniards. Soldiers know that their names will not be gazetted. I do not see what glory there was to be earned by the poor people of Leyden, who still held out against the Spaniards, when reduced to famished skeletons, despite ravenous hunger, fever, and total exhaustion, unless we call glory that which a man feels within him when he sacrifices himself to his duty, to the liberty of his country, to the cause of mankind and his religion.

bury, strange to say, came to agree with bishop Watson. At a still later period, political economy, viewing national transactions chiefly in the light of their immediate and pecuniary results, was more and more studied, while, on the other hand, wars on a gigantic scale were carried on by Napoleon, and many states since then have enjoyed the sweets and rapid improvements of peace. Thus people were easily carried to another extreme, and while in former times military glory was almost the only, certainly the highest, title to political distinction, now persons are induced to decry military talent as having a merely brutal character, and glory, even though it be earned in a noble cause, as ludicrous; nay, even patriotism as beneath either high religious feeling, or pure utilitarian perception unalloyed by any dross of feeling.

XVIII. A just war implies that we have a just cause, and that it is necessary; for war implies suffering on the part of some, and it is a principle of all human actions that, in order to be justified in inflicting suffering of any kind, we must not only be justified, but that there is a necessity for the infliction. I shall speak more of just wars further below.

If a war is just, the Christian religion does not prohibit it. If it did, one of two things must be true, either war must be directly prohibited, or the prohibition must be fairly implied in other direct commandments. This would be necessary for the Protestant; for the Catholic there might be a third supposition, namely, that the church from earliest times should have traditionally prohibited all war Neither of these positions, however, can be maintained; while there are strong biblical reasons which support the advocates of just war. The Bible nowhere directly prohibits war. Indeed, it may be answered, So there are many vices and offences not specifically prohibited, for instance suicide. But war is positively enjoined in the Old Testament, and not only war but even conquest; while in the New Testament it is not prohibited, although war was raging in the world, and the subject was brought almost directly before Christ and the apostles: still they said not a word of it. Compare, for instance, Luke vii. 8 and iii. 14.[1] To this we may add Paul's words, "For he [the ruler, magistrate] beareth not the sword in vain." (Romans xiii. 4.) What is the sword? An edged weapon to compel if need be by force, even at the risk of the opponent's life. If Paul acknowledges this power to compel or overawe as lodged in some one at home, if he acknowledges in the ruler not only the right to wear the sword but to use it, for "he does not bear it in vain," if he acknowledges the right of having armed servants, for this is evidently meant by the sword, since the ruler alone cannot use the sword, and of using these armed servants not only to compel subjects and citizens but actually to avenge, it is very plain that the ruler must have a still greater right to protect his subjects against unjust aggression and oppression; for, be it said at this early stage of our inquiry, the question as to the original and moral legality of war is no other than the general one of resistance—that is, ought force to be resisted by force?

Lastly, the fathers of the church amply acknowledge the right of war, and not only this, but it is acknowledged that war once declared and justly declared, the Christian may carry it on by open force or by fraud, that is, stratagem. See St. Augustine, Quest. 10, in Josuam.[2]

Against this it is said that our religion is eminently peaceful in its character, commands that we should love one another, prohibits revenge and hatred, commands to overcome evil with good, that we should be meek, etc.[3] Some point at passages such as, "I say unto you, that ye resist not evil, but whosoever shall smite thee on thy right cheek, turn to him the other also" (Matthew v. 39), and, "Put up again thy sword

---

[1] Both passages mentioned by Paley, Moral and Political Philosophy, vi. ch. xii.

[2] [The words are, "cum justum bellum susceperit, utrum aperta pugna utrum insidiis vincet, nihil ad justitiam interest." Quæst. in Heptateuch, on Joshua, cap. viii. (iii. 1, 906, Paris reprint of Benedict. ed. 1836). All sorts of fraud are not here allowed.]

[3] See the cited work of Dymond, and the last chapter of Wayland's Elements of Moral Science, New York, 1835.

into his place, for all they that take the sword shall perish with the sword" (Matthew xxvi. 52), or the commandment, "Thou shalt not kill," as containing more direct or typical commands for the Christian never to use the sword.

Upon this it is to be answered, that although Christ came among other things to preach and diffuse love, forbearance, charity, and even love of our enemy, he by no means intended to abolish thereby all relations of right, all law, all defence of right, for this would necessarily lead—and actually has misled crazy religionists more than once—to the abolition of all magistracy and of the institution of the state itself. How often in history has not this advent of dissolution been preached by fanatics, such as the Anabaptists, who ended, as nearly all these fanatics do, by using every species of cruelty and ferocity in order to compel others into their belief of non-resistance! Christ came to infuse the spirit of kindness, not to abrogate the principles of God's creation. A stone is attracted by the centre of the earth now, as before Christ; a conclusion drawn according to the logical laws of reasoning is now as binding as before Christ; and the eternal principles of justice are now as strong, as imperative, and as sacred as before Christ. Let the law do justice and full justice alone, and leave love to the individual; for, sacred as it is, it becomes so only if added to justice, but not if put in the place of justice. Every one ought to be reminded again and again that mutual love is a great virtue, but before all we must be just, which is not so easy.

Christ as well as the apostles acknowledged positively law, the state, and the magistracy. A citizen who fights because called upon by his government, a man who fights in a just cause, does not on that account hate his military enemy; he does not shoot at him from hatred or revenge.[1] He would do

---

[1] It is well known that enemies, as soon as overcome, that is, as soon as made harmless, treat each other without any feeling of personal malignity, and even with chivalrous acknowledgment of their gallantry. Whatever cases may occur to the contrary, they are, among civilized nations, considered with universal disapproval, and form exceptions. A very striking instance that war does not beget

this if he were to fight for the sake of fighting, but the object of just fighting is peace, the obtaining of right and its protection, and he fights against the enemy only because he cannot obtain these ends without removing the wanton obstacle in the way of obtaining it—that is, the enemy. This appears from the fact that all personal cruelty is prohibited, and that after a battle the wounded enemy is taken care of equally with the wounded friend.

As to the supposed injunctions never to fight, we must understand these passages as all the others, and as anything expressed in human language, that is, in conjunction with other passages, in the spirit of the whole document or text, and without losing sight of the first key of all interpretation, that is, of common sense and good faith; we must take what is tropical as tropical, what is hyperbolical as hyperbolical. It stands, Thou shalt not kill. Does not this mean, Thou shalt not unjustly kill? For killing means violently depriving of life. If we apply the commandment to every violent extinction of human life—and it is difficult to see how this can be done, since the commandment is in the Old Testament, in which war was absolutely commanded by the same authority from which this commandment proceeded—we may as well extend it to all animal life, as indeed some sects have done. Nor is there any reason why we should stop here. Plants have undoubtedly life too, and the commandment might be supposed to extend to vegetable as well as animal life. Here, every one would exclaim, This is against all sense! This is precisely the answer which is the correct one to be given to those who take the precept literally.

The other passage must be likewise understood in conjunction with the whole Bible; and we have seen already that

---

personal hatred occurred in the year 1838, when Marshal Soult, who had commanded the French in the Peninsular war against the British under Wellington, visited England. The marshal was received by the duke, as well as by the whole British people, wherever he went, with the greatest respect, and a warmth of feeling which was acknowledged by Soult himself as well as by the French nation was highly conducive towards increasing the good feeling now subsisting between those two great nations.

Paul speaks of the necessity of the sword to the magistrate, and that Christ does not seize upon those opportunities which we may fairly suppose he would have improved had he intended to prohibit war altogether. The expression that when smitten on one cheek we ought to turn the other is as evidently hyperbolical, in order to teach in a strongly impressive figure of speech the general principle of love and forgiveness, as are the similar passages which command us to give our cloak when robbed of our coat, or when compelled to go a mile to go twain. Christ taught principles, not absolute mathematical formulas, but addressed them to rational beings, who therefore must apply them with reason. If the various passages of the Bible were to be taken literally, no book would contain greater contradictions or render it more impossible for any one to obey all commands at the same time. In addition it ought to be observed that I should actually commit a moral wrong in literally following these precepts and in not resisting without hatred wicked attacks, for I should thus induce the evil-doer to commit still more wrong or crime. Literally when asked for a coat to give a cloak besides, to offer the one cheek if the other has been smitten, to walk two miles if bidden to march one, would amount to an invitation to the robber, the insolent, and the oppressor to proceed in their path of crime. Respecting the typical sense of Christ's command to his disciple to put up the sword, we must observe that no typical sense can be supposed to exist where we have not otherwise the means to find out that it is typical; else how could we know that it is typical? In this case, we ought to know from other parts of the Bible that war is absolutely prohibited before we can maintain that this passage is typical. It would be surprising indeed if a command should be given in typical form and leave men therefore in doubt!

XIX. On the score of ethics alone the objections against war may be comprehended under the following divisions: Men—that is, rational beings—ought to contend with one another by argument, that is, by the strength of reason, and not by force, by which they sink to the level of animals. We do not prove our right even if we obtain victory, which is, nevertheless, doubtful. In war those suffer who probably had little or no hand in bringing it about. War is immoral, because it is a cessation of morality, and in addition it breeds immorality. The effects of the most successful wars are always disproportionate to the evils which they entail. Finally, war being necessarily caused by an act of injustice, of immorality on one side if not on both, it is at least evident that it must cease with a state of diffused morality, and might be stopped, on a very large scale at any rate, if a large number of independent states would adopt among themselves the same rule which the various civilized societies adopt within themselves, namely, to prohibit the obtaining of right by force, and to allow it to be obtained by argument, by reasoning, on the powerful ground of justice alone.

XX. As to the first objection, that men are rational beings and ought to decide all differences by reason, we have to observe that although they ought to do it there are many who will not do it, and that it is not in the power of the good always to prevent those who will not from doing so. Throughout human life we resort to force if we cannot obtain our right otherwise. Resorting to physical force is not on that account brutish. Raising a wall around our garden, fastening our doors by locks and bolts, is resorting to physical means, because we know the thief would not allow himself to be argued away, or we have no time or obligation to watch the door until he come that we may argue with him. We chastise a child, that is resort to force, when it is so young that we cannot yet reason with it and an evil disposition shows itself so prominently as to need to be controlled. We prevent people from using a path by blocking it up, that is we resort to physical force, because a mere tablet, with a request to passengers not to use it, would be without effect. Going to law, is in all cases in which there is a malign intent on one side, resorting to force, only with this difference, that we wisely give up, or are *forced* to give up, private force, and resort to public. For we all know full well that our unjust adversary would not do the bidding of the court and abide by its decision were it not supported by public force. We do not go to the court to convince our adversary, but to convince the judge. A lawsuit against a wicked person amounts to this: A has wronged B; B goes to the executive and demands assistance against A. The executive says, "I will lend assistance, but I must first be convinced that you are not mistaken, or that A did not mean, perhaps, to wrong you. Go to C, who has been appointed to see, in such cases, who is right. He is a judge; and if he says that you are right, come back, and I will lend you force to obtain right from A." Let us go farther. My child is attacked by a murderer: have I not the right in this case to protect him, which protection may make absolutely necessary not only the parrying off of the assassin's blows but also the rendering him innocuous? I have the right to kill an animal which attacks me and endangers my life. If a murderer attacks me he thereby lowers himself for that moment to an animal, and he puts it out of my power to use any other means than those I would use against the animal, so long as I must avert the danger to which, like an animal, he exposes me; and whatever danger or suffering accrues from it is his own doing, not mine. I am bound to protect my life, for my Creator has given it to me for various solemn purposes. Were I not to protect it, brute force would rule, and the most sacred ends of humanity would be set at naught. Man is a reasonable being indeed, but he is not ordered to act by reason alone. But against killing a human being this objection has been made: You settle the doom of the killed. The answer is, that if a human being is killed according to the principles of justice and perfect right and the necessity of the case brought on by the assailant, we must needs suppose that this was intended to be his final hour, whatever consequences may be attached to it, because the principles of justice and right come from the Creator and are essentials in his vast system. If then they were to militate with others of his intentions, there would be contradiction in his government of the world, which it is absurd to suppose. In brief, the ancient "vim vi repellere licet" is not only justifiable, but is one of the principles of God's whole creation, and the abolition of it would create universal moral and physical disorder.

We do not prove our right by victory. This is very true, as it is likewise true that our injustice is not proved by defeat; but no one maintains that wars are undertaken to prove anything; they are not, like the ancient ordeals, a supposed trial of justice. We undertake wars in order to obtain right, and if victory is doubtful and we still undertake it, we do so because we believe the loss by submission would be so great that we must at least try to protect ourselves and hope that God will grant victory to the just cause: with such a hope the Swiss fought for their liberty against Austria, and the Americans resorted to arms because without it they were to be subjected by British arms, or made to submit to legislation which they thought disgraceful.

In war those suffer generally most who were least the cause of wrong. This is undoubtedly true; but first it is not in the power or the choice of those whom we suppose unjustly assailed to avert the evil,—they only protect themselves; and secondly the evil, though great, as has been admitted, is not so great as is often supposed. For it is the plan of the Creator that government and people should be closely united in weal and woe: no state of political civilization, no high standard of national liberty and general morality, is possible where this is not the case. History offers no more deplorable objects for the historian's contemplation than those nations which, owing to whatever cause, take no part in their government, are unconnected by feeling with it, and change allegiance as rapidly as the fate of battle may change, like the people of the kingdom of Naples in the seventeenth century. If, however, this union of government and people is desirable, the evil above alluded to cannot be averted. But, however this may be, it is not for those who are threatened with war to submit because innocent persons under the assailing government may suffer. The same principle applied to municipal matters would infallibly bring confusion and ruin upon society; for there is hardly a single sentence inflicted upon a criminal which does not affect in the infinite catenation of human connections, morally or physically, some innocent person—children who depend upon the father, a mother who mourns the disgrace of her son, or an innocent wife or a friend.

XXI. We come now to consider the last positions : War is immoral and begets immorality; it never furnishes advantages which can compensate for the evils it entails ; and, as rational beings, nations ought to settle, and might easily settle, their differences in the same way as those of individuals are settled.

An unjust war is not only immoral, but it is one of the greatest crimes—murder on a large scale; wars undertaken for plunder, or for the unrighteous end of compelling men in their belief, beget immorality and crime, annihilate the fixed standard of morality and pure justice, and are on this account alone, were there no other reasons, destructive to civil liberty, the government of law and right. So is unjust litigation immoral in its effects as well as in its cause. Yet, for all this, there would be much greater immorality and unrighteousness were there no courts of justice, and were people to suffer the wicked to commit their wrong without any litigation. So-called religious wars, or wars of plunder, are ruinous in the very highest degree both to society at large and to the individuals who engage in them. But just wars are not demoralizing. As protracted peace is not unalloyed with evil (for instance, in frequently begetting sordid selfishness and degrading submissiveness, increasing with each generation, as we see to be the case in China), so is a just war not without its great advantages. Public spirit, founded upon the very principle of unselfishness, is roused by few national events so much and

raised to such a pitch as by a just war. The tone of morality
of those who engage in a patriotic war is eminently raised; no
one who is acquainted with all the details can deny that the
whole moral tone of the German nation was greatly raised by
their struggle for national independence against the French
in 1812–14—a moral elevation which showed itself in all
spheres and all branches; and it was universally observed at
the time that the soldiers had returned from those wars with
high and elevated tone of moral feeling. The Americans certainly came out of their revolutionary struggle none the worse
in their morals; and is not the nation to this day intellectually
and morally feeding, as it might be called, upon their struggle
for liberty? Whence do the Americans habitually take their
best and purest examples of all that is connected with patriotism, public spirit, devotion to common good, purity of motive
and action, if not from the daring band of their patriots of the
Revolution? If war frequently, nay generally, makes party
spirit run high in a free country, and very often leads to calamitous consequences, we must not forget that, notwithstanding all warmth and undue, nay dangerous, zeal, parties during
wars are generally much purer than those which, growing
up in protracted peace, are founded, like court factions of
corrupt monarchies, on the worst principles of selfishness,
intrigue, and avidity for plunder. The British parties of
Pitt and Fox are certainly not the worst in English history.
High as the American parties ran during the last war, who
would say that they were not purer than those of some later
periods in the American history? Many nations have been
morally rescued by wars, which imparted new vigor to them.
In no situation whatever are so frequently pure, close, and
lasting friendships concluded, after the first period of unsus-
picious youth has passed, as in a just war. Is this not an act
eminently moral in its character? To no period whatever do
men look back in their old age with such animating delight
as to that in which they fought for a good cause. Poets cannot delight or animate a nation except by that which is founded
or finds a responding chord in the better part of the human

soul, as has been already observed by Mackintosh; but what has been the most unceasing theme of all the inspired bards of all nations and all periods—times of general depravity only excepted, when tartness of spicy wit must succeed to generous feeling which no longer exists, or satire against vice must stand in the place of admiration of virtue and greatness—if not death for our country? Has this been so by agreement, or were the poets paid for it, or is it not the general, spontaneous burst of men's noblest emotions? Wherever we find in a nation or period a general incapacity of feeling the heart-stirring beauty of this theme, we may set them down as lost to every thing that goes beyond self-interest and consequently appertains to the best traits of human society. Soldiers are proverbially known for frankness and generosity. Who that has any practical knowledge would be so bold as to assert that the soldiers engaged in a national war are as a class immoral? Who, indeed, would maintain that the officers even of a standing army are less moral than any other class on a similar level of education? Who would maintain that officers are less moral, for instance, than lawyers? Facts speak against it. Actions in court against officers are in fact peculiarly rare. But though the severest charges against war and soldiers on the score of diffusing immorality were true, it is equally true that the immoral consequences of submission to foreign conquerors, and of habitual submission to injustice, plunder, and insult, are still greater, and penetrate deeper, for they tend to extinguish that lively feeling of justice without which no free state can flourish.

XXII. That wars never compensate for the evils which they entail is as sweeping a remark as if a person were to assert that men would be all the healthier for having no such profession as that of medicine. Even if it were true in a physical point of view, the remark would yet be far too sweeping. But it is not true even thus considered. Nations are sometimes so situated that, for instance, the possession of the estuary of their largest river is of the greatest importance to their whole industry, while those who inhabit the country around the mouth of that river may likewise be greatly benefited by being united with the interior, and a war which unites both may become a great and lasting advantage to both. The continual efforts requisite for a nation to protect themselves against the ever-repeated attacks of a predatory foe may be infinitely greater than the evils entailed by a single and energetic war which forever secures peace from that side. Nor will it be denied, I suppose, that Niebuhr is right when he observes that the advantage on the score of power and national vigor to Rome of having conquered Sicily were undeniable. But, even if it were not so, are there no other advantages to be secured? No human mind is vast enough to comprehend in one glance, nor is any human life long enough to follow out consecutively, all the immeasurable blessings which have resulted to mankind from the ever-memorable victories of little Greece over the rolling masses of servile Asia, when they were nigh sweeping over Europe like the high tides of a swollen sea, carrying ruin over all the germs of civilization, liberty, and taste, and nearly all that is good and noble. Think what we should have been had Europe become an Asiatic province, and the Eastern principles of power and stagnation so deeply infused into her population that no process ever after could have thrown it out again. Has no advantage resulted from the refusal of the Hebrews in the times of the Maccabees' to be ground in the dust, and ultimately annihilated, by stifling servitude, and from the wars which followed their resolution? The war of independence in the Netherlands has had a penetrating and decided effect upon modern history, and, in the eye of all who value the most substantial parts and elementary ideas of modern civil liberty, a highly advantageous one, both directly and through Great Britain. Wars have frequently been, in the hands of Providence, the means of disseminating civilization if carried on by civilized people, as in the case of Alexander, whose wars had a most decided effect upon the intercourse of men and extension of civilization; or of rousing and reuniting people who had fallen into lethargy, if attacked by less civilized and numerous hordes. Frequently we find in history that the ruler and victorious tribe is made to revive civilization, as it were already on the wane, in a refined nation. Paradoxical as it may seem at first glance, it is nevertheless amply proved by history that the closest contact and consequent exchange of thought and produce and enlargement of knowledge between two nations otherwise severed is frequently produced by a war. War is indeed a state of suffering, but it is often one of those periods of struggle without which no great and essential good ever falls to the share of man. Suffering, merely as suffering, is not an evil. Religion, philosophy, every day's experience, prove it. No maternal rejoicing brightens up a mother's eye without the anxiety of labor.

Of what good, however, it has been asked, is war to those who fail in a war by which we may suppose one nation ultimately to be benefited? Both the merest utilitarian and many religious people have fallen into the error of never considering man except in his isolated capacity, the one with respect to material advantages, the other with regard to mental. Men, however, are social beings, not only as they are destined to help out one another better to obtain their isolated benefits, but because societies, nations, have their destinies as such, and men are destined to live for one another, one man for his brother, and one generation for another. All that is noblest in man is connected with his sociality, his denial of self, and his living and striving in close union with others. If it were not so, nothing could be more absurd, and indeed a more direct self-contradiction, than the idea of sacrificing one's self for another, for one's children, one's country, for truth, which of course can mean only truth in so far as it shall become known by and therefore part of others; yet "greater love hath no man than this, that a man lay down his life for his friend."

XXIII. One word respecting the proposed plan of settling national disputes by a congress of nations, according to an international code, on the plan of a petition lately laid before the congress of the United States.[1]

The idea of a perpetual peace has been repeatedly conceived by modern writers, as by St. Pierre, Bentham, and Kant, and has been a favorite one with associations for the promotion of peace.[2] The way of settling amicably what at other times would have led to bloodshed has of late become more frequent, and is undoubtedly upon the whole an evidence either of a more generally diffused love of peace, or of the fact that governments have, in the course of civilization, more or less changed their character from cabinet governments to national governments. Nations also have not in the present state of things as frequent desires for war as formerly, or as individuals may be supposed to have; though we should be unjust if we were to ascribe the many former wars always to the warlike spirit of princes. It was the spirit of the times, and in not a few cases were the princes urged by the people to a war in which they reluctantly engaged.

Yet we err if we suppose that the settlement of international questions by congresses of ambassadors has not had in some cases most grievous consequences for some nations. It is impossible to bring nations into such close contact as those congresses allow, and yet to separate the international ques-

---

[1] I would refer the reader to a very able report made by Mr. Legaré, from the committee on foreign affairs of the house of representatives, June 13, 1838, on a memorial of the New York Peace Society, praying to refer the subject in dispute between the United States and Mexico to a third power for arbitration, and that the government of the United States should send a proposal to those of other nations " that they would unite with it in the establishment of a great international *board of arbitration*, or a *congress of nations*, to which to refer international disputes; and also for the purpose of digesting and preparing a *regular code of international law*, obligatory on such nations as may afterwards adopt it."

[Of the two, a congress of nations and compromissory arbitration by arbiters whom the parties choose, the latter, of which many instances are to be met with in modern diplomacy, has in the present state of the world the advantage.]

[2] On Perpetual Peace, a Philosophical Sketch, written in 1795, in vol. vii. of Kant's Complete Works, Leipsic, 1838.—This paper, much as there is contained in it for reflection, belongs certainly to the weaker productions of that philosopher.

tions strictly from questions which, though domestic, are of general interest. Domestic interference is an almost necessary consequence. Wherever people meet, the most powerful must sway, in politics as in every other sphere; and wherever parts of nations or entire nations meet nominally on terms of parity, it is unavoidable that the most powerful must sway the less powerful. Independent national development, therefore, one of the most necessary requisites of a general, diverse, and manifold civilization, in law, language, custom, and literature, would be as seriously interfered with by such a proposed congress of nations as it was for a long time in the middle ages by the papal power. All legislation at a distance becomes inconvenient, not unfrequently ruinous, because unadapted to the specific case. A congress on the banks of the Po, or on the Bosphorus, for Asia, Europe, and America, would make galling decisions for people near the Rocky Mountains. All the inconveniences and hardships of so-called universal monarchies would be felt. Nor can many international questions possibly be settled like mathematical questions. The difference of nations, which nevertheless is necessary, must needs lead to very different wants and views. Something similar takes place in many law cases. Right and wrong are frequently not so strictly divided in complex cases that we can demonstrate it with absolute mathematical certainty. Still I may be answered, They are settled by the courts. They are settled, indeed; but how? Are both parties satisfied? They abide by the decision for two reasons: because public opinion compels them to do so, and because if they would not, there is the executive, the compelling power, without which no state could exist. The one of these agents would be very weak, the other would not exist at all, in those decisions of a supposed congress. Moreover, international law is one of the proudest victories of civilization, despite whatever incongruities there may still exist in it as it appears in the best authorities. Yet why is it so? Where does its force lie? Because it has gradually developed itself out of the intercourse in peace and war of civilized nations, and a united feeling of justice or fairness, mutual advantage and honor; but a mere legislation even of the wisest men of all nations, should we suppose them ever to agree, would fall to the ground like any other legislation, if not founded upon existing circumstances and customs. Finally, we Americans should be the very last to propose such a congress, because we might be sure that our republican ministers would play a very subordinate part in a congress of ambassadors consisting almost entirely of monarchical deputies, whose principles and views, therefore, would always be prevalent.

XXIV. A war, to be justifiable, must be undertaken on just grounds—that is, to repel or avert wrongful force, or to establish a right; must be the last resort—that is, after all other means of reparation are unavailable or have miscarried; it must be necessary—that is, the evil to be averted or redressed should be a great one; and it must be wise—that is, there must be reasonable prospect of obtaining reparation, or the averting of the evil, and the acquiescence in the evil must be greater than the evils of the contest.[1]

---

[1] The following passage on war comes from so excellent a writer, and contains such just views, that I feel authorized in transcribing it:

"The war of a people against a tyrannical government may be tried by the same tests which ascertain the morality of a war between independent nations. The employment of force in the intercourse of reasonable beings is never lawful but for the purpose of repelling or averting wrongful force. Human life cannot lawfully be destroyed, or assailed, or endangered, for any other object than that of just defence. Such is the nature and such the boundary of legitimate self-defence in the case of individuals. Hence the right of the lawgiver to protect unoffending citizens by the adequate punishment of crimes; hence, also, the right of an independent state to take all measures necessary to her safety, if it be attacked or threatened from without; provided always that reparation cannot otherwise be obtained, that there is a reasonable prospect of obtaining it by arms, and that the evils of the contest are not probably greater than the mischiefs of acquiescence in the wrong; including, on both sides of the deliberation, the ordinary consequences of the example, as well as the immediate effects of the act. If reparation can otherwise be obtained, a nation has no necessary, and therefore no just, cause of war; if there be no probability of obtaining it by arms, a government cannot, with justice to their own nation, embark it in war; and if the evils of resistance should appear, on the whole, greater than those of submission

Just wars may be:

Wars of insurrection, to gain or regain liberty, as in the late case of the Greeks; for man is not bound to suffer oppression. His moral character is deeply involved in it.

Wars of independence; for instance, if a colony has grown into sufficient strength to provide for its own safety by independent legislation [and is treated oppressively by the mother country].

Wars to quell armed factions, like those of Henry IV. in France.

Wars to unite distracted states of the same nation, or in a country destined by nature to form one political society, as the wars of the Swedish monarchs who united the conflicting states and parts of Sweden.

Wars of defence; for instance, against invasion or conquest. A war may be essentially defensive, and yet we may begin it, for instance, if we must prevent an invasion which is under preparation. Wars undertaken to assist an ally according to a previous treaty of common defence are wars of defence.

Wars of chastisement. A nation which habitually would suffer insult, depredation, and plunder would soon sink into meanness and lose its own respect. What in the first generation might have been mistaken generosity—I say mistaken, for it is the business of the state to protect its subjects— would be meanness in the next. It is one of the prominent

---

wise rulers will consider an abstinence from a pernicious exercise of right as a sacred duty to their own subjects, and a debt which every people owes to the great commonwealth of mankind, of which they and their enemies are alike members. A war is just against the wrong-doer when reparation for wrong cannot otherwise be obtained; but it is then only conformable to all the principles of morality when it is not likely to expose the nation by whom it is levied to greater evils than it professes to avert, and when it does not inflict on the nation which has done the wrong sufferings altogether disproportionate to the extent of the injury. When the rulers of a nation are required to determine a question of peace or war, the bare justice of their case against the wrong-doer never can be the sole, and is not always the chief, matter on which they are morally bound to exercise a conscientious deliberation. Prudence in conducting the affairs of their subjects is, in them, a part of justice." Mackintosh, History of the Revolution in 1688, chap. ix.

features in the Roman history, which showed that they had an elevated view of the state, that at an early period they considered the state pledged to protect the individual against foreign injury. They early saw the essence of the state. The Roman ambassador, when sent to remonstrate with the Epirote queen for the piracies committed by her and her subjects against Romans, said, "We Romans have the admirable custom of avenging with the whole force of the state offences done to private individuals, and aiding those who have undergone injustice. By the aid of the gods, therefore, we shall speedily and vigorously endeavor to constrain you to ameliorate the royal regulation of Illyria."

The German empire and the republic of the Netherlands, but a short time previously so great and powerful, and indeed all the neighbors of France, were fast sinking into degradation and sustained incalculable moral and physical evil when they allowed Louis XIV. to commit his endless and insulting iniquities in robbing land and cities, and in other ways, during times of peace, from the conclusion of the Peace of Nimeguen to the breaking out of the third war in 1688; and no man can calculate what would have become of all Europe, how deep it might have sunk in utter degradation, through the loss of the sense of justice and love of liberty, had not salvation ultimately come from England, whence, as William justly wrote in 1681 to Lord Hyde (Clarendon Corresp., i. 56, 59), salvation for Europe alone was possible. We are apt to consider the revolution of 1688 only in its mighty effects upon British and, through it, upon European and American civil liberty. But William is no less a great British king than he is a great European hero, for having stemmed the current which was fast enslaving and politically demoralizing all Europe, and was the more dangerous as it was accompanied by the dazzling yet unsound grandeur of an unprincipled monarch. The year 1688 was probably no less portentous for Europe than the years 590 and 580 before Christ had been, when the gallant Greeks stemmed the Asiatic invasion. A nation which at the proper time does not know how to un sheathe the sword can never be considered as resting its liberty or morality on a certain and firm basis.

Those cases of war where the possession of some place or province becomes absolutely necessary for the safety or existence of a state or nation, clearly seeing that its destiny is to exist as a nation and to manifest itself as such, to which I have alluded before, must be considered as exceptions produced by the clashing interests of various parties. Although these cases have been frequently made the iniquitous pretexts for the worst wars, truth, nevertheless, binds us to acknowledge that such cases of extreme necessity do actually occur.[1]

XXV. War does not rest on the contest of argument or reason; but it by no means absolves us from all obligation towards the enemy, for various reasons. They depend in part on the object of war, in part on the fact that the belligerents are human beings, that the declaration of war is, among civilized nations, always made upon the tacit acknowledgment of certain usages and obligations, and partly on the fact that wars take place between masses who fight for others or not for themselves only.

I repeat that I do not intend by any means to give here an outline of the law of war, but shall merely touch upon some points of importance in public ethics.

War does not absolve us from all obligations to the enemy. The Romans acknowledged—no matter how far they practised upon it—that "war had its rights as well as peace, and that the Romans had learned to conduct war justly no less than gallantly." These are, according to Livy (v. 27), the words of Camillus. ("Sunt et belli sicut pacis jura, justeque ea non minus quam fortiter gerere didicimus.") Cicero, de Leg. ii. 14, acknowledges the same principle. What then is permitted, and what not?

So soon as war is declared, or the respective parties are

---

[1] [Rather dangerous ground. What is the necessity of a nation's existence, compared with the necessity of adherence to the right?]

fairly in a state of war, it is understood that they appeal to force and stratagem. I may deceive the enemy whenever, and must injure him wherever, I can.[1] Deceit is allowed, but not perjury; and as to the injury I do to the enemy, it must be remembered that I must injure him as an enemy, that is, so far as he is there to oppose me in obtaining the ends which I consider as the next object of the war—for instance, that of obtaining possession of the capital or the country, or that of gaining the ultimate object of the war, which among civilized nations is always peace, on whatever conditions that may be. "Truth and Peace" was Cromwell's remarkable watchword in the battle of Winceby, or Horncastle, near Lincoln.[2]

From these positions we shall derive important consequences, after having settled who the enemy is. Properly speaking, the enemy is the hostile state, next represented for the belligerent in the hostile army, but also represented in all its citizens from whom the means of carrying on the war are drawn or who furnish them. The armed enemy, therefore, whether he actually have arms in hand or not (Bynkershoek, Law of War, ch. i.), provided he would or can use them, must be repelled and injured by arms; the unarmed enemy, in supplying the means for the war directly or indirectly.

I have not the right to injure my enemy without reference to the general object of the war or to that of the battle. We do not injure in war in order to injure, but to obtain the object of war. All unnecessary infliction of suffering, therefore, remains cruelty as among private individuals. All suffering inflicted upon persons who do not impede my way, for instance upon surgeons or other inoffensive persons, if it can possibly be avoided, is criminal; equally so is all turning of the public

---

[1] "The law of nature," says Heeren, "as applied to war, or pure military law, recognizes no further principle than 'I injure my enemy wherever I can.'" An Examination of the Questions respecting the Claims of the Armed Neutrality. In his Historical Treatises, translation, Oxford, 1836. I remind the reader of the necessity of remembering who the enemy is.

[2] Which took place October 11, 1643. Forster's Cromwell, vol. vi. of Eminent British Statesmen, London, 1838.

war to private ends, such as extorting money for private use, all use of arms or of the power which I enjoy as a soldier for private purposes, as for the satisfaction of lust, all unnecessary destruction of private property,[1] all avoidable destruction of works of art or science in particular, and all unnecessary destruction of any kind. No pain can be inflicted nor harm be done in war which does not aid the operations of war directly. As soon as an enemy is rendered harmless by wounds or captivity, he is no longer my enemy, for he is no enemy of mine individually. On the same ground I have no right to employ assassins, even if the general principle of honor did not make us abhor it. I ought not only to abstain from injuring the harmless, but to protect them against the unlawful attack of others, simply because this becomes a perfectly private case.

XXVI. On the other hand, I am not only allowed—which is altogether an unimportant question in war—but it is my duty to inflict on my enemy, as such, the most serious injury I can, in order to obtain my end, whether this be protection or whatever else. The more actively this rule is followed out, the better for humanity, because intense wars are of short

---

[1] The question of privateering cannot be discussed here. I will only say that those who defend it do it chiefly on the ground that when war is declared my avowed object is to injure my enemy as much as possible, in order to compel him to peace at my will. So far as this object is in view, I use and have a right to use all means. Capture of private property in land wars is not generally resorted to, because it would not serve the purpose; but no general would be pardoned for not taking it if it were to support the enemy in his endeavors to injure me, for instance if it consisted of grain. Now, there is very frequently no other way of injuring the enemy so that he feel it than by making maritime prizes. Ten captured vessels may dispose the enemy more to peace than a lost battle. The injustice of the case, it is maintained, is lessened, so far as the war is with the state; and all are bound to one fate, although it is admitted that it is a peculiarly hard case for those who lose the prize, yet no more than, for instance, in the case of the soldier who is crippled. This too is an individual hardship.

[Since this was written, most of the nations of Christendom have agreed to abolish privateering, and to allow enemies' goods on neutral vessels engaged in innocent trade to go unharmed. Every merchant can now put his goods on a safe vessel, so that nearly entire exemption from capture is already reached.]

duration. If destruction of the enemy is my object, it is not only my right, but my duty, to resort to the most destructive means. Formerly, when there were so many wars, in which only the amount of suffering interested the nations concerned, and which the belligerents were often conscious of undertaking for trifling or unjust causes, it was natural that many niceties should be considered as laws of war. Wars were somewhat like duels, or tournaments, and the laws which regulated them were carried over to the wars. Certain arms, advantages, and means of destruction were declared to be unlawful, or not considered honorable. The "Chevalier" lost his battle against King George, because he thought it unfair to take advantage of the battle-ground! When nations are aggressed in their good rights, and threatened with the moral and physical calamities of conquest, they are bound to resort to all means of destruction, for they only want to repel. First, settle whether the war be just; if so, carry it out vigorously: nothing diminishes the number of wars so effectually. It was formerly much debated whether it was right to poison wells, on the ground that it was not fair, because the enemy was not prepared for it. But it is one of the things I want against a wrongful aggressor in war that he be not prepared. Should I not surprise him? Who would blame the Athenians if, in retiring from Attica to their ships, they had poisoned the wells, in order to make the Persians retire the sooner? A just war is not made for the pleasure of fighting. The only consideration can be this: Do we inflict an evil upon the individual which will cruelly afflict him after he has ceased to be an enemy, and which we can avoid? If so, let us avoid it by all means. As for the destruction alone, in whatever number or by whatever means, it is lawful and advisable, for the reasons already given.[1]

---

[1] See Bynkershoek, Law of War, translated by Peter S. Duponceau, Philadelphia, 1810, chap. i.—[In 1863, Dr. Lieber prepared a code of laws of war at the request of the United States government, which is entitled Instructions for the Government of Armies of the United States in the Field. He there says (article 70, under section iii.), "The use of poison in any manner, be it to poison

Respecting deception we must observe that within the sphere of war it is perfectly lawful, but not beyond. Hence capitulations must be kept; for peace is the end of war; peace is founded upon confidence, but the breaking of capitulations would destroy it. A capitulation or any agreement, for instance an armistice, or a permitted convoy, is evidently above the declaration of war; an exemption from it; founded upon confidence, otherwise it would not be made. For the same reason we are bound to observe those provisions of treaties which were made for the case that war should break out at some future period between the contracting powers. These stipulations must be faithfully kept; if not, it was absurd to make them, and the confidence necessary for the basis of a future peace is destroyed; but, as was observed, peace being the ultimate object of just war, we destroy the very object of the war in which we are engaged. Indeed, if no degree of confidence remained between the belligerents, every war would become an internecine war; and such is the case between all savage tribes, who have lost all confidence in one another. The treaty between the United States and Prussia of 1785 (Treaties of the United States, 1871, p. 706 and onw.) stipulates, among other things, that in case of war merchants of either nation residing in the country of the other shall have nine months' time to wind up their business, and be authorized to carry off all their property; no artisan, etc., thus residing is to be molested; no letters of marque are to be given,

---

wells or food or arms, is wholly excluded from modern warfare. He that uses it puts himself out of the pale of the law and usages of war." He had, as this shows, learned something since this chapter was published, in which he seems to follow too much the somewhat savage and questionable doctrines of Bynkershoek in his Quæst. Jur. Publ., book first. Great lawyers are apt to be harsher than great military officers who are not imbruted by selfish lust of acquisition; for the former see war only in its abstract features, the latter see it written out in letters of blood. Dr. Lieber here approves of poisoning, but two pages back justly condemns the employment of assassins. But to kill a general in an underhand way is surely no worse than to poison half a regiment. Our author's mature and well-digested opinions in the code of war do him the highest honor, and modify what he says in this chapter in several particulars.]

and private property is to be safe on land or sea; prisoners are not to be sent into unhealthy climates, etc. In all treaties between maritime powers, a certain time is stipulated, in case of wars, for private vessels in distant regions, during which they shall not be molested though war be declared. Such conditions ought to be most punctiliously and most cheerfully fulfilled, for they are the moral points remaining in a state of force. Yet they have often been broken—for instance, when Charles II. seized the Dutch vessels in the Mediterranean, in 1672, long before six months after the declaration of war had elapsed, although by the Peace of Breda this time had been stipulated to give the citizens of the two states time to remove their property. (State Tracts of William III., i. 35.)

For the same reason that capitulations or treaties must not be broken, perhaps, or because the injury done in war beyond the necessity of war is at once illegitimate, barbarous, and cruel, works of art generally ought not to be carried off by the victorious party; because it galls the conquered nation *beyond* the time of war, and, as peace requires mutual good will, and war of itself causes irritation, the carrying off of these works would awaken feelings opposed to continued peace. Yet I candidly confess that I cannot see the jural ground on which the right of carrying off books and works of art, provided they belong to the nation, is denied. It is universally admitted that levying a contribution for the sake of chastisement for a wrongful war, beyond the expenses of the war, is lawful, as it undoubtedly is. Why then should it be wrong to carry away works of art for the sake of chastisement? If they are truly national, connected with the history and feelings of a nation, and were carried off for vain-glorious exhibition, it would be cruel. Nothing must be done in war but what is considered necessary. The destruction of works of art is vandalism, and, as their removal exposes to destruction, this is an additional ground why it ought but very rarely to be resorted to. Still, this is merely an adventitious reason, not one founded in the subject itself. The works of art may thus be injured; but they may also not. They may be saved from destruction by being carried off by the victor. What should we possess of the wonders of ancient art, had Rome's conquering sword not collected them? There would be no Vatican.

Wars are undertaken under the silent acknowledgment of certain usages, which, therefore, must be kept; both on the common ground of honor, and because they are necessary, either for mitigating the evils of war and bringing it within the sphere of civilization, or for obtaining the end of peace. Thus, flags of truce must be honored; heralds were sacred in most ancient times; indeed, with them begins, we may say, international law. Envoys must be kept sacred; they are, indeed, the remaining representatives of reason, in the state where force is chiefly appealed to.[1]

---

[1] I do not know that the entire denial of our right to use arms, or, in other words, of the legality of war, was ever adopted into any system, except by Quakers, before the publication of Wayland's Elements of Moral Science, New York, 1835. It may be proper, therefore, to notice his objections in detail. On page 443, under the head of Redress of Grievances, under which he comprehends the violation of treaties, he says,—

1. That the fact that a nation solely relied upon the justice of its measures and the benevolence of its conduct would do more than anything else to prevent the occurrence of injury.

This might be true in some cases, in others not. Besides, there are two points left out of consideration. National measures are in many cases not so absolutely just or unjust that they cannot appear in very different lights to different persons. We see this daily with respect to municipal questions; but respecting international questions there is the additional difficulty of nations forming separate communities, large enough to be, in a degree, their own world, and separated by language, history, law, views, prejudices, desires, etc. Secondly, benevolence is a delicate feeling, depending upon the individual view and disposition of men. Where many have to decide, as is the case in national questions, it is not often possible that problems be solved by delicacy of feeling, which depends so much on individuality. All we can and ought to desire is to see the questions solved upon the rules of strict justice; and even upon this it is not always easy to unite a number of men. We must not forget that governments have their power in trust, and as I might do a thousand things with my own money which I dare not do if I am a guardian, so government cannot act in many cases by way of benevolence, but must go by the principles of justice.

2. If wrong is done, the proper appeal for moral beings upon moral questions is not to physical force, but to the conscience of men.

This prohibits us from going to war before we have tried every other means But it is not wrong to trust to physical force against a thief—for instance, as was

XXVII. Connected with the subject of war is that of armies. All we have to observe with regard to the soldier, to his con-

---

said above, by way of a lock. Those who deny the right of using physical force almost always commit the error of arguing against force altogether. Yet no Quaker hesitates in using strictly defensive force—for instance, an iron chest. The question then is not, as stated here by Wayland, whether we are permitted to use force instead of applying to conscience, but whether we are allowed to use compelling force, and, above all, whether we are allowed to kill fellow-men in our endeavor to apply compelling force. For, I repeat it, neither destruction nor killing is the object of war. The object of war is either my defence or the compulsion of another, and in effecting this, owing to my being impeded in my way by the enemy, arms are used. If the question is thus reduced, it remains to be answered whether we are prevented from killing men under any circumstances. The Quakers say yes; we deny it. If I am attacked by a murderer, I hold it to be my solemn duty to kill him in order to save myself, because God does not want murder to triumph, because it is right according to the moral order of things that the wicked meet with their desert, because my life, being that of an innocent man, is worth more than the murderer's, and for a number of other reasons, unnecessary to state here. Puffendorf says, very justly, " If, then, some one treads the laws of peace under his feet, forming projects which tend to my ruin, he could not without the last degree of impudence (impudentissime) pretend that after this I should still consider him as a sacred person who ought not to be touched; in other words, that I should betray myself and abandon the care of my own preservation in order to give way to the malice of a criminal that he may act with impunity and with full liberty. On the contrary, since he shows himself unsociable towards me, and since he has placed himself in a position which does not permit me safely to practise towards him the duties of peace, I have only to think of preventing the danger which menaces me; so that, if I cannot do this without hurting him, he has to accuse himself only, since he has reduced me to this necessity." (De Jure Nat. et Gent., lib. ii. ch. v. 1.) The same applies to wars. I would recommend the perusal of the whole second book with reference to this subject.

3. Suppose this method to fail, that is, the appeal to the consciences of men; why, then let us suffer the injury.

I have already shown the reasons why I believe this to be against the Bible, against God's law " written in our hearts," against reason, and subversive of all right and righteousness. Why not apply the same principle much sooner to the daily and municipal intercourse of men? Reason with a defaulter or a robber, and if he will not listen, why, suffer the evil. For it will not be said that in appealing to courts we appeal to reason alone. Courts are not arbitrations. They decide upon reason, no doubt, but their decision is to be enforced if not willingly obeyed. All the arguments of the first part of p. 444 of Wayland's work would apply with much more strength to municipal courts.

By adopting the law of benevolence, as Wayland calls the adoption of the

duct towards his own country, and to his right of independent action, is this:

He does not decide upon the justness of war, and is free of all obligation respecting this point.[1] Cases of the utmost extremity, such as revolutions, when, as mentioned, he is ordered to fire upon his fellow-citizens for resisting unlawful and ruinous decrees of government, form exceptions, and cannot be brought under any general rule. He must decide whether it is a case of utmost extremity and whether the most sacred duties do conflict. In all other cases obedience for him is a

---

principle never to use force between men, a nation would render the event of being subjugated highly improbable. He adds, "There is not a nation in Europe that could be led on to war against a harmless, just, forgiving, and defenceless people."

But history does not only show that states or societies have been attacked again and again that would not fight, but even such as could not fight have been attacked and swallowed up, just as readily as the ancient New Englanders used force with the Quakers, despite their non-resistance principle. The fact is, an undefended state known to have the rule of suffering everything would become the prey of all the others. What should prevent the African or Asiatic pirates from plundering such a nation—for instance, from attacking our vessels trading to China, should we adopt the "law of benevolence"?

If, however, says Wayland, such a case of subjugation should nevertheless occur, we ought to suffer.

We must not forget that an individual in bondage may be free, but a nation cannot: for the individual may have a rare elevation of mind and be born free; were he born in a jail, he could not but be base, unless he were particularly instructed. Every nation in servitude becomes debased. Strange, indeed, that we are expected willingly to sacrifice everything divine—our moral elevation, civilization, government of law and right, and God's own liberty for which he made men—simply in order to avoid doing one single thing, that is, resisting; as if it were said anywhere that this was absolutely the greatest evil. As life is not the greatest good, so dying is not the greatest evil.

[1] * A question which in 1846, when the United States went to war with Mexico, became of great practical importance, is, whether a man whose government has gone to war has *a right to volunteer*, if he considers the war unjust, —whether he can say, In my individual opinion the war is wrong, but it is, after all, an individual opinion, and my country has thought differently, and I am not answerable for it. But who is the country? For instance, in the present case the president plunged us into the war, and congress was obliged to follow. Had it not been for this ethical consideration, I should probably have solicited a commission, and, I dare say, should have got one.

principal point of honor. The very meaning of an army is founded upon obedience. He therefore destroys his own character if he does not obey and does not do this as a duty. He may rest assured that in the same degree as he aids to infuse any other spirit than that of patriotism, obedience, and gallantry into the army, he injures the cause of liberty. A disobedient army is a curse to its country. The soldier, therefore, must under no circumstances allow the army to become deliberative, or a politically agitated body. Let the soldier, if he have a right, go to the poll, but the necessity of subordination ought to deprive the army of its political character. I believe officers in actual service ought not, in political delicacy, to offer themselves as candidates for the place of representative where they are allowed to sit in the legislature.

Never, except in cases of the utmost extremity, ought the citizens of a republic to elect an officer of the army, in service, as their chief magistrate. The Americans have had a glorious exception in General Washington; but the exception cannot invalidate a rule so sound and clear in itself, and so well proved by all history and our own times. When civil feud distracts the country, such a selection may become necessary. So are many evils necessary to overcome greater ones. But where it is customary to select candidates for chief magistracy from the army, we must not look or hope for liberty.[1]

---

[1] [Since this was written, two men, never distinguished in civil life, have been elected presidents of the United States on account of their reputation as military officers, and two others were brought into notice, although insignificant enough in themselves, by their participation in war. With a great army in a country this would be dangerous. But as supplies, recruiting, and much else must precede the subversion of the national liberties, the danger from military officers in this country is not very imminent. There are in this country so few prominent persons, and of these the real statesmen are so far above the power of the people to estimate them, that some conspicuity is needed in the head or the figure-head of a party of a sort to strike the popular mind. Our problem must be to carry government on with the minimum of talent. Add to this that politicians have been before the country and have made enemies. A new man comes in more easily. Moreover, the people justly dread the schemes, bargains, mutual insurances and assurances of old foxy politicians.]

Lastly, it is the imperative duty of the soldier, that is, of every man under arms regularly embodied in a corps, to show himself superior to adversity, to show his courage and strength as much in suffering and in performing harassing service as in fighting, to observe the strictest discipline, not to murmur for want of pay, dress, or food, to show great moral strength and alacrity in tiresome sieges, not to maraud or oppress, to alleviate as much as in him lies the evils of war, neither to be rash nor backward, to remember the great cause which is at stake in a just war, and that the success of war depends mainly upon the willing and perfect performance of duty by every individual: and let his country and his God be ever before his eyes.

THE END.

www.ingramcontent.com/pod-product-compliance
Lightning Source LLC
Chambersburg PA
CBHW032001300426
44117CB00008B/852